The Design and Evaluation of Physical Protection Systems

Second Edition

The Design and Evaluation of Physical Protection Systems

Second Edition

Mary Lynn Garcia, CPP

Sandia National Laboratories

AMSTERDAM • BOSTON • HEIDELBERG • LONDON • NEW YORK • OXFORD
PARIS • SAN DIEGO • SAN FRANCISCO • SINGAPORE • SYDNEY • TOKYO

Butterworth-Heinemann is an imprint of Elsevier

Acquisitions Editor:	Pamela Chester
Publisher:	Amorette Pedersen
Marketing Manager:	Marissa Hederson
Publishing Services Manager:	Greg deZarn-O'Hare
Project Manager:	Ganesan Murugesan
Cover Design:	Joanne Blank

The US Government holds a nonexclusive copyright license in this work for government purposes. This book was authored by Sandia Corporation under Contract DE-AC04-94AL85000 with the US Department of Energy.

Recognizing the importance of preserving what has been written, Butterworth-Heinemann prints its books on acid-free paper whenever possible.

Library of Congress Cataloging-in-Publication Data
Garcia, Mary Lynn.
  The design and evaluation of physical protection systems / Mary Lynn Garcia. – 2nd ed.
     p.   cm.
  Includes bibliographical references and index.
  ISBN-13: 978-0-7506-8352-4 (alk. paper)
  ISBN-10: 0-7506-8352-X (alk. paper)
  1. Security systems.   I. Title.
  TH9705.G37 2007
  658.4'73—dc22   2007029245

British Library Cataloguing-in-Publication Data
A catalogue record for this book is available from the British Library.

The publisher offers special discounts on bulk orders of this book.
For information, please contact:
Manager of Special Sales
Butterworth-Heinemann
30 Corporate Drive, Suite 400
Burlington, MA 01803
Tel: 781-313-4787

For information on all Butterworth-Heinemann publications
available, contact our World Wide Web home page at: http://www.bh.com

12 13   10 9 8 7 6

Printed in the United States of America

To the men and women, past and present, of the Security Systems and Technology Center at Sandia National Laboratories, for 35 years of exceptional service.

"In the future days, which we seek to make secure, we look forward to a world founded upon four essential human freedoms... The fourth is freedom from fear... anywhere in the world".

Franklin D. Roosevelt, January 6, 1941

Contents

Preface

This book was first published in April 2001, just a few months before the horrific attacks of 9/11. I was personally gratified that this meant that our book was available to help address the security issues that arose out of these attacks. At the same time, we didn't include details that might have addressed this new threat motivation and capability. How could we—we never imagined that this sort of attack would be launched against civilian targets. The attacks of 9/11 are exactly the type of security event the approach described here is most effective for—high consequence, low probability events that require the most rigorous attention to detail we have available.

The world has gone through many changes since that time, particularly with respect to the security of its citizens. Wars in Afghanistan and Iraq provide a terrorist training ground; malevolent attacks on trains in Madrid, London and Mumbai, nightclubs in Bali, even a school in Beslan, Russia, are all examples of the tactics of emerging threats against ordinary citizens engaged in ordinary activities. Though the evolution of threat capability is not new, the renewed vigor of adversaries fighting for their ideology has caused a corresponding increase of security awareness by citizens—ask anyone who has flown since the attacks of 9/11. In this new environment, it is fitting that we revisit the principles and concepts of effective security and provide necessary updates.

Most of the changes in this version of the text are focused on new threat capabilities, legal and other changes that have occurred since 9/11, and discussion of some emerging technologies that may be useful in the future. Related to emerging technologies, we have included a maturity continuum in Chapter 6 "Exterior Intrusion Detection" that may serve as a guide to the selection of new technologies to counter adversary threats. In addition, because the basic principles of security are the same regardless of the application, a new chapter that discusses the use of these principles in executive protection, ground transportation of cargo, and cyber systems (computers and networks) has been added. This version also includes a discussion of the use of neutralization (defeat of the adversary using force during an attack) as another performance measure of facility response and risk assessment.

This edition follows the recent release of another text on vulnerability assessment (VA) by this author (referenced in appropriate chapters throughout this work). The two books are meant to work together in a very complementary way. This book describes the overall process and approach, while the VA book describes how the process is applied to verify effective protection of assets.

As with the first edition, this book describes a problem-solving approach. It discusses defining and understanding the problem prior to designing the system, and describes methods used to evaluate the design before implementation. This book addresses the use of the many components that exist to support a security system, but it primarily shows how these elements are integrated to deliver an effective system. The process culminates in a risk assessment that predicts how well the protection system performs and helps senior management quantify the remaining risk and inform their decisions. The core of the process is the discipline of systems engineering. All options must be considered for their cost and performance effectiveness and we implement those elements that are supported by science and engineering principles, test data, and meet customer objectives.

As with any work of this magnitude, there are a great many people to whom I owe a debt of gratitude. At Sandia they include Jake Deuel, Greg Elbring, Frank Griffin, Bruce Green, John Hunter, Willie Johns, Miriam Minton, Dale Murray, Cindy Nelson, Chuck Rhykerd, Charles Ringler, JR Russell, Steve Scott, Mark Snell, Regan Stinnett, Boris Starr, Basil Steele, James Stevens, Dave Swahlan, Drew Walter, Ron Williams, Tommy Woodall, and Dennis Miyoshi. The expert information presented in this text belongs to them; any errors are strictly mine. This assertion, though often repeated, is nonetheless sincere.

At Elsevier Butterworth–Heinemann, Pam Chester, Mark Listewnik, Jenn Soucy, Kelly Weaver, Greg deZarn-O'Hare, Ganesan Murugesan, and Renata Corbani quickly and competently handled the publishing process. I am also grateful to Mark Potok and the Southern Poverty Law Center for permission to use the map that appears in Chapter 3, "Threat Definition" and Don Utz at Kontek and David Dickinson from Delta Scientific for pictures in Chapter 11 "Access Delay." Chapter 16 "Other Applications" required assistance from others outside of Sandia with specific expertise, and so my particular thanks to Joe Carlon and Dick Lefler for their expert guidance and input on executive protection, and Weston Henry for providing the section on cyber security. Finally, my special thanks to Doug, Fuzzy, and Kasey.

As with the first edition, I hope you find this book helpful.

Mary Lynn Garcia

1

Design and Evaluation of Physical Protection Systems

A physical protection system (PPS) integrates people, procedures, and equipment for the protection of assets or facilities against theft, sabotage, or other malevolent human attacks. The design of an effective PPS requires a methodical approach in which the designer weighs the objectives of the PPS against available resources and then evaluates the proposed design to determine how well it meets the objectives. Without this kind of careful assessment, the PPS might waste valuable resources on unnecessary protection or, worse yet, fail to provide adequate protection at critical points of the facility. For example, it would probably be unwise to protect a facility's employee cafeteria with the same level of protection as the central computing area. Similarly, maximum security at a facility's main entrance would be wasted if entry were also possible through an unprotected cafeteria loading dock. Each facility is unique, even if generally performing the same activities, so this systematic approach allows flexibility in the application of security tools to address local conditions.

The process of designing and analyzing a PPS is described in the remainder of this chapter. The methodology presented here is the same one used by Sandia National Laboratories when designing a PPS for critical nuclear assets (Williams, 1978). This approach and supporting tools were developed and validated over the past 25 years through research funded by the Department of Energy (DOE) and development totaling over $200 million. While other industrial and governmental assets may not require the highest levels of security used at nuclear weapons sites, the approach is the same whether protecting a manufacturing facility, an oil refinery, or a retail store. The foundation of this approach is the design of an integrated performance-based system. Performance measures (i.e., validated numeric characteristics) for various system components, such as sensors, video, or response time, allow the use of models to predict system performance against the identified threat. This effectiveness measure can then be used to provide the business rationale for investing in the system or upgrade, based on a measurable increase in system performance and an associated decrease in risk to the facility. Looking at system improvement compared to costs can then support a cost–benefit analysis. By following this process, the system designer will include

1

elements of business, technology, and the criminal justice system into the most effective design within the constraints and budget of the facility. Before describing this process in more detail, however, it is first necessary to differentiate between safety and security.

Safety Versus Security

For the purposes of this book, safety is meant to represent the operation of systems in abnormal environments, such as flood, fire, earthquake, electrical faults, or accidents. Security, on the other hand, refers to systems used to prevent or detect an attack by a malevolent human adversary. There are some overlaps between the two: for example, the response to a fire may be the same whether the fire is the result of an electrical short or a terrorist bomb. It is useful, however, to recognize that a fire has no powers of reasoning, while adversaries do. A fire burns as long as there is fuel and oxygen; if these elements are removed, the fire goes out. An attack by a malevolent human adversary, on the other hand, requires that we recognize the capability of the human adversary to adapt and thus eventually defeat the security system.

In the event of a safety critical event, such as a fire, security personnel should have a defined role in assisting, without compromising the security readiness of a facility. In this regard, security personnel should not be overloaded with safety-related tasks, as this may increase exposure of the facility to a security event during an emergency condition, particularly if the adversary creates this event as a diversion or takes advantage of the opportunity. In addition, security personnel may not possess the specific knowledge or training to respond to safety events. For example, in case of a fire, security personnel should not be expected to shut down power or equipment. This task is better left to those familiar with the operation and shutdown of equipment,

power, or production lines. Procedures describing the role of security personnel in these events should be developed, understood, and practiced in order to assure adequate levels of protection and safety.

Deterrence

Theft, sabotage, and other malevolent acts at a facility may be prevented in two ways—by deterring the adversary or by defeating the adversary. Deterrence occurs by implementing measures that are perceived by potential adversaries as too difficult to defeat; it makes the facility an unattractive target, so the adversary abandons or never attempts an attack. Examples of deterrents are the presence of security guards in parking lots, adequate lighting at night, posting of signs, and the use of barriers, such as bars on windows. These are features that are often implemented with no additional layers of protection in the event of an attack. Deterrence can be very helpful in discouraging attacks by adversaries; however, it is less useful against an adversary who chooses to attack anyway.

It would be a mistake to assume that because an adversary has not challenged a system, the effectiveness of the system has been proven. The deterrence function of a PPS is difficult to measure, and reliance on successful deterrence can be risky; thus it is considered a secondary function and will not be discussed further in this text. The deterrent value of a true PPS, on the other hand, can be very high, while at the same time providing protection of assets in the event of an attack. The purpose of this text is to describe a process that produces an effective PPS design, validates its performance, and relates the improvement in system effectiveness to the cost. Application of this process allows the design of a PPS that will protect assets during an actual attack, as well as provide additional benefits through deterrence.

As more research is done on the measurable and long-term value of deterrents, these may be incorporated into protection system design. To date, however, there is no statistically valid information to support the effectiveness of deterrents. There are, however, studies that indicate that deterrence is not as effective after implementation as is hoped (Sivarajasingam and Shepherd, 1999).

Process Overview

The design of an effective PPS includes the determination of PPS objectives, the initial design or characterization of a PPS, the evaluation of the design, and, in many cases, a redesign or refinement of the system. To develop the objectives, the designer must begin by gathering information about facility operations and conditions, such as a comprehensive description of the facility, operating states, and the physical protection requirements. The designer then needs to define the threat. This involves considering factors about potential adversaries, such as class, capabilities, and range of tactics. Next, the designer should identify targets. Targets may be physical assets, electronic data, people, or anything that could impact business operations. The designer now knows the objectives of the PPS, that is, what to protect against whom. The next step is to design the new system or characterize the existing system. If designing a new system, people, procedures, and equipment must be integrated to meet the objectives of the system. If the system already exists, it must be characterized to establish a baseline of performance. After the PPS is designed or characterized, it must be analyzed and evaluated to ensure it meets the physical protection objectives. Evaluation must allow for features working together to assure protection rather than regarding each feature separately. Due to the complexity of protection systems, an evaluation usually requires modeling techniques. If any vulnerabilities are found, the initial system must be redesigned to correct the vulnerabilities and a reevaluation conducted.

PPS Design and Evaluation Process—Objectives

A graphical representation of the PPS methodology is shown in Figure 1.1. As stated above, the first step in the process is to determine the objectives of the protection system. To formulate these objectives, the designer must (1) characterize (understand) the facility operations and conditions, (2) define the threat, and (3) identify the targets.

Characterization of facility operations and conditions requires developing a thorough description of the facility itself (the location of the site boundary, building location, building interior floor plans, access points). A description of the processes within the facility is also required, as well as identification of any existing physical protection features. This information can be obtained from several sources, including facility design blueprints, process descriptions, safety analysis reports, and environmental impact statements. In addition to acquisition and review of such documentation, a tour of the site under consideration and interviews with facility personnel are necessary. This provides an understanding of the physical protection requirements for the facility as well as an appreciation for the operational and safety constraints, which must be considered. Each facility is unique, so the process should be followed each time a need is identified. Compromises must usually be made on all sides so that operation can continue in a safe and efficient environment while physical protection is maintained. Additional considerations also include an understanding of liability and any legal or regulatory requirements that must be followed.

Next, a threat definition for the facility must be made. Information must be

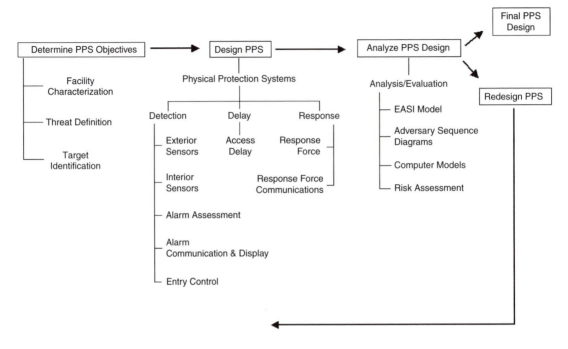

Figure 1.1 Design and Evaluation Process for Physical Protection Systems. The process starts with determining objectives, then designing a system to meet the objectives, and ends with an evaluation of how well the system performs compared to the objectives

collected to answer three questions about the adversary:

1. What class of adversary is to be considered?
2. What is the range of the adversary's tactics?
3. What are the adversary's capabilities?

Adversaries can be separated into three classes—outsiders, insiders, and outsiders working in collusion with insiders. For each class of adversary, the full range of tactics (deceit, force, stealth, or any combination of these) should be considered. Deceit is the attempted defeat of a security system by using false authorization and identification; force is the overt, forcible attempt to overcome a security system; and stealth is any attempt to defeat the detection system and enter the facility covertly.

For any given facility there may be several threats, such as a criminal outsider, a disgruntled employee, competitors, or

some combination of the above, so the PPS must be designed to protect against all of these threats. Choosing the most likely threat, designing the system to meet this threat, and then testing to verify the system performance against the other threats will facilitate this process.

Finally, target identification should be performed for the facility. Targets may include critical assets or information, people, or critical areas and processes. A thorough review of the facility and its assets should be conducted. Such questions as "What losses will be incurred in the event of sabotage of this equipment?" will help identify the assets or equipment that are most vulnerable or that create an unacceptable consequence.

Given the information obtained through facility characterization, threat definition, and target identification, the designer can determine the protection objectives of the PPS. An example of a protection objective might be to interrupt a criminal adversary equipped with hand tools and a vehicle before finished CPUs (central processing units or microprocessors) can be removed from the shipping dock. The process of determining objectives will be somewhat recursive. That is, definition of the threat will depend on target identification and vice versa. This recursion should be expected and is indicative of the complex relationships among protection system objectives.

PPS Design and Evaluation Process—Design PPS

The next step in the process, if designing a new PPS, is to determine how best to combine such elements as fences, barriers, sensors, procedures, communication devices, and security personnel into a PPS that can achieve the protection objectives. The resulting PPS design should meet these objectives within the operational, safety, legal, and economic constraints of the facility. The primary functions of a PPS are detection of an adversary, delay of that adversary, and response by security personnel (guard force).

Certain guidelines should be observed during the PPS design. A PPS performs better if detection is as far from the target as possible and delays are near the target. In addition, there is close association between detection (exterior or interior) and assessment. The designer should be aware that detection without assessment is not detection. Another close association is the relationship between response and response force communications. A response force cannot respond unless it receives a communication call for a response. These and many other particular features of PPS components help to ensure that the designer takes advantage of the strengths of each piece of equipment and uses equipment in combinations that complement each other and protect any weaknesses.

PPS Design and Evaluation Process—Evaluate PPS

Analysis and evaluation of the PPS design begin with a review and thorough understanding of the protection objectives the designed system must meet. This can be done simply by checking for required features of a PPS, such as intrusion detection, entry control, access delay, response communications, and a response force. However, a PPS design based on required features cannot be expected to lead to a high-performance system unless those features, when used together, are sufficient to assure adequate levels of protection. More sophisticated analysis and evaluation techniques can be used to estimate the minimum performance levels achieved by a PPS. These techniques include qualitative and quantitative analysis. Systems that are designed to protect high-value critical assets generally require a quantitative analysis. Systems protecting lower-value assets may be analyzed using less rigorous qualitative techniques. In order to complete a quantitative analysis, performance data must be available for the system components.

An existing PPS at an operational facility cannot normally be fully tested as a system. This sort of test would be highly disruptive to the operation of the facility and could impact production schedules, as well as security effectiveness (i.e., create a vulnerability). Because direct system tests are not practical, evaluation techniques are based on performance tests of component subsystems. Component performance estimates are combined into system performance estimates by the application of system modeling techniques.

The end result of this phase of the design and analysis process is a system vulnerability assessment. Analysis of the PPS design will either find that the design effectively achieved the protection objectives or it will identify weaknesses. If the protection objectives are achieved, then the design and analysis process is completed. However, the PPS should be analyzed periodically to ensure that the original protection objectives remain valid and that the protection system continues to meet them.

If the PPS is found to be ineffective, vulnerabilities in the system can be identified. The next step in the design and analysis cycle is to redesign or upgrade the initial protection system design to correct the noted vulnerabilities. It is possible that the PPS objectives also need to be reevaluated. An analysis of the redesigned system is performed. This cycle continues until the results indicate that the PPS meets the protection objectives.

Physical Protection System Design

A system may be defined as an integrated collection of components or elements designed to achieve an objective according to a plan. The designer of any system must have the system's ultimate objective in mind. The ultimate objective of a PPS is to prevent the accomplishment of malevolent overt or covert actions. Typical objectives are to prevent sabotage of critical equipment, theft of assets or information from within the facility, and protection of people (executive protection or workplace violence). A PPS must accomplish its objectives by either deterrence or a combination of detection, delay, and response.

The PPS functions of detection and delay can be accomplished by the use of equipment and guards. Facility guards usually handle response. There is always a balance between the use of equipment and the use of guards. In different conditions and applications, one is often the preferable choice. As technology improves, the mix of equipment and guards will change and increase system effectiveness. The key to a successful protection system is the integration of people, procedures, and equipment into a system that protects assets from malevolent adversaries.

Detection, delay, and response are all required functions of an effective PPS. These functions must be performed in this order and within a length of time that is less than the time required for the adversary to complete their task. A well-designed system provides protection-in-depth, minimizes the consequence of component failures, and exhibits balanced protection. In addition, a design process based on performance criteria rather than feature criteria will select elements and procedures according to the contribution they make to overall system performance. Performance criteria are also measurable, so they aid in the analysis of the designed system. These principles will be discussed in more detail in Chapter 5, "Physical Protection System Design."

PPS Functions

The purpose of a PPS is to prevent an adversary from successful completion of a malevolent action against a facility. There are several functions that the PPS must perform. The primary PPS functions are detection, delay, and response. It is essential to consider the system functions in detail, since a thorough understanding of the definitions of these functions and the measure of effectiveness of each is required to evaluate the system. It is important to note that detection must be accomplished for delay to be effective. Remember that the system goal is to protect assets from a malevolent adversary. For a system to be effective at this objective there must be awareness that there is an attack (detection) and slowing of adversary progress to the targets (delay), thus allowing the response force enough time to interrupt or stop the adversary (response).

Detection

Detection is the discovery of an adversary action. It includes sensing of covert or overt actions. The measures of effectiveness for the detection function are the probability of sensing adversary action and the time required for reporting and assessing the alarm. The probability of assessed detection for a particular sensor captures both of these measures. Included in the detection function of physical protection is entry control. Entry control refers to allowing entry to authorized personnel and detecting the attempted entry of unauthorized personnel and material. The measures of effectiveness of entry control are throughput, false acceptance rate, and false rejection rate. Throughput is defined as the number of authorized personnel allowed access per unit time, assuming that all personnel who attempt entry are authorized for entrance. False acceptance is the rate at which false identities or credentials are allowed entry, while the false rejection rate is the frequency of denying access to authorized personnel.

The response force can also accomplish detection. Guards at fixed posts or on patrol may serve a vital role in sensing an intrusion. However, this decision must be carefully considered. Once an alarm is initiated and reported, assessment begins. An effective assessment system provides two types of information associated with detection. This information includes whether the alarm is a valid alarm or a nuisance alarm and details about the cause of the alarm—what, who, where, and how many.

Delay

Delay is the second function of a PPS. It is the slowing down of adversary progress. Delay can be accomplished by personnel, barriers, locks, and activated delays. Response force personnel can be considered elements of delay if they are in fixed and well-protected positions. The measure of delay effectiveness is the time required by the adversary (after detection) to bypass each delay element. Although the adversary may be delayed prior to detection, this delay is of no value to the

effectiveness of the PPS, because it does not provide additional time to respond to the adversary. Delay before detection is primarily a deterrent.

Response

The response function consists of the actions taken by the response force to prevent adversary success. Response can include both interruption and neutralization. Interruption is defined as a sufficient number of response force personnel arriving at the appropriate location to stop the adversary's progress. It includes the communication to the response force of accurate information about adversary actions and the deployment of the response force. Neutralization describes the actions and effectiveness of the responders after interruption. The primary measure of response effectiveness is the time between receipt of a communication of adversary action and the interruption of the adversary action. Response time is the primary measure because responders must be at the correct location in order to neutralize the adversary. At sites where there is no immediate response, it is assumed that the asset can be lost and this is an acceptable risk. In these cases, the primary response may be after-loss-event investigation, recovery of the asset, and criminal prosecution.

Deployment describes the actions of the response force from the time communication is received until the force is in position to interrupt the adversary. The effectiveness measure of this function is the probability of deployment to the adversary location and the time required to deploy the response force.

Design Goals

The effectiveness of the PPS functions of detection, delay, and response and their relationship has already been discussed.

In addition, all of the hardware elements of the system must be installed, maintained, and operated properly. The procedures of the PPS must be compatible with facility operations and procedures. Security, safety, and operational objectives must be accomplished at all times. A PPS that has been well engineered will be based on sound principles, including protection-in-depth, minimum consequence of component failure, and balanced protection. Each of these principles will be discussed in more detail in Chapter 5, "Physical Protection System Design."

Design Criteria

Any design must include criteria (requirements and specifications) against which elements of the design will be evaluated. A design process using performance criteria will select elements and procedures according to the contribution they make to overall system performance. The effectiveness measure will be overall system performance.

A feature criteria (also called compliance-based) approach selects elements or procedures that satisfy requirements for the presence of certain items. The effectiveness measure is the presence of those features. The use of a feature criteria approach in regulations or requirements that apply to PPSs should generally be avoided or handled with extreme care. Unless such care is exercised, a feature criteria approach can lead to the use of a checklist method to determine system adequacy based on the presence or absence of required features. This is clearly not desirable, since overall system performance is of interest, rather than the mere presence or absence of system features or components. For example, a performance criterion for a perimeter detection system would be that the system is able to detect a running intruder using any attack method. A feature criterion for the same detection system might be that

the system includes two different sensor types.

Performance Measures

The design and evaluation techniques presented in this text support a performance-based approach to meeting the PPS objectives. Much of the component technology material will, however, be applicable for either performance criteria or feature criteria design methods. The performance measures for a PPS function include probability of detection; probability of and time for alarm communication and assessment; frequency of nuisance alarms; time to defeat obstacles; probability of and time for accurate communication to the response force; probability of response force deployment to adversary location; time to deploy to a location; and response force effectiveness after deployment.

Analysis

A PPS is a complex configuration of detection, delay, and response elements. Computerized techniques are available to analyze a PPS and evaluate its effectiveness (Bennett, 1977; Chapman and Harlan, 1985). Such techniques identify system deficiencies, evaluate improvements, and perform cost-versus-effectiveness comparisons. These techniques are appropriate for analyzing PPSs at individual sites. Also, the techniques can be used for evaluating either an existing protection system or a proposed system design.

The goal of an adversary is to complete a path to a target with the least likelihood of being stopped by the PPS. To achieve this goal, the adversary may attempt to minimize the time required to complete the path. This strategy involves penetrating barriers with little regard to the probability of being detected. The adversary is successful if the path is completed before guards can respond. Alternatively, the adversary may attempt to minimize detection with little regard to the time required. In this case, the adversary is successful if the path is completed without being detected.

The measure of effectiveness for interrupting an adversary used in this text is timely detection. Timely detection refers to the cumulative probability of detecting the adversary at a point where there is enough time remaining on the adversary path for the response force to interrupt the adversary. The delay elements along the path determine the point by which the adversary must be detected. That point is where the minimum delay along the remaining portion of the path just exceeds the guard response time. The probability of interruption (P_I) is the cumulative probability of detection from the start of the path up to the point determined by the time remaining for the guards to respond. This value of P_I serves as one measure of the PPS effectiveness. At high security facilities with an immediate on-site response (often armed), another measure of response is the probability of neutralization (P_N), which is defeat of the adversary after interruption.

Physical Protection System Design and the Relationship to Risk

The design and analysis of a PPS include the determination of the PPS objectives, characterizing the design of the PPS, the evaluation of the design, and, possibly, a redesign or refinement of the system. The process must begin by gathering information about the facility, defining the threat, and then identifying targets. Determination of whether or not assets are attractive targets is based mainly on the ease or difficulty of acquisition and the value of the asset. The next step is to characterize the design of the PPS by defining the detection, delay, and response elements. The PPS is then analyzed and evaluated to ensure

it meets the physical protection objectives. Evaluation must allow for features working together to assure protection rather than regarding each feature separately.

The basic premise of the methodology described in this text is that the design and analysis of physical protection must be accomplished as an integrated system. In this way, all components of detection, delay, and response can be properly weighted according to their contribution to the PPS as a whole. At a higher level, the facility owner must balance the effectiveness of the PPS against available resources and then evaluate the proposed design. Without a methodical, defined, analytical assessment, the PPS might waste valuable resources on unnecessary protection or, worse yet, fail to provide adequate protection at critical points of the facility. Due to the complexity of protection systems, an evaluation usually requires computer modeling techniques. If any vulnerabilities are found, the initial system must be redesigned to correct the vulnerabilities and a reevaluation conducted. Then the system's overall risk should be calculated. This risk is normalized to the consequence severity if the adversary could attain the target. This means that the consequence of the loss of an asset is represented numerically by a value between zero and one, where the highest consequence of loss is represented by one and other lower consequence losses are assigned correspondingly lower values. This method ranks the consequence of loss of assets from unacceptably high down to very low or no consequence. This is explained in Chapter 4, "Target Identification." The facility manager is then able to make a judgment as to the amount of risk that remains and if this is acceptable.

The risk equation used is

$$R = P_A{}^*[1 - (P_E)]^*C$$

Each term in the equation will be elaborated more fully throughout the text. At this time, it is sufficient to note that the measure of PPS effectiveness, P_E, can be related to the probability of attack (P_A) and the consequence associated with the loss (C) to determine risk. In addition, P_E is the product of the probability of interruption (P_I) and the probability of neutralization (P_N), assuming both interruption and neutralization are part of the response.

Once the risk value is determined, the security manager can justify the expenditure of funds based on a scientific, measurable, and prioritized analysis. This information can be presented to executive management of the corporation or facility to demonstrate how the security risk is being mitigated and how much risk exposure remains. The analysis can then form the basis for a discussion on how much security risk can be tolerated or how much to increase or decrease the budget based on risk. This analysis can also serve to demonstrate to any regulatory agencies that a careful review of the security of the facility has been performed and that reasonable measures are in place to protect people and assets. The analysis will allow the facility to state the assumptions that were made (threat, targets, risk level), show the system design, and provide detailed information to support system effectiveness measures.

This process only describes the evaluated risk of the security system and its effectiveness. It should be noted that there are multiple risk areas for a facility or corporation, of which security is only one part. Other areas of risk that need to be considered within the business enterprise include financial risk management, liability risk financing, property/net income financing, employee benefits, environmental health and safety, and property engineering (Zuckerman, 1998). It should be clear that the security program is one that contributes to the bottom line of the corporation, by protecting assets from malevolent human threats. The security manager should be capable of allocating available resources to best protect corporate assets and adjusting resources as required in the face of changing threats.

This is the role of the security manager or director in the corporate structure.

Summary

This chapter introduces the use of a systematic and measurable approach to the implementation of a PPS. It emphasizes the function of detection, followed by delay and response, and presents a brief description of the relationship of these functions. Deterrence of an adversary is compared to defeat of an adversary, along with the caution not to rely on deterrence to protect assets. Specific performance measures of various components of a PPS are described, along with how these measures are combined to support a cost–benefit analysis. The process stresses the use of integrated systems combining people, procedures, and equipment to meet the protection objectives. In support of this concept, the difference between safety and security is described to emphasize the difference between accidents or natural disasters and malevolent human attack.

Additional chapters in this text will provide the specific details incorporated by this approach. The concepts presented here are somewhat unique in the security industry as a whole, but have been demonstrated to be effective in protecting critical nuclear assets for the past 25 years. Although a particular facility may not require the same level of protection or have the same unacceptably high consequence of loss—the loss of a nuclear weapon or material could result in the death of thousands of people, while the loss of a piece of jewelry from a retail store is much less—the process described in these pages can still be applied to protect targets against the appropriate threats. Ultimately, this leads to an effective system design that can be used to explain why certain security components were used, how they contribute to the system effectiveness, and how this system mitigates total risk to the facility or corporation.

References

Bennett, H.A. The EASI approach to physical security evaluation. SAND Report 760500 1977; 1–35.*

Chapman, L.D., and Harlan, C.P. EASI estimate of adversary sequence interruption on an IBM PC. SAND Report 851105 1985; 1–63.

Sivarajasingam, V., and Shepherd, J.P. "Effect of closed circuit television on urban violence." *Journal of Accident and Emergency Medicine* 1999; 16(4): 255–257.

Williams, J.D. "DOE/SS Handbooks: A means of disseminating physical security equipment information." *Journal of the Institute of Nuclear Materials Management* 1978; 7(1): 65–75.

Zuckerman, M.M. "Moving towards a holistic approach to risk management education: Teaching business security management." Presented at 2nd Annual American Society of Industrial Security Education Symposium, August 13–15, 1998, New York, NY.

Questions

1. Explain the difference between the goals of safety systems and operations and security systems and operations.
2. Discuss the strengths and weaknesses of deterrence as the goal of a security system.
3. What are the functions of a good security system? How are these functions applied? Why?

---

* SAND Reports are available from National Technical Information Service, US Department of Commerce, 5285 Port Royal Road, Springfield, VA 22161. Phone: 800-553-NTIS (6847) or 703-605-6000; Fax: 703-605-6900; TDD: 703-487-4639; http://www.ntis.gov/help/ ordermethods.asp?loc=7-4-0 or US Government Printing Office, 732 North Capitol St. NW, Washington, DC 20401. Phone: 202-512-1800 or 866-512-1800; Fax: 202-512-2104; E-mail: ContactCenter@gpo.gov; http://www.access.gpo.gov.

PART ONE

Determining System Objectives

2

Facility Characterization

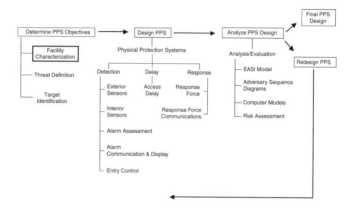

The first step in designing a new PPS or upgrading an existing system is to characterize the facility to be protected. Before any decisions can be made concerning the level of protection needed, an understanding of what is being protected and the surrounding environment is essential. Too often this crucial step is overlooked and security systems are designed that either overprotect a nonessential component or fail to adequately protect a vital portion of the facility. The cost of an overdesigned system can be enormous, and the possible results of inadequate protection can be disastrous. Thus, it is absolutely essential that a facility be understood fully in terms of constraints, expected performance, operations, and the circumstances in which the facility exists.

When characterizing a facility, information about as many different aspects of the facility as possible must be obtained and reviewed. While this may appear to be an overwhelming task at first, there are several areas of special interest that can serve as the basis for this data collection

effort. Major areas of investigation for facility characterization include:

- physical conditions
- facility operations
- facility policies and procedures
- regulatory requirements
- legal issues
- safety considerations
- corporate goals and objectives

As data is collected, other related areas of interest may emerge. The process of characterizing a facility is the most subjective and least constrained aspect of designing a PPS. The process may start out very structured, but eventually may uncover information that can be surprising and lead to additional unanticipated areas. During interviews conducted at a site, it is not uncommon to discover aspects of a facility's operation or policies that are unknown to some subsets of employees. The reaction to this new information ranges from mild interest to total shock. Interviews conducted at one entertainment complex, across a vertical slice of personnel levels, revealed that when power was lost at the facility the policy was to give guests complimentary one-day admission tickets as they left the park. This came as something of a surprise to some of the senior managers observing the interview! This anecdote also emphasizes the value of personal interviews of people around the facility, in addition to the documentation reviews, tours, and briefings that are normally used to collect information.

Physical Conditions

Perhaps the easiest area to characterize, physical conditions include the site boundary, the number and locations of buildings in the complex, room locations within buildings, access points, existing physical protection features, and all infrastructure details. This information is normally available in blueprints and drawings of the facility. Physical infrastructure that should be reviewed includes heating, ventilation, and air conditioning systems (HVAC); communication paths and type (fiber-optic, telephone, computer networks, etc.); construction materials of walls and ceilings; power distribution system; any unique environmentally controlled areas of the facility; locations of any hazardous materials; and exterior areas. Physical aspects of a site also include an understanding of the topography, vegetation, wildlife, background noise sources (such as airports, rail yards, major highways, or electromagnetic interference), climate and weather, and soil and pavement. This information can be used to predict adversary paths into a facility, establish target locations, and identify potential sources of nuisance alarms for protection equipment.

Existing physical protection features include fences, sensors, cameras, entry control systems, barriers, and response force availability. It will also be important to know whether a facility has an immediate, on-site guard force (contract or proprietary) and the capability of this force or if the facility will depend on other off-site response forces, such as local law enforcement. This information will determine, to a large extent, how effective the final PPS will be.

Several sources of checklists exist to help conduct the physical survey of a site (Barnard, 1988; Burstein, 1994; Fennelly, 1996). While these lists can be useful, excessive dependence on them is not recommended. No single checklist can be written that will cover all the pertinent questions for all different types of facilities or can predict what additional unique sources of information should be utilized. Existing survey tools, however, can form the basis for a checklist at a specific facility and can be modified to reflect the special circumstances of the facility.

Facility Operations

Another major area for investigation is facility operations. This will include such things as major products of the facility, processes that support these products, operating conditions (working hours, off-hours, emergency operations), and the types and numbers of employees. A large part of this stage of data collection is the review of the procedures that are used to accomplish the mission of the facility. This mission is related to the products made at the facility and can include manufactured parts, research data, retail sales, or other products. It should be apparent that any security system should not have an overly restrictive effect on the work of the facility.

Operational review of the facility should also include an evaluation of the supporting functions available at the site. This includes procurement procedures, computing resources and distribution, maintenance activities, asset tracking, operational involvement and location of senior executives, workflow, shift changes, employee benefits, shipping and receiving, accounting functions, and any other supporting functions. This information will establish constraints when implementing security technology or procedures and will help in the identification of facility vulnerabilities later in the process.

Operational details can reveal important transition periods at a facility. For example, at a shift change many employees may be entering and exiting the facility. This can be an important input into the design of any entry controls for the facility or parking areas. The system must be designed to accommodate this high throughput of personnel, even though it may only happen twice a day for a total of 60 minutes. Knowledge of the workloads and schedule at the shipping and receiving dock will help when designing an asset tracking system or implementing controls over the movement of raw materials or product into and out of a facility. This information will establish the operational needs to be accommodated by any security upgrades. Vehicle activity into and out of a facility, as well as within the facility (if it is a large industrial complex), will also provide a basis for vulnerability assessment and establish operational constraints that must be considered as part of the security system design.

In summary, operational issues need to be understood in order to design a system that is effective in protecting targets, while not having an undue effect on the work of the facility. This impact will be part of any trade-off analysis that is performed once a PPS design has been proposed.

Facility Policies and Procedures

One of the most critical areas for study at a facility includes an understanding of the written and unwritten policies and procedures used at a site. Although many companies maintain well-documented collections of this information, it is not uncommon to find that employees use other, undocumented procedures to do their work. This lack

of alignment can at times cause serious discrepancies in the way things are expected to be done and the way they are, in fact, accomplished. These discrepancies may only be minor, but occasionally cause major risk and expose large liabilities for the corporation. Due to the casual nature of unwritten policies and procedures, they can be hard to uncover. This is why it is very useful to spend some time at a facility observing how things are done. One way to do this is through guided tours of the facility accompanied by knowledgeable or responsible personnel, but it can also be revealing to spend time independently visiting all of the areas of the facility, within safety limits, and watching the general ebb and flow of work. Though this sort of unrestricted access can be difficult to obtain at times, it should be presented in the context of trying to help mitigate risk and reduce liability, not as a license to criticize. It is even possible that the unwritten procedures are more effective than the official versions, so their discovery and use could lead to very positive change. One way of reducing the implicit criticism that may be felt by management during this process is through the use of a nondisclosure agreement, whereby security consultants agree not to divulge any of the information they acquire without express permission from the facility. This will be less of a problem if the security system designer is a direct employee of the facility.

Corporate policies should exist that document to all employees their right to privacy or corresponding work locations where they should have no expectation of privacy; the policy on bringing drugs, alcohol, or weapons onto corporate premises; the use of force by site guards; and other notifications to employees of corporate expectations. Corporate procedures should then reinforce the policies by detailing what to do, when they apply, who is responsible, and through appropriate training for employees and contractors.

Training on the correct interpretation and application of corporate procedures must be provided at the facility. If there is a corporate expectation that everyone receives safety training once a year, it is incumbent on the organization to communicate this openly to the employee and then to provide access to training. A lack of alignment between corporate requirements and training in how to meet them can reduce employee morale and productivity and increase the chances for a safety or security incident. In a like manner, if employees are expected to maintain certain security levels, but have no training on what this means on a day-to-day basis, there can be disappointment on all sides. Corporate training should be available to solidify the expectations for employee behavior and show that management is fully committed to the policy. If management is not committed, the policy should be revised or removed. Employee training is a major part of the implementation of any corporate system, but especially for security, because employees can be one of the best sources of prevention and detection.

The presence or absence of well-documented, consistently applied and trained policies and procedures can be an indication of the corporate culture at a facility. A culture that is accustomed to clear expectations and the support to meet those expectations will be better able to accommodate the discipline necessary to support an effective security system. If the corporate culture is one that is less disciplined or more autonomous, a security system may not be embraced willingly by the employees, which can be a serious impediment to the success of the system. This point will be further discussed later in this chapter, under "Corporate Goals and Objectives."

Regulatory Requirements

All facilities, no matter what their product or business, are responsible to some regulatory authority. This may include the local fire department; safety and health regulators; federal agencies including the Departments of Labor, Energy, Defense, or Commerce; or any of a number of special regulatory agencies, such as the Nuclear Regulatory Commission or the local Corporation Commission. In addition, every facility must meet certain standards in their work practices. These may be standards imposed by professional organizations, such as Certified Public Accountant, or they may be best practices within an industry. Many facilities utilize a variety of standards approved by Underwriters Laboratories (UL, 2000). All construction must meet a variety of state and local building codes. Regardless of the formality of the regulation, it is important to understand the nature of all the regulations a facility may be expected or required to meet.

For example, a small bookkeeping office may only have to meet minimal state and local fire codes, while a major petrochemical producer will be expected to conform to additional state and local regulations. Federal agencies such as the US Occupational Safety and Health Administration (OSHA, 2006), the Department of Labor, the Environmental Protection Agency (EPA, 2006), and perhaps the National Labor Relations Board may also regulate the petrochemical producer. These requirements must be considered as a security system is designed. Obviously, any security system that is implemented cannot put the company at risk of violating any regulations. These regulations then become an important supplement to the design and implementation of the security system. Safety-related aspects of these regulations are discussed in more detail in the next section.

Safety Considerations

As previously discussed in Chapter 1, "Design and Evaluation of Physical Protection Systems," safety and security do not have the same goal, although they are complementary functions. Consider the desired behaviors of a group of employees during a fire at a facility. The facility safety representative will say: stop what you are doing right now, leave the area or building in a calm and orderly manner, and go to a certain designated location and wait for more information. However, the facility security manager will say: stop what you are doing, secure the critical information or asset you are using, then leave the building. This creates the classic conflict between safety and security—safety people want evacuation as fast as possible, and security people want to be sure that no asset is stolen or left unprotected during the fire (which may only be a diversion). This conflict, though difficult, must be resolved by the two parties working jointly to meet both their individual functional objectives and the bigger objectives of the corporation.

While no security manager would want to put a person in physical danger to protect an asset, it is prudent to design technology systems and procedures to meet all needs. One example of this is the use of a short (10–15 s) time-delay on fire exits from critical areas. This can allow safety or security personnel time to ascertain that there really is a fire or to broadcast instructions to personnel in the facility. Some fire systems now include an override feature that will allow a safety officer to continually reset the delay on a door, when they are certain there is no imminent danger (i.e., a false alarm). Some facilities dispatch a security officer to the critical location to guard the asset until the safety event ends or it is no longer safe to be in the area. In many jurisdictions, waivers to applicable codes in specific situations can be granted, if a strong case can be made to justify the exception. Either way, it is important to incorporate this kind of thinking into the facility security system.

A different example of the conflicts that can arise from safety and security systems is demonstrated by an incident at a major power-producing plant. A fire started in a limited access room in the plant and some people were hurt. In response to the fire, the automatic sprinklers were activated. The water shorted out the electric door locks on the room entrances, which prevented the immediate entry of medical personnel into the area. This is a good example of how safety and security systems must be designed to work together under all conditions.

It should be clear that an important voice in the design of an effective security system will be the facility or operational safety officer. Many companies base their safety systems on the standards published by Underwriters Laboratories (UL, 2006). Safety and security personnel must work together to design systems that will be effective in normal (daily operations), abnormal (e.g., a fire), and malevolent conditions (e.g., an attack on the facility by a human adversary). Conflicts between the two should be resolved by sound and integrated solutions; if this fails, the decision should be made based on some reasonable criteria determined in advance by the organization. This may include the consequence of the loss of the asset, the increased liability to the company for injury or death or the trade-off between the two.

Legal Issues

Perhaps the most visible and complex aspect of facility characterization is a thorough review of the legal issues that should be considered when designing and implementing a security system. Legal issues cover liability, privacy, access for the disabled, labor relations, employment practices, proper training for guards, the failure to protect, and excessive use of force by guards, to list only a few. A good understanding of the criminal justice system will be a very useful component in the design and implementation of a PPS.

It would be nearly impossible to give a complete overview of all the legal issues that a facility (or corporation) confronts every day, without the added burden that poorly designed or implemented security systems add. For this reason, a brief discussion of only some of the major considerations that fall under legal issues will be presented. Each facility will need to make its own assessment of which legal issues are concerns and what actions will be taken based on this information. It should be emphasized that an organization should not choose to ignore security issues just because the legal complexities seem overwhelming. This very act could put the enterprise at risk for some liability, by not acting to prevent crimes that have occurred on the premises (or similar ones in other locations) in the past. An excellent example of this is the lodging industry. Case law is full of examples where hotels, after a rape, robbery, or assault occurs on the premises, are expected to implement measures to protect guests from similar attacks. When they do not implement these measures, the penalty is much more severe at the next occurrence (Slepian, 2006). It is strongly suggested that an attorney be retained to consult with the facility to resolve these issues. An excellent overview of security and the law has been written by Kennedy (2006).

Security Liability

Within the context of liability incurred as a result of security system implementation, most businesses are sued for deficient proactive security services and practices (failure to provide reasonable security for persons, property, or information), and intrusive, improper, and abusive reactive services and practices when responding to an incident. To better define what is meant, a few examples will be discussed. Thorough reviews of the legal issues encountered by a security organization

are available (Hess and Wrobleski, 1996; Fischer and Green, 2006).

Failure to Protect

This can refer to a variety of instances, including the negligence of security guards to protect patrons at a restaurant or other site, loss of property through employee embezzlement or fraud, and loss of information such as a trade secret. Failure to protect would also include loss of intellectual property, such as patents, copyrights, or trademarks, and loss of confidential information, including employee personnel files, patient records, or business records.

Overreaction

The liability incurred for overreaction involves incidents such as excessive use of force by a security officer, invasion of privacy by an investigator or technology, and false imprisonment by a security officer (Timm and Christian, 1991). While these issues are resolved through clear policies at the facility and training to reinforce the policy, many companies still do not align their policies and procedures with their practice. This exposes them to increased liability with respect to these types of events. A surprising number of companies do not train their security force in proper procedures on use of force or detaining an employee or other suspect for questioning. Because many guards are not sworn peace officers, they have no power of arrest, so this can be a liability.

Labor/Employment Issues

Many companies have organized labor (union-represented) employees and so must be aware of federal law pertaining to union membership drives, strikes, and conduct of disciplinary interviews and interrogations of union members. Other aspects of this area include workers' compensation claims, termination of employment for security violations, and negligent hiring practices. While these cases do not represent a large number at any one facility, they are issues that have surfaced at times and need to be considered within the broader context of how a company chooses to operate. In addition, the law is clear that if an employee is hired and commits an illegal act on behalf of the company, the company is liable. This sort of finding has led many companies to initiate background checks on employees for certain sensitive positions, such as security guards and supervisors.

There are volumes of information available on legal issues and security, as well as other publications that track and report on case law for security, such as the *Private Security Case Law Reporter* (Strafford Publications, Atlanta). As facility information is collected and legal questions arise, consult with an attorney or review the many information sources on law and security to help develop guidelines, policies, and procedures that limit corporate liability while effectively protecting assets.

Corporate Goals and Objectives

When designing a PPS, it will be important to understand how the corporation or facility views the role of the security organization. If security is seen as a required function that adds no value, it will be difficult to establish an integrated security system using people, procedures, and equipment to meet the desired goals. It is important for senior management to see the security function as a part of the total business operation and a partner in the strategic plan for reaching corporate goals. For this reason, it is vital that the security system designer has the support of senior management. If senior management is not convinced of the importance

of security to the business, they may be reluctant to commit any resources towards system development or improvement. In addition, the security manager should be apprised of any impending major actions at the facility. Some examples include the purchase of a new operating division or site, anticipated layoffs, expansion or addition of production capacity, or scheduled meetings or visits by corporate executives or other officials to a site. This information is required in order to assure continued protection for assets or personnel.

The first job of the security system designer, then, may be to convince executives of the value and importance of at least evaluating a facility to see if there are any vulnerabilities, and then to present system improvements in a manner that shows them what value has been added. This is the goal of this textbook. The approach described throughout this text is meant to provide a business rationale to executives that will allow them to see the benefit of their investment, while at the same time helping the facility security manager to apply available resources most effectively. Later in this book, a more detailed description of risk analysis will be presented, which will tie together all of the system pieces presented in the different chapters.

Other Information

The political environment in the surrounding community and internal to the facility can provide additional information for facility characterization. Local politicians or councils can have an effect on operations at a facility, and internal power struggles could have an effect on the value placed on security systems or functions. Liaison between the facility and local law enforcement can also be important, particularly if the facility will depend on this group for any response to a security event. The existence of or membership in any mutual aid agreements with other industries in the area should also be investigated, because these agreements can provide additional resources to respond to or collect information from concerning threats. This will also allow links to others in the community for dealing with any emergency conditions.

Finally, it should be noted that the collection of data across different types of facilities will have some things in common (i.e., people are allowed in), some things that are different (a power company would have more infrastructure elements than a retail store), and some that are unique (a dam). As a result, there is no one-size-fits-all list of data or sources. This is also a dynamic process; as progress is made, additional data may be required or some data may become extraneous.

Summary

This chapter describes the process of collecting information to characterize a facility. Prior to designing a PPS, as much information as possible should be gathered to understand the activities at the facility and the facility layout. This will help identify constraints, document existing protection features, and reveal areas and assets that may be vulnerable. Areas of investigation include physical conditions, facility operations, facility policies and procedures, regulatory requirements, legal issues, safety considerations, and corporate goals and objectives. As more information is collected, additional areas of interest may emerge. When collecting information, a variety of sources should be used, including drawings, policies and procedures, tours, briefings, reference material, and personal interviews.

Security Principle

In order to design a system that will be effective, the PPS design must accommodate the safety, process, and mission needs of the corporation and the facility.

References

Barnard, R.L. *Intrusion Detection Systems,* 2nd ed. Boston: Butterworth-Heinemann, 1988, 7–15.

Burstein, H. *Introduction to Security.* Englewood Cliffs, NJ: Prentice Hall, 1994, 217–230.

EPA-Environmental Protection Agency: Laws and Regulations. http://www.epa.gov/epahome/rules.html, last accessed December 2006.

Fennelly, L.J. *Handbook of Loss Prevention and Crime Prevention,* 3rd ed. Boston: Butterworth-Heinemann, 1996, 33–54, 370–374.

Fischer, R.J., and Green, G. *Introduction to Security,* 7th ed. Boston: Butterworth-Heinemann, 2006, 103–128.

Hess, K.M., and Wrobleski, H.M. *Introduction to Private Security.* St. Paul: West Publishing, 1996, 72–90.

Kennedy, D.B. "Forensic security and the law" in Gill, M., ed., *The Handbook of Security.* New York: Palgrave Macmillan, 2006, 118–145.

OSHA (Occupational Safety and Health Administration)—Regulation and Compliance Links. http://www.osha.gov/, last accessed December 2006.

Slepian, C.G. Developing and Managing a Hotel /Motel Residence Security Program. Foreseeable Risk Analysis Center. May 22, 2006. http://www.frac.com/storage/docs/Amended-Slepian_Charles.doc.

Timm, H.W., and Christian, K.E. *Introduction to Private Security.* Pacific Grove: Brooks-Cole Publishing, 1991, 224–227.

Underwriters Laboratories Inc.: Standards Catalog. May 22, 2006. http://ulstandardsinfonet.ul.com/.

Questions

1. Pick three different facility types, for example, a retail store, a museum, and a power company, and describe the kinds of information needed to characterize the facility and where it might be obtained.
2. In groups of three, play the role of the security system designer for each of the facilities in Exercise 1 and discuss how your facility is the same as and different than the others.
3. Discuss how the collection of data about a facility requires information about the business goals for the company, use of security technology, and aspects of the criminal justice system.
4. What impediments to a new or upgraded security system could a protection system designer encounter? What would convince you, as the system designer, that a PPS could be effective at a facility?

3

Threat Definition

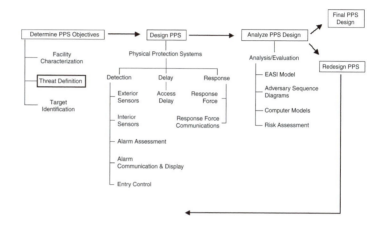

The possibility that criminals or terrorists might attempt to steal assets or information, sabotage a facility, extort a person, or perform other criminal activities at industrial or government sites has created special problems for the protection of assets. The designers of PPSs and those in charge of setting requirements make certain assumptions about the intentions and capabilities of their perceived adversaries. Assumptions are made when people in government or industry make budgetary allocations for physical protection measures. Assumptions are made when a decision is reached to acquire or not to acquire certain kinds of hardware or to hire additional personnel. A study of the capabilities and intentions of potential criminals or adversaries, although sometimes speculative, provides a basis for making such assumptions. The basis for making the needed assumptions should be predicated upon a thoughtfully developed threat statement that defines a reasonable assessment of the possible intentions, motivations, and physical capabilities of likely adversaries. In addition, the availability of on-site or local law enforcement response

personnel is an important consideration. Once adversary types are identified, additional thought can go into determining the design basis threat or the threat against which the facility or target will be protected. This chapter will describe one approach that can be used to develop a definition of threat for a specific facility. The threat definition must be considered when determining the objectives or evaluating the effectiveness of an existing PPS.

The concept of the design basis threat (DBT) is often used to establish the expected threat to a facility. The DBT is used as a management and design tool that helps facilitate informed decision-making by executives and establishes technical requirements for designers. For management, the DBT documents the assumptions that were used for the evaluation or design; the technical requirements for a system that protects assets from vandals will be much less than those for protection against armed criminals. Threats may range from vandals up through sophisticated terrorists. If a facility performs experiments on animals or provides abortion services, extremists may try to disrupt or stop operations. Government buildings and sites have become targets for various extremists, who have expressed their disagreement with government policies in violent and dramatic ways (see Figure 3.1). Collecting this information, organizing it, and using it to determine which threat(s) a particular facility may encounter form the basis of defining the threat. Since the attacks of 9/11, many agencies and private industries have spent considerable time defining expected threats, especially to critical infrastructures. In addition, the new US Department of Homeland Security (DHS), formed in 2002, has been working with private industry to define benchmark threats that can be used in vulnerability assessments and establish levels of risk to critical infrastructures (see http://www.asme-iti.org/RAMCAP/RAMCAP.cfm).

PPSs must be designed to protect against these threats. As an example, the threat for US Department of Energy (DOE) facilities is defined in the *DOE Design Basis Threat Policy*. Parts of this policy include classified information that is not available to the general public. The Nuclear Regulatory Commission (NRC) specifies another, but similar, threat that commercial nuclear facilities use in the design and analysis of their PPS. Without a defined threat, it is virtually impossible to design an effective PPS because designers need to understand the capabilities and motivation of the threat in order to select the appropriate components of the system. An analogy would be asking an automobile company to design a car without any idea of its desired characteristics. Car designs are usually targeted to certain demographics, which can include price point, age, gender, educational level, and other characteristics. In addition, each car has a set of features and specifications that are important to many buyers, such as reliability, comfort (air conditioning, power windows, etc.), seating capacity, and gas mileage. Lacking this sort of input to the automobile design process, engineers would be hard-pressed to create a car that meets the objectives. In a like manner, without an understanding of the expected threat to a facility, designers will have no basis for selecting equipment, establishing procedural controls, or training personnel on the use and operation of the PPS.

Steps for Threat Definition

The threat at one facility may not be the same as the threat for another. The threat may vary even for facilities making the same products or using the same operations. In addition, one facility may face several different threats. It should be noted that threats are based on targets, so these objectives must be considered in parallel.

The physical threat to a facility must be defined as part of determining the objectives of the PPS. A threat definition results in a detailed description of the physical threat by a malevolent adversary to the system. The description includes information about the potential actions, motivations, and physical capabilities of the potential adversary.

The methodology for threat definition consists of three basic parts:

1. List the information needed to define the threat.
2. Collect information on the potential threat.
3. Organize the information to make it usable.

Each of the parts is important in deriving a complete definition of the threat(s) for a specific site.

List Threat Information

Before time is spent collecting information, it is important to decide what kind of information is needed to complete a definition

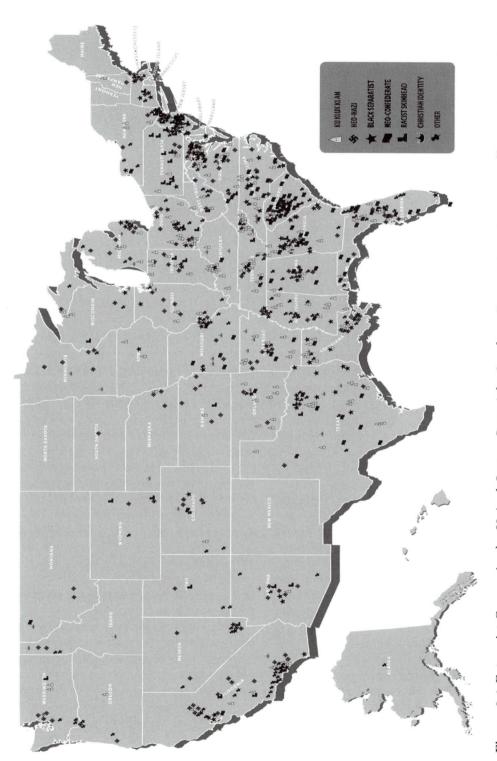

Figure 3.1 Extremist Groups in the United States. Copyright Southern Poverty Law Center, Intelligence Project. Visit their web site at http://www.splcenter.org for additional information

of threat for a site. A list of necessary information about adversaries includes:

- motivation
- potential goals based upon targets
- tactics
- numbers and capabilities

A definition of threat must include a description of the type of adversary. In this book, adversaries are characterized into three broad groups—outsiders, insiders, and outsiders working in collusion with insiders.

Outsiders

Outsiders might include terrorists, criminals, extremists, or hackers (Freedman and Mann, 1997). Motivations that might prompt potential adversaries to undertake criminal actions against an enterprise or facility can be grouped into three broad categories:

1. *Ideological motivations* are those linked to a political or philosophical system. They would include those of political terrorists, antinuclear extremists, and certain groups of philosophical or religious fanatics. Some examples include anti-abortion, animal rights, militia, and various hate groups.
2. *Economic motivations* involve a desire for financial gain. Criminals might view material or information as potentially attractive targets for schemes of theft for ransom, sale, or extortion.
3. *Personal motivations* pertain to the special situations of specific individuals. Personal reasons for committing a crime could range from those of the hostile employee with a grievance against an employer, to those of the psychotic individual. Some attacks are a form of recreation, such as those initiated on computer

systems by hackers. Other motivations may be based on drug or alcohol dependencies or mental instability.

A discussion of the potential goals of the adversary includes what sorts of crimes these various adversaries are interested in and capable of carrying out and which of these crimes are of concern to the specific site. Some of the potential goals of adversaries related to protecting information, assets, and people include theft, sabotage, extortion, kidnapping, or violence against persons, misuse of the facility, and disclosure of classified or proprietary information.

Insiders

An insider is defined as anyone with knowledge of operations or security systems and who has unescorted access to facilities or security interests. A full range of insider threats would include an individual or individuals who are passive (e.g., provide information), active nonviolent (e.g., facilitate entrance and exit, disable alarms and communications), or active violent (participate in a violent attack). The active violent insider is a very difficult adversary to protect against. Although more than one insider is possible, emphasis is placed upon addressing the single insider, the most probable insider threat. Hollinger and Davis (2006) have written an excellent discussion of employee theft.

Recent surveys indicate that insiders are responsible for the majority of security breaches in both physical and computer security systems (Computer Security Institute [CSI], 1998; Radcliff, 1998; Pinkerton, 1997; National Retail Security Survey, 2002). When considering the threat of the insider, it must be recognized that insiders can have the same motivations as outsiders. Any employee may pose a potential insider threat, even trusted plant managers and security personnel. It should not be assumed that since a person is an employee that he or she will be free from greed and dissatisfaction or invulnerable to cooperating with adversaries as a result of coercion. Insiders have three characteristics that distinguish them from other adversaries:

1. system knowledge that can be used to their advantage;
2. authorized access to the facility, assets, or PPS without raising suspicions of others; and
3. opportunity to choose the best time to commit an act.

Protecting against insiders can be very challenging. Insiders may exploit their knowledge of facility operations and security system performance. They may also maximize their chance of success because they have access to critical areas or information and can choose their own time and strategy. Insiders also may abuse their authority, through their proximity to information and assets or as security personnel. Guard forces represent a special and vexing problem. In one study at a facility, guards were responsible for 41% of crimes committed against assets (Hoffman et al., 1990).

Figure 3.2 shows the protection approaches used across the entire threat spectrum. It shows that outsiders acting alone are deterred or denied by physical protection (physical security), while insiders are primarily defeated through additional procedural measures related to accounting for and tracking of critical assets (i.e., inventories, random searches, or scans). In the case of collusion between outsiders and insiders, strict control of critical assets is added to existing procedures and physical security measures. In this case, additional access controls and specific controls are placed on the movement of assets around or out of a facility. For example, in a manufacturing plant, an assembler of VCRs may collude with the driver of the food service truck

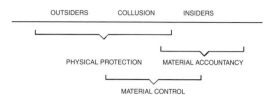

PROTECTION APPROACHES

Figure _3.2_ Protection Approaches Across the Threat Spectrum. Physical protection provides the best effectiveness against outsiders or collusion, while the control of and accounting for assets are useful against insiders. Control and accounting are accomplished through the use of procedures, audits, and inventorying

to remove finished VCRs. This act may be countered by eliminating the capability of the employee to move items out of the production area or by tracking production items manually or automatically.

Physical protection provides the most effective barrier to outsiders acting alone or in collusion with insiders, while the control of and accounting for assets are useful against insiders. Control and accounting are accomplished through the use of procedures, audits, and inventorying.

Additional procedural protection measures against insiders include the use of personnel security assurance programs, such as pre-employment background checks and periodic updates and separation of job responsibilities, so that two or more employees are required to complete sensitive tasks. This will decrease the probability of adversary success, because the cooperation of others is required and, as more people are aware of an imminent attack, there is a higher likelihood of it being reported. Many insider opportunities are the result of procedural failures, not failures of technology. A recent notable example of this is the case of Aldrich Ames. Ames single-handedly compromised the entire US intelligence gathering network in Russia (Earley, 1997). In this case, a knowledgeable insider with access to critical information was allowed to remain in a sensitive position, despite warning signs that should have been acted on during routine security clearance investigations. Other common examples of insider attacks are bank fraud and armored car robberies.

Capability of Adversary

Of utmost concern to the designer of a PPS is the capability of the potential adversary. The number of attackers to be defended against has always been a question of primary concern. It is also valuable to know how the adversary might be armed. Will the adversary have weapons and explosives and, if so, what kind? Other factors that describe adversary capabilities include a list of the adversary's tools and equipment, their means of transportation (truck, helicopter, etc.), extent of technical skills and experience, and whether or not they might have insider assistance.

In addition to weapons, various tools can be used by the adversary to penetrate the security system. Part of threat definition is an assessment of which tools the adversary may use. Tools may include hand tools such as bolt-cutters, pliers, or hacksaw blades, power tools, burn bars, or cutting torches, as well as any tools or equipment located at the facility. This might include such things as chemicals, forklifts, or facility vehicles. Figure 3.3 shows some

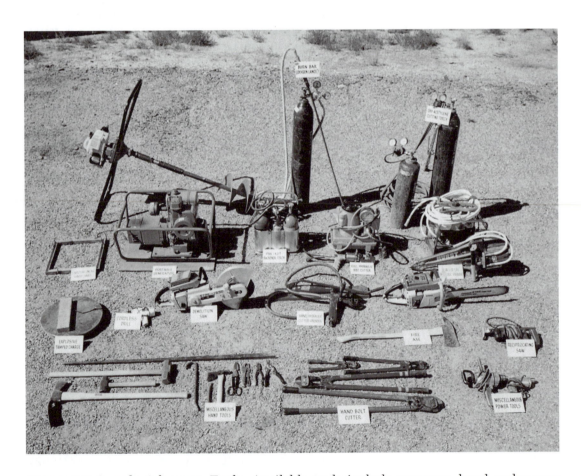

Figure 3.3 Sample Adversary Tools. Available tools include weapons, hand and power tools, and cutting torches, as well as any equipment located at the site of the attack

of the tools an adversary may choose to bring or adapt for use if located on-site.

The sarin attacks on the Tokyo subway, the attacks on 9/11, anthrax attacks in New York and Florida in the fall of 2001, and the Madrid and London train bombings (search http://en.wikipedia.org/wiki/Main_Page for information on these events) have led analysts to include weapons of mass destruction (WMD) as emerging adversary capabilities. WMD include chemical, biological, radiological, or explosive materials, which have the ability to cause mass casualties, public fear, and lasting contamination. While these capabilities may not be used against all facilities, they are a large part of the post-9/11 threat definition for critical industrial and government locations.

Adversary Tactics

Adversaries will be expected to use any tactics that increase their chances of achieving their objective. These tactics include force, stealth, and deceit. A force tactic is one in which the adversary overpowers the system or personnel at a facility, with no attempt to hide their intention. The adversary will penetrate the security system with no concern for being observed and will likely have a weapon to compel others to cooperate. Stealth refers to the adversary trying to enter a facility covertly to meet their objective. The goal is to remain undiscovered for as long as possible. Deceit implies the use of real or forged credentials to gain access to information or assets and remove them under the guise of authorized access.

Clearly, different groups of adversaries will employ different tactics. Although insiders could use any tactic, they benefit most through the use of deceit; that is, they bear legitimate credentials and authorization to be near the target. Workplace violence incidents may be the most common use of force by an insider. A criminal might use a combination of

stealth and deceit, and a terrorist might use a combination of stealth, then force. Consideration of the adversary tactic or combinations of tactics should be part of the threat definition for a facility.

Terrorism has become a larger part of the threat spectrum since 9/11. During the 1990s, Islamist terrorist groups carried out numerous attacks in a variety of countries. A bomb attack against the World Trade Center in New York in 1993 and the Paris Metro attacks in 1995 were amongst the earliest of these, but later in the decade many more attacks were made in other countries, including in Saudi Arabia, Egypt, Tanzania, Kenya, and Yemen. The attacks of 9/11 and significant attacks in predominantly Muslim countries such as Pakistan, Tunisia, Morocco, Qatar, Jordan, Indonesia, and Turkey; in India; as well as attacks in Egypt, Saudi Arabia, and Yemen are examples of evolving bomb attacks. There have also been significant attacks in Europe, as noted in the discussion above on WMD.

Potential Actions

When an adversary attacks a facility, they have specific goals in mind. Potential actions of an adversary include theft, industrial espionage, sabotaging equipment or processes, extortion, blackmail, coercion, violence against others, or kidnapping. It is important to understand the actions of a potential adversary before designing a system so that appropriate protection elements can be included. For example, if a company finds that their expected threat is from an outside competitor gathering information through unauthorized access to computer systems, adding a high-security perimeter intrusion detection system may not reduce the likelihood of attack. However, if the threat is a group of criminals with help from a passive insider, a PPS can be very effective.

Collect Threat Information

The local environment provides information about the threat for a specific site. Conditions outside the facility and inside the facility should be considered. Conditions outside the facility, such as the general attitude of the community, whether the surrounding area is urban or rural, and the presence of organized extremist groups, can provide information on threats. Conditions inside the facility, such as the workforce, labor issues, industrial relations policies, public relations policies, security awareness, and human reliability programs, may also affect the potential threat.

A review and characterization of the local and national population can be useful in determining a potential threat to a specific facility. Any discontented or disgruntled faction of the population should be reviewed. For this faction, special attention should be given to combat veterans, technically skilled people, political extremists, and employees with experience in or access to similar facilities.

There are several features of a facility that may make it more or less attractive to an adversary if there is a perception that these features can be used to adversary advantage. Geographic and structural differences of the facility, the attractiveness of specific assets, and the adversary's assessment of PPS effectiveness are a few of these features.

To determine the threat, information should be sought for regional, national, and international threats, depending on the mission and location of the facility. Sources for this information include:

- intelligence sources
- crime analysis, studies
- professional organizations and services
- published literature
- government directives and legislation

Intelligence Sources

Intelligence sources can provide detailed information about the current activities of groups, which might pose a threat to facilities. It is important that current information be received and reviewed constantly. In the aftermath of the 9/11 attacks, there has been considerable focus on collecting actionable intelligence, in the hope of disrupting attacks before they occur. This is certainly desirable, but security managers are cautioned not to rely on apprehension of adversaries prior to a planned attack, especially for critical assets.

It is also important to establish a network for talking with and receiving information from national law enforcement and intelligence sources. Establishing this relationship early provides an advantage in receiving important information. Security concerns and interests must be expressed clearly and specifically to these sources. They need to understand what information is desired and why. Information that should be provided to help them understand your problem includes the following:

- specific facility or facilities of concern;
- adversary objectives to be prevented, such as theft, sabotage, industrial espionage, and the targets to be protected; and
- information about the kinds of incidents at your facility or other facilities (burglaries, trespassing, espionage).

Requests that are too general may go unanswered. The United Kingdom provides some useful information at intelligence agency web sites (MI5, 2006 and MI6, 2006).

The advantage of establishing a network for talking with local law enforcement and intelligence sources is to gain their cooperation and to obtain approvals for receiving information from national sources. Once again, since 9/11, the sharing of intelligence data with local authorities has proven problematic, due to concerns about revealing sources and classification issues. Specifically, many local authorities, who may have assets that are potential targets of attack, do not have the proper clearances to allow access to the intelligence information. This in turn has made it difficult for the various groups to work together effectively. Efforts are well underway to obtain clearances and develop procedures for local officials to allow better sharing of intelligence information (Kaplan, 2006).

Crime Studies

A review of past and current crimes committed locally, nationally, and internationally can provide useful information in characterizing the potential threat. Lacking an adequate sample of incidents from which to build a profile of adversaries, analysts might expand their study to include actual crimes outside the specific domain of the site that are in some way analogous to possible, but uncommitted, crimes. For facilities with high-value or high-consequence assets, review sophisticated burglaries, major armed robberies, and industrial sabotage. Crimes committed by well-educated professionals may provide additional insight. Thoroughly research incidents involving political extremists, such as terrorist assaults and symbolic bombings, where a political statement—and not the destruction of the target—was the primary aim. Examine the criminals (arsonists, psychotic bombers, and mass murderers) as well as the crimes themselves for clues about the criminals' sometimes bizarre motivations and capabilities.

Professional Organizations and Services

Nongovernment networks for information exchange can provide information on the assessment of threat. Academic, research, and industrial organizations meet periodically to discuss current topics, and security issues and problems are often included. A network can be established to compare perceptions of the threat problem at local, national, and international levels. National professional organizations, such as ASIS International (see http://www.asisonline.org) and the Computer Security Institute (CSI, 1998), publish surveys on insider threats, costs of crime in industrial facilities, and threats from hackers.

In addition to the use of professional organizations, some professional services are also available to help in threat definition. Consultants in investigation, surveillance, business intelligence, due diligence, and computer systems have the expertise and insight to provide useful threat information to corporations or enterprises. Other professional services may include behavioral psychologists, criminologists, and attorneys, who can provide profiling information or advice on recent court cases and rulings that may help identify emerging threat areas.

Published Literature and the Internet

A complete search of current literature can provide extensive information concerning the threat. Information can be obtained from open sources and from library and research organizations. Open literature sources include national information services and publications, newspapers, news broadcasts, and publications on specific topics. Library and research organizations have electronic databases, newspaper microfilm banks, and cross-references for material that make it easy to find information concerning a threat if it exists. The Federal Bureau of Investigation (FBI) maintains a bomb data center and has a web page that contains crime statistics and recent publications (FBI, 2006). Under the auspices of the

National Institute of Justice, JUSTNET is maintained by the National Law Enforcement and Corrections Technology Center (NLECTC) and is a comprehensive source of law enforcement and corrections information, including recent news items regarding threats (NLECTC, 1999). Of particular interest may be articles or reports discussing emerging threats, such as chemical/biological attacks, nonstate-sponsored terrorist acts, international crime including narcotics trafficking, and information warfare. The US Department of State (DOS; US Department of State, 2006) publishes a yearly report describing global terrorist threats and the US Secret Service, in conjunction with Carnegie-Mellon University, has published reports on insider threats to computer systems (Keeney et al., 2006).

Government Directives and Legislation

Various pieces of government legislation and directives provide information about expected or emerging threats. These sources may provide additional insight regarding potential threats to a facility or industry and may also serve advance notice to some industries of government interest in protecting certain targets against threats.

The recent presidential Combating Terrorism directive (PDD-62) highlights the growing threat of unconventional attacks against the United States. It details a new and more systematic approach to fighting terrorism by bringing a program management approach to US counter-terrorism efforts. The directive also establishes the office of the National Coordinator for Security, Infrastructure Protection, and Counter-Terrorism, which will oversee a broad variety of relevant policies and programs, including areas such as counter-terrorism, protection of critical infrastructure, preparedness,

and consequence management for WMD (Environmental Protection Agency, 2006).

The Critical Infrastructure Protection directive (PDD-63) calls for a national effort to assure the security of the increasingly vulnerable and interconnected infrastructures of the United States (Environmental Protection Agency, 2006). Such infrastructures include telecommunications, banking and finance, energy, transportation, and essential government services. The directive requires immediate federal government action, including risk assessment and planning to reduce exposure to attack. It stresses the critical importance of cooperation between the government and the private sector by linking designated agencies with private sector representatives.

Moreover, Executive Order 13010, which formed the President's Commission on Critical Infrastructure Protection (PCCIP), was signed by President Clinton on July 15, 1996. This order mandates that those facilities that are part of the national critical infrastructure be reviewed and adequately protected as a matter of national security. The list includes:

- information and communications
- electrical power systems
- gas and oil transportation and storage
- banking and finance
- transportation
- water supply systems
- emergency services
- government services

Legislation passed by Congress in the past few years shows an increased emphasis on the emerging threats of chemical and biological warfare, domestic terrorism, and the preparedness of state and local agencies to counter these threats. For example, the 1996 Anti-Terrorism Act increases penalties for conspiracies involving explosives, expands penalties for possession of nuclear materials, and criminalizes the use of chemical weapons within the United States or against

Americans outside of the United States. This act also directs the Attorney General to issue a public report on whether literature or other material on making bombs or weapons of mass destruction is protected by the First Amendment, authorizes the Secretary of State to designate groups as terrorist organizations, and authorizes more than $1 billion over 5 years for various federal, state, and local government programs to prevent, combat, or deal with terrorism. This legislation and others may provide additional useful information when identifying threats to certain assets or targets. Related to this effort, studies have been performed for the government that provide information in defining threats, as well as state and local capability to respond (Riley and Hoffman, 1995).

Since the attacks of 9/11, additional legislation has been enacted. A review of the most important acts and links to additional information is provided below:

- Uniting and Strengthening America by Providing Appropriate Tools Required to Intercept and Obstruct Terrorism Act of 2001 (USA PATRIOT ACT)

    Signed into law within 2 months of the 9/11/2001 attacks, the Patriot Act greatly expanded the powers of US law enforcement in an effort to thwart future terrorist attacks. Containing 10 major titles and hundreds of section and sub-sections, this legislation was passed with broad bipartisan support in the wake of the 9/11 attacks, though its provisions have grown more controversial as concerns over civil liberties infringements have arisen. Provisions of the legislation include expanded authority for surveillance of suspected terrorists, increased powers to track and prevent international money laundering, increased assistance to law enforcement agencies and first responders, and many more.

    Link: http://thomas.loc.gov

- Aviation and Transportation Security Act

    Signed November 19, 2001, this law established the Transportation Security Administration (TSA) within the Department of Transportation and gave it responsibility for security in all modes of transportation, but with particular emphasis on aviation security. TSA took on responsibility for screening air passengers, including the development of new screening technologies such as explosives detection and biometric identification, and greatly expanded the Air Marshall program to protect flights en route. The law also requires TSA to periodically conduct a comprehensive systems analysis using vulnerability assessment, threat attribute definition, and technology roadmap techniques to review the security of civil aviation.

    Link: http://thomas.loc.gov

- Maritime Transportation Security Act of 2002 (MTSA)

    Signed into law on November 25, 2002, the MTSA is intended to protect the nation's ports and waterways from a terrorist attack. This sweeping legislation requires threat and vulnerability assessments to be conducted at dozens of critical ports, security plans to be developed for over 10,000 seagoing vessels and 5000 related facilities, security verification and audit teams to inspect 2500 foreign ports, private operators of critical ports to develop security incident response plans to be submitted for Coast Guard approval, a Transportation Worker Identification Credential (TWIC) program to be implemented for access control at key nodes in the nation's transportation infrastructure network, Coast Guard Maritime Safety and Security Teams to be established at strategic locations on the east and west coasts for rapid response to seaborne threats, Operation Safe

Commerce and other programs to identify ways to improve cargo container security, and much more.

Links: http://www.uscg.mil/hq/g-cp/comrel/factfile/Factcards/MTSA2002.htm and http://www.uscg. mil/news/Headquarters/MTSAPressKit.pdf

- Homeland Security Act of 2002

Also signed on November 25, 2002, this law established the cabinet-level Department of Homeland Security (DHS). Composed of 22 existing federal agencies, the new department was given the mission of protecting the nation from future terrorist attacks. Major agencies falling under the purview of DHS after the reorganization include Immigration and Customs Enforcement, the Transportation Security Administration, Customs and Border Protection, the Secret Service, and the Coast Guard.

Link: http://www.whitehouse.gov/deptofhomeland/bill/

- Homeland Security Presidential Directive 7:

Critical Infrastructure Identification, Prioritization, and Protection

This directive, part of a series of new Homeland Security Presidential Directives (HSPD) begun after the 9/11/2001 attacks, instructs all federal departments to identify, prioritize, and coordinate the protection of critical national infrastructure and assets. The directive seeks to reduce the vulnerability of such assets and infrastructures "in order to deter, mitigate, or neutralize terrorist attacks." It also mandates the DHS and other federal agencies to perform vulnerability assessments for their sectors of responsibility and encourages the use of risk management strategies to protect against and mitigate the effects of terrorist attacks.

Link: http://www.whitehouse.gov/news/releases/2003/12/20031217-5.html

Organize Threat Information

After all of the threat information has been collected, it is necessary to put it in a form that makes it usable. Table 3.1 lists the type of information required and presents a way to organize the information to define an outsider threat. The table is designed to address three outsider adversary groups: terrorist, criminal, and extremist. Other outsider groups could be added to the table or could replace one of the originals. For each outsider adversary group, assessments of the likelihood of potential actions concerning theft, sabotage, or some other action are provided. The assessments are qualitatively judged to be high, medium, or low. In the same way, judgment of the category of motivations for each outsider adversary group can be high, medium, or low. Finally, outsider adversary capabilities can be tabulated. For each adversary group, specific data should be listed for each topic under capabilities.

Information to define an insider threat is described in Table 3.2. The different types of insiders at a facility should be listed in the left column and the information in the table completed for each type of insider. Types of insiders might include the PPS designer, security console operator, maintenance person, engineer, clerical workers, security manager, and so on. Questions are asked about how often each type of insider has access to the asset or vital equipment or the PPS. Based upon this access information, assessments of the likelihood of theft, sabotage, and collusion are made. The assessments for each type of insider are high, medium, or low.

After all of the information has been completed in the tables, the adversary groups can be compared and ranked by type in order of their threat potential. This threat definition provides the designer or analyst of a PPS with the information needed for a specific site. However, even though one threat is identified as the highest potential (and becomes

Table 3.1 *Outsider Adversary Threat Spectrum.*

Each threat is rated in each category to summarize outsider threat data. Additional groups can be added or used as a replacement for those shown. Capabilities are assessed at a high, medium, or low ranking.

	Type of Adversary		
Potential Action Likelihood (H, M, L)	Terrorist	Criminal	Extremist
Theft			
Sabotage			
Other			
Motivation (H, M, L)			
Ideological			
Economic			
Personal			
Capabilities			
Number			
Weapons			
Equipment and tools			
Transportation			
Technical experience			
Insider assistance			

the design basis threat), the PPS must be evaluated against the entire threat spectrum.

Sample Threat Statements

The following is a sample design basis threat that is used to design and evaluate safeguards systems for nuclear power plants for protection against acts of radiological sabotage and theft of special nuclear material. The threat is considered to include a determined, violent external assault, attack by stealth, or deceptive actions, of several persons with the following attributes, assistance, and equipment:

- well-trained (including military training and skills) and dedicated individuals;
- inside assistance, which may include a knowledgeable employee in any

Table 3.2 *Insider Adversary Threat Spectrum.*

Different types of insiders are listed and information describing the threat is shown in the table.

Insider	Access to Asset (often, seldom, never)	Access to PPS (often, seldom, never)	Theft Opportunity (H, M, L)	Sabotage Opportunity (H, M, L)	Collusion Opportunity (H, M, L)

position who attempts to participate in a passive role (e.g., provide information) or an active role (e.g., facilitate entrance and exit, disable alarms and communications, participate in a violent attack) or both;

- suitable weapons, up to and including hand-held automatic weapons, equipped with silencers and having effective long-range accuracy;
- hand-carried equipment, including incapacitating agents and explosives for use as tools of entry or for otherwise destroying reactor, facility, transporter, or container integrity or features of the safeguards system;
- land vehicles used for transporting personnel and their hand-carrier equipment; and
- the ability to operate as two or more teams.

This threat statement also considers the potential for a conspiracy between individuals in any position who have access to and detailed knowledge of nuclear power plants or the facilities or items that could facilitate theft of special nuclear material (e.g., small tools, substitute material, false documents, etc.) or both.

The following is another threat statement that identifies and characterizes

a potential threat for a semiconductor manufacturer: Facility interests shall be protected against theft of product, production materials, tools and equipment, personal computers or components, and personal property for financial gain. The threat may include up to three people who perpetrate criminal acts for economic gain. Normally this group does not commit acts of violence in furtherance of the crime, but they may resort to less than deadly force to resist or avoid capture. This individual or group typically commits crimes of opportunity and frequently targets easily accessible and removable assets that can be personally used or readily sold. Attack methods include stealth and deception, may be an insider or assisted by one, may have extensive knowledge of the facility, and may use weapons other than firearms to avoid capture but will not use explosives. Additional threats to this facility may be disgruntled employees and industrial espionage, each of which would require their own specific characterization.

Another sample design basis threat statement reads as follows:

The design basis threat shall serve to:

- establish a safeguard and security program and requirements;

- provide a basis for site safeguards and security program planning implementation and facility design;
- provide a basis for evaluation of implemented systems;
- support counterintelligence programs and requirements; and
- provide a basis for evaluation of counterintelligence risks posed to interests.

This threat statement describes a baseline threat spectrum. In the development of this threat, site-specific geographical, environmental, or other unique facility or location characteristics were not considered. Site-specific threat statements should be modified to take into account unique local and regional threat considerations to supplement the design basis threat.

For example, types of adversary groups that could be included within the site-specific threat definition include:

- Terrorists—persons or groups who unlawfully use force or violence against persons or property to intimidate or coerce a government, the civilian population, or any segment thereof, in furtherance of political or social objectives.
- White Collar Criminal—individual who seeks classified and/or sensitive unclassified information or material or attempts to alter data maintained for the purpose of gaining economic advantage for the individual or the individual's employer.
- Organized Criminals—persons who perpetrate criminal acts for profit or economic gain.
- Psychotic—person suffering from a mental disorder of sufficient magnitude to experience periodic or prolonged loss of contact with reality.
- Disgruntled Employee—individual who engages in vindictive, violent, or malicious acts at or directed against the place of employment.

- Violent Activists—a group or individual who commits violent acts out of opposition to programs for ecological, political, economic, or other reasons.
- Intelligence Collector—individual who uses human intelligence methods and engages in clandestine intelligence gathering on behalf of a foreign intelligence service.

In conclusion, a well-constructed threat statement should be established by an appropriate group with relevant information, undergo periodic review and update, supplement corporate policy with local threat assessment, address insider potential, and provide threat details including numbers, equipment, weapons, transportation, and motivation. Once this information has been collected and summarized it should be protected as classified or sensitive and access to it should be limited.

Summary

One approach for completing a definition of the threat for a specific site has been presented. The approach suggests the type of information required and possible sources of that information to develop a description of the threat. The information can be summarized and used in ranking the adversaries in order of their threat potential. The summary comprises the threat spectrum, from which the design basis threat can be selected. The design basis threat is the maximum credible threat to a facility. The final threat definition for a specific site is required information for the PPS designer and system analyst. Once established, this information should be protected and its distribution limited. This design basis threat should be reviewed and updated periodically or as events dictate.

Security Principle

Design Basis Threat—A facility PPS is
designed based on the maximum credible threat to the facility. The final design
should be checked against the entire threat
spectrum. Once established, the design
basis threat should be protected as classified or sensitive proprietary data. The
threat statement should be reviewed periodically and updated as necessary.

References

Computer Security Institute (CSI) and
Federal Bureau of Investigation (FBI).
*1998 CSI/FBI Computer Crime and
Security Survey*. Computer Security
Issues and Trends IV(1), 1998, 1–12.
http://www.gocsi.com.

Earley, P. *Confessions of a Spy: The Real
Story of Aldrich Ames*. New York: G.P.
Putnam's Sons, 1997, 1–36.

Environmental Protection Agency, 2006.
http://www.epa.gov/radiation/rert/
authorities.htm#pdd, last accessed
December 2006.

Federal Bureau of Investigation (FBI).
http://www.fbi.gov, last accessed
December 2006.

Federal Bureau of Investigation. May 22,
2006. http://www.fbi.gov/publications.
htm.

Freedman, D.H., and Mann, C.C. Cracker.
U.S. News and World Report. June 2,
1997, 57–65.

Hoffman, B., Meyer, C., Schwarz, B., and
Duncan, J. Insider Crime: The threat to
nuclear facilities and programs. RAND
Report, U.S. Department of Energy.
February 1990; 42.

Hollinger, R.C., and Davis, J.L. "Employee
theft and dishonesty," in Gill, M., ed.,
The Handbook of Security. New York:
Palgrave Macmillan, 2006, 203–228.

Keeney, M., Kowalski, E., et al. Insider
threat study: Computer system sabotage

in critical infrastructure sectors. May
2005. http://www.cert.org/archive/pdf/
insidercross051105.pdf and http://www.
secretservice.gov/ntac_its.shtml, last
accessed October 28, 2006.

Kaplan, D.E. Spies among us. *U.S. News
and World Report*. May 8, 2006, 41–49.

National Law Enforcement and Corrections Technology Center (NLECTC).
http://www.nlectc.org/, last accessed
December 2006.

National Retail Security Survey,
2002. Summary available at http://
retailindustry.about.com/od/statistics_
loss_prevention/l/aa021126a.htm, last
accessed December 2006.

Pinkerton Service Corp. "Top organizational and professional issues for
today's security director." *Pinkerton
Organization Security Issues Study*,
1997, 1–19.

Radcliff, D. "Physical security: The danger
within." *Info World* April 20, 1998;
20(16).

Riley, K.J., and Hoffman, B. Domestic
terrorism: A national assessment of state
and local preparedness. RAND Report
1995; 1–66.

United Kingdom, MI5 home page
http://www.mi5.gov.uk/, and MI6 home
page http://www.mi6.gov.uk/output/
Page79.html, last accessed August 2006.

United States Department of State
Office of the Coordinator for Coun-
terterrorism Country Reports on
Terrorism 2005, April 2006, United
States Department of State Publication 11324. http://www.state.
gov/documents/organization/65462.pdf,
last accessed November 2006.

Questions

1. Using Tables 3.1 and 3.2, pick a
sample facility and create a threat
spectrum. Select a design basis threat
and explain your selection.

2. Why is it so important to complete a threat definition before designing a physical protection system?

3. What work conditions are important in the evaluation of the insider threat?

4. Explain why threat definition considers international threat in addition to a local or national threat.

5. What are the other sources of information on threat?

6. What are the different ways that an insider can help an outsider adversary?

4

Target Identification

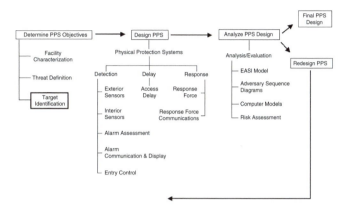

Target identification provides the basis for PPS design by focusing on what to protect, while PPS design addresses how to protect. Target identification is an evaluation of what to protect without consideration of the threat or the difficulty of providing physical protection. In other words, target identification determines areas, assets, or actions to be protected and generally are those that have undesirable consequence of loss to the enterprise. The threats to these items, and the ease or difficulty of protecting the items against a particular threat, are considered after the items are identified. In this chapter, the terms target and asset are used interchangeably; in succeeding chapters, asset will refer to any target of an adversary attack. Primary targets may be physical assets, electronic data, people, or anything that could impact business operations. Secondary targets can also include PPS components that can be attacked to reduce system effectiveness and facilitate an attack. Identification of both types of assets is often required, depending on the threat goals, capability, and motivation, and the consequence of loss of the asset.

Figure 4.1 summarizes the steps involved in target identification. These steps are discussed in the following sections.

Undesirable Consequences

It is not possible or practical to protect all assets at a facility. Effective security protects a minimum, yet complete, set of items. The criteria for selecting items to protect depend on the undesirable consequences to be prevented. Some undesirable consequences are:

- loss of life
- loss of material or information through industrial espionage
- environmental damage due to release of hazardous material by theft or sabotage
- interruption of critical utilities such as water, power, or communications
- degraded business operations
- workplace violence, extortion, blackmail
- building collapse

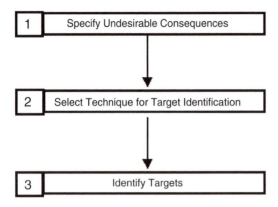

Figure 4.1 Steps in Target Identification. Following a structured process helps ensure that all assets that are targets of an attack are identified

- damage to reputation
- legal liability

It should be apparent that the consequence of the loss may cover a spectrum, from unacceptable (loss of life) to financial loss (industrial espionage) to the relatively less severe (damage to reputation). The process of target identification uses the consequence of the loss to help determine which assets should be protected and to what extent. For example, the loss of proprietary data from a facility, while undesired, could not be compared to the loss of a life. Thus, we assume that loss of life is the highest consequence event, and other undesired consequences are lower in comparison. After the attacks of 9/11, loss of many lives has become a common criterion for selecting critical targets for protection. This does not mean that loss of life is the only high consequence event at a facility.

Consequence Analysis

A major result of target identification will be the prioritization of targets based on the consequence of the loss of the asset. This is accomplished by first listing all the targets at a facility or within an enterprise, determining the level of the consequence of loss (i.e., high, medium, or low), estimating the probability of the occurrence of the event, and, finally, assessing where a particular threat fits. The consequence measure may be in dollars, loss of life, loss of reputation, or a combination of these, but it should establish consistency among targets to allow for relative ranking of the consequences. The probability of occurrence, which is the likelihood that an adversary will attack, may be obtained through use of historical records or based on information obtained during threat definition. This process can be expedited through the use of a matrix, as shown in Table 4.1.

In Table 4.1, the target is a pump station at a water utility. Consequence analysis of the station yields the matrix shown in the table. Thus, the highest consequence event appears to be the threat of a terrorist using a chemical or biological agent to contaminate the water supply. A lower consequence event is the possibility of sabotage by an insider or a citizen with a grudge against the company or the town. The lowest consequence event is characterized as vandals spraying graffiti on walls, equipment, or other property. In addition to the ranking of consequence, it is also important to establish the probability of occurrence of the event. In the pump station example, there is a high probability that vandals will spray graffiti on pump station property. Although this has a high probability of occurring, the consequence of this is much less than the consequence of contamination of the local water supply. In a like manner, the probabilities of the terrorist attack and sabotage event have been assessed to be a medium probability. This analysis shows that there is a moderate probability of a terrorist attack or a sabotage event, but the consequence of the terrorist attack is higher, so preventing contamination of the water supply is the highest priority.

This matrix is a quick way to relate consequence, probability of occurrence,

Table 4.1 *Consequence Analysis of Pump Station.*

The threat goal and (type) is placed inside the table at the place where the consequence of the loss and the probability of adversary attack intersect.

High Consequence		Chem/Bio Contamination (Terrorist)	
Medium Consequence		Sabotage (Insider, upset citizen)	
Low Consequence			Graffiti (Vandals)
	Low Probability	Medium Probability	High Probability

and threat. This matrix helps to determine the risk to a facility across a threat spectrum and at varying consequence levels. This information will be useful in allocating resources within the protection system design and for more complete risk analysis, which will be covered in more detail in Chapter 15, "Risk Assessment." In a quantitative analysis, consequence values fall between 0 and 1.0, with 1.0 being the highest consequence loss. Consequence values may also be established using a qualitative scale of high, medium, and low, based on the relative consequence of loss. Because this book is a broad overview of PPS design and evaluation, specific details of consequence analysis will not be covered; however, additional details are provided in Chapter 4 of the vulnerability assessment textbook (Garcia, 2005).

Targets

When target identification is focused on theft, all assets of concern must be protected. When target identification is concerned with sabotage, choices of target sets to protect may exist. For example, a dam will have a control room and various valves and pumps to control the flow of water. Protection of certain components within selected systems may prevent malevolent flooding

if components of other systems are sabotaged. That is, sabotage concerns may sometimes be addressed by protecting one critical set from among a number of sets of items. The selection of a set to be protected is determined by the ease and operational impact of providing protection, and the consequence of the loss. Targets may also include people, such as workplace violence against any employee or focused on senior executives. When targets include people or executive protection, additional information and planning may be required. Executive protection is not a specific focus of this book (a brief description of application of protection principles is provided in Chapter 16, "Process Applications"). Many good references are available for details regarding this activity (Braunig, 1993; Oatman, 1997; Hawley and Holder, 1998). If senior executives are identified as targets, additional personal protection will be required. This book is mainly focused on protection of assets and information at a facility, where one of the assets will be people.

The selection of a limited set of components to be protected against sabotage is intended to minimize the difficulty of providing protection. The PPS is designed to protect a minimum number of critical components to a high degree. This set of components must be complete; that is, protection of the minimum set must completely prevent the undesirable result regardless of sabotage of components not included in this protection set.

There is one final note concerning targets. In large, complex facilities, there may be many theft, sabotage, or other targets. Very often these targets are distributed throughout the facility. For example, there may be multiple buildings, each with critical assets, or a large building with many smaller targets, such as finished product, laptop computers, proprietary information, and tools. For large facilities with distributed targets, a PPS must be designed around the entire area containing the assets. On the other hand, some facilities, while complex, may contain certain localized targets. Examples include explosive storage facilities, power substations, transmission towers, dams, and computer equipment rooms. In this case, the PPS may be concentrated on a smaller area. This reduction in size can be a very cost-effective method for protecting critical assets.

Techniques for Target Identification

The two techniques for target identification discussed in this chapter are manual listing of targets and use of logic diagrams to identify vital areas. A section explaining logic diagrams is provided below as an introduction to vital area identification.

Manual Listing of Targets

For theft of localized items such as computers, tools, proprietary information, or work-in-process, the manual listing of targets is an appropriate technique. This technique consists of listing all significant quantities of assets of concern and their locations. The list provides the targets to be protected.

The manual technique can also be applied to theft of product-in-process (such as semiconductors or drugs) or sabotage of critical components if the facility is simple. For complex facilities, the manual technique is limited for both of these concerns. Product-in-process may include pills just ready to be packaged or filled bottles waiting to be loaded into cases. These intermediate process steps may be good theft targets, particularly for insiders. If a production line is very complex or there are multiple production lines at work, the opportunities for theft of these drugs may be broadly distributed throughout the plant, not limited to the end of the production line. In addition, storage and shipping areas are also areas of interest. Or, consider a large petrochemical plant with sabotage as a concern. Many complex systems, each with hundreds of components, interact to produce, route, and store the finished products. Furthermore, many support systems such as electrical power, ventilation, and instrumentation are interconnected to primary components such as pump motors in a complex manner. Target identification must consider which systems and components to protect and their interaction with other support systems.

When the facility is too complex for a manual identification of targets, a more rigorous identification technique may be used. The following sections discuss this technique in detail. They describe a methodical, comprehensive way to logically consider which systems and components must be protected to prevent an undesirable result.

Logic Diagrams

The logic diagram is a useful tool for determining the potential theft and sabotage targets for a complex facility. One type of logic diagram, called a fault tree (Fussell, 1976), graphically represents the combinations of component and subsystem events that can result in a specified undesired state. A simple logic diagram for

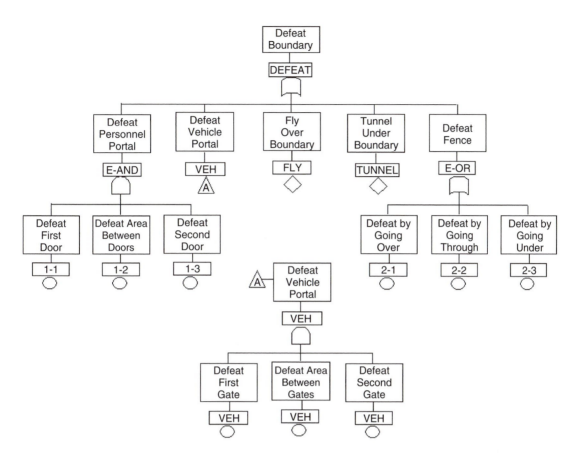

Figure 4.2 Simple Logic Diagram. The diagram develops all the ways to penetrate the outer boundary of a facility

penetrating the outer boundary of a site with some physical protection components present is shown in Figure 4.2. The following discussion on logic diagrams borrows heavily from the notation used in digital electronics (Putman, 1986).

In this example, the undesired event is defeat of the boundary, which can be accomplished by defeating the personnel or vehicle portals, by passing over or under the boundary, or by defeating the fence. Further elaboration of the actions required to defeat the personnel and vehicle portals, as well as defeating the fence, is also shown.

In a more complex example, one undesired consequence (or event) for a dam is the uncontrolled release of large quantities of water as a result of sabotage of

critical components. The PPS is intended to prevent sabotage of these components. Logic diagrams that are intended to identify the sets of components an adversary would have to sabotage to cause the consequence are called sabotage fault trees and are used for vital area analysis. They describe the actions an adversary must accomplish to cause sabotage and can be used to identify the areas (locations) to be protected in order to prevent sabotage.

Figure 4.3 illustrates the symbols that are used in logic diagrams. The logic diagram shown represents relationships between events. Each event will have a written description in the large rectangle in the logic diagram. A smaller rectangle placed immediately under the description will show the event name or label. Event names

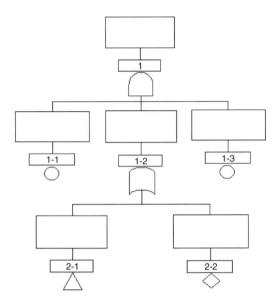

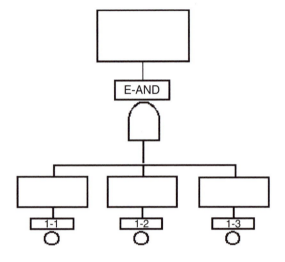

Figure 4.4 Example of an AND Gate. All inputs must occur for the output to occur

Figure 4.3 Logic Diagram Symbols. The logic diagram is a graphical representation of combinations of events that can result in a specified state or event. Each symbol has a specific meaning

1-2, and 1-3. Event E-AND will occur if, and only if, Events 1-1, 1-2, and 1-3 all occur.

should be brief and may be formed from combinations of letters and numbers.

The symbols of the logic diagram shown in Figure 4.3 will be discussed in detail. These include symbols for logic gates, events, and transfer operations. Two kinds of logic gates, the AND gate and the OR gate, are used in the logic diagrams. Gates have inputs and an output. Inputs enter the bottom of the gate; outputs exit the top of the description rectangle above the gate.

OR Gate
The shape of the OR gate is a pointed arch with a curved bottom (see Figure 4.5). For the undesired event described above

AND Gate
The shape of the AND gate is a round arch with a flat bottom (see Figure 4.4). For the undesired event described above for the AND gate to occur, all the events that have an input into the AND gate must occur. Thus, if any one of the input events can be prevented, the event described above the AND gate will be prevented. For example, assume Event E-AND is generated by an AND gate whose inputs are Events 1-1,

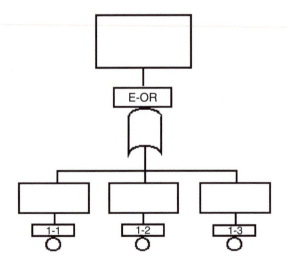

Figure 4.5 Example of an OR Gate. Any one of the inputs must occur for the output to occur

the OR gate to occur, any one (or more) of the events that input to the OR gate must occur. All the input events must be prevented in order to prevent the event described above the OR gate. For example, in Figure 4.3, Event E-OR is defined by an OR gate whose inputs are Events 1-1, 1-2, and 1-3. Event E-OR occurs if one or more of Events 1-1, 1-2, or 1-3 occur.

Events

There are several types of events in logic diagrams. They include end events, intermediate events, and primary events. If an event is not used as input to another gate, it is called an end event. Logic diagrams have only one end event, the topmost event of the tree. In Figure 4.3, Event 1 is the end event. Sometimes this event is also called the treetop. Events that have both inputs and outputs are called intermediate events. In Figure 4.3, Event 1-2 is an intermediate event.

Primary Events are events that do not have an input. They represent the start of actions that ultimately generate the end event. Two types of primary events are distinguished by the symbol that appears immediately below the name of the primary event: the basic event and the undeveloped event.

The basic event is symbolized by a circle below the rectangle, as shown in Figure 4.6. A basic event can be understood and evaluated qualitatively or quantitatively, depending on the purpose of the

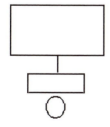

Figure 4.6 Basic Event. These are the starting events that lead to the end event

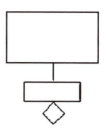

Figure 4.7 Undeveloped Event. These are events where causes are not sufficiently understood to be included in the logic diagram

analysis, without further development of the event into causes or specific cases. In Figure 4.3, Events 1-1 and 1-3 are basic events.

Figure 4.7 shows an undeveloped event, symbolized by a diamond below the rectangle. An undeveloped event is an event whose causes are insufficiently understood to be included in the logic diagram. For the purpose of evaluation, the undeveloped event is treated as a basic event. The conclusions drawn from the analysis of a tree that contains an undeveloped event are tentative and subject to revision if the event is better characterized. In Figure 4.3, Event 2-2 is an undeveloped event.

Transfer Operation The transfer operation is represented by an upright triangle. The transfer operation is used to make the graphic display of the logic tree more compact and readable. Because many logic diagrams, as they are developed, occupy a wide left-to-right space across a page, it might be necessary to disconnect the development of an event and place it at a more convenient position on the page or on another page. To connect the event and its development without drawing a line between separate figures the transfer symbol is used.

An example of the transfer symbol is shown in Figure 4.8. The diagram shown contains one transfer symbol. The transfer

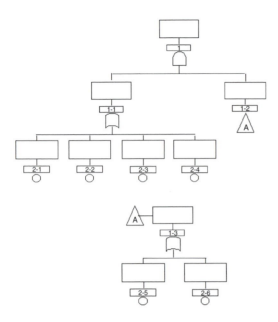

Figure 4.8 Example of the Transfer Operation. Event A has been developed in a different location on the diagram. Transfer operations make the logic diagram more compact and readable

operation is shown at the bottom as a separate diagram. The development of Event 1-2 is transferred. Event 1-2 is shown twice: once in the diagram whose development is truncated by the transfer and once at the top of the subdiagram that develops Event 1-2. In general, an event may occur at several places in a logic diagram and the common development of that event may be transferred. The development will appear only once on the page. The A which appears within the transfer symbol to the left of Event 1-2 is the name of the event for which Event 1-2 is an input. In general, there will be a list of every event to which the transferred event is an input.

Vital Area Identification

To develop a PPS for a facility, it is necessary to determine which assets are attractive for theft, the equipment that a saboteur must damage in order to halt

or reduce production, and the location of that equipment within the facility. Material that is attractive for theft is relatively easy to designate. Because both the function and structure of a given facility can be very complex, the choice of components and facility areas to protect as vital in the prevention of undesired events is usually not obvious. Locations containing equipment to be protected against sabotage are called vital areas. To identify the vital areas of a facility in a comprehensive and consistent way requires a rigorous structured approach. This section presents techniques that are useful to the performance of the required analysis. Many times, once the vital area identification has been performed, it may be reused for other similar facilities, where the construction and layout of the facility are the same or where operations are located in the same areas.

The basic steps used to identify vital areas in facilities are summarized in Figure 4.9. These steps are applicable to any facility. The following discussion uses a dam as an example of the vital area identification process.

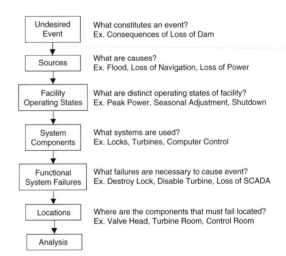

Figure 4.9 Steps in Vital Area Identification. Using a dam as an example, the steps are followed to determine the areas that require sabotage protection

First, the undesirable consequences for a given facility must be defined. This level, in turn, determines the events that must be considered and helps to establish the required scope of the analysis. The second step is to identify the sources of the undesired consequences.

Third, the facility's operating states must be identified. For a dam, operating states include peak power operation, adjustment to seasonal climate (such as a rainy or dry season), and shutdown. Some of the equipment necessary to prevent a consequence during one operating state may not be required during another. Thus, it may be appropriate to identify different sets of vital areas for the different modes of operation at a facility.

In the fourth step, the system failures that could lead to an event must be determined. This step can be the most complicated and time-consuming part of the process in a complex facility with redundant systems or multiple operations. A systematic analytical technique is required in order to ensure that the many possible failure mechanisms are rigorously taken into account and comprehensively reviewed. This will require identification of the systems in use. This will lead to the next step: determining what functional failures are required to cause the undesired consequence.

In order to identify vital areas it is necessary, in step six, to determine all the locations in the facility at which each failure can be accomplished. After the detailed information on system failure and component locations is collected, the sabotage fault trees are analyzed using a computer code for Boolean algebra manipulation as the final step in the process. Analysis of the fault trees with the code yields the vital areas for the facility being analyzed. The procedures used in the computer code can also be carried out by hand, depending on the size of the fault tree. Sabotage fault trees are discussed in more detail in the following sections.

Sabotage Fault Tree Analysis

Sabotage fault tree analysis procedures are used to identify the sabotage events that, in certain combinations, can lead to undesired consequences. A fault tree is a logic diagram that graphically represents the combinations of component and subsystem events that can result in a specified undesired system state. The undesired state for our example is the release of significant amounts of water by the dam as a result of sabotage. In the sabotage fault tree analysis, the undesired event is developed, in turn, until primary events terminate each branch of the tree. Primary events are individual sabotage acts such as the disabling of a pump or the severing of a pipe. As an example, Figure 4.10 is an abbreviated version of a sabotage fault tree for a dam. In this figure, the undesired event is developed into intermediate events that represent primary sources of failure. Each gate in the tree represents the logical operation by which the inputs combine to produce an output. Each branch of the tree is developed by identification of the immediate, necessary, and sufficient conditions leading to each event.

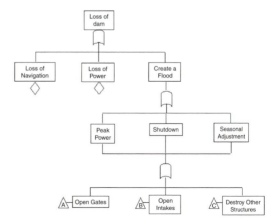

Figure 4.10 Partial Fault Tree for a Dam. In this example, events that can lead to a flood are described

Generic Sabotage Fault Trees

Many facilities have a number of features in common. Because of these common characteristics, portions of the sabotage fault trees will have very similar structures. Generic sabotage fault trees that can be applied to a broad spectrum of similar facilities can be developed.

The specific details of facility design and layout are usually not common to different facilities. The systems used to provide the functions necessary to prevent the undesirable event, the subsystems and components comprising these systems, and, particularly, the locations of components can vary significantly from facility to facility. Because of these site-specific differences, the details of the sabotage fault trees and, consequently, the number and locations of vital areas will be different for different facilities, even if the operations or processes at the facilities are of the same type. General procedures have been developed to gather appropriate site-specific information and incorporate that information into generic sabotage fault trees to produce detailed sabotage fault trees for specific facilities (Fussell, 1976). The advantages of using generic sabotage fault tree procedures are that they (1) make it unlikely that a sabotage event will be overlooked in the development of sabotage fault trees for specific facilities; (2) reduce the time required to develop the specific trees; and (3) make it possible for someone with minimal knowledge of fault tree analysis to develop the detailed trees efficiently.

Location of Vital Areas

Once the trees have been made site-specific, an analysis is performed on the trees to find the combinations of events that are sufficient to cause an undesirable consequence. Each combination of events represents a scenario for sabotaging the facility. The next step in vital area identification is to find the locations in the facility where the sets of events can be performed. This is done by associating an area (location) with every primary event. Then the combinations of events that cause sabotage are transformed to combinations of locations from which sabotage can be accomplished. Typically, this transformation reduces the size of the tree.

The next step in the procedure is to identify minimum sets of locations (minimum critical location sets) that, if protected, will prevent an adversary from accomplishing sabotage. This is the set of locations that, if protected, will interrupt all possible sequences leading to the event. Clearly, AND functions can greatly help in the protection of a facility, particularly if the equipment is located in different areas or sectors of the facility. This is true because in order for an output event to occur as a result of an AND function, all the inputs must be present. This can be used to the designer's advantage, if critical components can be located some distance from each other, because this will force the adversary to attack several locations simultaneously (requiring more people) or attack several locations sequentially, which takes more time. This sort of design has been used in nuclear power facilities outside the United States, to reduce the probability of a successful sabotage event by an adversary. This approach may also have some use in critical infrastructure protection within the United States, such as power, water, telecommunications hubs, banks, and transportation systems. In choosing which sets of locations to protect, such things as the cost of protection and the impact on operability for each location should be considered. Some locations may be cheaper and easier to protect or may have less of an operational effect if protected. If these areas are part of an AND function, selection of areas with these characteristics will be preferred. Once the fault tree and the protection set are generated, this data should be protected as sensitive proprietary information with limited distribution.

In practice, the above procedure is carried out using a computer for the lengthy manipulation of equations representing the fault tree. After the generic fault trees have been made site-specific, the computer code operates on the Boolean representation of the tree to find the sets of locations where sabotage can occur and the minimal set of locations that, if protected, will prevent a successful sabotage attack (Fussell, 1976). These computer codes make use of identities from Boolean algebra. Figure 4.11 illustrates the connection between Boolean algebra operations and the methodology just described.

A complete set of locations to be protected can be identified by hand without using a computer. In this case, a listing of every input to OR gates and any

single input to AND gates can be used to generate location protection sets.

Summary

Target identification is the process of identifying specific locations, actions, or assets to be protected to prevent undesirable consequences. Techniques for target identification range from a manual listing to a more rigorous logic approach. A manual listing of targets can be used for theft of localized items. For simple facilities, it can also be used for theft of product-in-process and sabotage of critical components.

Vital area identification is a structured approach of target identification based on logic diagrams called fault trees. Fault tree analysis provides a disciplined, logical, repeatable method for determining vital areas in complex facilities. The sabotage fault trees clearly document the assumptions made in the analysis and allow an examination of the effect of different sets of assumptions on the number and location of vital areas. The results are consistent in form and level of detail for every facility analyzed; therefore, that uniform criterion can be applied. The analysis identifies the minimum set of areas that must be considered as vital and thus will help reduce costs of physical security. The use of generic sabotage fault trees makes it possible to quickly develop detailed fault trees for specific complex facilities.

Once a facility has been characterized, the design basis threat determined, and targets based on threats and consequences identified, the design of the PPS can begin. In Part II, the detection, delay, and response elements that are applied to meet the system objectives will be addressed.

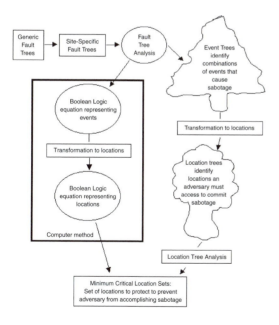

Figure 4.11 Vital Area Identification— Boolean Logic Compared to Fault Tree Methodology. Fault tree information is captured in Boolean logic expressions for analysis by hand or using a computer

Security Principle

Target identification is used to determine what to protect. Targets may be susceptible to theft, sabotage, or personal harm. Priorities of targets are based on the analysis of the consequence of the loss and the threat.

References

Braunig, M.J. *The Executive Protection Bible*. Aspen: ESI Education Development Corp., 1993, 1–606.

Fussell, J.B. *Fault Tree Analysis: Concepts and Techniques, Generic Techniques in Systems Reliability Assessment*. Groningen, The Netherlands: Noordhoff Publishing, 1976, 133–162.

Garcia, M.L. *Vulnerability Assessment of Physical Protection Systems*, Boston: Butterworth-Heinemann, 2005, 72–77.

Hawley, D.L., and Holder, P.T. *The Executive Protection Professional's Manual*. Boston: Butterworth-Heinemann, 1998, 1–144.

Oatman, R.L. *The Art of Executive Protection*. Baltimore: Noble House, 1997, 1–296.

Putman, B.W. *Digital and Microprocessor Electronics*. Englewood Cliffs, NJ: Prentice-Hall, 1986, 10–15.

Questions

1. Using the symbols and process described in this chapter, draw a logic diagram for some task that you routinely do. Examples might include making dinner, changing a flat tire, or painting a room.
2. Using the manual listing technique, list some theft targets for a few selected facilities. List the target type, such as computers, people, tools, or information, and its location. Note the consequence of the loss of the item (use High, Medium, or Low). Selected facilities might include schools, retail stores, malls, museums, water or power utilities, and so on.
3. Discuss how the process of target identification could be used at a movie theatre, a museum, and the local telephone switching station. Use Table 4.1 to summarize your analysis for each facility.
4. What sources of information could be used to aid in target identification?

PART TWO

Design Physical Protection System

5
Physical Protection System Design

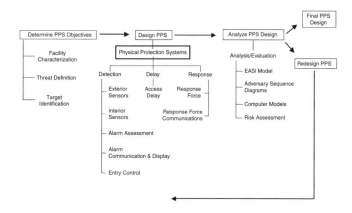

The designer now knows the objectives of the PPS, that is, what to protect and against whom. The next step is to design the new system or characterize the existing system. If designing a new system, we must determine how best to integrate people, procedures, and equipment to meet the objectives of the system. Once a PPS is designed or characterized, it must be analyzed and evaluated to ensure that it meets the physical protection objectives. The PPS design must allow the combination of protection elements working together to assure protection rather than regarding each feature separately. Implementation of the PPS design then addresses the systematic and integrated protection of assets in anticipation of adversary attacks, rather than in reaction to attacks after they occur.

If designing a new PPS, the designer must determine how best to combine such elements as fences, barriers, sensors, procedures, communication devices, and security personnel into a PPS that can achieve the protection objectives. The resulting PPS design should meet these

objectives within the operational, safety, legal, and economic constraints of the facility. The primary functions of a PPS are detection of an adversary, delay of that adversary, and response by security personnel (guard force). These functions and some of their components are shown in Figure 5.1.

Certain guidelines should be observed during the PPS design. A PPS system performs better if detection is as far from the target as possible and delays are near the target. In addition, there is close association between detection (using exterior or interior sensors) and assessment. It is a basic principle of security system design that detection without assessment is not detection, because without assessment the operator does not know the cause of an alarm. If the alarm is the result of trash blowing across an exterior area or lights being turned off in an interior area, there is no need for a response, since there is no valid intrusion (i.e., by an adversary). Another close association is the relationship between response and response force communications. A response force cannot

57

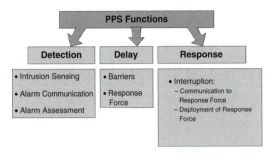

Figure 5.1 Functions of a Physical Protection System. The PPS functions include detection, delay, and response

respond unless it receives a communication call for a response. These and many other particular features of PPS components help to ensure that the designer takes advantage of the strengths of each piece of equipment and uses equipment in combinations that allow them to complement each other and protect any weaknesses.

Design of the PPS begins with a review and thorough understanding of the protection objectives that the designed system must meet. This can be done simply by checking for required features of a PPS, such as intrusion detection, entry control, access delay, response communications, and a protective force. However, a PPS design based on required features cannot be expected to lead to a high-performance system unless those features, when used together, are sufficient to assure adequate levels of protection. Feature-based designs only check for the presence of a particular number or type of component, with no consideration for how effectively the component will perform during an adversary attack. A good PPS is designed using components that have validated performance measures established for operation. Component performance measures are combined into system performance measures by the application of system modeling techniques.

Physical Protection System Design

A system may be defined as a collection of components or elements designed to achieve an objective according to a plan. The ultimate objective of a PPS is to prevent the accomplishment of overt or covert malevolent actions. Typical objectives are to prevent sabotage of critical equipment, theft of assets or information from within the facility, and protection of people. A PPS must accomplish its objectives by either deterrence or a combination of detection, delay, and response. Listed below are the component subsystems that provide the tools to perform these functions. Each of these component subsystems will be discussed in detail in the remainder of Part Two.

Functions and Component Subsystems

Detection
    Exterior/Interior Intrusion Sensors
    Alarm Assessment
    Alarm Communication and Display
    Entry Control Systems
Delay
    Access Delay
Response
    Response Force
Response Force Communications

The system functions of detection and delay can be accomplished by the use of either hardware and/or guards. Guards usually handle response, although automated response technologies are under development. There is always a balance between the use of hardware and the use of guards. In different conditions and applications, one is often the preferable choice. The key to a successful system is the integration of people, procedures, and equipment into a system that protects assets from threats. This integration requires a tradeoff analysis of cost versus performance, so if a designer decides to use more guards and less hardware, there should be a corresponding analysis that supports this decision. Keep in mind that humans are generally not good detectors, while equipment is very good at the repetition and boredom associated with constant close monitoring.

Detection, delay, and response are all required functions of an effective PPS. These functions must be performed in this order and within a length of time that is less than the time required for the adversary to complete his or her task. A well-designed system provides protection-in-depth, minimizes the consequence of component failures, and exhibits balanced protection. In addition, a design process based on performance criteria rather than feature criteria will select elements and procedures according to the contribution they make to overall system performance. Performance criteria are also measurable, so they can help in the analysis of the designed system.

PPS Functions

The primary PPS functions are detection, delay, and response. It is essential to consider the system functions in detail, since a thorough understanding of the definitions of these functions and the measure of effectiveness of each is required to evaluate the system. It is important to note that detection must be accomplished for delay to be effective. Recall that the highest priority system goal is to protect critical assets from theft or sabotage by a malevolent adversary. For a system to be effective at this objective, there must be notification of an attack (detection), then adversary progress must be slowed (delay), which will allow the response force time to interrupt or stop the adversary (response).

Detection

Detection is the discovery of an adversary action. It includes sensing of covert or overt actions. In order to discover an adversary action, the following events need to occur:

1. A sensor reacts to a stimulus and initiates an alarm.
2. The information from the sensor and assessment subsystems is reported and displayed.
3. A person assesses information and judges the alarm to be valid or invalid. If assessed as a nuisance alarm, detection has not occurred. Detection without assessment is not considered detection. Assessment is the process of determining whether the source of the alarm is due to an attack or a nuisance alarm.

These events are depicted in Figure 5.2 and show that detection is not an instantaneous event. Included in the detection function of physical protection is entry control. Entry control allows entry to authorized personnel and detects the attempted entry of unauthorized personnel and material. The measures of effectiveness of entry control are throughput, false acceptance rate, and false rejection rate. Throughput is defined as the number of authorized personnel allowed access per unit time, assuming that all personnel who attempt entry are authorized for entrance. False acceptance is the rate at which false identities or credentials are allowed entry, while false rejection rate is the frequency of denying access to authorized personnel.

The measures of effectiveness for the detection function are the probability of sensing adversary action, the time required

Figure 5.2 Detection Functions in a PPS. Detection starts with sensor activation and ends with assessment of the alarm to determine the cause

for reporting and assessing the alarm, and nuisance alarm rate. A sensor activates at time T_0, then at a later time a person receives information from the sensor and assessment subsystems. If the time delay between when the sensor activates and when the alarm is assessed as short, the probability of detection, P_D, will be close to the probability that the sensor will sense the unauthorized action, P_S. The probability of detection decreases as the time before assessment increases. Figure 5.3 shows that a long time delay between detection and assessment lowers the probability of detection, because the more the time required to make an accurate assessment, the less likely it will be that the cause of the alarm is still present. For example, if sensor alarms are assessed by sending a guard to the sensor location, by the time the guard arrives there may no longer be an obvious alarm source. In this case, the delay between sensor initiation and assessment was so lengthy that no assessment could be made. This is why P_D decreases. In addition, the delay between detection and assessment favors the adversary due to the further progression of the adversary toward the target before the response force has been notified of an attack.

Response force personnel can also accomplish detection. Guards at fixed posts or on patrol may serve a vital role in sensing an intrusion. An effective assessment system provides two types of information associated with detection: information about whether the alarm is valid or nuisance, and details about the cause of the alarm—what, who, where, and how many. However, even when assisted by a video-assessment system, humans do not make good detectors. Studies have shown that brief instances of movement are missed by 48% of human observers using video monitors (Tickner and Poulton, 1973).

An additional performance measure of sensors is the nuisance alarm rate. A nuisance alarm is any alarm that is not

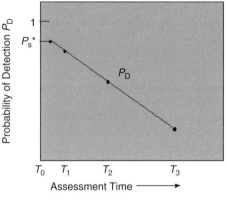

*Probability that sensor alarms

Figure 5.3 Relationship between Assessment Time and Probability of Detection. The probability of detection will decrease as assessment time increases

caused by an intrusion. In an ideal sensor system, the nuisance alarm rate would be zero. However, in the real world all sensors interact with their environment and they cannot discriminate between intrusions and other events in their detection zone. This is why an alarm assessment system is needed: not all sensor alarms are caused by intrusions.

Usually nuisance alarms are further classified by source. Both natural and industrial environments can cause nuisance alarms. Common sources of natural noise are vegetation (trees and weeds), wildlife (animals and birds), and weather conditions (wind, rain, snow, fog, lightning). Industrial sources of noise include ground vibration, debris moved by wind, and electromagnetic interference. False alarms are those nuisance alarms generated by the equipment itself (whether by poor design, inadequate maintenance, or component failure).

Delay

Delay is the second function of a PPS. It is the slowing down of adversary progress. Delay can be accomplished by people,

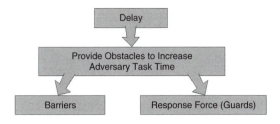

Figure 5.5 Response Function. Response components include communication, proper deployment of the response force, and interruption of the adversary prior to attack completion

Figure 5.4 Delay Function. Delay components include barriers and members of the response force. Barriers include active and passive barriers

barriers, locks, and activated delays. The response force can be considered elements of delay if they are in fixed and well-protected positions. The measure of delay effectiveness is the time required by the adversary (after detection) to bypass each delay element. Although the adversary may be delayed prior to detection, this delay is of no value to the effectiveness of the PPS since it does not provide additional time to respond to the adversary. Delay before detection is primarily a deterrent. There are some situations where barriers are placed before detection; however, this application is meant to force adversaries to change or abandon their tactic. For example, the use of speed bumps or placement of jersey bounce barriers along the sides of a road will slow down or prevent an adversary in a vehicle from leaving the road. Figure 5.4 summarizes the function of delay in a PPS.

Response

The response function consists of the actions taken by the response force to prevent adversary success. Response consists of interruption and neutralization. Interruption is defined as a sufficient number of response force personnel arriving at the appropriate location to stop the adversary's progress. It includes the communication to the protection force

of accurate information about adversary actions and the deployment of the response force. An additional measure of response force effectiveness, neutralization, is also used in some high-security applications. Neutralization is a measure of the outcome of a confrontation between the response force and adversaries. Neutralization can range from chasing away vandals up through an armed engagement with well-armed attackers. This concept will be discussed further in Chapter 12, "Response." The measures of response force effectiveness include the time between the receipt of communication of adversary action and the interruption of the adversary action (response force time), and the success of the response team after interruption (neutralization) function, shown in Figure 5.5.

The effectiveness measures for response communication are the probability of accurate communication and the time required for communication. The time after information is initially transmitted may vary considerably depending on the method of communication. After the initial period, the probability of valid communication begins to increase rapidly. As shown in Figure 5.6, with each repeat, the probability of correct and current data being communicated is increased. There can be some delay in establishing accurate communication due to human behavior. On the first attempt to communicate, the operator is alerted that there is a call, but may not have heard all the relevant information. Then a request for a second transmission is made to repeat the information,

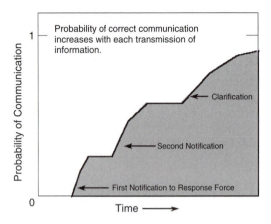

Figure 5.6 Variation of Probability of Communication with Time. As the time to establish accurate communication increases, the probability of communication increases

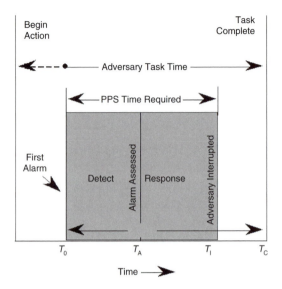

Figure 5.7 Interrelationship of PPS Functions. Detection begins upon receipt of the first alarm and ends when the alarm is assessed. The delay function slows down the adversary in order to allow the response force time to deploy. The PPS must provide enough time for the response force to stop the adversary from successfully completing the task

and finally, the operator understands the call and asks for clarification.

Deployment describes the actions of the protective force from the time communication is received until the force is in position to interrupt the adversary. The effectiveness measure of this function is the probability of deployment to the adversary location and the time required to deploy the response force.

Relationship of PPS Functions

Figure 5.7 shows the relationships between adversary task time and the time required for the PPS to do its job. The total time required for the adversary to accomplish the goal has been labeled Adversary Task Time. It is dependent upon the delay provided by the PPS. The adversary may begin the task at some time before the first alarm occurs, which is labeled on the diagram as T_0. The adversary task time is shown by a dashed line before this point because delay is not effective before detection. After the alarm, the alarm information must be reported and assessed to determine if the alarm is valid. The

time at which the alarm is assessed to be valid is labeled T_A, and at this time the location of the alarm must be communicated to the members of the response force. Further time is then required for the response force to respond in adequate numbers and with adequate equipment to interrupt adversary actions. The time at which the response force interrupts adversary actions is labeled T_I and adversary task completion time is labeled T_C. Clearly, in order for the PPS to accomplish its objectives, T_I must occur before T_C. It is equally clear that the first alarm should occur as early as possible and T_0 (as well as T_A and T_I) should be as far to the left on the time axis as possible.

Consideration of chemical, biological, and radiological attacks does not change the time relationship among the PPS functions. There still must be detection with enough time to allow whatever response is required—shelter-in-place, evacuation, put on protection equipment, and so on. Some facilities have used different strategies to address these attacks, such as always filtering incoming air, but the filters must be replaced periodically to maintain effective capability. In this case, sensors can still provide detection, and delay components include filters or turning off the heating and ventilation system to slow the spread of the agent. The basic principle is the same—the spread of the agent must be delayed so there is enough time to implement whatever response is desired. Implementation of the appropriate detection, delay, and response elements must be considered for the overall system against the defined threat.

Characteristics of an Effective PPS

The effectiveness of the PPS functions of detection, delay, and response and their relationships have been discussed. In addition, all the hardware elements the system must be installed, maintained, and operated properly. The procedures of the PPS must be compatible with the facility procedures and integrated into the PPS design. Training of personnel in policies, procedures, and operation of equipment is also important to system effectiveness. Security, safety, and operational objectives must be accomplished at all times. A well-engineered PPS will exhibit the following characteristics:

- protection-in-depth
- minimum consequence of component failure
- balanced protection

Protection-in-Depth

Protection-in-depth means that to accomplish the goal, an adversary should be required to avoid or defeat a number of protective devices in sequence. For example, an adversary might have to defeat one sensor and penetrate two separate barriers before gaining entry to a process control room or a filing cabinet in the project costing area. The actions and times required to penetrate each of these layers may not necessarily be equal, and the effectiveness of each may be quite different, but each will require a separate and distinct act by the adversary moving along the path. The effect produced on the adversary by a system that provides protection-in-depth will be:

- to increase uncertainty about the system;
- to require more extensive preparations prior to attacking the system; and
- to create additional steps where the adversary may fail or abort the mission.

Minimum Consequence of Component Failure

It is unlikely that a complex system will ever be developed and operated that does not experience some component failure during its lifetime. Causes of component failure in a PPS are numerous and can range from environmental factors (which may be expected) to adversary actions beyond the scope of the threat used in the system design. Although it is important to know the cause of component failure in order to restore the system to normal operation, it is more important that contingency plans are provided so the system can continue to operate. Requiring portions of these contingency plans to be carried out automatically (e.g., redundant equipment automatically takes over the function of disabled equipment) may be highly desirable in some cases. An example of this is the presence of backup power at a facility. In the event that an adversary disables the primary power source, generators or batteries can be used to power the security system. Some component failures may require aid from sources outside of the facility in order to minimize the impact of the failure. One example of this is the use of local law enforcement to supplement airport security personnel at times of higher alert status. In this case, the component failure is the temporary lack of sufficient response forces under new threat conditions.

Balanced Protection

Balanced protection means that no matter how an adversary attempts to accomplish the goal, effective elements of the PPS will be encountered. Consider, for example, the barrier surface that surrounds a room. This surface may consist of:

- walls, floors, and ceilings of several types;
- doors of several types; equipment hatches in floors and ceilings; and
- heating, ventilating, and air conditioning openings with various types of grills.

For a completely balanced system, the minimum time to penetrate each of these barriers would be equal, and the minimum probability of detecting penetration of each of these barriers should be equal. However, complete balance is probably not possible or desirable. Certain elements, such as walls, may be extremely resistant to penetration, not because of physical protection requirements, but due to structural or safety requirements. Door, hatch, and grille delays may be considerably less than wall delays and still be adequate. There is no advantage in over-designing by installing a costly door that would take several minutes to penetrate with explosives, if the wall with the door were standard drywall, which could be penetrated in a few seconds with hand tools.

Finally, features designed to protect against one form of threat should not be eliminated because they overprotect against another threat. The objective should be to provide adequate protection against all threats on all possible paths and to maintain a balance with other considerations, such as cost, safety, or structural integrity.

Design Criteria

Any design process must have criteria against which elements of the design will be evaluated. A design process based on performance criteria will select elements and procedures according to the contribution they make to overall system performance. The effectiveness measure will be overall system performance. By establishing a measure of overall system performance, these values may be compared for existing (baseline) systems and upgraded systems and the amount of improvement determined. This increase in system effectiveness can then be compared to the cost of implementation of the proposed upgrades and a cost/benefit analysis can be supported.

A feature criteria approach selects elements or procedures to satisfy requirements that certain items are present. The effectiveness measure is the presence of those features. The use of a feature criteria approach in regulations or requirements that apply to a PPS should generally be avoided or handled with extreme care. Unless such care is exercised, the feature criteria approach can lead to the use of a checklist method to determine system adequacy, based on the presence or absence of required features. This is clearly not desirable, since overall system performance is of interest, rather than the mere presence or absence of system features or components. For example, a performance criterion for a perimeter detection system would be that the system be able to detect a running intruder using any attack method.

A feature criterion for the same detection system might be that the system includes two specific sensor types, such as motion detection and a fence sensor.

The conceptual design techniques presented in this text use a performance-based approach to meet the PPS objectives. Much of the component technology material will, however, be applicable for either performance criteria or feature criteria design methods.

The performance measures for the PPS functions are:

Detection
- Probability of detection
- Time for communication and assessment
- Frequency of nuisance alarms

Delay
- Time to defeat obstacles

Response
- Probability of accurate communication to response force
- Time to communicate
- Probability of deployment to adversary location
- Time to deploy (interruption)
- Response force effectiveness (neutralization)

Additional Design Elements

As emphasized above, an effective PPS will combine people, procedures, and equipment into an integrated system that will protect assets from the expected threat. The use of people and technology components are important design tools that often form the basis for protection systems. The use of procedures as protection elements cannot be overstated. Procedural changes can be cost-effective solutions to physical protection issues, although when used by themselves they will only protect assets from the lowest threats. Procedures include not only the operational and maintenance procedures previously described, but also the training

of facility personnel in security awareness and of guards or other response forces in when and how to stop an adversary. Another procedural design tool is the use of investigations. Investigation may be the response to a loss event or may be used to anticipate a threat, such as in background investigations of potential employees. Regardless of how the investigation tool is used, it is an important design element in a PPS and should be used when appropriate. Of course, for critical high-consequence loss assets, an investigation after the fact may be too late. In these cases, more immediate responses will be required to prevent loss of or damage to the critical asset.

In addition to use of the investigative tool, some corporations are applying more resources to the use of technical surveillance countermeasures, such as sweeps and searches for electronic bugging devices. This is an additional aspect of a security system that, like executive protection, must be part of an integrated approach to asset protection. The use of hotels and other nonproprietary sites for seminars or meetings provides the opportunity for industrial espionage. For these threats, a security manager may choose to send personnel to the meeting location and assure that a room or area is free of any recording or other surveillance equipment. Technical surveillance techniques may also be used within a facility, either on a daily basis or for some special events, such as on-site Board of Directors meetings, to prevent theft of information.

The performance measures for investigative and technical surveillance techniques do not lend themselves to quantification as readily as technical protection elements. In these cases, discovery of the person responsible for the theft or damage or the presence of surveillance devices serves as the measure of performance for the design element. These tools are very useful, but may not be sufficient for protection of critical assets at sites. As with any design, the design elements used to achieve the protection system objectives will depend on the threat, the likelihood of an attack, and the consequence of loss of the asset.

There are a wide variety of procedural elements that can be incorporated into an effective system design at a facility. These are too numerous to be listed in detail here, but as general guidelines, procedures can supplement a good technical design and training. Procedures that can be considered, depending on the threat and the value of the asset, include shredding of all papers before disposal, locking procedures for safes, password control and update for computer systems, random drug searches in accordance with company policies and legal requirements, periodic audits of employee computer files, and issuing parking permits to employees and authorized visitors. Regardless of the type of procedure that is used, these procedures are another design tool that falls into one of the three functions of a good PPS—detection, delay, and response.

Summary

This chapter described the use of a systematic and measurable approach to the design of a PPS. It emphasizes the concept of detection, followed by delay and response, and presents a brief description of the relationship of these functions. Specific performance measures of various components of a PPS are described, as well as desired characteristics of a good PPS, including protection-in-depth, minimum consequence of component failures, and balanced protection. The process stresses the use of integrated systems combining people, procedures, and equipment to meet the protection objectives. Emphasis is placed on the design of performance-based systems, rather than feature-based, since systems based on performance will indicate how successful the design is at meeting the protection objectives, not just the presence or absence of components. The use of performance measures will

also enable a cost/benefit analysis that can compare increased system effectiveness to cost of implementation.

Security Principles

The functions of a PPS are detection, delay, and response. They represent the integration of people, procedures, and equipment to meet the system objectives.

Detection is placed before delay, with detection most effective at the perimeter and delay more effective at the target. Detection is not complete without assessment.

The total time for detection, delay, and response must be less than the adversary's task time to protect critical assets.

Characteristics of a good PPS include protection-in-depth, minimizing the effect of component failure, and balanced protection.

Performance-based design criteria are better than feature-based when measuring overall system effectiveness.

Reference

Tickner, A.H., and Poulton, E.C. "Monitoring up to 16 television pictures showing a great deal of movement." *Ergonomics* 1973;16(4):381–401.

Questions

1. It is often said that the role of physical protection is to encourage the adversary to attack someone else's plant. Is that the role of physical protection? Explain.
2. If all analyses point out that the earlier the adversary is detected, the better our chances of defeating him or her, then what prevents us from moving sensors out to the very limits of our property?

3. Explain the difference between alarm communication and response communication?
4. If we were to use guard towers around the site, which of the PPS system functions (detection, delay, or response) would be enhanced the most?
5. What is the advantage of a system with protection-in-depth compared to one that is very secure at one level?
6. Explain balanced protection.
7. What is the difference between performance criteria and feature criteria?

6

Exterior Intrusion Sensors

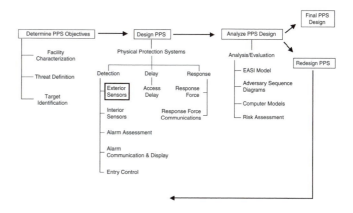

Intrusion detection systems consist of exterior and interior intrusion sensors, video alarm assessment, entry control, and alarm communication systems all working together. Exterior sensors are those used in an outdoor environment, and interior sensors are those used inside buildings.

Intrusion detection is defined as the detection of a person or vehicle attempting to gain unauthorized entry into an area that is being protected by someone who is able to authorize or initiate an appropriate response. The intrusion detection boundary is ideally a sphere enclosing the item being protected so that all intrusions, whether by surface, air, underwater, or underground, are detected. The development of most exterior intrusion detection technology has emphasized detection on or slightly above the ground surface, with increasing emphasis being placed on airborne intrusion and tunneling. This chapter will primarily cover ground-level intrusion.

Performance Characteristics

Intrusion sensor performance is described by three fundamental characteristics—probability of detection (P_D), nuisance alarm rate, and vulnerability to defeat. An understanding of these characteristics is essential for designing and operating an effective intrusion sensor system.

Probability of Detection

For the ideal sensor, the P_D of an intrusion is one (1.0). However, no sensor is ideal, and the P_D is always less than 1. The way that P_D is calculated does not allow a P_D of 1. Even with thousands of tests, the P_D only approaches 1. For any specific sensor and scenario (e.g., a specific facility at night, in clear weather, a crawling attacker), the two values P_D and confidence level (C_L) are used to describe the effectiveness of the sensor. The sensor will detect the intrusion with probability of detection P_D for confidence level C_L. This means that, based upon test results and with probability C_L, the sensor's true, but unknown, probability of detection is at least P_D. For an ideal sensor the P_D would be 1.0 with a C_L of 1.0 or 100%. In reality, a P_D or a C_L equal to 1.0 will not occur, because complete knowledge of a sensor's effectiveness is never achieved. Also, the pair (P_D, C_L) is not unique; based upon the same test results, it is possible to calculate different P_Ds for different C_Ls. Most commonly, values of 90, 95, or even 99% are used for C_L, although a value of 99% would require very extensive testing. Although technically incorrect, manufacturers will often state values of P_D without stating the corresponding value of C_L. When this happens, it is reasonable to assume that they are inferring a value of at least 90% for C_L against a low-level threat.

The probability of detection depends primarily on:

- target to be detected (a walking, running, or crawling intruder; tunneling; etc.)
- sensor hardware design
- installation conditions
- sensitivity adjustment
- weather conditions
- condition of the equipment
- acceptable nuisance alarm rate

All of the above conditions can vary, and thus, despite the claims of some sensor manufacturers, a specific P_D cannot be assigned to each component or set of sensor hardware. Due to this variation, any P_D assigned to a sensor is conditional, based on the assumptions made about the conditions in which the sensor operates.

For example, an intrusion sensor may have one P_D for a low-level threat such as a vandal and another lower P_D against a more sophisticated threat. This is an area where the design basis threat drives system design. If the design basis threat is three

criminals with considerable knowledge and skill, it would be better to use a sensor that has a higher P_D, since we are faced with a more capable adversary. If the threat is expected to be teenagers vandalizing property, a lower P_D can be tolerated, since the threat is correspondingly less. Similarly, it would be impractical to use a microwave sensor in an area that received deep snow accumulation during the winter, since this could allow an adversary to tunnel undetected into the facility through the snow. For these reasons, sensor selection must be matched to the application and environment.

It is important that the system designer specify the detection criteria required or expected of a sensor or sensor system. This specification should be clear as to what will be detected, what actions are expected, any other considerations such as weight or speed of movement, and what P_D is required. An example of a detection criterion might be as follows: the perimeter intrusion detection system shall be capable of detecting a person, weighing 35 kg or more, crossing the detection zone by walking, crawling, jumping, running, or rolling, at speeds between 0.15 and 5 m/s, or climbing the fence at any point in the detection zone, with a detection probability of 90% at 95% confidence. This represents a clear and measurable set of conditions, not just a statement such as "successful detection should occur most of the time." Notice that the former specification is clear that the system will perform as expected with the implication that this should happen day or night, good weather or bad, while the latter will be hard to objectively measure. When a high P_D is required 24 h a day under all expected weather conditions, the use of multiple complementary sensors is recommended. Sensors are considered to be complementary when one sensor's weaknesses are complemented by another sensor's strengths. For example, an e-field sensor may experience an elevated nuisance alarm rate if flowing water is running under the e-field sensor line. In this instance a complementary sensor could be a fence-mounted fiber optic sensor. The fiber optic sensor will not respond to water flowing under the fence, hence it complements the e-field sensor. Sensors can be complementary with respect to nuisance alarm issues or vulnerability issues. Generally speaking, complementary sensors will have different sensor phenomenologies. Contingency plans and procedures should exist so that compensatory measures can be implemented in the event of loss of any or all sensors.

Nuisance Alarm Rate

A nuisance alarm is any alarm that is not caused by an intrusion. Nuisance alarm rate (NAR) is a function of the number of nuisance alarms over a given time period. In an ideal sensor system, the nuisance alarm rate would be zero (0.0). However, in the real world all sensors interact with their environment, and they cannot discriminate between adversary intrusions and other events in their detection zone. This is why an alarm assessment system is needed—not all sensor alarms are caused by intrusions. This is also why it is ineffective to have the guard force respond to every alarm. Assessment, then, serves the purpose of determining the cause of the alarm and whether or not it requires a response. This is why we say that detection is not complete without assessment.

Usually nuisance alarms are further classified by source. Both natural and industrial environments can cause nuisance alarms. Common sources of natural noise are vegetation (trees and weeds), wildlife (animals and birds), and weather conditions (wind, rain, snow, fog, lightning). Industrial sources of noise include ground vibration, debris moved by wind, and electromagnetic interference.

False alarms are those nuisance alarms generated by the equipment itself (whether by poor design, inadequate maintenance, or component failure). Different types of intrusion sensors have different sensitivities to these nuisance or false alarm sources, as is discussed in detail later in this chapter.

As with P_D, it is important to specify an acceptable false alarm rate (FAR). For example, the FAR for the total perimeter intrusion system shall not average more than one false alarm per week, per zone, while maintaining a P_D of 0.9. This statement is much more meaningful than: a higher FAR and NAR may be tolerated if this does not result in system degradation. In this case, system degradation takes on a very subjective meaning and so becomes harder to measure. Establishing specific values for false alarm rates also helps the operator determine when a sensor should be reported to maintenance personnel.

Vulnerability to Defeat

All sensors can be defeated; a security system designer uses a sensor's strength to make the system very difficult and costly to defeat. Different types of sensors and sensor models have different vulnerabilities. Vulnerabilities can be accomplished by exploiting the sensor physics, signal processing, installation, degradation factors, or site conditions. There are two general ways to defeat a sensor:

- Bypass—Because all intrusion sensors have a finite detection zone, any sensor can be defeated by going around its detection volume.
- Spoof—Spoofing is any technique that allows the intruder to pass through the sensor's normal detection zone without generating an alarm

Preliminary testing or past experience will often indicate vulnerabilities or suggest additional testing to better characterize specific vulnerabilities. If results of sensor tests conducted under ideal conditions do not compare well with required performance, it is not likely that additional vulnerability tests will be conducted. Simply stated, if the sensor does not work under ideal conditions it is unlikely to work in an operational environment and, thus, is not a good candidate for use at a site.

There are several questions regarding vulnerabilities that concern every security designer. They include:

1. Can a vulnerability of a selected security technology be exploited, thereby circumventing the security measure?
2. How damaging is the vulnerability to the effectiveness of the overall system?
3. What are the resources and skills required to identify and exploit the vulnerability?
4. Can the security system design (including people, procedures, and technology) be improved to remove or minimize existing vulnerabilities?

The answers to the first three questions give the security designer an indication of the severity of the vulnerability and are strongly tied to the defined threat capabilities. Addressing the last question requires analysis of the whole security system. A proficient designer will examine many options to improve the security system and will consider:

- cost of the design option—both installation and life cycle costs
- creation of additional vulnerabilities
- maintenance impacts
- safety issues
- increases in manpower
- increased training requirements
- design life
- system effectiveness against the specified threat
- possibly just accepting the risks associated with leaving a vulnerability in the design

Clearly, the issue of identification and mitigation of vulnerabilities in the design of a security system is complex. Every security designer faces these issues to varying degrees and part of their job is to minimize the existence and/or minimize the effects of vulnerabilities on the security design deployed. Vulnerability assessment is discussed in more detail in a recent textbook (Garcia, 2006).

Sensor Classification

There are several ways of classifying the many types of exterior intrusion sensors. In this discussion, five methods of classification are used:

1. passive or active
2. covert or visible
3. line-of-sight or terrain-following
4. volumetric or line detection
5. application

Passive or Active

Passive sensors detect some type of energy that is emitted by the target of interest or detect the change of some natural field of energy caused by the target. Examples of the former are mechanical energy from a human walking on the soil or climbing on a fence. An example of the latter is a change in the local magnetic field caused by the presence of a metal. Passive sensors utilize a receiver to collect the energy emissions. Passive sensor technologies include those based on vibration, heat, sound, magnetic and electric fields.

Active sensors transmit some type of energy and detect a change in the received energy created by the presence or motion of the target. They generally include both a transmitter and a receiver and include microwave, infrared, and other radio frequency (RF) devices. The distinction of passive or active has a practical importance. The presence or location of a passive sensor is more difficult to determine than that of an active sensor since there is no energy source for the adversary to locate; this puts the intruder at a disadvantage. In environments with explosive vapors or materials, passive sensors are safer than active ones because no energy that might initiate explosives is emitted. Active sensors, because of their stronger signals, more effectively eliminate nuisance alarms.

Covert or Visible

Covert sensors are hidden from view; examples are sensors that are buried in the ground. Visible sensors are in plain view of an intruder; examples are sensors that are attached to a fence or mounted on another support structure. Covert sensors are more difficult for an intruder to detect and locate and thus they can be more effective; also, they do not affect the appearance of the environment. Visible sensors may, however, deter the intruder from acting. Visible sensors are typically simpler to install and easier to repair and maintain than covert ones.

Line-of-Sight or Terrain-Following

Line-of-sight (LOS) sensors perform acceptably only when installed with a clear LOS in the detection space. This usually means a clear LOS between the transmitter and receiver for active sensors. These sensors normally require a flat ground surface or at least a clear LOS from each point on the ground surface to both the transmitter and the receiver. The use of LOS sensors on sites without a flat terrain requires extensive site preparation to achieve acceptable performance.

Terrain-following sensors detect equally well on flat and irregular terrain. The transducer elements and the radiated field follow the terrain and result in uniform detection throughout the detection zone.

Volumetric or Line Detection

Volumetric sensors detect intrusion in a volume of space. An alarm is generated when an intruder enters the detection volume. The detection volume is generally not visible and is hard for the intruder to identify precisely.

Line detection sensors detect along a line. For example, sensors that detect fence motion are mounted directly on the fence. The fence becomes a line of detection, since an intruder will not be detected while approaching the fence; detection occurs only if the intruder moves the fence fabric where the sensor is attached. The detection zone of a line detection sensor is usually easy to identify.

Application

In this classification method, the sensors are grouped by mode of application in the physical detection space. These modes are:

- buried line, in which the sensor is in the form of a line buried in the ground;
- fence-associated, in which the sensor either is mounted on a fence or forms a sensor fence; and
- freestanding, being neither buried nor associated with a fence, but mounted on a support in free space.

Sensor Technology

In this chapter, sensors are grouped by their modes of application. Table 6.1 summarizes the different exterior intrusion sensor technologies according to the different sensor classification schemes. Many sensor technology reviews have been published and supplement the material presented in this chapter (Barnard, 1988; Cumming, 1992; Fennelly, 1996; Williams, 1988).

Table 6.1 *Types of Exterior Sensors and Characteristics.*

	Passive or Active	Covert or Visible	LOS or Terrain-Following	Volumetric or Line Detection
Buried Line				
Seismic Pressure	P	C	TF	L
Magnetic Field	P	C	TF	VOL
Ported Coaxial Cable	A	C	TF	VOL
Fiber-Optic Cables	P	C	TF	L
Fence-Associated				
Fence-Disturbance	P	V	TF	L
Sensor Fence	P	V	TF	L
Electric Field	A	V	TF	VOL
Freestanding				
Active Infrared	A	V	LOS	L
Passive Infrared	P	V	LOS	VOL
Bistatic Microwave	A	V	LOS	VOL
Dual Technology	A/P	V	LOS	VOL
Video Motion Detection	P	C	LOS	VOL

Buried-Line Sensors

At present there are four types of buried-line sensors that depend on different sensing phenomena: pressure or seismic sensors, magnetic field sensors, ported coaxial cable sensor, and fiber-optic sensors.

Pressure or Seismic

Pressure or seismic sensors are passive, covert, terrain-following sensors that are buried in the ground. They respond to disturbances of the soil caused by an intruder walking, running, jumping, or crawling on the ground. Pressure sensors are generally sensitive to lower frequency pressure waves in the soil, and seismic sensors are sensitive to higher frequency vibration of the soil. A simple example of a pressure sensor consists of a reinforced hose that is filled with a pressurized liquid and connected to a pressure transducer. A balanced pressure system consists of two such hoses connected to a transducer to permit differential sensing and

to reduce nuisance alarms from seismic sources located far away.

A typical seismic sensor suite consists of a line or array of individual vibration sensors called geophones. A geophone consists of a permanent magnet suspended by a spring within a conducting coil. Motion of the geophone in response to ground vibrations causes the magnet to move relative to the coil, inducing a small voltage in the coil. Calibration of the geophone allows this voltage to be directly related to ground velocity, giving an accurate measure of the amount of vibration occurring at the geophone location. A variety of geophones are available that have differing vibration amplitude sensitivities and frequency ranges and should be chosen appropriately depending on the specific signatures of interest and ambient noise field.

Accelerometers offer an alternative vibration sensor and are most often based on piezoelectric crystals or piezoceramics that are compressed by a mass when the case is vibrated, creating a voltage output from the crystal. The downside of accelerometers is that they require a separate small power source and are less rugged, so are not the preferred option for long unattended monitoring. However, such accelerometers may have required characteristics in either frequency range or sensitivity and may have some application in special circumstances.

Seismic sensors are susceptible to several noise sources that can result in nuisance alarms, the most common being power line noise that results from interference by the omnipresent power grid. This noise source results both from signals generated by direct induction of the 60 Hz electric power into the geophone coil as well as 60 Hz vibrations transmitted into the ground by power poles. In all cases, this noise source is strongly band limited to 60 Hz and its harmonics and sub-harmonics. It is commonly removed with narrow notch filters that remove specific frequencies and by appropriate shielding of both the sensors and the cables connecting the seismic array.

The other most common noise sources are wind noise and cultural noise. Wind noise results from the interaction of the wind with objects anchored to the ground, such as poles, vegetation, and even buildings. Burying the sensors mitigates this noise source to some degree, but wind and weather conditions will be a consideration when looking at P_D measures. Cultural noise, on the other hand, is defined as the vibrations resulting from other activities within the immediate vicinity, such as traffic, machinery, and any other human activity that causes significant ground vibration. This type of noise is highly dependent on the amount of human activity and varies considerably by environment (e.g., urban versus rural) and time of day, with early morning hours typically being the quietest.

Coupling of the geophones is a critical consideration when installing seismic monitoring arrays. The sensors must be in intimate contact with the ground to preserve both the amplitude and frequency content of the vibrational energy. Often, sensors will be cemented in at depth and then backfilled to both ensure strong coupling and reduce the wind noise effects which attenuate rapidly with depth. Loose soil may have an effect on the quality of the signal received, but, in general, burying the sensor 2–3 ft in depth will provide sufficient coupling for good signal reception. Because these sensors are passive and buried, movement above the ground is not directly detected. If the location of the buried-line sensor is known, an adversary may defeat this sensor by forming a low bridge over the transducer line. However, vibrations from personnel movement will still be transmitted into the ground at the anchor points of the bridge and may be detectable.

Magnetic Field

Magnetic field sensors are passive, covert, terrain-following sensors that are buried in the ground. They respond to a change in the local magnetic field caused by the movement of nearby ferromagnetic material. Thus magnetic field sensors are effective for detecting vehicles or intruders with weapons.

This type of sensor consists of a series of wire loops or coils buried in the ground. Movement of metallic material near the loop or coil changes the local magnetic field and induces a current. Magnetic field sensors can be susceptible to local electromagnetic disturbances such as lightning. Intruders who are not wearing or carrying any metal will be able to defeat this type of sensor. Magnetic field sensors are primarily used to detect vehicle traffic.

Ported Coaxial Cables

Ported coaxial cable sensors are active, covert, terrain-following sensors that are buried in the ground. They are also known as leaky coax or radiating cable sensors. This type of sensors responds to motion of a material with a high dielectric constant or high conductivity near the cables. These

Figure 6.1 Installation of Ported Coaxial Cable. This type of ported coax uses two cables and is installed with one cable in each trench. The trenches must be consistently spaced and flat. Usually the trench bottom is partially filled with sand prior to laying the cable

materials include both the human body and metal vehicles. Figure 6.1 shows the installation of one type of ported coaxial cable.

The name of this sensor is derived from the construction of the transducer cable. The outer conductor of this coaxial cable does not provide complete shielding for the center conductor, and thus some of the radiated signal leaks through the ports of the outer conductor. The detection volume of ported coax sensors extends significantly above the ground: about 1.5–3.0 ft above the surface and about 3–6 ft wider than the cable separation. The sensitivity of this type of sensor in frozen soil actually increases slightly relative to thawed conditions. This is because some of the field energy is absorbed by conductive soil, and the conductivity of frozen ground is less than that of thawed ground.

Metal or water in the ported coax detection zone can cause two types of sensor problems. Moving metal objects and moving water are large targets for ported coax sensors and thus are a major potential source of nuisance alarms. Both flowing water and standing water (primarily flowing water) contribute to

this problem. The second problem is that fixed metal objects and standing water distort the radiated field, possibly to the extent of creating insensitive areas with no detection. Nearby metal objects or utility lines should be excluded from the detection volume. This includes above-ground fences and poles and underground water lines and electrical cables.

The P_D of ported coaxial cable is affected by the ported coaxial cable processor settings, orientation of the intruder, soil characteristics, and the presence of metallic objects. Large amounts of salt or metals in the soil will also degrade performance of this sensor.

Fiber-Optic Cables

Optical fibers are long, hair-like strands of transparent glass or plastic. Fiber-optics is the class of optical technology that uses these transparent fibers to guide light from one end to the other. As light travels through the fiber, it remains in the clear plastic core by reflecting off the surface of cladding material that has a different refraction index. Thus the fiber becomes a "light-pipe."

The fiber does not have to be straight since light reflects off a curved or straight surface. The light diffraction (speckle) pattern and the light intensity at the end of the fiber are a function of the shape of the fiber over its entire length. Even the slightest change in the shape of the fiber can be sensed using sophisticated sensors and computer signal processing at the far end (100 yards or more). Thus a single strand of fiber-optic cable, buried in the ground at the depth of a few centimeters, can very effectively give an alarm when an intruder steps on the ground above the fiber (Wolfenbarger, 1994). To ensure that an intruder steps above the fiber, it is usually woven into a grid and buried just beneath the surface. A typical installation of fiber-optic mesh on the ground is shown in Figure 6.2.

Because fiber-optic cable senses vibrations, nuisance alarm sources can be

Figure 6.2 Installation of Fiber-Optic Mesh as a Ground Sensor. Once installed, the mesh is covered with gravel or dirt. Stepping on the ground above the mesh causes the fiber to bend and changes the received signal. This change in signal causes an alarm

similar to those of seismic sensors. By decreasing the seismic coupling to the soil, for example, installing the sensor in gravel, seismic events can be minimized so the nuisance alarm rate will be much lower. It is useful to note that a fiber optic sensor does not respond to electric fields and may be a good candidate for regions with high lightning activity or areas close to high-power transmission lines.

Fence-Associated Sensors

There are three types of intrusion sensors that either mount on or attach to a fence or form a fence using the transducer material: fence-disturbance sensors, sensor fences, and electric field or capacitance sensors.

Fence-Disturbance Sensors

Fence-disturbance sensors are passive, visible, terrain-following sensors that are designed to be installed on a security fence, typically constructed with chain-link mesh. These sensors are considered terrain-following because the chain-link mesh is supported every 3 yards with a galvanized steel post, and thus the fence itself is terrain-following.

Fence-disturbance sensors can detect motion or vibration in the fence; thus, they are intended to detect an intruder who climbs on or cuts through the fence fabric. Several kinds of transducers are used to detect the movement or vibration of the fence. These include switches, electromechanical transducers, strain-sensitive cables, piezoelectric crystals, geophones, fiber-optic cables, or electric cable.

Fence-disturbance sensors respond to all mechanical disturbances of the fence, not just intruders. Common noise sources include wind and debris blown by wind, rain driven by wind, hail, and seismic activity from nearby traffic and machinery coupled to the fence through the ground. Good fence construction is important to minimize nuisance alarms, so rigid fence posts and tight fence fabric are required. Fence posts should not move more than 0.5 in. for a 50-pound pull applied 5 ft above the ground. Fence fabric should deflect no more than 2.5 in. for a 30-pound pull centered between fence posts. To eliminate nuisance alarms caused by rattles, do not place signs, loose ties, or other items on the fence. In addition, installing fence sensors on the inner fence of a two-fence system can reduce the NAR. This precaution will allow the outer fence to block blowing trash or other debris, and keep small animals away from the inner fence with a sensor.

Digging under the fence or bridging over the fence without touching the fence itself can defeat fence-disturbance sensors. A complementary sensor approach to address this concern can be accomplished by burying seismic sensors along the fence line to detect digging. Digging can be deterred by putting concrete under the fence. The bottom edge of the fabric can also be placed in the concrete. The P_D of fence-disturbance sensors is affected by the fabric tension, the fence processor settings, the rigidity of the fence, any noise coupled to the fence, and the aids used by the adversary to defeat the fence. For example, if the adversary defeats the fence by the use of a ladder and never touches the fence, the P_D will be very low or zero.

Sensor Fences

Sensor fences are passive, visible, terrain-following sensors that make use of the transducer elements to form a fence itself. These sensor fences are designed primarily to detect climbing or cutting on the fence. There are several common fence configurations.

Taut-wire sensor fences consist of many parallel, horizontal wires with high tensile strength that are connected under tension to transducers near the midpoint of the wire span. These transducers detect deflection of the wires caused by an intruder cutting the wires, climbing on the wires to get over the fence, or separating the wires to climb through the fence. The wire is typically barbed wire, and the transducers are mechanical switches, strain gauges, or piezoelectric elements. Taut-wire sensor fences can either be mounted on an existing set of fence posts or installed on an independent row of posts.

Sensor fences tend to be much less susceptible to nuisance alarms than fence-disturbance sensors because the transducers are not sensitive to vibrations and require a force of approximately 25 pounds on the wire to cause an alarm. However, because sensor fences also have a well-defined plane of detection, they are vulnerable to the same defeat methods as fence-disturbance sensors. Taut-wire fences attribute most nuisance alarms to large animals walking into the fence, improper installation or maintenance, and ice storms.

The P_D of taut wire fences is affected by the tension of the wires, wire friction, and wire spacing. If the spacing between two wires is large enough to allow a person to pass through undetected, the P_D will be much lower than if spacing is kept to 4 in. or less (Greer, 1990a,b).

Electric Field or Capacitance

Electric field or capacitance sensors are active, visible, terrain-following sensors that are designed to detect a change in capacitive coupling among a set of wires attached to, but electrically isolated from, a fence.

The sensitivity of electric field sensors can be adjusted to extend up to 1 m beyond the wire or plane of wires. A high sensitivity typically has a trade-off of more nuisance alarms. Electric field and capacitance sensors are susceptible to lightning, rain, fence motion, and small animals. Ice storms may cause substantial breakage and damage to the wires and the standoff insulators. Good electrical grounding of electric field sensors is important to reduce nuisance alarms. Other metal objects (such as the chain-link fence) in the sensor field must also be well grounded; poor or intermittent grounds will cause nuisance alarms. Because the detection volume extends beyond the fence plane, electric field sensors are more difficult than other fence-associated sensors to defeat by digging under or bridging over the fence (Follis, 1990).

The electric field or capacitance sensors can be mounted on their own set of posts instead of being associated with a security fence. The main differences in performance are due to the absence of the parallel grounded chain-link mesh. This results in two areas of improved performance: a wider detection volume for the sensitive electric field sensor and a lower nuisance alarm rate due to the elimination of noise from the motion of the chain-link fence. For the freestanding version of electric field sensors, some electronic signal-processing techniques employ additional wires in the horizontal plane to reduce the effects of distant lightning and alarms due to small animals.

Freestanding Sensors

The primary types of freestanding sensors currently used for exterior intrusion detection are infrared, microwave, e-field sensors, and video motion detection sensors.

Active Infrared

The infrared (IR) sensors used for exterior intrusion detection are active, visible, line-of-sight, and freestanding sensors. An IR beam is transmitted from an IR light-emitting diode through a collimating lens. Collimating lenses are used in active infrared sensors to convert the divergent beams of IR light into parallel beams, resulting in an efficient collection of the signal at the receiver. Without this lens, the light would disperse and provide a weaker signal at the receiver. The beam is received at the other end of the detection zone by a collecting lens that focuses the energy onto a photodiode. The IR sensor detects the loss of the received infrared energy when an opaque object blocks the beam. These sensors operate at a wavelength of about $0.9\,\mu m$, which is not visible to the human eye. One type of active infrared exterior sensor is shown in Figure 6.3.

Although single-beam IR sensors are available, multiple-beam sensors are normally used for high-level security applications because a single IR beam is too easy to defeat or bypass. A multiple-beam IR sensor system typically consists of two vertical arrays of IR transmitter and receiver modules (the specific number and configuration of modules depends on the manufacturer). Thus the IR sensor creates an IR fence of multiple beams but detects a single beam break. Multiple-beam infrared sensors usually incorporate some electronics to detect attempts at spoofing the beams with an alternative IR source.

Conditions that reduce atmospheric visibility have the potential to block or attenuate the IR beams and cause nuisance alarms. If the visibility between the two arrays is less than the distance between the two arrays, the system will probably produce a nuisance alarm. These conditions sometimes exist in fog, snow, and dust storms. In addition, grass, vegetation,

Figure 6.3 Freestanding Active Infrared Sensor. This picture shows one of the two units in the transmitter/receiver pair. Intrusions are detected when the IR beam is broken

and animals also add to nuisance alarms. The area between the IR posts should be kept clear of grass or other vegetation since even grass that is trimmed will move in the wind and can cause an alarm. Other sources of nuisance alarms include ground heave, optical alignment problems, and deep snow accumulations.

The detection volume cross-section of a multiple-beam IR sensor is typically 2 in. wide and 6 ft high, so IR sensors have a narrow plane of detection similar in dimensions to fence sensors. IR sensors are considered LOS sensors and require a flat ground surface because the IR beam travels in a straight line. A convex ground surface will block the beam, and a concave surface will permit passing under the beam without detection. Digging under the bottom beam is possible unless a concrete sill or paved surface has been installed. The PD is very high for a multiple beam sensor. Other methods of defeat include bridging, pole vaulting, stepping, sliding through beams, using sunshades on posts as a ladder.

Passive Infrared

Humans emit thermal energy due to the warmth of their body. On average, each human emits the equivalent energy of a 50 W light bulb, and passive infrared (PIR) detectors sense the presence of this energy and cause an alarm to be generated. For years, this technology was only usable in an interior application because the changes in heat, emitted by the ground as clouds passed overhead, caused too many false alarms. Current models, however, compare the received thermal energy from two curtain-shaped sensing patterns. A human moving into one area and then the other would cause an imbalance. Weather-related temperature changes such as the increases in temperature during a summer day would affect both areas equally and would not cause an alarm.

The PIR sensors should be mounted such that the motion of the intruder will most likely be across the line of sight because that is the most sensitive direction. Blowing debris, animals, birds, vegetation, standing water movement, and very heavy rain or snowfall could cause nuisance alarms. The passive infrared detector is most sensitive when the background is at a much different temperature than an intruder. Methods of defeat include bridging, tunneling, pole-vaulting, shielding the intruder to minimize the difference between his or her temperature and the background, or causing an identical change to both sensing patterns, such as blocking the field of view. Detection ranges can exceed 100 yards on cold days and can vary depending on the background temperature. Large hot objects, such as vehicles, may be detected well beyond the desired detection zone. PIR sensors will be discussed in more detail in the next chapter, "Interior Intrusion Sensors."

Bistatic Microwave

Bistatic microwave sensors are active, visible, line-of-sight, freestanding sensors. Typically, two identical microwave antennas are installed at opposite ends of the detection zone. One is connected to a microwave transmitter that operates near 10 or 24 GHz. The other is connected to a microwave receiver that detects the received microwave energy. This energy is the vector sum of the direct beam between the antennas and the microwave signals reflected from the ground surface and other objects in the transmitted beam. Microwave sensors respond to changes in the vector sum caused by objects moving in that portion of the transmitted beam that is within the viewing field of the receiver. This vector sum may actually increase or decrease, as the reflected signal may add in-phase or out-of-phase. One bistatic microwave antenna is shown in Figure 6.4.

Bistatic microwave sensors are often installed to detect a human crawling or rolling on the ground across the microwave beam, keeping the body parallel to the beam. From this perspective, the human body presents the smallest effective target to the bistatic microwave sensor. This

Figure 6.4 Bistatic Microwave Antenna. This sensor will detect humans crawling or rolling through the microwave beam. The other unit of the microwave pair is placed at the opposite end of the detection zone to establish the detection volume

has two important consequences for the installation of microwave sensors. First, the ground surface between the transmitter and receiver must be flat so that the object is not shadowed from the microwave beam, precluding detection. The surface flatness specification for this case is +0, −6 in. Even with this flatness, crawlers may not be detected if the distance between antennas is much greater than 120 yards. Second, a zone of no detection exists in the first few meters in front of the antennas. This distance from the antennas to the point of first crawler detection is called the offset distance. Because of this offset distance, long perimeters where microwave sensors are configured to achieve a continuous line of detection require that the antennas overlap one another, rather than being adjacent to each other. An offset of 10 yards is typically assumed for design purposes, thus adjacent sectors must overlap twice the offset distance, for a total of 20 yards. Other site requirements are that the antenna height is 18–24 in. above the sensor bed surface, and the slope of the plane of operation cannot allow more than a 1 in. elevation change in 10 ft from any point on the surface of the plane. Because the primary cause of nuisance alarms for a bistatic microwave is standing water, the sensor performs best when the sensor bed surface is made of 4 in. of riverbed gravel, no larger than 1.5 in. in diameter, with a neutral color preferred for assessment purposes. If the size of the gravel is greater than 1.5 in. in diameter, rain will still cause nuisance alarms. Crushed rock that will pass through a 1 in. screen may be used. Smaller stones quickly fill in with soil and do not drain properly.

The detection volume for bistatic microwave sensors varies with the manufacturer's antenna design but is large compared to most other intrusion sensors. The largest detection cross-section is at midrange between the two antennas and is approximately 4 yards wide and 3 yards high.

Microwave sensors tolerate a wide range of environmental conditions without producing nuisance alarms. However, nuisance alarms can be produced by a number of environmental conditions. Vegetation should be no higher than 1–2 in. tall in the area, and no vegetation at all is preferable. A nearby parallel chain-link fence with loose mesh that flexes in the wind will appear to the sensor as a large moving target and may cause nuisance alarms. Surface water from rain or melting snow appears to the microwave sensor as a moving reflector, therefore the flat plane required for crawler detection should have a cross slope for water drainage and gravel should be used to prevent standing water on the surface of the zone. Heavy blowing snow may produce nuisance alarms; snow accumulation will reduce the P_D, especially for the crawler; and complete burial of the antenna in snow will produce a constant alarm. Defeats by bridging or digging under are not simple due to the extent of the detection volume. More sophisticated defeat methods involve the use of secondary transmitters.

It is recommended that some form of fencing be incorporated in applications using exterior bistatic microwave sensors, to reduce the potential for nuisance alarms and to help maintain the carefully prepared area. These sensors are difficult or impossible to use in areas where hills, trees, or other natural features obstruct the beam.

Monostatic Microwave

Microwave detectors are also available in monostatic versions. In this configuration, the transmitter and receiver are in the same unit. Radio-frequency energy is pulsed from the transmitter, and the receiver looks for a change in the reflected energy. Motion by an intruder causes the reflected energy to change and thus causes an alarm. These sensors are range-gated, meaning that the site can set the range beyond which motion can occur without an alarm. A monostatic microwave sensor is pictured in Figure 6.5.

Figure 6.5 Monostatic Microwave Sensor. The receiver and transmitter are in the same unit

Dual-Technology Sensors

In an effort to reduce nuisance alarms, dual-technology sensors are becoming more popular. An example of dual technology would be to place both a passive infrared and a monostatic microwave in the same housing. The theory behind these devices is that the sensor will not give an alarm until both sensors have detected, thus avoiding common nuisance alarms from each of the technologies and only initiating an alarm for an actual intruder. In this mode, the sensitivity of each sensor could be set very high without the associated nuisance alarms. The reduction in nuisance alarms, however, is accompanied by a decreased P_D since an intruder must only defeat one sensor to bypass the detector.

Emerging Technology

In the wake of the devastation of the 9/11 attacks on the United States, security professionals were thrust into a new era of emerging threats. In this new era of terrorism, US adversaries are now very willing to overtly target US assets or US civilians on US soil. The terrorists of today are bolder, better organized, willing to stage attacks that take years to plan, and use attack teams that consist of larger numbers of individuals. Terrorists are just as likely to exploit procedural deficiencies associated with a security system design as they are to exploit technology limitations of sensors or detectors.

Given this state, security designers are exploring new technologies and strategies to improve the system effectiveness of future security designs. For fixed-site high-security applications, one strategy being considered is that of being able to detect and engage intruders beyond the traditional security boundaries of a site, referred to as extended detection. Various technologies are being developed with the intent of accomplishing extended detection, including:

- video motion detection
- passive scanning thermal imager
- active scanning thermal imagers
- ground-based radar
- wireless sensor network
- blue force tracking

These technology areas will be discussed in the following sections of this chapter.

Video Motion Detection

Video motion detectors (VMDs) are passive, covert, line-of-sight sensors that process the video signal from closed-circuit television (CCTV) cameras. These cameras are generally installed on towers to view the scene of interest and may be jointly used for detection, surveillance, and alarm assessment. Lighting is required for continuous 24 h operation. Readers unfamiliar with video in general or the use of alarm assessment may find it easier to read Chapter 8, "Alarm Assessment," before reading this section.

VMDs sense a change in the video signal level for some defined portion of the viewed scene. Depending on the application, this portion may be a large rectangle, a set of discrete points, or a rectangular grid. Detection of human body movement is reliable except during conditions of reduced visibility, such as fog, snow, heavy rain, or loss of lighting at night. The effectiveness of any VMD is primarily determined by the quality of the video signal (resolution). If the video is of low quality, that is, the resolution is not sufficient to allow an operator to quickly determine the source of an alarm, the VMD will not perform well. As a result, the first requirement for an effective VMD is to provide a video image of sufficient resolution such that the cause of the intrusion (or nuisance alarm) can be determined. If nuisance alarms rates are too high or the sensitivity is set too low to trigger an alarm, the use of VMD as the only means of detection is not recommended.

There are many potential sources of nuisance alarms for VMDs used outdoors. Application to exterior intrusion detection has been limited pending the development of new VMDs with signal processing to reduce nuisance alarms without significantly compromising detection. Nuisance alarms may be created by apparent scene motion due to unstable camera mounts; changes in scene illumination caused by such things as cloud shadows, shiny reflectors, and vehicle headlights; and moving objects in the scene such as birds, animals, blowing debris, and precipitation on or near the camera. Defeat tactics include taking advantage of poor visibility conditions, camouflaging the target into the background, and attack during times of reduced visibility (Ringler and Hoover, 1994; Matter, 1990). Video motion detection allows for alarm assessment by providing a video image to security personnel. The area of the image containing detected motion is generally highlighted to allow a quick and appropriate response. A single camera can protect a large area, limited only by the field of view that the lens provides and camera resolution, or it can protect

selected regions within the field of view through the use of masking (selecting only part or parts of the video scene that the VMD will protect, ignoring activity in the unmasked portions). Masking allows the VMD to discriminate between multiple zones created on one camera view. Depending on the performance desired, the system can be extremely sensitive, down to a single pixel of video. However, there is a tradeoff between the acceptable sensitivity and the rate of nuisance alarms; increased sensitivity results in an increase in the number of nuisance alarms.

Older VMDs use analog technology. These are still in production and can be very effective depending on the sensitivity settings of the system; however, they provide a limited ability to analyze an image and exclude false alarms, such as leaves on a tree or waves on a pool of water within the camera scene. Digital VMDs are becoming much more common. They are more expensive than their analog counterparts, but they address some of the shortcomings of analog VMDs. Digital VMDs use A/D (analog to digital) converters to sample the incoming video signal and electronically convert it to a digital value. The higher the resolution of the video signal, the greater the accuracy and performance of the VMD. High-resolution motion detection allows for longer detection zones, fewer cameras, and the detection of slower, smaller moving targets at longer distances.

Variables can be adjusted on a VMD to optimize detection capabilities and minimize nuisance alarms. As noted above, a masking feature will allow a variable number of detection areas and the modification of detection area dimensions. Target size and sensitivity can be adjusted to the particular application. Tracking features can be implemented to help in assessment video. Digital VMDs have some ability to accommodate for gradual illumination changes in the environment and for some vibration adjustments in the camera. There is also a limited ability to discriminate between wind, rain, snow, blowing leaves, and small animals or birds. Even with the optimized adjustment of variables, low-end analog VMDs are best suited for the purpose of detecting any type of motion in the scene. On the other hand, high-end digital VMDs are generally good at false alarm rejection, very small (pixel level) detection, and estimation of the direction of motion, using the proper settings. They can also be very effective in low contrast, poorly illuminated areas with slow movement.

VMD technology is best used in conjunction with other sensors. VMD developers are continually improving algorithms for use of the technology in a large range of applications. The use of VMD in interior applications has always been effective; with the advancement of digital VMDs, they are becoming increasingly popular in exterior environments. Developments in recent years have extended VMD technology to three dimensions. A three-dimensional VMD (3D VMD) increases the detection capabilities and provides 3D information that can be used to assist in assessment decisions, such as intelligent filtering of nuisance alarms, classification and targeting of moving objects, and providing a volumetric sensing capability.

VMD technologies are best suited for interior applications, providing good detection capability and low NARs. With respect to exterior VMD applications, further development is needed to reduce excessive NARs before deployment at high-security sites. If VMDs are used in conjunction with other exterior sensors, a lower sensitivity setting could be used to reduce nuisance alarms and still provide the operator with some visual assessment capability.

Passive Scanning Thermal Imagers

In an attempt to use VMD at night for extended detection, passive scanning thermal imagers (PSTIs) were developed. Current PSTIs have advertised detection ranges from 400 to 2500 m for a walking intruder. One of the attractive features of PSTIs is that intruders can be detected and assessed using one device. This should reduce costs because the purchase of a separate imager would not be necessary. A simple description of how an STI works follows.

During set-up the PSTI scans the horizon several times in order to establish a baseline image. As an intruder enters the detection envelop, a perturbation of the recorded baseline is detected. The intrusion is indicated on a monitoring screen by highlighting its location with a colored box. The operator can then take manual control of the PSTI, point it to the location of the intruder, and zoom in to assess the cause of the alarm.

Variables such as scan rate, detection threshold, and scan angle can be changed to optimize detection capability and minimize NARs. Some PSTIs are capable of masking out zones within scanning limits established by the user. Some of the challenges associated with PSTIs are:

- Large scan angles will increase the scan time, creating significant time gaps between scans. In some cases, this will decrease the detection performance.
- A PSTI is dependent on line-of-sight, requiring careful selection of the terrain to be scanned.
- A PSTI has the same limitations as thermal imagers, decreasing sensitivity on hot days. For this reason some PSTIs have also incorporated CCD imagers, providing better performance in hot backgrounds.
- CCD imagers will also see degradation in performance on hot days due to thermal turbulence.
- Most PSTIs were designed for a tactical environment and integration into common commercial monitoring systems was not a priority; hence, most PSTIs are stand-alone systems, requiring additional manpower to observe the sensor output.

- The most worrisome challenge of PSTIs in an extended detection application is high NARs. Shadows, moving foliage, drifting clouds, wildlife, and fog can cause hundreds to thousands of nuisance alarms a day.

PSTI developers continue to work to improve detection algorithms that will decrease nuisance alarms yet maintain high detection performance.

Active Scanning Thermal Imagers

In an attempt to address some of the limitations of passive PSTIs, developers considered supplying IR illumination. As a result, this technology is considered an active device, or an active scanning thermal imager (ASTI). The performance of an ASTI can be optimized to match the wavelength of the IR illumination, thereby improving detection performance. Supplying IR illumination has the potential to reduce nuisance alarm rates due to shadows or drifting clouds. This is because IR illumination, acting like a spotlight, will minimize but not eliminate the effects of shadows. Representative ranges of ASTIs vary from 500 to 1000 m, depending on the power of the illumination. If stronger IR illuminators are deployed, eye safety issues must be addressed. Their use around airports may be prohibited, depending on the power and wavelength of the illumination.

The basic operation of an ASTI is the similar to that of PSTIs. Currently, little test data is available and no claims on detection performance or NAR can be made.

Ground-Based Radar

Another extended detection technology currently being considered for fixed-site security applications is ground-based radar (GBR). Traditional GBR systems were designed for military tactical deployment by a team of highly trained individuals who used these long-range systems to monitor areas of interest for enemy movement. Operators used both audio and visual information from the GBR system to determine the legitimacy of targets based upon the available information. Fixed-site issues relating to integration, nuisance and false alarms, and operator overload were either not of concern, were mitigated with training, or were considered acceptable due to the hostile environment or the ability of the user to determine intent via other means. As a result, there are still some issues associated with their use in defensive fixed-site PPSs.

The standard tactical system has advertised range capabilities from 200 m out to 48 km under ideal conditions. These systems are based on a pulsed Doppler design, which uses time of flight to determine the targets range and a shift in the return signals' frequency and phase to determine the targets velocity and direction of travel.

Drawbacks of these Doppler systems include very little, if any, filtering of nuisance alarms; a dead zone for the first 65–200 m depending on the system; they are manpower intensive (one operator per system); poor angular and range resolution: high-power output (allows possible discovery by the adversary that radar is being used); cost; inability to effectively assess targets at distances greater than a few kilometers (less depending on the weather and time of day); a limited operator interface; and little consideration of system integration. A limitation of most extended detection technologies is that a clear LOS must exist in order to detect an intruder. Terrain and foliage issues may present gaps in GBR coverage, requiring additional sensor technologies that are not LOS dependent if a continuous detection zone is required. This increases cost and gives performance that is similar to the use of the additional sensor technologies alone, which makes this combination hard to justify. As processing power has increased, most new systems have improved filtering capabilities, a method for system integration (XML protocol), the capability to mask areas of non-interest, and can be easily combined with thermal and electro-optic imaging systems.

In addition to the pulsed Doppler systems, newer systems employ a frequency-modulated continuous wave (FMCW) design, which allows for less power to be transmitted. Less power makes it harder for the adversary to intercept the transmitted signal. There are a few variations of the FMCW design—some still use Doppler discrimination for adversary detection, while others establish an adaptive threshold based on the return signal. Due to the many possible combinations and use of modern detection algorithms, it is important to understand that there are differences and that all FMCW radars do not operate or filter target data the same way.

Variables for these systems include phenomenology (FMCW or pulsed Doppler), scan angle, range, minimum detection velocity settings, threshold settings, sensitivity settings, installation height, antenna tilt, and data throughput. As with any new technology planned for deployment, it is highly recommended that they be tested in an operational environment prior to procurement. It is critical to understand the detection performance, vulnerabilities, nuisance alarm sources, the NAR, and how the implementation of these systems will affect the overall system effectiveness. Some sites are establishing test beds to characterize performance of these devices. These results will determine if detection and nuisance alarm issues meet site requirements in the operational terrain, foliage, and weather conditions and provide more data on which to judge overall performance.

Wireless Sensor Networks

Advances in microelectronics have resulted in the ability to combine increased sensor capabilities, local data processing, and smart on-board control systems with networked wireless communications to create the foundation of wireless sensor networks (WSNs).

WSN concepts can apply to both interior and exterior sensor applications. They can also be used within traditional perimeter detection and assessment systems to supplement required sensor coverage. WSNs allow security system designers to quickly and easily place individual sensor/communication nodes at locations where security coverage is needed. Once the sensor nodes are in place and powered, they locate neighboring nodes and establish wireless communication paths back to the monitoring station. If a sensor node is destroyed or loses it ability to relay information, the sensor network will adapt by identifying alternate communication paths back to the monitoring station, hence the term self-forming ad hoc wireless network is used to describe this concept. The use of node-to-node communication paths would allow security coverage beyond the capabilities of traditional LOS sensor concepts. Each sensor node must be able to see at least one neighbor, but nodes can be positioned on hill tops and look down into ravines or canyons, providing the monitoring station non-LOS coverage.

The long-term vision for WSNs is to be able to provide reliable detection and assessment of intruders in native terrain, thus avoiding the expense of preparing the ground for sensor and camera deployment. The sensor nodes provide sufficient power for several years and the WSN would overlay existing power and communication infrastructures, minimizing the need to rebuild infrastructure. If this goal can be attained, significant construction cost savings could be realized and security system designs could be much different in the future.

However, before WSNs can be a reality at high-security sites some major issues must be resolved, including the following:

- cost of a node should approach that of a cell phone or less;
- secure and reliable wireless communication methods must be established (currently, neither DOE nor DoD will use wireless communications for security sensor information at high-security sites);
- inexpensive reliable power for sensor nodes under all weather conditions;
- inexpensive battery power storage;
- improved data algorithms are needed to convert simple sensor data into information, differentiating intruders from nuisance alarms;
- low power, inexpensive imagers are needed to assess causes of sensor alarms at long ranges;
- creation of networking technologies that enable data from large numbers of sensors to be reliably passed between nodes;
- architecture levels to enable distributed processing of data and information fusion;
- reduction of nuisance alarms in natural terrain and all weather conditions;
- information displays that do not overwhelm an operator; and
- adaptability to changing threats, including rapid adjustment of system functions and the ability to reprogram data analysis algorithms.

When WSNs are mature, reliable, inexpensive, and secure, a state of virtual presence may be possible. Pertaining to a security system, virtual presence is the ability to extend situational awareness around valuable assets by using large numbers of wireless sensor nodes to detect, track, and interact with intruders as they pass though security layers, communicating the information gathered back to a central alarm station in near real time. Similar systems carried by friendly forces can provide real time locations, tracking, and communications between them and other friendly forces.

WSNs may seem to be a very ambitious goal today; however, many government and commercial organizations are exploring the use of wireless sensor systems to provide added situational awareness. In the next few years, we expect to see sites begin to incorporate networked wireless sensor technologies that may provide early warning of intrusion and decreased vulnerability to threats at affordable cost. To facilitate this objective, WSNs are receiving considerable research and development funding from DoD, DOE, intelligence agencies, and industry.

Red/Blue Force Tracking

Establishing the capability of extended detection will improve the ability to detect and engage intruders beyond the traditional confines of an established perimeter. If an engagement between adversaries and responders does take place, there will be a need to manage the ensuing conflict. In order to accomplish this, knowing the location of the adversary (Red Force) and the responders (Blue Force) will be very important. As sensors continue to feed information indicating continued intrusions, the Battlefield Manager must distinguish Red Forces from Blue Forces.

This problem can be addressed if the location of Blue Force members can be tracked at all times, also referred to as Identification-of-Friend-or-Foe (IFF). Methods under development for Blue Force tracking include:

- GPS (global positioning satellite)
- RFID tags
- bluetooth technologies
- triangulation-based RF/wireless communications
- mesh networks
- ultra wideband technologies
- unmanned aerial vehicles (UAVs)

Some concepts under consideration for Red Force Tracking include range finding, position location, range finding binoculars, or other technologies to pinpoint the adversary's locations. Development issues relate to the problems of adding the Red Force points on a map and the use of more satellite technology to remove the LOS issues associated with high-frequency signals. It is important to note that for any system to be useful both Red and Blue Force tracking must be present—tracking only one side will not suffice. In security systems today, we already detect Red Forces; tracking of both Red and Blue Forces would advance our tactical response capabilities in the future.

One vision is to tie in mobile communications to Blue Force Tracking and add voice over internet protocols (VOIP) and Google maps. This would provide the capability to share data with all levels of command and let everyone see the same data that the front-line troops have.

As with research and development for WSN, many government and commercial organizations that require high security are exploring the use of Red/Blue Force tracking capabilities to provide added situational awareness. It is expected that Red/Blue Force tracking will be a viable capability in the next few years. While the emphasis today is on high-security suites, the use of Red/Blue Force tracking could become more prevalent at lower security sites in the future. For example, tracking capability for children, cars, and prisoners is already in use, so there is some reason to believe this is a natural evolution of technology as it matures.

Maturity Model for Security Technologies

Faced with increasing security threats, more government regulations regarding critical infrastructure protection and limited budgets, decision makers in both government and commercial sectors are continually searching for technologies that will provide enhanced security within a finite budget. When new technologies (as with some of those described above) hit the market, how does a decision maker (or a designer for that matter) determine if the technology is ready for deployment? A growing concern is that decision makers and designers of security systems may unknowingly accept significant risk if an immature security technology is fielded prematurely.

One approach used to address this concern is a maturity model for security technologies. The proposed model (see Figure 6.6) is tailored to reflect the status of both technology development and policy requirements prior to deployment of any technology at a site. The following is a brief

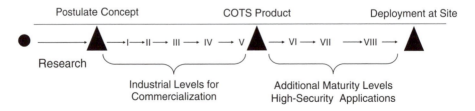

Figure 6.6 Maturity Model for Security Technologies. The maturity levels can be used to aid in the selection of candidate technologies when considering upgrades. Use of this model may help reduce technical risk by allowing designers and decision makers to understand how dependable a new sensor technology may be

Research	The scientific basis is established but the security application has not necessarily been identified. An example could be the discovery of the ferroelectric properties of lithium niobate, a material that has been used to sense IR energy in IR detectors.
Level I	Establish feasibility of the concept in a laboratory demonstration
Level II	Research prototype—hand built in a laboratory, breaks a lot, cannot withstand an operational environment
Level III	Engineering prototype—about 90% functionality, still working on reliability, does not break as often
Level IV	Field prototype—fully functional over complete operational environment, producing reliable repetitive results, user driven and accepted, ready to progress to full-scale production
Level V	Commercial off-the-shelf technology (COTS)—manufactured, production units with infrastructure in place for replacement parts and technology support
Level VI	Performance testing—to establish performance metrics such as probability of detection, NARs, vulnerability to defeat, performance degradation factors, sensor-to-sensor interference. This type of testing takes approximately 12 months for outdoor applications to observe performance under all weather conditions.
Level VII	Onsite testing—to determine actual performance in the desired operational environment, foliage, weather, terrain, integration into site monitoring station
Level VIII	Non-technical maturity factors—site concept of operations, how does the response force use the information provided, how do they respond, do legal or policy issues prevent use of the technology

description of the levels of the maturity model:

Although Figure 6.6 depicts the maturity model as a linear sequence, a good security system designer will not wait until the completion of Level VII to begin investigating Level VIII. Prior to purchase of a COTS item, the limitations imposed by non-technical factors including environmental, integration, legal, and policy constraints must be considered.

Perimeter Sensor Systems—Design Concepts and Goals

The material discussed thus far in this chapter summarized a variety of exterior intrusion sensor technologies. The next sections discuss the integration of individual sensors into a perimeter sensor system and consider the interaction of the perimeter system or subsystem with a balanced and integrated PPS. Before the detailed design and implementation of a perimeter sensor system are considered, some basic design principles and concepts for perimeter sensor systems should be understood.

Continuous Line of Detection

By definition, a perimeter is a closed line around some area that needs protection. A design goal is to have uniform detection around the entire length of the perimeter. The perimeter is divided into sectors to aid in assessment and response. This requires that sensors form a continuous line of detection around the perimeter. In practice, this means configuring the sensor hardware so that the detection zone from one perimeter sector overlaps with the detection zones for the two adjacent sectors. Also, in areas where the primary sensor cannot be deployed properly, such as a gate, an alternate sensor is used to cover that gap.

Protection-in-Depth

As applied to perimeter sensor systems, the concept of protection-in-depth means the use of multiple lines of detection; thus, a minimum of two continuous lines of detection are used in high-security systems. Many perimeter sensor systems have been installed with three sensor lines, and a few have four. For example, a perimeter sensor system might include a buried-line sensor, a fence-associated sensor, and a freestanding sensor. Multiple sensor lines provide additional detection, increased reliability, and in case of hardware failure, will fail-secure (i.e., still provide protection, although to a lesser degree). In this scheme, any single sensor can fail without jeopardizing the overall security of the facility being protected. Elimination of single-point or component failures is a major advantage in any security system, as this will assure balanced protection even in adverse conditions and will prevent the introduction of vulnerability based on the failure or defeat of only one component by the adversary.

Complementary Sensors

Significantly better performance by the perimeter sensor system can be achieved by selecting different and complementary types of sensors for the multiple lines of detection, for example, microwave and active infrared. In this way, different sensor technologies, with different PD, NAR, and vulnerabilities are combined to increase the effectiveness of the exterior perimeter intrusion detection system. Complementary sensors enhance the overall system performance because they use the best features of a particular technology, while at the same time providing effective backup in case of environmental change, component failure, or successful attack by the adversary. This design philosophy results in detection of a wider spectrum of intruders, allows operation of at least one sensor line during any conceivable environmental disturbance, and increases the difficulty of the task for the covert intruder attempting to defeat the system.

Use of complementary sensors can be an effective alternative to the use of dual-technology sensors because the individual sensors will perform at their maximum levels and not be compromised by co-location and filtering. While implementation of complementary sensors may be more expensive, they will also afford a higher protection level. Due to the higher protection provided by complementary sensors, they are the preferred choice in high-security applications.

Examples of exterior complementary sensors include microwave/infrared, microwave/ported coaxial cable, and ported coaxial cable/infrared combinations. The important point is that the detection patterns must overlap for the sensors to be complementary. For example, a microwave/fence sensor combination is not complementary because the detection patterns cannot overlap without serious nuisance alarm problems. In addition, bistatic/monostatic microwave combinations are not complementary since both are susceptible to the same defeat methods and nuisance alarm sources.

Priority Schemes

One disadvantage of multiple sensor lines is that more nuisance alarms will have to be processed. System effectiveness has not been increased if the system operator is overwhelmed with nuisance alarms. As discussed in Chapter 5, "Physical Protection System Design," the probability of detection decreases as the time to assess alarms increases. The assessment subsystem should aid the operator in evaluating alarm information. Many different methods have been used to deal with the alarm data from a combination of sensors. A recommended method currently in use requires the system operator to assess all alarms with the aid of a computer that establishes the time order of assessment for multiple simultaneous alarms. The computer sets a priority for each alarm based on the probability that an alarm event corresponds to a real intrusion. The alarms are displayed to the operator in order of decreasing priority; all alarms are eventually assessed. The alarm priority is typically established by taking into account the number of sensors in alarm in a given sector, the time between alarms in the sector, the order in which the alarms occur in relation to the physical configuration of the sensors, and alarms in the two adjacent sectors. This point will be discussed in more detail in Chapter 9, "Alarm Communication and Display."

Combination of Sensors

It is desirable that a sensor or sensor system have a high probability of detection (P_D) for all expected types of intrusion and a low NAR for all expected environmental conditions. No single exterior sensor presently available meets both of these criteria; all are limited in their detection capability and all have high NARs under certain environmental conditions. The two basic techniques for combining sensors are OR combinations and AND combinations.

A system can consist of two or more sensors with their outputs combined by an OR gate so that an alarm would be generated when any sensor is activated. This combination is useful for sensors that

make up for the deficiencies of each other; each sensor is intended to detect particular types of intrusions. Thus, sensors that detect above ground, overhead, and tunneling intrusions should be combined by an OR gate.

The nuisance alarm rate of the OR combination, or NAR (OR), will be the sum of the NAR of each sensor. Neglecting the possibility of simultaneous activation, the NAR of the combination will equal the sum of individual NARs:

$$NAR(OR) = \sum_{i=1}^{n} NAR_i$$

where NAR_i is the nuisance alarm rate of the ith sensor in a system of n sensors. Because this combination results in an increased NAR, it is most useful for sensors that individually have low NARs.

The NAR can be significantly reduced by combining sensors with an AND gate *if the nuisance alarms of the sensors are not correlated*. For example, a seismic sensor and an electric field sensor do not give correlated nuisance alarms because they have different nuisance alarm sources. If both are activated at about the same time, it is probable that they have detected an intrusion. In this configuration, a single intrusion attempt will not activate both sensors simultaneously, so the system can be designed to generate an alarm if both sensors are activated within a preselected time interval. A longer time interval is desirable to assure detection of intruders moving slowly, but if the interval is too long, the NAR may not be reduced enough. By installing sensors so they cover the same general area, thereby providing redundant coverage, the time interval can be kept small.

The detection probability of the AND combination, or P_D (AND), will be lower than the detection probability of each sensor. If detection performance is independent and coverage by sensors is redundant, the P_D of the combination will equal the product of the individual P_Ds. To assure a reasonable detection probability for the system, the detection probability of the individual sensors must be high.

The nuisance alarm rate of the AND combination, NAR (AND), will be less than the NAR of each sensor. If the sensor outputs are not correlated and occur at a random rate that is much less than one output per selected time interval, T, then for two sensors,

$$\mathrm{NAR(AND)} = \frac{T}{60}(\mathrm{NAR1})(\mathrm{NAR2})$$

where T is in minutes and NAR1 and NAR2 are in alarms per hour. The AND combination is desirable since nuisance alarms can be reduced by several orders of magnitude over the individual sensor's own NAR. The time interval T may be site-specific, depending on the installation geometry and sensor characteristics; however, it will probably be within the range of 15 and 120 s. The disadvantage of the AND scheme is that there is still the problem of reduced P_D because the intruder must only defeat one sensor.

Clear Zone

A perimeter intrusion detection system performs better when it is located in an isolated clear zone (or isolation zone). The purpose of the clear zone is to improve performance of the perimeter sensor system by increasing detection probability, reducing nuisance alarms, and preventing defeat. The clear zone also promotes good visual assessment of the causes of sensor alarms. The clear zone is usually defined by the presence of two parallel fences extending the entire length of the perimeter. The fences are intended to keep people, animals, and vehicles out of the detection zone. The area between the fences is usually cleared of all above-ground structures, including overhead utility lines; vegetation in this area is also removed. After the zone between the fences is cleared, only the detection

and assessment hardware and associated power and data lines are installed in the area. When clear zones bounded by two parallel fences are used, no sensors should be placed on the outer fence. This will reduce nuisance alarms from blowing debris and small animals and will eliminate the possibility of an adversary defeating the fence sensor without being seen by the video assessment system. Video assessment of anything outside the fence will be difficult due to the inability of the camera to see through the fence fabric. Clear zones and the associated use of multiple complementary sensors are generally reserved for use at high-security facilities, such as nuclear plants, prisons, military bases, or other government installations.

Sensor Configuration

The configuration of the multiple sensors within the clear zone also affects system performance. Overlapping the detection volumes of two different sensors within each sector enhances performance by creating a larger overall detection volume. Thus, defeat of the sensor pair is less probable because a larger volume must be bypassed or two different technologies must be defeated simultaneously. A third sensor can further enhance performance, not by overlapping with the first two, but by forming a separate line of detection. Physically separate lines of detection can reveal information useful for determining alarm priority during multiple simultaneous alarms. In particular, the order of alarms in a sector (or adjacent sectors) may correspond to the logical sequence for an intrusion.

Site-Specific System

Each site requiring physical protection has a unique combination of configuration and physical environment. Thus, a PPS designed for one site cannot be transferred to another. The physical environment will influence the selection of types of sensors for perimeter sensor systems. The natural and industrial environments provide the nuisance alarm sources for the specific site. The topography of the perimeter determines the shapes and sizes of the space available for detection, specifically the clear zone width and the existence of flat or irregular terrain. These factors generally help determine a preferred set of sensors. Although understanding of the interaction between intrusion sensors and the environment has increased significantly in recent years, it is still advisable to set up a demonstration sector on site using the possible sensors before making a commitment to a complete system. This test sector located on site is intended to confirm sensor selection and to help refine the final system design.

Tamper Protection

The hardware and system design should incorporate features that prevent defeat by tampering. This means the system should be tamper-resistant and tamper-indicating. Sensor electronics and junction box enclosures should have tamper switches. Aboveground power and signal cables should be installed inside metal conduit. Alarm communication lines should use some type of line supervision, which detects lines that have been cut, disconnected, short-circuited, or bypassed. The receiver electronics of bistatic sensors are generally more vulnerable to defeat than the transmitter electronics. In this case, the sensors can often be placed so that an intruder must be in or pass through the detection volume to approach the receiver.

Self-Test

To verify normal operation of a perimeter sensor system, its ability to detect must be regularly tested. Although manual testing is recommended, manpower requirements are usually restrictive. A capability for remote testing of trigger signals can be provided and initiated by the alarm communication and control system. Typically this is just a switch closure or opening. In an automatic remote test procedure, the central computer control system generates at a random time a test trigger to a given sensor. The sensor must then respond with an alarm. The control system verifies that an alarm occurred within a specified time and cleared within another specified time. Failure to pass the test indicates a hardware failure or tampering and produces an alarm message.

Pattern Recognition

The field of sensor technology is in a period of major change, caused by the development of inexpensive, powerful computers. These computers can now receive signals from sensors and analyze the signal pattern, looking for patterns that are particularly characteristic of an intruder. Using neural network or artificial intelligence software, the computers can actually learn these intruder signal patterns and then avoid nuisance alarms. Any sensor or combination of sensors that returns a signal beyond off and on can be analyzed by a small computer and possibly sense whether or not an intruder is present. Examples include intelligent infrared and fence sensors.

Effects of Physical and Environmental Conditions

The physical and environmental conditions that can affect exterior detection systems include:

- topography
- vegetation

- wildlife
- background noise
- climate and weather
- soil and pavement

These conditions are different at every site.

Topographic features such as gullies, slopes, lakes, rivers, and swamps must be considered when designing an exterior detection system. Grading may be required to reduce hills and slopes. Draining may also be required to reduce water flow through gullies and ditches to prevent seismic disturbances caused by running water. The perimeter system should avoid lakes, rivers, and swamps, since there are few commercial sensors suitable for use in water. If a security perimeter traverses water and land, there will be significant additional complications regarding sensor detection, NAR, intrusion assessment, and delay.

Sensor performance can be affected by vegetation in two ways: underground and above ground. Motion of trees or plants caused by wind may be transmitted to their root systems and cause a seismic sensor to generate a nuisance alarm. Above ground, large plants and trees can be used as cover by an intruder and also generate nuisance alarms. Additionally, vegetation tends to attract small animals, creating more nuisance alarms. If vegetation is a problem, it must be controlled by mowing, removal, soil sterilization, or surfacing.

In some locations, wildlife may cause some problems. Large animals may damage equipment by collision, and burrowing animals may eat through cable insulation material. Small animals, burrowing animals, birds, and insects also cause nuisance alarms that may be difficult to assess. Dual chain-link fences and chemical controls may be used to control wildlife; however, local regulations should be observed with regard to poisons and repellents. Removing vegetation from fence lines has been found to discourage some smaller animals.

A site survey along with information obtained from utility companies and onsite plant-engineering organizations may reveal many sources of background noise. These sources may include wind, traffic, electromagnetic interference, and seismic sources.

Disturbances related to wind are caused by the transfer of energy to the ground by trees, power and light poles, fences, and other items. High winds and wind-blown debris can also cause nuisance alarms from sensors mounted on fences by disturbing the fence.

Traffic from nearby roadways, railways, and airports creates nuisance alarms for seismic sensors. Roads should be kept smooth and the speed limit at a minimum to reduce the NAR. Seismic sensors are not practical near heavy air or railway traffic, because this type of traffic causes seismic disturbances even at long distances.

Examples of sources of electromagnetic interference include lightning, high-voltage power lines, radio transmitters, welding, and electrical transients. Shielding of the sources or the sensors can reduce nuisance alarms.

Specific data about climate and weather conditions should be obtained for the site. Information such as frequency, velocity, accumulation, and duration should be obtained about hail, electrical storms, rainfall, and wind. Mean minimum and maximum temperatures should also be noted as well as other weather and environmental conditions.

Water tables, soil, and pavement conditions can affect the operation of buried seismic sensors. The seismic conductivity of the medium is the determining factor—it should be high enough to make seismic sensors effective, but not so high that it causes nuisance alarms. Wet soil tends to have exceptionally good seismic conduction. However, wet soil also responds strongly to distant sources of seismic activity and thus causes excessive nuisance alarms. Buried systems of magnetic sensors and seismic sensors may have to be embedded in or installed under areas paved with concrete or asphalt. The sensitivity of a sensor embedded in the pavement is increased if the sensor is adequately coupled to the medium. If the sensor is not adequately coupled to the medium, its sensitivity may be much lower than when it is installed in soil or buried under the pavement. Soil conductivity can also affect the sensitivity of ported coaxial cable. Highly conductive soils greatly reduce the detection volume of the sensor. In addition, the time required for soil around a recently buried seismic sensor to regain the properties of undisturbed soil may take 3–6 months. During this period the coupling and the sensitivity may change as well.

Lightning Protection

Because exterior sensors are installed outdoors, they are exposed to electrical storms at most sites. Lightning can easily disable, damage, or destroy the sensitive electronics used in sensor equipment. There are three primary precautions for reducing lightning damage. First, all signal cables should be shielded, either by the internal cable construction or by using metal conduit. Second, a good ground system is required. This means eliminating ground loops and using grounds at a single point. Third, passive transient suppression devices can be installed at the ends of the cables. Fiber-optic transmission cables are not affected by lightning and have thus become very popular for transmitting signals for long distances outside a building.

Integration with Video Assessment System

Many perimeter security systems use a CCTV system to perform alarm assessment. For both the sensor and video systems to perform well, care must be taken to ensure that the designs of the two systems or subsystems are compatible. Assessment may take place via the use of CCTV systems or manually by people. Video assessment automatically tied to sensor activation greatly reduces the amount of time required to determine the alarm source, thereby maximizing the use of any remaining delay and increasing the chance of successful interruption of the adversary. Video assessment also allows remote evaluation of the alarm condition, which eliminates the need to constantly dispatch guards to determine the cause of the alarm—perhaps too late to make an accurate assessment. For maximum effectiveness, the sensors must be placed so that when an alarm occurs, the camera viewing the zone will have an unobstructed view of the entire zone.

One trade-off to be considered is the width of the clear zone. Sensor engineers desire a wide area for installing their sensors to reduce nuisance alarms. Video engineers desire a narrow area to assess so that they can achieve better resolution from the cameras. A compromise clear zone width is in the range of 10–15 yards.

Another trade-off is the location of the camera tower within the clear zone. The camera must be positioned to view the entire area being assessed. The sensors must be placed far enough away from the camera towers to prevent distortion of the detection volume and not cause nuisance alarms. Frequently, the camera towers are located 1–2 yards inside the outer fence of the clear zone to prevent their use in bridging attacks by an adversary. Video assessment is discussed in more detail in Chapter 8, "Alarm Assessment."

Integration with Barrier Delay System

Balanced and integrated PPSs usually incorporate some type of barrier or access denial systems to provide delay time for video assessment of the alarm source and for the response force to respond to an intrusion. In many cases, this includes some type of barrier installed at the perimeter; however, the barrier should not degrade the performance of the sensors. Perimeter barriers are usually installed on or near the inner clear zone fence so that an intruder cannot tamper with or defeat the barrier without first passing through the detection zone. This placement is important to ensure that the response action is initiated before the delay occurs. Barriers should not distort the sensors' detection volume, cause nuisance alarms, or obscure part of the camera's view.

Exterior Sensor Subsystem Characteristics

The finished exterior intrusion detection subsystem should incorporate many of the security principles and features described thus far. A diagram of a typical exterior system is shown in Figure 6.7.

This subsystem uses a continuous line of detection, protection-in-depth, complementary sensors, and a clear zone in the design. Not readily apparent but also

included is the use of alarm combination and priority schemes in alarm monitoring. The system shown uses CCTV to accomplish the assessment function. A look at how this sector might appear in actual use is shown in Figure 6.8. Notice the well-maintained clear zone, the consistency in width between fences, the placement of the sensors, lighting, and camera towers, and the overlap of sensors from one zone to the next. This is an excellent example of a well-designed exterior sensor subsystem on a high-security site perimeter.

Procedures

As this text repeatedly stresses, an effective security system represents the successful integration of people, procedures, and equipment. For exterior intrusion detection systems, the procedures related to installation, maintenance test, and operation should be established. Training in all of these procedures will also be required for new personnel and to stay abreast of new technology.

Proper installation instructions can be obtained from the manufacturer and

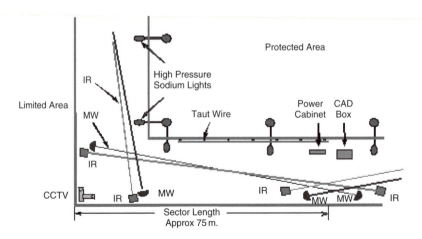

Figure 6.7 Schematic View of Exterior Sensor System Layout. The complementary IR and microwave sensors overlap to prevent defeat by crawlers or jumpers, the taut wire sensor is located close to the inner fence to reduce the NAR, and junction boxes are placed inside the detection volume

Figure 6.8 Typical Perimeter Using Exterior Intrusion Sensors. The isolation zone is clear of debris or vegetation, the fences are consistently spaced, and sensor detection zones overlap

provide an appropriate starting point. However, because many manufacturers cater to both the high- and low-end security market, it is common to find that some modification of these instructions will optimize sensor performance. For example, several microwave manufacturers publish literature stating that the units will operate at a separation of up to 300 yards, but at this distance the sensor will not detect a crawling intruder. Many fence sensor manufacturers also suggest using a fence-disturbance sensor around a corner, but it is not possible to assess this type of a sensor zone.

Maintenance activities on all sensors and associated components must also be performed on a periodic basis. Such things as calibration, sensitivity checks, alignment, and visual inspection should be performed regularly to keep the sensor components operating as effectively as possible. More importantly, poor maintenance will have a significant effect on P_D and NAR and perhaps make the system more vulnerable to defeat. Improper drainage of a sector may cause erosion that ultimately leads to defeat of a sensor.

In addition to maintenance activities, component operational tests should also be performed on a regular basis, to assure that the sensor element is contributing as expected to overall system effectiveness (Hayward, 1993a,b). These tests should be done both during the day and at night to verify that the sensor still performs as expected against the design basis threat. Different sensor types will require different specific tests; however, tests for walking and running speeds (slow and fast) and crawling tests should be performed to check sensor operation. Tests checking how slowly an object can move and avoid detection should also be performed. Standardized tests should be performed whenever possible. For microwave sensors, these tests consist of using an aluminum sphere to simulate a crawling intruder. This test results in more accurate, repeatable results than performing actual crawl tests. Another standardized test is to measure attenuation factors for infrared sensors.

Contingency plans and procedures should exist that will be implemented in the event that a particular sensor or other equipment is lost. These plans should clearly define when they will be used: for example, when two of the three perimeter sensors are lost. If the contingency plan for the loss of one or more sensors in a sector is to provide compensatory measures, these measures should also be clear. In some situations, it may be possible to use portable sensors. In other situations, the procedure may be to dispatch a guard to the sector to provide detection. This would be expected at a site with a large number of distributed targets. A site with a limited set of targets might choose to send a guard to the target location. The specific procedures should be defined in advance and readily available to system operators for implementation.

Once all of the procedures used to maintain, test, and operate exterior sensors are established, documentation should be collected, stored, and maintained by site personnel. Required, recommended, and troubleshooting procedures should be included, as well as maintenance logs for each sensor, training records for all employees, and outcomes of any unique instances, such as causes of any false alarms.

Summary

Exterior intrusion detection sensors have been discussed in terms of sensor classification and application, probability of detection, nuisance alarm rate, and vulnerability to defeat. The designer integrating individual sensors into a perimeter sensor system must consider specific design goals, the effects of physical and environmental conditions, and the interaction of the perimeter system with a balanced and integrated PPS.

Security principles incorporated into a good exterior intrusion detection system include protection in depth, use of complementary sensors, elimination of single-point failures, and integration of people, equipment, and procedures. Desired features include the use of a clear zone, proper configuration of sensors in the clear zone, alarm combination and priority schemes, tamper protection, and self-test capability. The design should be site-specific and suitable for the physical, environmental, and operational conditions that will be encountered. Finally, the exterior sensor subsystem should be well integrated with the video and barrier subsystems.

Major sensor component and subsystem characteristics include high probability of detection, low NAR, and low vulnerability to the defined threat. Other features include a fast communication system for sending and assessing alarms, good lighting and assessment systems, and a balanced system that provides adequate protection on all paths through the perimeter. Use of exterior perimeter intrusion detection systems is generally found only in high-security applications.

Security Principles

The performance measures for sensors are P_D, NAR, and vulnerability to defeat.

Use of multiple, continuous lines of detection provides protection-in-depth.

Use of complementary sensors or sensors that compensate for each other's weaknesses will increase system performance.

Single-point or component failures should be avoided to maintain balance within the system and to reduce the chance of successful adversary attack at a weak point in a protection layer.

The perimeter-intrusion detection system should be integrated with the alarm assessment and barrier delay systems.

References

Barnard, R.L. *Intrusion Detection Systems*, 2nd ed. Stoneham, MA: Butterworth Publishers, 1988, 71–143.

Cumming, N. *Security*, 2nd ed. Boston: Butterworth-Heinemann, 1992, 79–114.

Fennelly, L.J. *Handbook of Loss Prevention and Crime Prevention*, 3rd ed. Boston: Butterworth-Heinemann, 1996, 268–280.

Follis, R.L. Stellar Systems Inc. series 800–5000 E-field sensor evaluation. SAND90-1039 1990;1–39.

Garcia, M.L. *Vulnerability Assessment of Physical Protection Systems*. Boston: Butterworth-Heinemann, 2006, 382 pp.

Greer, G. Vindicator VTW-250 test report. SAND90-1824 1990a;1–41.

Greer, G. Vindicator VTW-300 test report. SAND90-0922 1990b;1–43.

Hayward, D.R. Automated sensor tester. SAND93-2063C 1993;1–8.

Hayward, D.R. Intrusion detection sensor testing tools. SAND94-1068C 1993;1–5.

Matter, J.C. Video motion detection for physical security applications. SAND90-1733C 1990;1–12.

Ringler, C.E., and Hoover, C. Evaluation of commercially available exterior video motion detectors. SAND94-2875 1994;1–120.

Williams, J.D. Exterior alarm systems. SAND88-2995C 1988;1–25.

Wolfenbarger, F.M. A field test and evaluation of exterior fiber-optic intrusion detection sensors. SAND94-1664 1994;1–39.

Questions

1. Discuss the following application considerations:
   a. Sensors should always be installed with proper overlap at sector boundary.
   b. If relocation of existing pipes or lines is not feasible, then additional sensors may be required.
   c. Sensors should not be installed in locations where assessment may be difficult.
   d. A high-security perimeter system requires more than a single sensor type.
   e. Sensors with the same susceptibility to nuisance alarms should not be combined.
2. Why is the distinction between passive and active sensors important?
3. What are some of the advantages of combining sensor inputs in an AND configuration?
4. What are some of the disadvantages of combining sensor outputs in an AND configuration?
5. What are some of the advantages of using sensor outputs in an OR configuration?
6. What are some of the disadvantages of using sensor outputs in an OR configuration?
7. In what situations would a member of the protective force (guard) be used instead of an exterior intrusion sensor? How effective is detection under these conditions and why?
8. Why should field-testing of sensors be performed at the site where the sensors may be used in a system?
9. When are false alarms considered excessive?
10. Does a high probability of intrusion sensing always imply a high probability of detection?
11. How does surface water cause an unreliable condition for microwave sensors but not for infrared sensors?
12. What are some advantages and disadvantages of sensors incorporating pattern recognition?
13. Assume an exterior bistatic microwave sensor has been tested for a running man. The man runs straight through the detection volume at 15 ft/s and is detected 25 out of 28 times. What is the P_D for this sensor against this attack? Is this the value you would use when you do your analysis?

7

Interior Intrusion Sensors

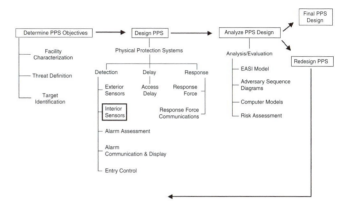

The design of an interior intrusion detection system requires a thorough knowledge of the operational, physical, and environmental characteristics of the facility to be protected. In addition, the designer must be familiar with the broad spectrum of sensors available, how the sensors interact with the adversary and the environment, and the physical principles on which each of the sensors depends for its operation. This chapter will address interior intrusion sensor technology. Figure 7.1 shows the example interior layout that will be used throughout this chapter.

Interior intrusion sensors, when integrated into a system using administrative procedures, access controls, and material monitoring, can be highly effective against insider threats. Using interior intrusion sensors that are correctly placed, installed, maintained, and tested, an alarm can be generated by unauthorized acts or the unauthorized presence of insiders as well as outsiders.

Performance Characteristics

As described in Chapter 6, "Exterior Intrusion Sensors," intrusion sensor performance is described by three fundamental characteristics:

1. probability of detection (P_D)
2. nuisance alarm rate (NAR)
3. vulnerability to defeat

An understanding of these characteristics is essential for designing and operating an effective intrusion detection system. Refer to the discussion in Chapter 6 for detailed information on performance characteristics.

As with exterior sensors, specific criteria for measuring the effectiveness of interior sensors are required, as in the statement "Devices and equipment used in interior-intrusion detection systems shall meet the requirements of UL 639 and shall be functionally tested per established procedures at a documented period." For example,

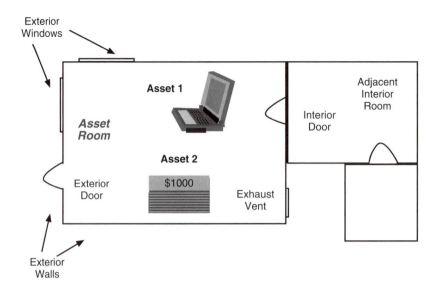

Figure 7.1 Sample Interior Area. The area shows a boundary, interior areas, and asset locations

the statement "Volumetric sensors shall detect an individual moving at a rate of 1 foot per second or faster within the total field of view of the sensor" is a clear and measurable specification for interior sensor performance. Additional information on performance characteristics specific for interior intrusion sensors follows.

As with exterior sensors, a nuisance alarm is any alarm that is not caused by an intrusion. Common sources of nuisance alarms for interior sensors include electromagnetic, acoustic, thermal, meteorological, seismic, and optical effects and wildlife (birds, insects, animals). False alarms are those nuisance alarms generated by the equipment itself (whether by poor design, inadequate maintenance, or component failure). Different types of intrusion sensors have different sensitivities to these nuisance or false alarm sources, as is discussed in detail later in this chapter.

An interior intrusion detection system is vulnerable to both outsiders and insiders. These terms were fully discussed in Chapter 3, "Threat Definition." Because

insiders have authorized access to an area or facility, many perimeter exterior sensors are not in the detection path of the insider. Interior sensors, on the other hand, can still be useful for detecting insider theft or sabotage, as well as any attacks by outsiders.

Interior sensors are often placed in access mode during regular working hours, making them more susceptible to tampering by an insider. In many alarm-monitoring systems, access mode means that the sensor alarms are temporarily masked so that alarms are not displayed at the alarm-monitoring station. An insider among maintenance personnel probably has the greatest opportunity and the technical skills necessary to compromise sensors or the system compared to other employees. Vulnerabilities created by a technically capable insider include reducing sensor sensitivity, shifting a sensor's coverage area, or changing the characteristics of a zone area. These actions may not totally disable a sensor, but could create a hole in detection.

Sensor Classification

There are several ways of classifying the types of intrusion sensors. In this discussion, the following methods of classification are used for interior intrusion sensors:

- passive or active
- covert or visible
- volumetric or line detection
- application

Active or Passive

A useful way of looking at interior sensors and their interaction with the environment is to consider the sensors in two categories: active and passive. Active sensors transmit a signal from a transmitter and, with a receiver, detect changes or reflections of that signal. The transmitter and the receiver may be separated, in which case the installation is called bistatic, or they may be located together, in which case the installation is called monostatic. The principal point is that these active sensors generate a field of energy when the sensor is operating, and a very sophisticated adversary could use this field to detect the presence of the sensor prior to stepping into the active sensing zone.

Passive sensors are different from active sensors in that they produce no signal from a transmitter and are simply receivers of energy in the proximity of the sensor. This energy may be due to vibration (from a walking man or a truck), infrared (from a human or a hot object), acoustic (sounds of a destructive break-in), or from a change in the mechanical configuration of the sensor (in the case of the simpler electromechanical devices). The distinction of passive or active has a practical importance. The presence or location of a passive sensor can be more difficult to determine than that of an active sensor; this puts the intruder at a disadvantage. In environments with explosive vapors or materials, passive sensors are safer than active ones because no energy that might initiate explosives is emitted.

Covert or Visible

Covert sensors are hidden from view; examples are sensors that are located in walls or under the floor. Visible sensors are in plain view of an intruder; examples are sensors that are attached to a door or mounted on another support structure. Covert sensors are more difficult for an intruder to detect and locate, and thus they can be more effective; also, they do not disturb the appearance of the environment. Another consideration, however, is that visible sensors may deter the intruder from acting. Visible sensors are typically simpler to install and easier to repair than covert ones.

Volumetric or Line Detection

The entire volume or a portion of the volume of a room or building can be protected using volumetric motion sensors. An advantage of volumetric motion sensors is that they will detect an intruder moving in the detection zone regardless of the point of entry into the zone.

Forcible entry through doors, windows, or walls of a room can be detected using line-type sensors. These sensors only detect activity at a specific location or a very narrow area. Unlike volumetric sensors, line sensors only detect an intruder if he or she violates a particular entry point into a detection zone.

Application

Sensors may be grouped by their application in the physical detection space. Some sensors may be applied in several ways. There are three application classes for interior sensors:

1. Boundary-penetration sensors detect penetration of the boundary to an interior area.
2. Interior motion sensors detect motion of an intruder within a confined interior area.
3. Proximity sensors can detect an intruder in the area immediately adjacent to an object in an interior area or when the intruder touches the object.

Sensor Technology

In the following discussion of interior sensor technologies, the sensors are grouped by their application. Excellent reviews of interior intrusion sensor technologies have been written by Barnard (1988), Cumming (1992), and Rodriguez et al. (1991).

Boundary-Penetration Sensors

This class of sensors includes vibration, electromechanical, infrasonic, capacitance proximity, and passive sonic sensors. The interior area best protected by boundary penetration sensors is shown in Figure 7.2. This area includes ceilings and floors of rooms as well as walls and doors.

Vibration Sensors

Boundary-penetration vibration sensors are passive line sensors and can be either visible or covert. They detect the movement of the surface to which they are fastened. A human blow or other sudden impact on a surface will cause that surface to vibrate at a specific frequency determined by its construction. The vibration frequencies are determined to a lesser extent by the impacting tool.

Vibration sensors may be as simple as jiggle switches or as complex as inertial switches or piezoelectric sensors. Inertial switches use a metallic ball mounted on metal contacts as the sensing element. The body of the sensor is mounted on the

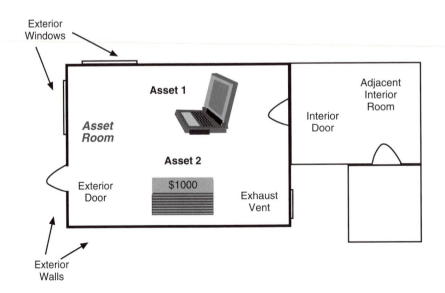

Figure 7.2 Boundary Penetration Sensor Location. Boundaries for interior areas are usually established by walls, doors, and windows

vibrating surface and the ball tends to remain stationary relative to the surface. As the body of the sensor is moved, the inertia of the ball causes the ball to momentarily lose contact with the mount, causing an alarm. The vibration frequencies detected by an inertial sensor are usually 2–5 kHz. The sensing element of a piezoelectric sensor is also mounted directly on the vibrating surface and moves relative to the mass of the sensor body. This motion flexes the piezoelectric element, causing a voltage output that can be processed for the proper combination of amplitude, frequency, and duration to detect an intrusion. The vibration frequencies detected by a piezoelectric vibration sensor are 5–50 kHz.

Glass-break sensors that mount directly to the glass are vibration sensors. These are specifically designed to generate an alarm when the frequencies more nearly associated with breaking glass are present. These frequencies are normally above 20 kHz. Active glass-break sensors introduce a vibration into the protected glass (e.g., a window) and listen for the signal received by a second transducer located elsewhere on the glass. Breaking the glass causes the retrieved signal to change and generate an alarm. Active glass-break sensors are more expensive than other glass-break sensors, but their NAR is much lower.

The more recent models of fiber-optic intrusion sensors also detect vibration. These are passive, line sensors, and can be either visible or covert. Fiber-optic sensors of this type detect microbending of fiber-optic cable. Microbending is caused by cable movement or bending, even minute movement of the cable such as vibration of the surface to which the cable is attached. A processing unit that is part of the fiber-optic sensor transmits light down the cable and also receives the light at the other end. Microbending causes changes to the light at the receiving end, and these changes are detected. The processing unit also includes a number of user-adjustable parameters such as low- and high-frequency filtering,

amplitude filtering, and pulse duration and count. The adjustable parameters aim to reduce sensitivity to nuisance sources, while maintaining enough sensitivity to intrusion activity. However, when proposing use of a fiber-optic sensor for vibration detection, the coincidence of intrusion activity frequencies and nuisance source frequencies (such as vibrations caused by nearby machinery, vehicles, trains, and air traffic near airports) must be considered. Filtering of the nuisance frequencies is possible, but this may also reduce intrusion sensitivity if there are no intrusion-induced frequencies beyond the nuisance frequencies.

The primary application advantage of vibration sensors is that they provide early warning of a forced entry. When applying vibration sensors, the designer must be aware that the detector might generate nuisance alarms if mounted on walls or structures that are exposed to external vibrations. If the structures are subject to severe vibrations caused by external sources such as rotating machinery, vibration sensors should not be used. However, if the structures are subject to occasional impacts, vibration sensors with a pulse accumulator or count circuit might be effective. These circuits will allow a limited number of impacts to occur, as long as the number remains below a predetermined threshold.

Electromechanical Sensors

Electromechanical sensors are passive, visible, line sensors. The most common type is a relatively simple switch generally used on doors and windows. Most of these switches are magnetic switches, which consist of two units: a switch unit and a magnetic unit. Figure 7.3 shows a magnetic reed switch and its components in the closed and open positions.

The switch unit, which contains a magnetic reed switch, is mounted on the stationary part of the door or window. The

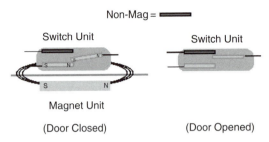

Figure 7.3 Simple Magnetic Switch. When the door is closed, the magnet holds the switch closed. When the door opens, the magnetic field is removed, the switch opens, and generates an alarm

magnetic unit, which contains a permanent magnet, is mounted on the movable part of the door or window, adjacent to the switch unit. With the door or window closed, the spacing between the switch unit and magnet unit is adjusted so that the magnetic field from the permanent magnet causes the reed switch to be in the closed (or secure) position. A subsequent opening of the door or window (removal of the magnet) results in the decrease of the magnetic field at the switch, causing movement of the switch to the open (or alarm) position. Placing a strong magnet near the switch unit and forcing the switch to the secure position, allowing undetected access through the door, easily defeats these switches.

An additional bias magnet in the switch unit that can be adjusted to help prevent defeat is also available. Magnetic sensors with bias magnets are generally referred to as balanced magnetic switches (BMS). Other variations include multiple reed switches and multiple magnets; fusing and voltage breakdown sensing devices; and shielded case construction. Some units incorporate internal electromagnets for self-testing, which have complex interactions with the switch units, increasing the complexity of the unit and decreasing its vulnerability to defeat.

BMSs provide a higher level of protection for doors and windows than either

magnetically or mechanically activated contacts or tilt switches. However, the protection is only as good as the penetration resistance of the door or window. These sensors are only adequate if the intruder opens the door or window for entry. If the intruder cuts through the door, the BMS will be bypassed. Sample design criteria for a BMS might be, "a BMS shall initiate an alarm whenever the door is moved 1 inch or more from the jamb . . . A BMS shall NOT initiate an alarm for door movements of 1/2 inch or less."

A relatively new type of magnetic switch is known as a Hall effect switch. This switch is totally electronic without mechanical reed switches. It contains active electronics and requires power. It is intended to provide a higher level of security than BMSs. Similar to other magnetic switches, it consists of a switch unit and a magnetic unit. Operation of the switch is based on Hall effect devices in the switch unit that measure and monitor the magnetic field strength of the magnetic unit. The Hall effect is a phenomenon that occurs when a current-carrying wire (or metallic strip) is exposed to an external magnetic field. In this state, the magnetic field causes charge carriers to be accelerated toward one side of the wire, resulting in a charge separation across the wire. The amount and polarity of the charge separation is proportional to the magnetic field strength and magnetic polarity. The separation of charge in the wire is called the Hall effect. The amount of charge can be measured across the sides of a metallic strip. In the Hall effect switch, if significant enough magnetic field changes occur as measured by the Hall effect devices, an alarm condition is generated. Both BMS and Hall effect sensors provide better protection against insider tampering and defeat than does the simple magnetic switch. The Hall effect switch also provides increased tamper and defeat protection over the BMS. An insider will be required to be more knowledgeable as the sensor technology progresses from simple magnetic switch to BMS and then to Hall effect.

Another electromechanical sensor, the continuity or breakwire sensor, is usually attached to or enclosed in walls, ceilings, or floors to detect penetration through many types of construction materials. The sensor consists of small electrically conductive wires and electronics to report an alarm when the conductor is broken. The wires can be formed in any pattern to protect areas of unusual shape. Printed circuit technology can be used to fabricate continuity sensors if desired. Breakwire grids and screens can be used to detect forcible penetrations through vent openings, floors, walls, ceilings, locked storage cabinets, vaults, and skylights. NARs for this class of sensor are very low since the wire must be broken to initiate an alarm. Breakwire sensors should be electrically supervised to decrease the chances of tampering. Since these sensors require a break or cut to detect, they can be defeated through the use of a jumper around a cut or by movement of the wire to allow penetration. Another version of a breakwire sensor uses optical fibers instead of electrical wire. The principle is the same—the optical fiber must be broken or damaged enough to stop or significantly reduce light transmission. These are considered fiber-optic intrusion sensors, but are very different and much simpler than the fiber-optic intrusion sensors described earlier under vibration sensors.

Capacitance Sensors

Capacitance sensors are most commonly proximity-type sensors; however, they can be applied for boundary-penetration detection. They establish a resonant electrical circuit between a protected metal object and a control unit, making them active sensors. The capacitance between the protected metal object and a ground plane becomes a part of the total capacitance of a tuned circuit in an oscillator. The object to be protected is electrically isolated from the ground plane. The

capacitive dielectric is usually the air that surrounds, or is between, the protected object and the ground plane. The tuned circuit may have a fixed frequency of oscillation, or the oscillator frequency may vary.

Oscillators whose frequency is fixed have an internally adjustable capacitance, which is used to compensate for different capacitive loads. A loop of wire, known as the protection loop, is connected between the conductive object or objects to be protected and the control unit, which contains the tuned circuit. Once the connection is made, the circuit is adjusted to resonance. Then any change in capacitance within the protection loop (which now includes the metal objects to be protected) will disturb the resonance condition, thereby causing an alarm. Humans very close to or touching the protected object will change the capacitance of the protection loop. Alarms can be generated by a person being very close or actually touching the object based on the sensitivity settings of the control unit.

Infrasonic Sensors and Passive Sonic Sensors

Infrasonic sensors are a class of intrusion sensors that operate by sensing pressure changes in the volume in which they are installed. A slight pressure change occurs whenever a door leading into a closed room is opened or closed, for example. The sound pressure waves thus generated have frequencies below 2 Hz. They are passive sensors that can be centrally located in a building some distance from exit doors. Air blowing into the closed volume can cause nuisance alarms with an infrasonic sensor. These sensors are best used in environments where there is only occasional access, such as a storage area.

Passive sonic sensors are covert, volumetric sensors. They are one of the simplest intrusion detectors, using a microphone to listen to the sounds generated in the area within the range of the microphone. If sounds of the correct amplitude, frequency content, and duration or repetition rate corresponding to a destructive penetration are heard, an alarm is generated. It is possible to make the sensor respond only to frequencies in the ultrasonic frequency range. This kind of sensor is then termed a passive ultrasonic sensor. Passive sonic sensors have limited effectiveness and are seldom used anymore. There are some applications, such as in bank vaults, where they may still be in use.

Active Infrared Sensors

Active infrared (IR) sensors are visible line sensors. These sensors establish a beam of infrared light using an infrared light source or sources (mated with appropriate lenses) as the transmitters and photodetectors for receivers. Several transmitters and receivers are usually employed to provide a system with multiple beams, and the beams are usually configured into a vertical infrared fence. A pulsed, synchronous technique may be used to reduce interference and the possibility of defeat by other sources of light. Infrared light is invisible to the human eye.

The narrow vertical plane in which this sensor operates does not provide any significant volume coverage, and the PPS designer must carefully consider its installation in order to avoid easy defeat or bypass. These sensors can also be used over short ranges in applications for filling gaps, such as for gates, doors, and portals. They may also be used in applications with long ranges up to about 100 m. To reduce the vulnerability of an intruder bypassing the active IR sensor, at least two detectors should be installed to form a barrier. Mirrors can also be installed to reflect the IR beam back and forth to form a fence-like pattern across an entrance.

Active IR sensors are susceptible to several nuisance alarm sources. Smoke and dust in the air can scatter the beam until, depending on the density of the particles, the energy at the receiver is reduced to a level that causes the sensor to initiate an

alarm. Falling objects, small animals, or anything that could interrupt the IR beam long enough can cause an alarm.

Fiber-Optic Cable Sensors

These sensors are passive line detectors and can be either visible or covert. They can be applied as either a boundary penetration or a proximity sensor. A fiber-optic sensor typically consists of a length of fiber-optic sensing cable and an alarm processor unit. Both ends of the fiber are usually connected to the processor unit, which has a light source, a light receiver, and signal alarm processing electronics. One of the major advantages of a fiber-optic cable is its immunity to radio and electromagnetic frequencies and to changes in temperature and humidity. Fiber-optic sensors can be separated into two major categories: continuity-type and microbend-type sensors.

A fiber-optic continuity sensor is primarily sensitive to damage or breaks in the fiber loop, which causes a severe loss of signal amplitude at the receiver. The signal alarm processor detects the loss of signal and then initiates an alarm. Schemes such as time-of-flight techniques and synchronous detection, which are based on injecting pulses of light into the fiber, may recognize attempts to splice or bridge portions of the optical fiber.

A microbend fiber-optic sensor is sensitive to both applied pressure and movement of the cable. Pressure and movement cause microbends in the fiber cable, which are detected. There are two techniques being implemented by the various brands of fiber-optic sensors for detection of microbending, including speckle pattern and interferometry. The speckle pattern technique utilizes multimode fiber-optic cable through which light travels in many different paths. Because of the many paths, light at the end of the cable appears as a speckle pattern of light and dark patches when focused onto a detector surface. When the cable is stationary, the pattern is stationary; when microbending occurs, the speckle pattern changes. A photodiode detector converts the changes to electrical signals. Single-mode fiber is used with the interferometry technique. Wavelength-division multiplexing is employed using a beam-splitter, which generates multiple light signals at different wavelengths to travel down the same fiber in opposite directions. When pressure is applied to the fiber cable, changes to the interference between the signals occur. These changes are detected and converted to electrical signals for processing.

With either technique, the alarm processor performs electrical signal processing of the microbending events that occur along a fiber sensor cable. The processing is aimed at detecting intruder movement and rejecting nuisance alarm sources. The amount of processing varies among the different models. Examples of the processing are sensitivity and threshold levels, event counting, event timing, and low- and high-pass frequency filtering.

The sensing area covered by a fiber-optic sensor depends on how the cable is laid out or arranged and the maximum length of cable supported by the fiber processor. Systems currently being offered can support in the ranges of 1000–2000 yards of sensor cable, depending on the system.

When properly installed, fiber optics used as continuity sensors are a reliable means of intrusion detection as a structural boundary penetration sensor. These sensors depend on severe cable damage or breakage for detection. The cable must be installed so that it will be damaged or broken when surfaces such as the walls or ceiling of a building are being cut or broken through. Fiber-optic microbend sensors are a newer technology than the continuity type. Possible interior applications include installation in walls, ceilings, or doors, or under carpets (Vigil, 1994; Sandoval and Malone, 1996). One advantage of using a fiber-optic microbend sensor over a continuity sensor is that a

microbend sensor can give earlier warning that an intrusion is being attempted. For example, when used in protecting a wall the sensor can detect the vibrations caused by the intrusion attempt.

Interior Motion Sensors

Sensors that use several different types of technology fall into this category of motion sensors. Figure 7.4 shows the interior areas best suited to motion sensors.

Microwave Sensors
Microwave sensors are active, visible, volumetric sensors. They establish an energy field using energy in the electromagnetic spectrum, usually at frequencies on the order of 10 GHz. Interior microwave motion sensors are nearly always in the monostatic configuration with a single antenna being used both to transmit and receive. Intrusion detection is based on the Doppler frequency shift between the transmitted and received signal caused by a moving object within the energy field.

The Doppler shift requires a sufficient amplitude change and duration time to cause an alarm. In practical terms, this

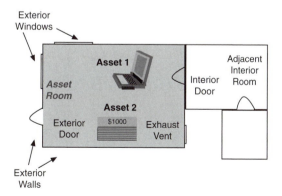

Figure 7.4 Interior Volume Protection Area for Motion Sensors. Volume protection can detect an intruder regardless of the point of entry

means that the microwave transmitter sends out a known frequency and if a higher or lower frequency is returned to the receiver, this is an indication that a target is moving closer or further away from the sensor. Due to this operating principle, optimum detection for microwave sensors is achieved when the target is moving towards or away from the sensor, not across the detection zone. Placement of microwave sensors should then be made so that the adversary is forced to move in this manner.

The shape of the detection zone is governed by the design of the antenna and is roughly similar to an elongated balloon. The antenna is typically a microwave horn but may be a printed circuit planar or phased array. Figure 7.5 shows a typical relationship between the antenna and pattern shape. It should be noted that these patterns are approximate; a truer representation of a microwave detection pattern is shown in Figure 7.6. The differences in the typical pattern and the true pattern should be considered when using

microwave sensors. If the target to be protected or the critical area falls within the concave portion of the true pattern, the sensor can be defeated.

This pattern feature is desirable if the sensor is to be used at a location where the microwave energy can penetrate beyond the walls of the area or room being protected. Microwave energy will readily penetrate most glass, as well as plaster, gypsum, plywood, and many other materials used in normal wall construction. Such penetration can cause unwanted interference with effective sensor operation. Metal objects, such as large bookcases or desks and screens or fencing within the protected area, can cause shadow zones and incomplete coverage. On the other hand, metal objects reflect the microwave energy, which can result in improved detection in an area that might be considered a shadow zone.

The fact that microwave energy can penetrate walls has both advantages and disadvantages. An advantage occurs when an intruder is detected by the microwave energy penetrating partitions within a protected volume; but detecting someone or something moving outside the protected area, or even outside the building, is then a

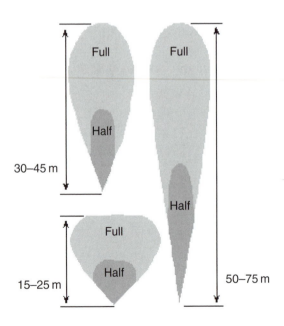

Figure 7.5 Typical Microwave Detection Patterns. The detection pattern varies based on antenna design

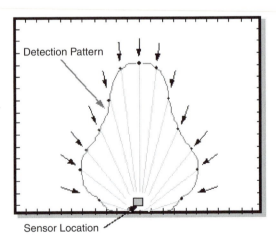

Figure 7.6 True Microwave Detection Pattern. The actual pattern has places where the pattern is not perfectly symmetrical

disadvantage and would cause a nuisance alarm. Because microwave energy is difficult to contain, special care should be taken when locating and directing the energy within the area requiring protection.

Other advantages of microwave detectors include:

- invisible and inaudible detection pattern;
- reliable low-maintenance device;
- low cost for area of coverage;
- high probability of detection;
- immune to high air turbulence, temperature and humidity changes; and
- variety of detection patterns available.

For all of their good qualities, there are a few disadvantages to the use of microwave sensors, in addition to those described above. These are:

- require a completely rigid mounting;
- susceptible to pattern drift;
- tendency to reflect off metallic objects; and
- extra considerations are required when considering installing in an area with light construction (glass, plaster board, wood).

Monostatic microwave devices can also be used as point sensors to provide limited coverage of a point or area in which other sensors may provide inadequate coverage or may be vulnerable to tampering. A common commercial application of monostatic microwave sensors is the automatic door openers used in supermarkets and airports.

Microwave detectors should be mounted high, near the ceiling of the area being protected. They should be aimed in the direction of desired coverage, yet pointed away from metal objects that might reflect microwave energy and cause nuisance alarms. Multiple microwave sensors used within the same area must

be set at different frequencies. Sensors at the same frequency will interfere with each other and cause continual nuisance alarms. Some manufacturers offer microwave sensors with different operating frequencies. Common sources of nuisance alarms for microwave sensors include movement of objects (i.e., nonhuman) within and outside the detection zone, small animals or birds, and vibration due to poor sensor installation and mounting. The ionized gas in fluorescent lights can reflect microwave energy. This can cause nuisance alarms due to the 60 Hz rate of the ionization, so fluorescent lights should not be within the detection area of a microwave sensor. Some models have filters that will ignore the Doppler shift created by fluorescent lights. Microwave sensor vulnerabilities include slow-moving targets, absorption or reflection of the microwave energy, blockage of the field of view (such as stacking boxes or moving furniture around in a room), and motion along the circumference of the detection pattern.

Ultrasonic Sensors

Ultrasonic sensors are active, visible, volumetric sensors. They establish a detection field using energy in the acoustic spectrum typically in the frequency range between 19 and 40 kHz. Ultrasonic sensors may be monostatic, and as is the case with monostatic microwave sensors, detection is based on the frequency shift between the transmitted and received signals caused by the Doppler effect from a moving object in the beam. The magnitude and range of the frequency shift depend on the moving target's size, velocity, and direction. The shape of the detection zone is similar to the monostatic microwave sensor detection zone, but the effective shape can be changed by the installation of deflectors.

Most common solid materials such as walls, cardboard, and windows will stop or deflect ultrasonic waves. Large objects in a protected volume, such as bookcases, desks, and partial wall partitions, will create shadow zones. Coverage of a volume by several of the sensors can usually overcome this problem.

A feature of ultrasonic energy is that it will not penetrate physical barriers such as walls; therefore, it can be easily contained in closed rooms. Since acoustical energy will not penetrate physical barriers, the walls of the protected room will either absorb or reflect the energy. Because most walls absorb very little ultrasonic energy unless they are covered with a very soft material, such as heavy drapes, most of the energy is reflected. This reflected energy helps fill the detection zone, making it more difficult for an intruder to escape detection.

Mechanically produced stimuli such as air turbulence or miscellaneous acoustic energy sources within the protected zone can cause nuisance alarms. Air turbulence from heating or air conditioning ducts, drafts, and so on can reduce the effectiveness by limiting the coverage of ultrasonic sensors and, at the same time, cause nuisance alarms. Acoustic energy generated by ringing bells and hissing noises, such as the noises produced by leaking radiators or compressed air, contains frequency components in the operating frequency band of ultrasonic sensors. These sources of ultrasonic energy sometimes produce signals similar to an intruder that can confuse the signal processor and cause nuisance alarms.

Another environmental condition that can affect ultrasonic sensor performance is the climate within the protected area. Appreciable changes in the relative humidity can change the detector's sensitivity until, in some installations, a sensor can become overly sensitive to the environment, which could cause nuisance alarms. Ultrasonic sensors may also be bistatic, and detection is based on a combination of Doppler effect and signal amplitude variation. In a bistatic installation, receivers and transmitters are placed (usually on the ceiling) to obtain the desired coverage. Individual receivers will have range adjustments.

Other characteristics will be similar to monostatic ultrasonic sensors.

Active Sonic Sensors

Sonic sensors are active, visible, and volumetric. They establish a detection field using energy in the acoustic spectrum at frequencies between 500 and 1000 Hz. These units can be used in monostatic, bistatic, or multistatic modes of operation. Since a much lower frequency is transmitted, good reflections are obtained, and standing waves will be established in the protected volume even in the monostatic configuration. For proper operation, it is necessary to establish standing waves to prevent drastic reduction of the detection range.

The frequencies used for these sensors are well within the hearing range of the human ear and are quite unpleasant to the listener. Further, in addition to a remote alarm indication, one of these sensors will give an electronic siren type of alarm varying between 350 and 1100 Hz at 3 cycles/s for 90 s. This audible alarm can be adjusted in audio level up to 135 dB. For this reason, they are seldom found in normal operating environments where there is significant human activity or interaction.

Passive Infrared Sensors

Passive infrared (PIR) sensors are visible and volumetric. This sensor responds to changes in the energy emitted by a human intruder, which is approximately equal to the heat from a 50 W light bulb. They also have the capability to detect changes in the background thermal energy caused by someone moving through the detector field of view and hiding in the energy emanating from objects in the background if there are sufficient differences in the background energy. These systems typically employ special optical and electronic techniques that limit their detection primarily to an energy source in motion; therefore, reliance on background energy change for detection is discouraged.

There are four major characteristics of infrared radiation. First, all objects emit infrared radiation. The intensity of the infrared is related to the object's temperature. Second, infrared energy is transmitted without physical contact between the emitting and receiving surfaces. Third, infrared warms the receiving surface and can be detected by any device capable of sensing a change in temperature. Fourth, infrared radiation is invisible to the human eye. PIR sensors respond to infrared energy in the wavelength band between 8 and 14 nm.

The PIR sensor is a thermopile or pyroelectric detector that receives radiation from the intruder and converts this radiation into an electrical signal. The signal is then amplified and processed through logic circuits, which generally require that the source of radiation move within the field of view of the sensor. If the signal is strong enough and the required movement occurs, an alarm is generated. Detection is based on the difference in temperature between the intruder and the background and is referred to as the minimum resolvable temperature (MRT). Some manufacturers specify an MRT as low as 1°C.

A pyroelectric detector is based on the principle that certain dielectric materials of low crystal symmetry exhibit spontaneous dielectric polarization. When the electric dipole moment occurs it is dependent on the temperature at which the material becomes pyroelectric. Through the use of segmented parabolic mirrors or Fresnel lens optics, infrared energy is focused onto the pyroelectric detector. These optics provide a single long conical field of view or a multiple segment field of view. Long single-segment sensors are used to protect corridors, and those with multisegments are used to protect large open areas. Figure 7.7 shows a representation of the detection zones present in a multisegment sensor. As with microwave sensors, it should be noted that the detection pattern is not a perfect shape, so caution should be used when placing these devices. In addition, due to the operating

principles of the device, a PIR will be most effective if the target is forced to cross the detection pattern, thereby entering and exiting multiple detection segments over a period of time. Figure 7.8 shows the

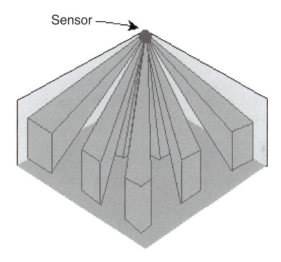

Figure 7.7 Passive Infrared Sensor Multi-segment Detection Zones. As a person passes across the detection segments, each segment will detect an increase or decrease in temperature, which will trigger an alarm

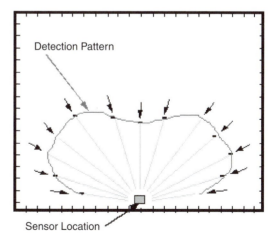

Figure 7.8 True Passive Infrared Detection Pattern Determined by Testing. The pattern has some concave spots, which may create holes in the detection coverage

true detection pattern of a PIR sensor determined via testing.

Birds and small flying insects can cause nuisance alarms with PIR sensors. Birds flying near the sensor can block the background energy from the thermal sensors, and if the birds' motions satisfy the alarm criteria, the result is a nuisance alarm. An insect crawling on the lens can cause large temperature changes, also resulting in a nuisance alarm.

Infrared energy does not penetrate most building materials, including glass, and therefore sources of infrared energy that are located outside buildings will not typically generate nuisance alarms. Nuisance alarms can be generated indirectly, however, from sources outside the buildings due to local heating effects. For example, while glass and Plexiglas® window materials are effective filters for infrared energy in the wavelength region of interest (8–14 nm), sunlight passing through windows can produce locally heated surfaces that can radiate energy in this band.

Infrared sensors should be located away from any heat sources that could produce thermal gradients in front of the sensor's lens. In addition, heat sources within the sensor's field of view should be avoided. For instance, an infrared detector should never be mounted over or near radiators, heaters, hot pipes, or other heating elements. Radiant energy from these sources can produce thermal gradients in the view of the detector's lens that might change the background energy pattern. Depending on the intensity of the heat source, the thermal gradients might cause nuisance alarms. An unshielded incandescent light that is within 3–5 yards of the sensor might also cause an alarm if it burns out or goes out due to loss of power.

PIRs offer several advantages, including:

- totally passive device;
- well-defined detection zones;
- no interaction between multiple devices;

- low to moderate cost; and
- relatively few nuisance alarms.

The disadvantages of PIRs include:

- moderate vibration sensitivity;
- sensitivity changes with room temperature;
- it is a line-of-sight device and the field of view is easily blocked; and
- sources of rapid temperature change are potential nuisance alarm sources.

Dual-Technology Sensors

This sensor can be active and passive, visible, and volumetric. This sensor type attempts to achieve absolute alarm confirmation while maintaining a high probability of detection. Absolute alarm confirmation is ideally achieved by combining two technologies that individually have a high probability of detection and no common nuisance alarm-producing stimuli. Currently available dual-channel motion detectors (dual-technology) combine either an active ultrasonic or microwave sensor with a PIR sensor. When used in combination, alarms from either the active ultrasonic or microwave sensor are logically combined with the alarms from the infrared sensor in an AND gate logic configuration. The AND gate logic requires nearly simultaneous alarms from both the active and passive sensors to produce a valid alarm.

Dual-technology sensors usually have a lower NAR than single technology sensors—when the detectors are properly applied and assuming each has a low NAR. But it is important to understand that when two sensors are logically combined using an AND gate, the probability of detection of the combined detectors will be less than the probability of detection of the individual detectors. For instance, if an ultrasonic sensor has a probability of detection of 0.95 and it is combined with an infrared detector that also has a probability of detection of 0.95, the dual sensor has the product of the individual probabilities of detection, or only 0.90. Also, ultrasonic and microwave detectors have the highest probability of detecting motion directly toward or away from the sensor, but infrared sensors have the highest probability of detecting someone moving across the field of view. Therefore, the probability of detection of the combined sensors in a single unit will be less than if the individual detectors are mounted perpendicular to each other with overlapping energy patterns and fields of view. To optimize the probability of detection for combined sensors, separately mounted, logically combined sensors are recommended. For high-security applications, a single dual-technology sensor should never be used in place of two separately mounted sensors. If dual-technology sensors are to be used, multiple sensor units should be installed, with each unit offering overlap protection of the other.

Video Motion Detection

A video motion detector (VMD) is a passive sensor that processes the video signal from a CCTV camera. These were discussed in some detail in Chapter 6, "Exterior Intrusion Detection." The assessment camera is an integral part of a VMD sensor. Camera characteristics affect both detection capability and NAR. A low-contrast output from a camera reduces detection capability. High noise levels from a camera can cause nuisance alarms. Enough light is required for proper operation of CCTV cameras, and the light must be uniform to avoid excessively dark or light areas.

Because a VMD detects changes in the video brightness level, any change can cause an alarm. Flickering lights, camera movements, and other similar movements can lead to excessively high NARs. Also, very slow movement through the detection zone can defeat most VMDs.

Many VMDs are effective for interior use, because nuisance alarm sources like snow, fog, traffic flow, and clouds are not present.

Performance tests should be completed on any VMD prior to installation in a facility. Tests should be performed with a low-profile target, such as a crawler, and with higher velocity and profile targets, such as people walking or running. These tests should be performed under the lowest contrast lighting condition expected. Vigil (1993) has written an excellent evaluation of a number of commercially available interior VMDs. The following factors should be considered before selecting a VMD:

- consistent, controlled lighting (no flickering);
- camera vibration;
- objects that could cause blind areas;
- moving objects such as fans, curtains, and small animals; and
- changing sunlight or shadows entering through windows or doors.

Proximity Sensors

This class of sensors includes capacitance and pressure sensors. Figure 7.9 shows the interior areas best protected by proximity sensors.

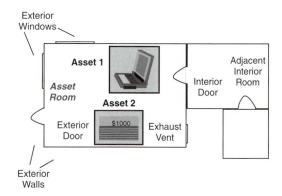

Figure 7.9 Proximity Sensor Areas. Proximity sensors are placed near or on an asset to provide detection

Capacitance Proximity Sensors

Capacitance proximity sensors are active, covert line sensors. They can detect anyone either approaching or touching metal items or containers that the sensors are protecting. These sensors operate on the same principle as electrical capacitors. A capacitor is an electronic component that consists of two conductor plates separated by a dielectric medium. A change in the electrical charge or dielectric medium results in a change in the capacitance between the two plates. In the case of the capacitance proximity sensor, one plate is the metal item being protected and the second plate is an electrical reference ground plate under and around the protected item. The metal item in this application is isolated from ground by insulating blocks. This leaves only air around and between the metal object and ground, so air is the dielectric medium.

Variable frequency oscillators use a phase-locked loop and use the correction voltage for sensing. This type of capacitance proximity sensor generally balances itself in a short time (usually less than 2 min) after being connected to the conductive metal object to be protected. Once the sensor is balanced, any change in capacitance between the object to be protected and ground will disturb the balance condition, thereby causing an alarm. Capacitance proximity sensors are operated at frequencies below 100 kHz and can often be set to detect capacitance changes of a few picofarads.

During operation, the metal object is electrically charged to a potential that creates an electrostatic field between the object and reference ground. The electrical conductivity of an intruder's body alters the dielectric characteristic as the intruder approaches or touches the object. The dielectric change results in a change in the capacitance between the protected item and the reference ground. When the net capacitance charge satisfies the alarm criteria, an alarm is activated. Figure 7.10 illustrates a typical arrangement

for connecting a capacitance proximity sensor to a safe or file cabinet.

For applications where the object to be protected must be grounded, the object can be considered the ground plane. This requires the fabrication of a capacitance blanket for draping over the protected object as shown in Figure 7.11. If the

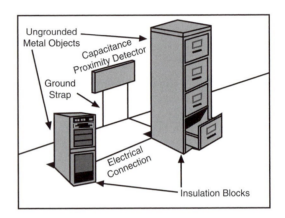

Figure 7.10 Depiction of Capacitance Proximity Sensor for Safe and File Cabinet. Isolating all of the pieces from ground on one side and connecting them to the sensor, which has a ground connection, sets up a dielectric field. If the field is disturbed by entry of a person, an alarm is triggered

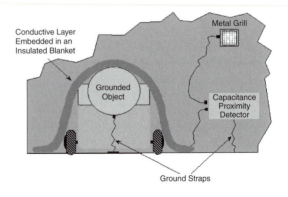

Figure 7.11 Capacitance Blanket Proximity Sensor. The sensor detects any movement of the blanket, which disturbs the capacitive field and triggers an alarm. This application will also keep the object out of plain sight

blanket is made large enough to cover the object entirely, any access attempts will cause blanket movement, capacitance change, and alarm. This can also be useful to keep the object out of plain sight, as for some classified components or proprietary equipment.

The sensitivity of capacitance sensors is affected by changes in relative humidity and the relocation of other metal objects closer to or away from the protected item. Changes in the relative humidity vary the dielectric characteristics, which can either increase or decrease the air conductivity. Capacitance sensors use a self-balancing circuit to adjust automatically to the change in relative humidity and relocation of metal objects close to the protected object. If the sensor's sensitivity is adjusted to detect an intruder several meters from the object, this change in conductivity could be enough to initiate a nuisance alarm.

Sometimes objects requiring protection are located in areas with poor grounding conditions. In such places, a reference or ground plane can be established by installing a metal sheet or screen under the object. The use of wooden blocks to isolate the protected metal object from the ground plane should be avoided. Wooden blocks might absorb enough moisture over a period of time to change the dielectric enough that the protective object is no longer isolated from ground, resulting in nuisance alarms. Hard rubber material, similar to a hockey puck, has been found to be a very effective insulator in this application.

Pressure Sensors

Pressure sensors, often in the form of mats, can be placed around or underneath an object. These sensors are passive, covert, line detectors. Pressure mats consist of a series of ribbon switches positioned parallel to each other along the length of the mat. Ribbon switches are constructed from two strips of metal in the form of a ribbon separated by an insulating material. They are constructed so that when an

adequate amount of pressure, depending on the application, is exerted anywhere along the ribbon, the metal strips make electrical contact and initiate an alarm.

When using pressure mats in security applications, the mats should be well concealed under carpets or even under tile or linoleum floor coverings. If the intruder is aware of their existence, he or she can just step over or bridge over the mat. Pressure mats alone should be used only to detect low-skill intruders. However, pressure mats can be used along with other sensors in a system designed to provide a higher level of protection. Table 7.1 provides a summary of technologies used for interior sensors.

Wireless Sensors

The most common wireless sensors are the RF transmission type. In the United States, these systems typically operate in the 300 or 900 MHz bands. Some systems utilize spread-spectrum techniques for transmission. A typical RF wireless sensor system consists of sensor/transmitter units and a receiver. The sensor/transmitter unit has both the sensor and transmitter electronics integrated into one package and are battery powered. Advertised battery life is 2–5 years, depending on the number of alarms and transmissions. Each sensor/transmitter unit is programmed with a unique identification code. The number of individual sensors that can transmit to one receiver and the transmission range varies with the system. In most systems, the receiver can output alarm messages in the form of RS-232, logic levels, or relay contact operation. In order to conserve battery power, the transmitters are in a sleep mode until an event requires a transmission. Events consist of alarms, tampers, and state-of-health messages. Alarms and tampers are transmitted when they occur. State-of-health messages verify that the sensor is still present and operating. They typically

Table 7.1 *Summary of Interior Sensor Technologies.*

For specific applications, one type may be preferred over another, depending on the surrounding environment and desired performance.

	Passive or Active	Covert or Visible	Volumetric or Line
Boundary Penetration Sensors			
Electromechanical	P	C/V	L
Infrared	B*	V	L
Vibration	P	C	L
Capacitance	P	C	L
Fiber-Optic Cable	P	C/V	L
Interior Motion Sensors			
Microwave	A	V	V
Ultrasonic	A	V	V
Sonic	A	V	V
Passive Infrared	P	V	V
Proximity Sensors			
Capacitance	A	C	L
Pressure	P	C	L
* Both active and passive types exist.			

consist of battery status, alarm status, and tamper status and are transmitted to the receiver at user-specified intervals. The receiver is programmed to expect state-of-health messages at the specified intervals. If they are not received, the receiver will indicate a fault condition.

Most wireless systems use PIR, microwave, dual-technology, and magnetic switches as sensor types. They also typically have what is known as a universal transmitter. The universal transmitter allows interfacing to other sensors or controls by monitoring the alarm contacts of the separate sensor.

Some of the concerns when using a RF sensor system include collisions, signal fade, and interference. Collisions occur when multiple signals, such as state-of-health, are received simultaneously, resulting with neither message being read by the receiver. Fading can occur when the path between the transmitter and the receiver is too far or is blocked by too much material that shields the RF signal, such as large metal objects, metallic building siding, and so forth. Interference occurs when other RF sources transmitting in the same frequency range overpowers the signal sent by the sensor/transmitter unit. Techniques such as spread-spectrum transmission and dithering the state-of-health timing can help reduce these problems. Testing to verify a good transmission path and possible interference sources prior to final location and installation of transmitters and receivers is recommended and will help reduce problems.

Miscellaneous Technologies

Any quantity or parameter in a volume or area that changes when an intrusion takes place can be used to detect the intrusion. The most common ones have already been discussed. Other technologies that have been exploited include light and electric field.

Light sensors monitor the average light level within their field of view. If the light level changes by a predetermined amount, the possibility of an intrusion exists. The light sensor is designed to produce an alarm when such a change occurs. Electric field sensors are similar to capacitance proximity sensors except they may cover larger areas. They consist of sets of wires, along a wall for example, which generate an alarm when a person approaches or touches the wires.

One additional sensor technology uses active infrared energy in a continuous plane (like a curtain) to create an invisible detection pattern. The sensor uses a mechanical rotating mirror and reflective tape for protection. Laboratory testing revealed that flies and moths resting on the protective tape caused nuisance alarms, but a single fly passing quickly through the plane will not cause alarms. Additional sensors under development are based on human presence detection and look for human heartbeats, carbon dioxide changes, or other human characteristics.

Effects of Environmental Conditions

A large number of environmental conditions can produce noise in the same energy spectra that the intrusion sensors are designed to detect. These outside noise sources can degrade sensor performance and may cause the sensor to generate an alarm even when an intruder is not present. The following sections discuss several factors that can degrade a sensor's performance. Environmental conditions that can affect interior sensors include:

- electromagnetic
- nuclear radiation
- acoustic
- thermal
- optical
- seismic
- meteorological

Electromagnetic Environment

Sources of electromagnetic energy that could affect the performance of a particular type of interior detection system include lightning, power lines and power distribution equipment, transmission of radio frequencies, telephone lines and equipment, lighting, computer and data processing equipment. Other sources are various electric powered vehicles, such as forklifts and elevators, television equipment, automotive ignition, electrical machinery or equipment, intercom and paging equipment, and aircraft.

Construction of the building or room to be monitored will play an important role in determining the nature of the electromagnetic energy that is present. If the structure is made primarily of wood or concrete, neither of which provides electromagnetic shielding, then a high background of electromagnetic energy generated by sources outside the building or room is possible.

The best way to minimize the effects of stray electromagnetic energy is to provide electromagnetic shielding to all system components (including all data transmission links) and to ensure that all the components have a common, adequate electrical ground.

Nuclear Radiation Environment

Nuclear radiation can damage various components within the sensor. The most susceptible elements are semiconductors. Research has shown that current systems cannot be made totally invulnerable to the effects caused by some radiation environments. The appropriate design and choice of components and shielding where possible can reduce system vulnerability. Generally speaking, neutrons will degrade the performance of semiconductor devices and integrated circuits. The degradation primarily depends on the total dose.

Acoustic Environment

Acoustic energy is generated by many sources within an internal area. Also, energy generated by outside sources can be transmitted into an area to be protected. Some of the forms of acoustic energy that can affect the performance of interior sensors are noise from meteorological phenomena; ventilating, air-conditioning, and heat equipment; air compressors; television equipment; telephone electronic equipment; and exterior sources such as aircraft, vehicles, and trains.

Thermal Environment

Changes in the thermal environment can result in stimuli that affect the performance of interior intrusion sensors. These stimuli include uneven temperature distribution that causes air movement within the area and expansion and contraction of buildings. Causes of changes in the thermal environment include weather, heating and air-conditioning equipment, machinery that produces heat, interior lighting, chemical and radioactive reactions producing thermal outputs, and fluctuations of sunlight through windows and skylights.

Optical Effects

The sources of optical phenomena that affect interior intrusion sensors include light energy from sunlight, interior lighting, highly reflective surfaces, and infrared and ultraviolet energy from other equipment.

Seismic Effects

Seismic phenomena affect interior intrusion devices by producing undesirable vibrations in interior areas. Seismic phenomena include earth tremors, machine equipment, vehicular traffic, trains, thunder, and high winds.

Meteorological Effects

Meteorological phenomena, such as lightning, thunder, rain, hail, temperature, wind, earth tremors, high relative humidity, and sunlight that adversely affect interior intrusion sensors have already been discussed within the individual sensor sections.

Sensor Selection

Sensor selection consists of identification of the equipment and installation methods that best meet the intrusion detection system objectives for a given facility. Consideration of the interaction among equipment, environment, and potential intruders is integral to the selection of the proper technological type of equipment necessary to ensure the desired intrusion detection functions. Two important physical conditions that affect sensor performance are the building or room construction and the various equipment or objects that occupy the same area or room to be monitored.

The relative susceptibility to nuisance alarms of several types of interior sensors suitable for fixed site applications is

Table 7.2 *Relative Susceptibility of Interior Sensors to Nuisance Alarms.*

	Environment			Small	Electrical Interference			
	Wind	Temp	RH	Animals	Lightning	Power	RF	Seismic
Boundary penetration sensors								
Active Glass Break	L	VL	VL	VL	L	L	L	L
Continuity	VL	VL	VL	VL	VL	VL	VL	VL
Simple magnetic switch	VL	VL	VL	VL	L	L	L	L
BMS	VL	VL	VL	VL	L	L	L	L-M
Passive Ultrasonic	M	L	L	M-H	L	L	L	L
Vibration	L-M	L	L	L	L	L	L	H
Fiber optic	L-M	L	VL	VL	VL	VL	VL	L-M
Volumetric Sensors								
Active Sonic	M	L	L	L	L	L	L	L
Microwave	L	L	L	M	M	M	M	L
PIR	L	H	L	M	M	M	M	L
Ultrasonic	L	L	M	M	M	M	M	L
VMD	L	L	L	M	M	M	M	L
Proximity Sensors								
Capacitance	L	L	M	M	M	L	L	L-M
Pressure	L	L	L	L	L	L	L	L
Fiber Optic	L	L	L	M	VL	VL	VL	M

Key: H = High, M = Medium, L = Low, VL = Very Low.

shown in Table 7.2. It is usually possible to identify appropriate sensors that will perform acceptably in the environment in question since the environment associated with interior areas is normally controlled and is usually predictable and measurable. However, correct sensor choice requires that the particular nuisance alarm stimuli to which it is susceptible be known, as well as whether these stimuli are contained in the environment in question. This is particularly true of the motion detectors (ultrasonic, microwave, infrared, and sonic), all of which can be installed to provide acceptable detection coverage and which typically have nuisance alarms from different stimuli. Figure 7.12 shows a possible arrangement of interior sensors for an interior area similar to the one used in this chapter. Optimum performance of an interior intrusion detection system can be achieved by an appropriate combination of sensors and sensor technologies. Adams (1996) has published a useful summary of operational issues.

Procedures

Procedures such as two-person rules, sensor effectiveness testing, and good maintenance practices and documentation

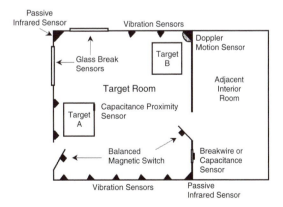

Figure 7.12 Sample Layout of Multiple Interior Sensors. A variety of boundary, volumetric, and proximity sensors are combined to provide protection-in-depth

ensure an effective interior intrusion detection system. When procuring sensors, select those that come closest to meeting performance goals and protection requirements while demonstrating compatibility with future systems to achieve the best integration.

The two-person rule is a procedure requiring two knowledgeable people to be involved in a situation or activity in order to prevent compromising facility security by a single insider. The two-person rule is applicable to functions such as granting access within the site and handling of critical assets, information, or equipment. Each person involved in a two-person rule task must be technically qualified to detect tampering by the other. The two-person rule is effective as long as the individuals involved do not relax the requirement because of long-term friendship or association.

For testing purposes, it can be very useful if a sensor has an audible or visible alarm indicator that can be recognized from 10 to 35 ft away. This indicator should be deactivated during operational use. Conduct walk tests every day to start, then periodically, based on successful results of the daily tests. All sensors should be performance tested after maintenance activities. A sensitivity analysis or effectiveness test can confirm the performance of a sensor, verify sensor coverage, and check for blind areas created by changes in room layout. Self-test mechanisms, whether part of a sensor or a separate device, will allow frequent operational testing of the sensor and alarm communication system. Self-testing should be activated on a random basis (Graham and Workhoven, 1987).

Installation and maintenance of sensors should be at least to manufacturer specifications, although testing may show ways to optimize performance beyond manufacturers' recommendations. Periodic inspections of sensors and components will ensure that they conform to the required configuration and specifications.

Possible alterations and modifications to components should be looked for during inspections. Acceptance tests, operational tests, and logs of maintenance calls on each piece of equipment will help determine how many and what kind of spares to keep on hand. Thorough inspections of spare parts should be performed prior to installation. Spare parts should be secured during storage in order to deter tampering.

Inspection of sensors after maintenance should also be performed. All sensors monitored by a data-collection control panel should be walk-tested after that control panel has undergone maintenance. Requiring approval of plant modification plans by security personnel prevents any changes that would degrade system performance. This should include changing the location of detectors, adding objects that may cause nuisance alarms, and relocating large objects in the protected area. Readjustment of detector sensitivity may be necessary following remodeling.

Documentation should be readily available showing theory of operation of equipment, functional block diagrams, cabling diagrams, schematics, and parts lists showing manufacturers and commercial equivalent part numbers. Maintenance logs can be used to monitor reliability of equipment and problem components or areas.

System Integration

System integration is the process of combining individual technology elements, procedures, and personnel into one system for providing security at a facility. This requires a balance among hardware, personnel, and operational procedures. As with exterior sensors, interior intrusion sensors must be integrated with the display and control subsystem, the entry-control subsystem, and delay mechanisms. This integration should include consideration of protection-in-depth, balance along all paths into the facility, and the use of backup systems and contingency plans.

Line supervision is the means for monitoring the communication link between a sensor and the alarm control center. Use of supervised lines between the sensor and host alarm system as well as continuously monitored sensor tamper switches will also help protect against the insider. The interior intrusion subsystem designer should be familiar with the range of line supervision techniques that are available for the communication lines that connect a sensor alarm relay to the alarm-reporting system. Line supervision techniques, such as reverse polarity, sound monitoring, radio class C, steady direct current class B, tone, and digital classes A and AB, cover the full range of security levels. Line supervision techniques will be explained further in Chapter 9 "Alarm Communication and Display." If a series of interior sensors is connected to a single alarm processor, line supervision is required between the processor and each detection sensor.

Summary

This chapter discusses interior intrusion detection sensors in terms of application, probability of detection, NAR, and vulnerability to defeat. The integration of individual sensors into an interior sensor system must consider the skill level of the intruder, the design goals, and the effects of environmental conditions, as well as the interaction of the interior system within a balanced and integrated PPS.

Security Principles

The performance measures for interior sensors are P_D, NAR, and vulnerability to defeat. Physical operation of a sensor should determine sensor placement to achieve optimum performance. Sensor detection areas should overlap.

Consideration of the interaction among equipment, environment, and potential intruders is integral to the selection of the proper technological type of equipment necessary to ensure the desired intrusion detection system functions.

References

Adams, D. Operational tips for improving intrusion detection systems performance. SAND96-0468C 1996;1–4.

Barnard, R.L. *Intrusion Detection Systems*, 2nd ed. Stoneham, MA: Butterworth Publishers, 1988, 147, 217.

Cumming, N. *Security*, 2nd ed. Boston: Butterworth-Heinemann, 1992, 115–171.

Graham, R., and Workhoven, R. Evolution of interior intrusion detection technology at Sandia National Laboratories. SAND87.0947 1987;1–10.

Rodriguez, J., Dry, B., and Matter, J. Interior intrusion detection systems. SAND91-0948 1991;1–114.

Sandoval, M.W., and Malone, T.P. Evaluations of fiber-optic sensors for interior applications. SAND96-0514 1996;1–41.

Vigil, J.T. An evaluation of interior video motion detection systems. SAND92-1987 1993;1–43.

Vigil, J.T. An evaluation of fiber-optic intrusion detection systems in interior applications. SAND94-0020 1994;1–42.

Questions

1. Discuss the following general application considerations for interior intrusion sensors:

   a. Use of more than one sensor or sensor type is recommended.

   b. Sensor installation should be considered during the selection process.

    c. Salesmen must demonstrate or provide independent verification of their claims.

    d. Sensors should be placed on stable mountings.

    e. Line supervision should be considered.

    f. Sensor field of view should be kept clear of clutter.

    g. Motion sensors should not be used in an area that has moving things other than people, such as small animals, birds, or insects.

    h. The line supervision circuits should be continually monitored even when an area or sensor is in the access mode.

    i. Rather than place wiring in the open, use conduit.

    j. Tamper switches should be installed in junction boxes.

    k. The sensor should be placed before the delay mechanism in the adversary's path.

    l. Motion sensors should not be installed next to or over openings, such as doorways or windows.

    m. To provide protection, sensor detection areas should overlap.

    n. Outside influences, such as trains, trucks, should be taken into account.

    o. Power line transients can cause nuisance alarms.

    p. The installer may be inexperienced.

    q. Radio frequency sources, for example portable radio transmitters, may have adverse affects on the sensor system.

2. Discuss the following application considerations for ultrasonic motion sensors:

    a. Ultrasonic motion sensors in the same area should be from the same manufacturer.

    b. Ultrasonic motion sensors should be installed away from sources of ultrasonic noise, such as air leaks, air filters, dripping water, clanging metal (telephone bells).

    c. A monostatic ultrasonic motion sensor should be aimed so that the most likely intruder path is towards or away from the sensor.

    d. Ultrasonic motion sensors should be installed so that they cannot see moving objects, such as moving machinery and banners.

3. Discuss the following application considerations for PIR motion sensors:

    a. A PIR motion sensor should be aimed so that rapidly changing heat sources, such as space heaters, are out of its field of view.

    b. A PIR motion sensor should not be aimed so that hot, turbulent air flows through or into the sensor's field of view.

    c. A PIR motion sensor should be aimed away from the floor if mice or other small animals are present.

    d. A PIR motion sensor should be placed so that sunlight will not fall directly on the face.

    e. A PIR motion sensor should be installed so that the least likely direction an intruder will move is directly at or away from the sensor.

4. Discuss the following application considerations for microwave motion sensors:

    a. Microwave energy can penetrate many common wall types.

    b. Multiple microwave motion sensors installed in the same area should be operated on different frequencies.

    c. Radar speed detectors operate in the same frequency band as microwave motion sensors.

    d. Microwave motion sensors should not be placed so that they can "see" microwave ovens.

e. Large metal objects can reflect the area of coverage.

f. Microwave motion sensors should be aimed away from metal air ducts that can direct the energy into other areas.

g. Microwave motion sensors should be placed so that they are unable to see metallic (or conductive) moving objects, such as fan blades and moving machinery.

h. People should not look directly into an operating microwave motion sensor antenna at very close ranges (<30 cm).

i. Fluorescent lighting tubes should be outside the microwave sensor field of view, particularly at distances less than 3 m.

j. A microwave motion sensor should be installed so that the most likely intruder path is not across its field of view.

5. Discuss the following application considerations for other sensors:

   a. A capacitance proximity sensor should not be used if there are mice or other small animals present in the area.

   b. Passive sonic or passive ultrasonic sensors should be avoided in an extremely noisy environment.

   c. Balanced magnetic switches mounted on ferrous (steel) doors or frames must use 1/2 in. nonferrous spacers.

   d. Balanced magnetic switches should not be mounted on the outside of the protected surface.

6. Discuss the following application considerations for interior sensor maintenance:

   a. A sensor system should not be installed and forgotten.

b. Walk-test should be conducted periodically to verify sensor operations.

c. Only authorized personnel should adjust sensitivities.

d. A modification in the system should be accepted only after testing has verified proper operation.

e. The NAR should not be reduced by lowering sensor sensitivity, because lowering sensitivity also reduces system coverage.

f. Building maintenance should be performed even if it may cause nuisance alarms.

7. What are some of the differences in the detection capabilities of infrared, microwave, and ultrasonic sensors?

8. What kind of environmental conditions can affect interior sensor systems?

9. A total of 28 tests have been performed to estimate P_D for a new PIR sensor but one-half of the tests were performed using each of two different tactics. One tactic is a walk across the detection pattern of the sensor at 1 ft/s. (A normal walk is approximately 2–3 ft/s.) This tactic shows 13 detections in 14 tests. The other tactic is a crawl at 0.5 ft/s and shows 10 detections out of 14 tests. What is the P_D for this sensor? Should we use two P_Ds or just one?

8

Alarm Assessment

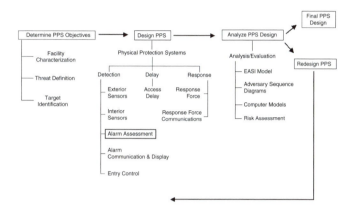

Primary and secondary assessment is essential to identify the cause of an alarm and to effectively end the detection function. Alarm assessment can be provided through closed-circuit television (CCTV) camera coverage of each sensor sector or by visual checks by personnel. With a CCTV alarm assessment system, authorized personnel can rapidly assess sensor alarms at remote locations and avoid unnecessarily sending guards or other responders to an area. The premise of this chapter is that alarm assessment will be accomplished through the use of CCTV cameras. We call this primary video alarm assessment or just assessment. Secondary assessment is the use of other cameras or resources at the site to provide additional information. This is discussed further under the section "Assessment versus Surveillance" below.

There are two purposes of assessment. The first is to determine the cause of each sensor alarm. This includes determining whether the alarm is due to an adversary or a nuisance alarm. The second purpose of assessment is to provide additional information about an intrusion that can be relayed to the response force.

This information includes specific details such as who, what, where, and how many. These two purposes roughly coincide with primary and secondary assessment, respectively.

A key principle in the design and evaluation of a PPS is that detection is not complete without assessment. This principle is based on the premise that the primary goal of a security system is to protect assets from loss or damage. As explained in some detail in Chapter 5, "Physical Protection System Design," to meet this objective effectively a facility must detect that an attack has started and delay the adversary long enough to allow an appropriate response to the attack. There is an important distinction between detection and assessment. Detection is the notification that a possible security event is occurring; assessment is the act of determining whether the event is an attack or a nuisance alarm. As described previously, exterior or interior sensors best accomplish detection. Humans are better at assessing an event. Longstanding studies have shown that humans are not good detectors, particularly over long time periods. In one study using 16 television monitors, it was shown that after 60 min human effectiveness at detecting suspicious events dropped significantly, even though operators were told to expect the events (Tickner and Poulton, 1973). Other studies have shown similar results after 30 min (Ware et al., 1964; Mackworth, 1961). Tickner and Poulton also demonstrated that human operators could successfully observe up to nine large monitors, but reduction of monitor size, distance of incident from the camera, duration of the incident, and disruptions such as telephone calls also reduced operator effectiveness (Tickner et al., 1972; Tickner and Poulton, 1973).

These results emphasize the importance of separating the act of detection from the act of assessment. Cameras are not detectors; they are imaging devices. When combined with humans or sensors, cameras can provide an immediate method to assess a scene of interest. The camera operates the same whether or not an intruder is in the scene; detection is accomplished through the use of a sensor or human monitoring. To be successful at protecting assets, it is not sufficient to provide remote CCTV monitoring of an area and expect that human operators will detect undesired or suspicious events. Based on the scientific evidence demonstrating that this approach starts to degrade after 30 min and is not reliable after 1 h, effective protection systems must incorporate some sensor technology to assist in the detection function and reduce the load placed on the human operator. Sensors detect events and do not suffer from fatigue or boredom, while humans are good at viewing an image and deciding on the appropriate response. In low-security applications, the use of humans for detection may be accepted, but the probability of their detecting an event is very low. In these systems, frequent rotation of human operators can be implemented in order to counter this effect.

Assessment Versus Surveillance

In this text, the term assessment is different than surveillance. Assessment refers to immediate image capture of a sensor detection zone at the time of an intrusion alarm. The detection zone is then also termed an assessment zone. A live or recorded image or image stream can then be reviewed to determine the cause of the alarm and initiate the proper response. The response to the alarm may be to dispatch a guard in the case of an adversary attack, to initiate an investigation, or to log the alarm as a nuisance or false alarm. The most effective systems will use CCTV to capture and record the cause of the alarm and enable immediate assessment. Surveillance, on the other hand, uses live CCTV to continually monitor activity in an area, without benefit of an intrusion sensor to direct attention to a specific event or area. Many surveillance systems also do not use human operators, but record video acquired using fixed or pan-tilt-zoom (PTZ) cameras for later review. This brings us back to primary and secondary assessment.

Primary assessment is generally provided through the use of fixed cameras; most surveillance systems use PTZ cameras. Although primary assessment cameras can provide some supplementary information, secondary assessment or surveillance PTZ cameras that have variable fields of view may provide more opportunities to gather this supporting information. A note of caution is appropriate here. While PTZ cameras provide flexibility that may allow for more information gathering, there is often limited overall night lighting that prevents recording of useful video. This is exacerbated by the fact that, by their nature, PTZ cameras are not always aimed at the area where there is activity. Additionally, many sites have areas in the camera field of view that allow an intruder to hide and avoid discovery. In this text, secondary assessment is the use of the surveillance cameras (fixed or PTZ) to obtain additional information after an alarm event has occurred. Secondary assessment might be used in a chemical or biological attack at a facility, that is, after an alarm event has occurred, a security operator using surveillance cameras observes that personnel outside are lying on the ground. This observation might alert the operator to caution the response force that gas masks or some equivalent tactic should be used when responding to the event.

The use of assessment or surveillance relates to the value of the asset and the timeliness of the response that is required. If the asset to be protected has a consequence of loss that can be tolerated, use of surveillance systems may be appropriate. However, if the consequence of loss of the asset is unacceptably high, assessment systems represent the better alternative. It is important to emphasize that the assumption throughout this text is that high-consequence losses cannot be allowed, and those assets require the use of an immediate and effective on-site response. High-consequence losses include the loss of life, damage to critical infrastructures such as telecommunications systems or utilities, and loss of control of hazardous assets. Assets that have lower consequences if lost or damaged may use surveillance systems with human review after occurrence of the event to initiate the proper response.

As an example, if a clerk in a convenience store is killed during the commission of a robbery, the CCTV surveillance system in place to monitor the store using videotape recording may collect information as to the identity of the perpetrator but did nothing to prevent the death of the employee. In this case, a high consequence (death) was realized and the system did not protect the employee. Although the surveillance tape may supply evidence to help identify, capture, and prosecute the felon, the system failed to prevent the death of the employee, resulting in a high-consequence loss.

Regardless of whether the video system is to be used for assessment or surveillance, the technical guidance in this chapter will still apply. Gill (2006) has written an excellent review of CCTV effectiveness, which summarizes the evidence both for and against the uses of CCTV and provides an extensive list of references on the subject. Readers are strongly encouraged to read this review when considering the use of CCTV for security.

Video Alarm Assessment System

The basic components of a video alarm assessment system are shown in Figure 8.1. Whether the assessment system uses analog or digital devices, the basic functions will remain the same, but may be referred to by different names or executed by software instead of hardware. The assessment system is composed of cameras at the remote sensor areas, display monitors at the local end, and various transmission, switching, and recording systems. Major components include:

- camera and lens
- lighting system

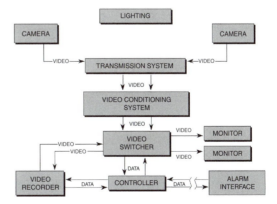

Figure 8.1 Block Diagram of Video Assessment System Components. The video assessment system uses CCTV cameras to capture images of intrusion in detection zones, then transmits it to a recording or immediate review location

- transmission system
- video switching equipment
- video recorder
- video monitor
- video controller

Kruegle (2007) and Damjanovski (2000) have written outstanding books discussing video systems and their component pieces in considerable depth.

Camera and Lens

The basic function of the camera and lens system is to convert an optical image of the physical scene into an electrical (video) signal, suitable for transmission to a remote display area. The camera and lens system is sized and located to assess a defined area.

Selection of an analog or digital camera and lens for a video assessment system must start with the determination of the degree of resolution to be required. The camera selection should also take into consideration the following desirable characteristics:

- high sensitivity to best utilize available light;
- ability to maintain an adequate picture in the presence of bright sources;
- ability to retain picture clarity at all points in the scene when motion is present;
- long life; and
- if digital, output format, bandwidth and compression compatibility with the total system.

Before describing these characteristics, some background information is required. Readers who do not require an in-depth understanding of the technical basis for performance measures used in CCTV systems can skip to the "Resolution Limited Field of View" section below for

a discussion on the application of these concepts.

Basic Television Operation

An analog television (TV) image is developed in a scanning fashion. The image is "painted" by a spot of light moving from left to right repeatedly, all the while drifting down much like the eye scanning a page while reading. Each pass of the spot of light from left to right is referred to as a scan line. When the surface area is completely surveyed, the light spot returns (retraces) to the top, repeating the process. Some lines of scan are not visible but are blanked out while the spot retraces to the top (vertical blanking). The beam also is blanked as the spot rapidly retraces from right to left, from the end of one scanning line to the start of another (horizontal blanking).

Vertical deflection of the beam is continuous, causing lines to slope slightly downward as the scan is made from left to right. As developed electronically, the lines are distinctly visible. They do not merge but actually leave dark gaps between adjacent lines. The scan line itself is not a track of uniform brightness, but is brighter at the center than at the edges. Therefore, there is a visible background pattern, a striped effect, in all television images. When this technique was first developed it was presumed that the viewer would be far enough away from the display so that the striped effect was not visible.

The interlace technique was devised to overcome this objectionable effect in televised displays. Interlace arranges the scan sequence to survey a field with one-half the scan lines initially (Field 1), then retraces (Field 2), placing the scan lines of the second field between the lines developed in the first field. Thus the brightness refresh rate is in effect doubled, sufficiently rapid to be above the critical flicker frequency of human vision. The image appears whole due to the slow decay of brightness from the phosphor. Each field contains half the available information.

One frame contains two fields (odd and even, based on line number) and there are 30 frames per second. The development of two fields to make up a whole image (frame) is referred to as 2:1 interlace. This is not the case in modern applications, so the consideration becomes more complex as the use of digital displays (LCD or plasma) is becoming more prevalent in the security world. The difference in digital displays is that the picture elements, or pixels, are generated by turning them on or off, not by a scanning beam, and therefore, are capable of displaying an image with better resolution. Additionally, both cameras and monitors have the capability to use a progressive scan that displays each line in order and not as an odd and even field, thus providing a better focus on moving objects.

In this chapter, discussions of alarm assessment equipment assume television-scanning rates in terms of the US standard. Because commercial US power is furnished at a 60-Hz rate, 60 Hz is the field rate with 525 scan lines per frame (267.5 TV lines per field) for video systems in the United States. These specifications, with the addition of color information, comprise the National Television System Committee (NTSC) standard. In the International Radio Consultative Committee (CCIR) West European system, a 50 Hz power and a 625-line frame scan are used. Many manufacturers supply both NTSC (60 Hz, 525 line) and CCIR (50 Hz, 625 line) systems as options. The PAL (Phase Alternate Line) standard was developed by Walter Bruch of Telefunken. This system has a higher resolution than the American NTSC with 625 lines, but it runs at 25 frames per second. The French television standard, Sequential Couleur A'Memorie (SECAM), uses the same resolution and frame rate as PAL but is not compatible. This system is widely used in Russia and Eastern Europe. In the future, Digital Television (DTV) and High Definition Television (HDTV) will become the new standards. In the interim, high-resolution flat screen digital displays or computer workstation monitors are being used to display the digitized video from analog cameras or directly from digital cameras.

Resolution

Resolution is the ability to see fine details in an image. It is a measure of spatial frequency or the number of pairs of alternate black and white evenly sized lines that can be seen in a given linear distance, typically expressed in line pairs per millimeter. The line pairs designation is used primarily in the field of optics, but the term appears occasionally in television literature. There is no universally used terminology either in standards or in common practice to define resolution. Since the display is in a single plane, we are concerned with the ability to produce detail vertically (up and down) and horizontally (left and right). Separate considerations apply to each dimension.

The resolution of a TV camera is commonly measured on a resolution chart where groups of equally spaced black and white lines arranged in a wedge-shaped pattern form the basis for resolution measurement. A typical resolution chart is shown in Figure 8.2. A camera is positioned so that it views the full chart with no background visible. The resolution chart is marked at various intervals along the wedge patterns with the resolution values in TV lines, typically between 200 and 1600 lines.

Since sequential scanning lines produce the analog TV image, the resolution in TV lines is often confused with the number of scanning lines that produce the image. Although the vertical resolution in TV lines is dependent upon the number of scanning lines in the raster, they have different meanings. Due to the difficulty in interpreting wedge patterns on resolution charts, they are generally not used for evaluation of vertical resolution. In practice, vertical resolution is considered to be equal to the number of unblanked scan lines. Horizontal resolution can be

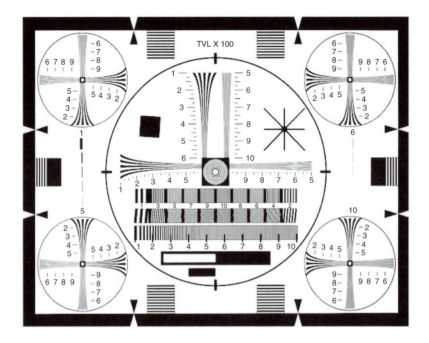

Figure 8.2 Sample Resolution Chart Used to Determine TV Camera Resolution in TV Lines. The patterns in the center of the chart are used to determine nominal camera resolution, while the patterns in the corners are useful to test monitor resolution across the entire display

measured using a resolution chart with the vertical black and white wedge patterns. The point where the converging vertical lines are just barely visible before fusing into a gray blur is defined as the limiting horizontal resolution in TV lines.

At the same time the NTSC technical specification was developed, the TV industry also adopted a viewing format with a width-to-height ratio of 4:3 (aspect ratio) and specified horizontal resolution in TV lines per picture height. Due to the aspect ratio, the horizontal field of view is greater than the vertical field of view by 33%. If the vertical and horizontal resolution were 300 TV lines each, there would be 400 pixels in the horizontal direction, but by definition the horizontal resolution would still be 300 TV lines. The horizontal resolution read from the chart is not defined by the width of the picture but by a distance equal to the picture height or three-fourths of the picture width. There are newer

imaging devices and displays that may not hold to this aspect ratio; therefore, these considerations must be adjusted for these digital devices (thermal imagers, megapixel square pixel cameras, square displays on computer workstations).

In summary, resolution is not a simple consideration. In addition to the specifications discussed above, contrast, bandwidth roll-off, use of color versus black-and-white cameras, compression of digital images, and method of measurement can also influence resolution. Specific testing for the proposed application should be performed to verify that the camera selected will provide the necessary resolution.

Resolution Limited Field of View
Now that a basic description of resolution has been presented, it is important to explain how this information is used when designing a video assessment

system. These same considerations will also be useful when integrating surveillance system components. For assessment purposes, three levels of resolution may be considered:

1. detection—the ability to detect the presence of an object in the area of interest;
2. classification—increased resolution provides sufficient information to determine what is present by class (animal, blowing debris, person);
3. identification—improved resolution sufficient to uniquely identify an object on the basis of details of appearance (Tom, not James);

These three levels of resolution are dependent on camera resolution as well as size and proximity of the object in question to the camera. For example, in a given situation it might be possible to identify a particular person, classify an object as a large dog, or detect an object the size of a small animal. Consideration of the object or target of the assessment is critical in determining camera placement and number.

In an exterior perimeter, a security system operator may need to classify a person crawling slowly through a clear zone at night. The crawler could be close to the camera or further away. This distance, combined with camera resolution, lighting, and other system performance characteristics, will determine how easily and quickly the operator can make the assessment. For exterior perimeter applications, resolution in the classification category is probably sufficient for the operator to differentiate between an adversary attack (a crawling person) or a nuisance alarm (a rabbit). At the other extreme, for some interior applications it may be desirable to identify the target. For example, in a retail application it may be necessary to identify a person suspected of shoplifting, as well as the item (perhaps a compact disc) being held. In many casinos,

CCTV systems are used to monitor players at tables or machines to discover any attempts to cheat. This may require the capability to identify the cards in a player's hand or the value of the currency being exchanged for chips. The level of resolution required in the exterior perimeter will use fewer, more widely spaced cameras than the other two cases, since there are different objectives for the video images.

This is why it is so important to consider the goal of CCTV prior to designing the video subsystem. Is the facility under attack by a stealthy adversary or trying to collect legal evidence for use in prosecution? It should be clear that understanding the threat and its tactics will play a large role in the proper selection and placement of cameras at a facility. Understanding the target to be assessed will also allow cost-effective decisions to be made using the level of resolution. If the need is for resolution to classify a stealthy adversary, a camera that meets a lower standard is sufficient. If, on the other hand, identification of a specific person is the goal, a higher-resolution camera is appropriate. Lower-resolution cameras are generally less expensive than higher-resolution cameras, so this is one method of controlling system costs.

Extensive testing at Sandia National Laboratories has shown that a minimum of 6 TV lines of horizontal resolution (8 pixels) is required to accurately classify a 1 ft target. This figure does not change with camera resolution but it does have a significant effect on camera placement and number. To be certain that a specific camera will meet the desired objective, cameras under consideration should be tested for their resolution and performance in the specific application prior to purchase. Reliance on manufacturer specifications is discouraged, because the test conditions used may not directly relate to the specific application. Application of this performance measure is discussed in more detail in the "Distance and Width Approximation" section later in the chapter.

Types of Cameras

There are a variety of camera types available including tube, solid state, intensified and thermal. Solid state cameras include low- or no-light, 3-in-1, digital, mega-pixel, and Internet Protocol addressable (IP). Each type is based on a different technology and together, along with the different models of each type, they provide a wide spectrum of solutions to specific applications, particularly when low light levels are expected. Solid state cameras use a silicon sensor pixel array in place of the older image tubes, and the pixels convert light energy (photons) into an electrical charge. The moving electrical charge across the sensor creates an electrical signal that is converted to a video image. The various types of solid state cameras can be used in a variety of applications, but caution should be used when selecting these cameras to be sure that the camera performs the intended task. The following brief descriptions provide an introduction to these cameras and associated cautions.

Low-light cameras usually have an extra amplification circuit to increase the video signal to an acceptable level. This camera attempts to minimize the signal-to-noise level during the amplification process, thereby producing a usable video signal under extremely low light conditions. It may have problems maintaining the best overall performance (video signal output) when the light levels change from extremely low to high. No-light cameras only produce a black and white image and may really be a misnomer or a marketing ploy. The camera may actually have a light emitting diode (LED) that is projecting near infrared light (covert) in front of the camera for the image sensor to pick up.

An integrating camera slows the internal clocking characteristics of the sensor imaging device to allow for more reflected light from the scene and objects in the scene to be collected (integrated) by the camera imager. This camera can produce an acceptable image under extremely low light conditions but not at the standard frame rate of 30 frames per second. If the frame rate is too slow (much less than one frame per second) there is a chance that items that are moving may not be reproduced in the picture. This would then provide inaccurate information when observing the image, which would result in an incorrect assessment.

The 3-in-1 cameras use color solid-state imaging sensors along with electronic and mechanical processes to provide a camera picture over a wide illumination range. This camera will produce a color image using multiple pixels of red, green, and blue to produce a color output during daylight hours. Eventually, when the outside light is below the color imaging illumination threshold, the camera's internal electronics switch to processing the pixels from the imaging chip to a black and white mode using every pixel, which provides a higher resolution picture. If the light level continues to decrease, the camera mechanically removes the IR cut filter used in the color mode, allowing near-IR light into the camera, thus switching operation to an IR camera. In the IR mode, the camera only receives near-IR reflected light from the scene and objects within the scene; it is not operating as a thermal camera.

A digital camera removes the digital-to-analog conversion of the imager information, which provides a better signal level than cameras that have to perform this conversion. The mega-pixel digital camera is an extension of this type of camera—the imager contains a large number of pixels to produce a very high resolution image. Many of these mega-pixel cameras transmit the digital picture using some type of compression to reduce the amount of transmitted data necessary to reproduce the image. These mega-pixel cameras usually require matched mega-pixel lenses to optimize the image quality.

Generally, IP cameras are digital in nature and have the same attributes of digital and mega-pixel cameras, but have the capability to communicate the digital information across a network (TCP/IP, Ethernet, etc.) communication system. Because the communication occurs directly on the network, other security issues that result from extending the security network infrastructure outside physical protection boundaries must be considered.

In some situations, lighting may not be adequate for the use of solid-state cameras. Some examples include dimly lit parking lots, covert surveillance activities, exterior outlying areas at large facilities, or streets. In these cases intensified cameras may be useful. These low light level cameras have a special electronics section to intensify the image by amplifying the reflected scene illumination and then pass this image to a standard CCTV sensor, where it is processed normally and sent to the monitor. They amplify the residual photon energy from sources such as stars, moonlight, or artificial lighting and illuminate an internal phosphor screen to produce an image for a standard camera sensor to process. While useful in low lighting conditions, intensified cameras are considerably more expensive than solid-state cameras, require more frequent replacement and maintenance, and, in older versions, are susceptible to loss of image if moving or bright sources of light are in the scene.

A thermal-IR camera is a night vision device that uses the difference in temperature of scene objects to produce a video image. They are passive devices that require no light and produce images based completely on the thermal signature of objects in the scene. The lower resolution and higher cost of these devices have limited their use; however, as improvements in the uncooled versions of these cameras continue, the lifecycle cost of these devices will challenge the lifecycle costs of standard cameras and its needed infrastructure.

In addition to the selection of camera technology, there is the more straightforward choice of color versus black-and-white cameras. Many system designers select color cameras because they feel that a monochrome (i.e., black-and-white) image is inferior. However, monochrome cameras have higher resolution, better signal-to-noise ratio, increased light sensitivity, and greater contrast than similarly priced color cameras. Although color imaging may provide some advantages, the human eye perceives spatial differences more clearly in gradients of black and white. In addition, some applications use a computer interface, which requires more processing time for color images and may not give significantly more information about the target. Terry (1992, 1993a,b) has published two reviews of color cameras comparing performance under controlled conditions.

Additional Considerations

Camera vulnerabilities can be created through positional errors in camera placement, mismatches in expected and actual resolution, overt or covert tampering, environmental conditions, and overall system-response time. The relationship between expected camera resolution and actual need was described above. It should be clear that if a camera is only capable of resolution sufficient for detection and the requirement is for identification, the video system would not be effective.

Covert tampering of a video signal can be accomplished by tapping into video transmission cables, inserting a recorded scene, or by switching video cables to display the wrong zone. Overt tampering modes include blinding of a camera with a bright light, covering the camera, cutting cables, or destroying the camera with a weapon. If these methods are of concern, the CCTV system should provide for tamper protection through the use of video loss detection, video authentication, and physical protection for cameras and cables. Additional methods of video tamper-proofing will be discussed Chapter 9, "Alarm Communication and Display."

Changing environmental conditions, such as the presence of rain, fog, snow, or shadows, can also introduce vulnerabilities into the video subsystem due to the loss of usable images. If these conditions are expected, contingency plans should be prepared in advance to allow for assessment during these times. The use of existing PTZ cameras positioned for secondary assessment or surveillance, or posting a guard to provide visual assessment, can be considered. Mounting the camera in an unprotected area could lead to undetected camera tampering. To detect camera tampering, the video line can be electronically supervised. Video presence detectors, which can monitor the video signal and produce an alarm if the video level increases or decreases by a preset amount, are commercially available. The video presence detector can also detect when the video sync signal amplitude has been reduced. Some inexpensive video presence detectors detect only the presence of the video sync signal. This may be helpful in detecting catastrophic camera or video line failure, but it is of little use if the camera scene is obscured, because the sync pulses would still be present even if the camera view were blocked.

Video presence detectors are usually placed at a central equipment location, such as a security control center. At this location, the video presence detector can also monitor the transmission path from the camera through any signal conditioning equipment and indicate a failure in any of this equipment.

Image Device

As previously stated, vertical resolution is primarily dependent upon the number of horizontal scanning lines. In monolithic, photosensitive-surface image tube cameras, the horizontal resolution is primarily dependent upon the bandwidth of the camera. In cameras with solid-state imagers, the horizontal resolution is determined by the number and spacing of the discrete elements in the horizontal dimension. The practical method for determining resolution is to read the resolution from the IEEE resolution chart as in previous examples. This will provide a common basis for the performance comparison among various types of cameras.

Frequently, only one resolution specification is listed in manufacturers' literature for image tube cameras. The listed specification should be assumed to be the horizontal resolution because the number of scanning lines fixes the vertical resolution. For most applications today, solid-state cameras are the preferred imaging device. Tube cameras are only used for special applications requiring high resolution or as replacements in older systems. Although tube cameras have slightly greater resolution and sensitivity, this performance degrades with tube age and a permanent image of a fixed bright scene can burn into the tube. Solid-state camera performance degrades little with age; image burn-in is not a problem; and they need relatively little maintenance. Solid-state and tube camera costs are about equal.

Solid-state cameras use a silicon array of photosensor pixels to convert the input light image into an electrical signal. Most solid-state sensors are charge-transfer devices and come in three types, based on manufacturing technology. These include the charge-coupled device (CCD), the charge-priming device (CPD), and the charge-injection device (CID). Another sensor type is the metal oxide substrate or MOS. All four types are in use, with the CID primarily used in special military and industrial applications.

Image Device Format   The image device format is related to the size of the photosensitive surface and is a measure of the diagonal of the scanned rectangular area. The most common formats for solid-state cameras are 1/2 and 1/3 in. but as silicon target densities improve, 1/4 and 1/8 in. cameras may become the standard.

Due to the increased use of silicon targets as the sensor device in cameras, it is common for cameras to be specified in terms of their horizontal and vertical pixel counts. These numbers can then be multiplied for an estimate of the total pixel area. A typical value is 200,000 pixels for a good 525-line CCTV system. For horizontal resolution in black and white cameras this is accomplished by multiplying the horizontal pixel count by 0.75. Color cameras use different algorithms and masks for producing the color content; therefore, determining the HTV lines from a color camera is not a straight forward calculation.

Lenses

After the geometry of an area to be assessed has been established, the selection of an appropriate lens system to be used with the associated camera is important. Several factors must be considered at the same time. They are interdependent variables and vary with the designer's objectives, including the manner in which the video assessment system will interface with the intrusion sensing system and the response force. In general, the main purpose of lens selection will be to cover as much of the desired area as possible with a minimal number of cameras while retaining an acceptable degree of overall resolution. The parameters that must be considered in proper lens selection include:

- lens and camera format;
- focal length and field of view;
- f-number; and
- distance and width approximations, including maximum field of view width and maximum usable zone length.

Lens Format

The lens format size defines the maximum usable image created by the lens. For optimal performance, the lens and camera formats must match, as well as whether the camera is standard or mega-pixel. Fixed focal length (FFL) lenses of one format may be used with smaller sensor formats, but never with larger sensor sizes. Use of lenses with larger camera sensor sizes will create image distortion and darkening (vignetting) at the edges of the field of view. Standard lens formats are 2/3, 1/2, 1/3 and 1/4 in. In addition to lens format, the type of iris to be used should be specified. The iris manually or automatically adjusts to optimize the amount of light reaching the camera sensor. Manual iris lenses are used when light levels are expected to be fairly consistent or the camera uses electronic shuttering; automatic iris lenses are useful when there are wide variations in the expected light, such as full daylight to lower level nighttime lighting.

Focal Length and Field of View

Focal length is the single most important factor in proper lens selection. It determines the relative magnification of the object. Since the format of a lens is known, the focal length will define the horizontal and vertical angles covered by the lens for any object distance. These coverage areas are referred to as the horizontal and vertical angular field of view.

For a desired minimum resolution, the range (length of the coverage) of a short focal length lens will be less than that of a long one, as Figure 8.4 illustrates. But once the width of the field of view spreads out to a certain distance, the low resolution past that point makes the camera and lens unusable for assessment purposes. This is called the resolution-limited field of view, also shown in Figure 8.3.

Angular fields of view can be drawn on site drawings using a conventional protractor and overlaying sheets of transparent (tracing) paper. These overlays can be located arbitrarily at various points surrounding the clear zone to obtain optimal focal length and format selection and coverage of the clear zone while

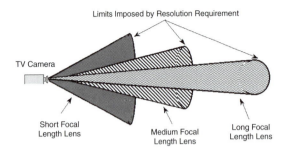

Figure 8.3 Practical Field of View Versus Focal Length of Lens. Three different fields of view are superimposed to show how the field of view gets longer and narrower as the focal length increases

using a minimal number of cameras. The following equations may be used to calculate the horizontal and vertical angular fields of view:

Horizontal angular field of view
(in degrees) $= 2 \times \text{Tan}^{-1}(W_\text{I}/2F)$

Vertical angular field of view
(in degrees) $= 0.75 \times$ (horizontal angular field of view)

where

$F =$ lens focal length (mm)
$W_\text{I} =$ width of imager active scan area (mm) and

If camera is:	2/3 in.	1/2 in.	1/3 in.	1/4 in.	1/8 in.
Then $W1 =$	8.8 mm	6.4* mm	4.8 mm	3.2 mm	1.6 mm

* Note: There are differences in imager width among manufacturers. Consult the specification for a particular camera to verify the width.

An alternate technique is to determine the geometry of the area to be assessed and analytically match a lens to it. This provides an excellent first approximation to lens requirements. This technique may result in calculated lens requirements that do not correspond to a commercially available lens with an f-number appropriate to planned lighting. Design iterations in which lens parameters, lighting requirements, camera type, camera placement, and sector geometry are varied will result in a suitable system design.

f-Number
An important lens parameter is its relative aperture (or lens speed), which is a measure of its ability to gather light. The relative aperture is expressed as the f-number. The smaller the f-number, the more light is admitted; therefore, a small f-number (1–1.8) is desirable for exterior assessment applications. For interior applications, larger f-numbers can be used. The depth of field (how much of the image is in focus) for the image is also affected by the f-number. The lower the f-number during low-light conditions, the smaller the depth of field of the scene.

Distance and Width Approximation
If standard lenses (having focal lengths of 3.5, 6.0, 12, 25, 50, 75 mm, etc.) are to be used, a fast and easy calculation can be made to determine either the width of the field of view at a given distance from the camera or the distance from the camera given a specific width. Either of these, distance or width, can be approximated as follows:

$$H_{\text{FOV}} = \frac{W_\text{I}D}{FL}$$

where

$H_{\text{FOV}} =$ horizontal field of view, in ft or m

$D =$ distance from camera (m or ft)

$FL =$ focal length (mm)

$W_\text{I} =$ imager width in mm (as shown above)

As described above, the vertical field of view can then be calculated as

$$V_{\text{FOV}} = 0.75\,(H_{\text{FOV}})$$

Although useful in this form, the horizontal field of view equation is generally manipulated into the alternative:

$$D = \frac{H_{\mathrm{FOV}}\mathrm{FL}}{W_I}$$

This representation allows calculation of distance from the camera, given the width of the assessment zone, imager width, or lens focal length. Normally, the camera distance from the beginning of the assessment zone is the unknown quantity that must be determined, in order to aid in camera placement and estimates for cable lengths and power.

As an example of distance and width approximation, a 65 ft wide area, assessed with a 8 mm format (1/2 in.) camera using a 25 mm focal length, 8 mm format lens, would have its camera placed approximately 254 ft away in order to see the entire 65 ft width. Using the formula above,

$$D = \frac{65\,\mathrm{ft}\ (25\,\mathrm{mm})}{6.4\ \mathrm{mm}} = 254\,\mathrm{ft}$$

The distance to the resolution-limited field of view width can also be determined. The resolution-limited field of

view width for assessment is based on experimental data to classify a 1 ft target. For a 600-HTV line resolution (800 pixel B/W) camera, this is located where the horizontal field of view is 100 ft wide (to give 6 HTV lines per foot or 8 pixels per foot). Using the previous example, the distance from the resolution-limited field of view to the camera would be 391 ft and is calculated by:

$$D = \frac{100\,\mathrm{ft}\ (25\,\mathrm{mm})}{6.4\,\mathrm{mm}} = 391\,\mathrm{ft}$$

Maximum Usable Zone Length

For the special case where an assessment system is being designed for perimeter use, the distance and width approximation may be used to determine the maximum zone length that may be assessed with a particular camera and lens combination. Figure 8.4 shows a typical exterior assessment zone. Note that the lower field of view (bottom of scene on TV monitor) is not normally the zone width. Likewise, the upper field of view is not normally the resolution-limited field of view width.

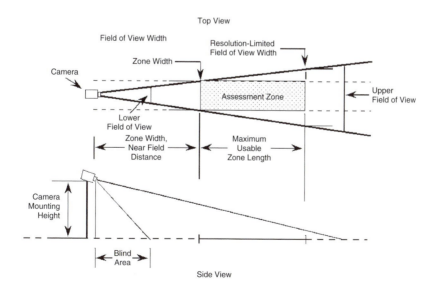

Figure 8.4 Perimeter Assessment Zone Geometry. The zone width determines the near field of view, while the resolution determines the far field

Also note that between the camera location and lower field of view, there is a blind area which cannot be seen by the camera. Determination of zone length through the use of these distance approximations will allow the designer to optimize system performance in terms of resolution while minimizing the number of cameras. It is important to note that one fixed camera per exterior assessment zone will provide the required resolution, reduce cost, and make integration of sensors and video much easier.

The maximum usable zone length is calculated based on zone width and resolution requirements at the end of the zone. It is the difference between the resolution-limited field of view distance (far field) and the zone width (near field) distance. For the previous example (65 ft wide zone width, 25 mm lens, and 1/2 in. format camera/lens), the maximum usable zone length is 137 ft ($391 - 254 = 137$). Using this technique it is easy to determine which focal length lens is best suited for a specific zone size. If the requirement were to assess a 65 ft wide, 165 ft long zone, then a 25 mm lens would not work. A longer focal length lens would be required. It is always wise to select a lens that provides adequate zone coverage and the closest camera location to the zone. Near field, far field, maximum usable zone lengths, proper lens size, and camera placement distances can all be calculated using the formulas above, by using mechanical aids such as the one sold by Cohu and other camera manufacturers and distributors, through the use of computer models or online website calculators.

Interior Assessment Zones

Camera layouts for interior assessment follow the same principles and guidelines as for exterior cameras. Due to the shorter distances generally found in interior applications, resolution sufficient for classification or identification is relatively easy to achieve. Interior cameras will still use the same resolution-limited field of view as exterior cameras, but this distance will be much closer to the camera. Interior cameras generally use lenses up to approximately 16 mm for 1/2 or 1/3 in. format cameras. Lighting levels suitable for human comfort and safety (30–100 footcandles) will be adequate for most cameras. Many interior cameras are now equipped with manual iris lenses and electronic shuttered lighting control on the image device.

Cameras mounted at the corners of a room just below the ceiling usually provide the best assessment. Corners away from entry points are preferred in order to eliminate camera tampering from someone below the camera and out of the camera's field of view. Due to the blind spot in the camera field of view, wide-angle lenses can be used to provide full wall-to-wall (90°) camera coverage. Tilted downward, the camera avoids the ceiling lights that would adversely affect the camera signal. This still allows viewing over the area and/or equipment. In typical interior applications, the assessment zone will normally contain items other than the asset being protected, which will effect the maximum usable zone length. When tall equipment is located in the room, a second camera may be required to observe the blind side. If a second camera is required, a good location may be the corner diagonally across from the first camera.

Two examples of interior camera placement will be discussed to illustrate these points. Figure 8.5 shows a simple room using one camera and one sensor. The room is typical of a small office, such as a school principal or manager's office. There is a safe that contains private information located in a corner of the room. There are various pieces of furniture located in the office including a desk, chairs, bookcases, a table, and filing cabinets. None are higher than 5 ft tall. A design using a microwave sensor and one camera is shown. Other variations are possible. Note that the camera has the sensor in

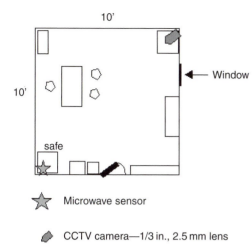

Microwave sensor

CCTV camera—1/3 in., 2.5 mm lens

Figure 8.5 Sample Camera Placement in a Small Office. The sensor is in the camera field of view and the microwave sensor detection volume covers the safe containing the assets

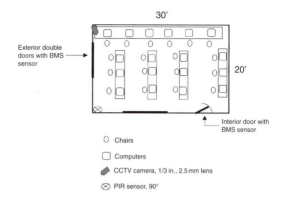

○ Chairs

▢ Computers

✎ CCTV camera, 1/3 in., 2.5 mm lens

⊗ PIR sensor, 90°

Figure 8.6 Sample Camera Placement in a Computer Classroom. The camera will view approximately half the room, including the exterior doors and the PIR sensor. The interior door is not covered very well because if it opens, the door will shield the intruder

its field of view, the safe (the asset to be protected) is covered by the detection pattern of the sensor, and the microwave sensor is placed so that the adversary will move toward or away from it to maximize performance. In addition, when microwave sensors are used, it is important to consider the door and wall materials so that nuisance alarms are eliminated. In this case, a short detection pattern would produce the best results. The window located across from the desk should be covered with fine wire mesh or other materials to eliminate interference with the sensor, as should fluorescent lights. To provide the maximum video coverage of the room, a board camera can be used, to reduce camera size and minimize the blind area under the camera.

Figure 8.6 shows a sample design in a slightly larger room such as in a library, a museum, bank, or storage area. Our example is a computer classroom. The room is 20 ft by 30 ft, has a set of double doors that exit to the outside of the building, one interior entry door, and 18 computers and related equipment on tables in the room.

Camera Mounting/Support Structures

It is highly recommended that exterior cameras be mounted on stable towers and mounts so that motion or movement in the wind is avoided. A wire-frame steel tower is unaffected by varying weather conditions and will not dry out and twist over time as do wooden poles. To compensate for the twisting action of the wood, cameras must be repositioned to maintain the proper view of the assessment area.

If east- or west-facing exterior cameras are positioned so that they look into the horizon, there may be a period of time each day when the rising or setting sun will blind the camera and allow an adversary to pass through the perimeter. Similarly, interior cameras aimed into lights will create glare or bright spots that will wash out any usable images. In addition, a camera focused under one type or level of light and operated under a different light level or with a different lens mount or format will result in poor focus. It is recommended that exterior solid-state cameras be focused with the iris fully open at dawn and dusk to get good focus through the entire depth of field. Incorrect camera placement can result in a horizontal field of view too narrow for the near field or not sufficient to see a person (or other target) at the end of the zone.

Cameras must be installed so that no light sources are in the field of view. Direct light can cause blooming of the image or allow the auto-iris lens circuitry to increase the lens aperture. Possible sources include perimeter lighting, the sky, exterior lighting, objects capable of reflecting light, and interior lighting. Viewing portions of the sky must be avoided to eliminate exterior camera blinding at dusk and dawn when the sky is considerably brighter than the ground, regardless of which direction the camera is facing. Cameras must never be angled to look above the horizon. Considerable care must be taken because camera blinding from unexpected light sources is difficult to predict prior to installation and is one of the most frequent problems later encountered. When there is a choice, north/south exterior perimeter sections should have the cameras facing north to minimize sun reflections at low sun angles. Illumination sources in the field of view may have to be reoriented and/or shielded to prevent camera blinding. A perimeter section adjacent to a roadway presents problems from vehicle headlights and taillights, even when the roadway is a considerable distance from the assessment camera.

Exterior cameras should be mounted at heights that permit them to be tilted down to view the entire assessment area. With the cameras tilted down, the horizon is not in the field of view and glare during sunrise and sunset is reduced. In addition, the chance of snow and ice getting on and sticking to the camera enclosure faceplate is reduced. A typical camera mounting height to achieve a good downward angle is 20–30 ft above the assessment area surface but below the lighting system.

Use of PTZ mounts and cameras should be avoided for assessment cameras due to timing, reliability, and operation issues. Use of PTZ cameras may introduce vulnerabilities due to the likelihood that they will be pointing in the wrong direction at the time of sensor activation and may not be able to rotate to the appropriate position fast enough to catch a fast-moving adversary, particularly over a short distance. This effect is magnified if a slow video recording system is used to help with the assessment. If the time for the PTZ and/or the recording system is not fast enough to capture one video frame at the time of the alarm and another frame a fraction of a second later, the system may not capture the adversary in time to present a useable assessment image. Can the PTZ rotate to the proper position in time to still catch an adversary penetrating a sensored location? If so, how many alarms can be processed in one second by the system? Depending on the application, fast alarm reporting and synchronization with alarm assessment equipment can make a critical difference in whether or not the operator will make an accurate assessment. An inaccurate assessment could result in dispatching the response force to a nuisance alarm or not sending the responders during an attack.

Pan/tilt camera mounts may be effectively used in surveillance or secondary assessment applications where remote control of the camera's position and pointing angles is desirable. In limited cases, this unit can provide a useful backup to assessment cameras if properly located. These mounts should not be used in place of fixed-focal-length assessment cameras that have been carefully placed to provide the maximum assessment value. Use of pan/tilt systems compromises effective, timely assessment.

Older pan/tilt mounts are rated by the maximum allowable load they can position and by the speed of rotation. Newer pan/tilt mounts can provide unlimited travel in the pan mode by the addition of electrical slip rings. Faster units cost more, and their controllability at high speeds is limited by the operator's orientation perceptions from a remote location. One major disadvantage of the pan/tilt system is the requirement for continuous operator attention while working with such a system. No other activities can be monitored by an operator while the pan/tilt unit is in motion.

Exterior cameras will require environmental housings to protect them from temperature extremes and precipitation. There are two types of enclosures to protect cameras from the elements. The first type is the integral environmental housing that forms the outer shell of the camera. It is quite rigid and sturdy and can be pressurized with dry nitrogen and equipped with thermostatically controlled integral heaters. A sunshade can be attached to overhang the lens and deflect light or precipitation from the glass faceplate. In high winds, the faceplate may not remain entirely free of precipitation, and some compromise in visual assessment can be expected.

The second option is to mount a camera inside a separate sheet metal or fiberglass housing, which permits access to the camera by a hinged or removable lid. These housings can be equipped with heaters, insulation, fans, defrosters, windshield washers, and windshield wipers. All these functions can be automatically controlled except the windshield washers and wipers. The washers and wipers must be remotely controlled from the central assessment station.

These separate housings must be large enough to contain the camera, lens, and cable connectors. Their chief advantage is the accessibility to the camera for adjustments, such as lens focusing. They cannot be pressurized, so some dirt and dust accumulation can be expected inside these housings. The windshield washers and wipers have proved to be a considerable maintenance problem, and the washers are not recommended unless very unusual environmental conditions exist. Washer reservoirs, which must be located at the camera, compel more frequent access to the camera location. The windshield wipers, if kept properly adjusted and free of ice, can maintain adequate assessment in high-precipitation situations where the nonwipered camera faceplate may have problems with assessment. Conditions at each site would determine the need for these devices after considering their added maintenance requirements.

A separate environmental housing will require additional wiring to provide the power necessary to operate the electrical equipment. A remote control system will be required for the operation of windshield wipers and washers, if used. These remote control systems can be furnished by the housing manufacturer or are available from other manufacturers, such as those providing remote control of other camera-related functions like pan/tilt mounts and zoom lenses.

Lighting System

For a given scene to be visible to a camera, it must be illuminated by natural or artificial light and must reflect a certain amount of this light into the camera lens. The function of the lighting system is to illuminate the assessment zone evenly with enough intensity for the chosen camera and lens system. Light fixtures should be mounted well above camera height. This will prevent these bright light sources from interfering with the camera's field of view.

Camera Sensitivity
The sensitivity of a CCTV camera can be defined as the minimum amount of illumination required to produce a specified output signal. The following factors are involved in producing a TV signal:

- Illuminance level of the scene
- Spectral distribution of the illumination source
- Object reflectance
- Total scene reflectance
- Camera lens aperture
- Camera lens transmittance
- Spectral response of the camera imager

- Video amplifier gain, bandwidth, and signal-to-noise ratio
- Electronic processing circuitry

Camera sensitivity is usually specified as the minimum illuminance level that will produce a full 1 V peak-to-peak video signal. The specification should state whether the indicated illuminance level is the scene illuminance or the faceplate illuminance. The illumination source is usually an incandescent lamp operating at a color temperature of 2854 K. In some cases, the parameters used to claim this sensitivity are unrealistically assumed to indicate a better performance. Two of the favored parameters are higher scene reflectances than are normally encountered and greater transmittance than is commonly available in standard auto-iris lenses with neutral-density spot filters.

Scene Illumination
The amount of light necessary to produce a usable video signal from any video camera is a function of:

- the type and brightness of the source;
- the amount of light energy illuminating the scene of interest;
- the portion of the light reflected from the scene;
- the amount of light transmitted by the lens to the imager; and
- the sensitivity of the imaging device itself.

An understanding of the relative levels of scene illumination produced by natural sources, the amount of light reflected from typical scenes, and the resultant faceplate illumination levels required by the variety of available cameras is important to the successful deployment of even the simplest CCTV system.

The percentage of light reflected from a scene (reflectance) depends on the incident light angle and on the texture and composition of the reflecting surface. For

Table 8.1 *Typical Scene Reflectances of Some Common Surfaces.*

Surface	Reflectance (%)
Empty asphalt surface	7–10
Sandy soil, wet	15–20
Grass-covered area with trees	20–25
Red brick building	30–35
Sandy soil, dry	30–35
Unpainted concrete	35–40
Smooth surface aluminum	60–65
Snow-covered field	70–75

natural illumination, the reflectance of various scenes is relatively independent of the angles of incidence and reflection. Table 8.1 lists some common surfaces and their approximate reflectances.

Parameters
The two most important parameters of a lighting system for CCTV are its minimum intensity and its evenness of illumination. The intensity must be great enough to ensure adequate performance of the chosen camera system. A minimum of 1.5 foot-candle (fc) is required for a camera system using an F1.8 or faster lens and a solid-state imager (Greenwoll, 1991). This assumes a ground-surface reflectivity of 25%. Of equal importance is the evenness of illumination, which is characterized by the light-to-dark ratio (maximum intensity to minimum intensity). An excessive light-to-dark ratio will produce unacceptable pictures in which the bright areas appear washed out and the darker areas appear black due to lack of light. A design ratio of 4:1 is preferred to allow for environmental and other degradation factors to achieve a 6:1 maximum over time.

Cameras are light-averaging devices, so when deploying them it is necessary to assure that the light level in not only the assessment area but also the entire camera field of view is illuminated evenly. As shown in Figure 8.7, light contours are distributed throughout the field of view, and the entire field of view contributes

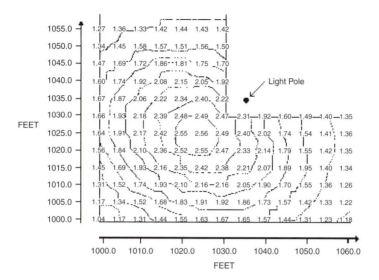

Figure 8.7 Computer Output of Light Contours in an Exterior Perimeter. The brightest and darkest spots are not necessarily located between the two fences. The areas under the light and outside the outer fence will also be in the camera field of view. These values will determine the light-to-dark ratio, not the values within the assessment zone

to the light-to-dark ratio, not just the area between the fences. Computer programs that model the expected light level from a variety of lamps are available and can be used to assist in the initial design and layout of exterior and interior lighting. These results should be validated by measuring actual light levels in an area with similar conditions as expected in the application. After implementation of the final lighting design, lighting surveys should be performed to establish a baseline light-to-dark ratio and periodically there-after, in order to establish the proper main-tenance and replacement schedule.

Types of Lighting

Light sources can be divided into two classes—natural and artificial. Natural lighting includes sunlight, moonlight, and stars. Sunlight and moonlight contain both visible light and IR radiation. In addi-tion, they are broadband sources, that is, they contain all colors and wavelengths of visible light. The spectral content of light is important when designing a video subsystem because a system using color cameras and monitors will need broadband light, while a system using black-and-white components will not. Outdoor lighting systems generally rely on sunlight during the day and add lighting for night-time operation. Occasionally, it may be necessary to supplement daylight with artificial light, such as on dark overcast days. Indoor systems can be supplemented by light coming in through windows or skylights, but generally they use some form of artificial lighting all the time.

Lighting sources include incandescent, mercury vapor, metal halide, fluorescent, and sodium vapor. Mercury vapor, metal halide, and sodium vapor sources are generally used in outdoor applications, while fluorescent and incandescent are typically used indoors. Incandescent lamps provide good color rendition, but are inefficient and have a relatively short lifetime. One interesting feature of incandescent lighting is that only a small portion of the radiation emitted is in the visible region. Most of the energy emitted is in the IR region, due to the characteristics of the tungsten filament (Illuminating Engineering Society, 1981).

Mercury vapor lamps are more efficient than incandescent and provide good color rendition. Most street lighting is mercury vapor. Metal halide lighting is similar to mercury vapor, but is more efficient and has better color rendition. Mercury vapor lamps have a rated life of 24,000 h compared to the 6000 h of metal halide lamps. Fluorescent lamps provide good color rendition, high efficiency, and long life (up to 1700 h) but cannot project light over long distances.

The most efficient forms of outdoor lighting include high- and low-pressure sodium. As the name implies, the difference between these two types is the pressure at which the sodium vapor forms and produces light (Illuminating Engineering Society, 1981). As a result of this pressure difference, low-pressure sodium lamps are more efficient, but emit almost monochromatic yellow light at approximately 589 nm, which makes them unusable with color cameras. High-pressure sodium lamps are less efficient but contain all visible frequencies (Illuminating Engineering Society, 1981), making them more effective when used with color CCTV cameras.

One additional note concerning lighting—if lighting is lost, varying times are required to restrike (reenergize) the light source. Incandescent lamps are instantaneous and fluorescent lighting is near instantaneous, depending on the time needed to create an arc in the tube (Illuminating Engineering Society, 1981). Mercury vapor lamps typically require 3–7 min, and metal halide lamps may take as long as 15 min (Illuminating Engineering Society, 1981). High-pressure sodium lamps generally restrike in less than 1 min and low-pressure sodium lamps in 7–15 min (Illuminating Engineering Society, 1981). Comprehensive reviews of lighting types and specifications are available (Illuminating Engineering Society, 1981; Kreugle, 2007; Fennelly, 1996).

In general, low-pressure sodium vapor lamps are a good choice for exterior illumination because of their energy efficiency. These lamps may become difficult to procure as time progresses, so compromises on the type of light must be made. Light fixtures should be mounted well above camera height. This will prevent these bright light sources from intruding on the camera's field of view.

In addition to lighting sources, lighting types include:

- continuous—a set of fixed luminaires that provide continuous illumination during the hours of darkness. This is the most common form of facility lighting.
- standby—similar to continuous in terms of placement, but luminaires are not continuously lighted. Instead they are activated when suspicious activity is suspected or detected by the guard force. The disadvantage to this method is that it can alert the adversary as to detection and allow for an adjustment of tactics.
- movable—this type of lighting can be stationary or portable and is used to supplement other lighting, such as manually operated searchlights.
- emergency lighting—may be used as a backup to the other types or in the event of power failures or other emergencies that may prevent the primary system from operating. This will depend on the presence of generators or batteries as alternate sources of power.

Transmission System

The overall function of a video transmission system is to connect the remote cameras to the local video monitors in such a way that no undesirable effects are introduced to the video signal. This transmission system should have a bandwidth at least that of the cameras being used in the assessment system.

Video transmission may be accomplished in a number of ways. One of the most widely used techniques for alarm assessment purposes using multiple cameras is coaxial cable transmission, which may be base-band video or video-modulated radio frequency. Fiber optics is also a good means for video transmission and is becoming more widely used. Microwave links and optical (infrared) systems are also used in some installations. IP-based cameras will use a standard network to send its information, but the network must have enough bandwidth to handle the other network traffic in addition to the video transmission loads.

Bandwidth

The transmission system bandwidth is related to the resolution of the cameras and monitors. Using the approximation of 80 lines of horizontal resolution being equivalent to 1 MHz of bandwidth (in a 525-line, 60 Hz system) and considering, for example, a camera with a specification of 600 lines of horizontal resolution, a 7.5 MHz bandwidth will be required. For maximum cost-effectiveness and optimum system performance, the bandwidth capabilities of all applicable system components should match. Monitor resolution and bandwidth capabilities are generally stated in lines of horizontal resolution, but of the two components, the camera is usually the limiting factor for optimized system bandwidth.

Line Loss

All copper/coaxial transmission lines, including video cables, will have resistive and reactive losses associated with them. With video cables, the loss is primarily a function of the distributed interconductor capacitance and core resistance. This loss is normally expressed in decibels (dB) per unit length (at various operating frequencies) or capacitance per unit length. Attenuation increases with both frequency and section length and varies widely with the particular cable type in

use. For a given distance and frequency, the cable attenuation in decibels may be determined. If cable loss is greater than about 3 dB at the uppermost system-operating frequency, some form of signal conditioning will be required to obtain satisfactory performance.

Signal Conditioning

The selection of equipment for signal conditioning is based primarily on the amount of attenuation experienced by the video signal during cable transmission and the amount of noise picked up during the transmission. This equipment includes video equalizers and hum clampers.

Video Equalizers Equalizers are used to compensate for cable attenuation at higher frequencies. An equalizer at the receiving end of the cable is commonly used in installations since many cable losses encountered are usually correctable with one equalizer at the receiving end. In addition, this location makes the necessary equalizer alignment much simpler, as the equalizer output can be adjusted while the video test signal is being monitored.

Most commercially available equalizers have an upper-frequency gain limit of about 30 dB. This corresponds to the loss experienced in about 1500 m of RG–11 cable at 10 MHz. Use of an equalizer at both ends of the cable (pre- and post-equalization) will extend the gain limit to about 60 dB.

Hum Clampers A clamper is a diode circuit used to change the DC level of a waveform without distorting the waveform. Of prime importance in the selection of a clamper is its ability to remove hum from the video input signal. Power-line induction or ground-loop currents, both of which might be eliminated with proper design, usually cause hum. A wide range of commercial hum clampers are capable of removing power line frequency hum. Isolation transformers are used to eliminate ground-loop currents.

Fiber-Optic Transmission Fiber-optic transmission does not require signal conditioning with equalizers and hum clampers. Fiber optics use an optical path rather than an electrical path for transmission. The conductor is a glass or plastic fiber rather than copper. A transmitter to convert the electrical signal to an optical signal is required at the camera end. At the display area, a receiver is required to convert the optical signal back to an electrical signal. Ground loops, induced noise, and surges from lightning, which can damage other video transmission equipment, do not occur with fiber optics (Malone, 1991).

Video Switching Equipment

Most alarm assessment systems use more cameras than display monitors. For this reason, a video switcher is used to connect the multiple video signals (cameras) with one or more monitoring devices (monitors and video recorders). The associated alarm-sensor system generally interfaces with the switching system in such a way that an alarm in any sector causes the associated camera output to be automatically displayed on a local monitor.

The simplest type of switcher connects one of a number of inputs to a single output. One input is connected at a time. Multiple output switchers can switch one or more inputs to any combination of outputs. In a fully connected switcher, any input can appear on any output, one input can go to all outputs, or different inputs can go to each output.

Switching can be either passive or active. In a passive switcher, control is by manual input. The actual switching is performed by pushbutton contacts, and the video signal is routed through the switcher with no electronic conditioning or timing. Active switchers include input and output amplifiers that provide signal isolation, impedance matching, and amplitude control. Electronic processing of the

video signal can be included to control the timing of switching between video signals. The switching path for the video signal is through relay contacts or semiconductors. In a digital-based network system the video switcher has become a data network server and the switching of video has been simplified to the transmission of digital data stored on hard drives of the network server or network video recorder.

Some widely used switching systems include:

- manual switching (passive system)
- sequential switching (all camera outputs are sequentially scanned)
- switching that is alarm activated (alarm sector camera information is automatically presented to the output regardless of the selected input before alarm activation)
- remote switching (some switching is done prior to entry of the signals into the security command center)

Switching that is computer integrated can be complex and expensive. It represents the ultimate in state-of-the-art sophistication for video assessment system control. With computer control, priority ranking of multiple alarm-sector displays, automatic recording control, sequential switching pattern control, and other features are also possible. Additional discussion of computer control and alarm priority will be presented in the next chapter.

Video Recording

The purpose of the video recording system is to produce a record of an event. In addition to providing historical information for subsequent study, it provides an aid to the real-time assessment by adding instant replay stop action to the system. The older system in use for CCTV recording is the helical scan system (videotape or VCR). This VCR system has been almost completely replaced by its modern equivalent, the digital video recorder (DVR) or the network video recorder (NVR).

Characteristics

Videocassette recorders (VCRs) provide long-term storage of large quantities of video, but mechanical components, such as recording or playback heads, gears and motors, and the video tape itself require more frequent maintenance to preserve recording capabilities than the newer DVR or NVRs.

DVRs are generally standalone units much like the VCRs. They record either analog or digital camera information and store the information on a hard disk drive. The DVR usually has a method of displaying the recording to a computer display that is directly attached to the DVR. Some units may not allow transfer of event recordings to other devices without compromising the legal use of the recording and, therefore, the unit may be confiscated by law enforcement as evidence. The quality and number of cameras that are recorded directly affects the length of time that a DVR is capable of retaining the recordings. As a result, to increase the amount of time and the number of recordings that can be made from various cameras to one DVR, most units allow for recordings to be compressed by one of many software or hardware algorithms. Depending on the amount of compression, the compressed image may not have the same quality as the original and could be challenged legally in some jurisdictions. The advantage of DVRs is that, other than the highly reliable hard drive and cooling fans of the computer system, there are no moving parts that require increased maintenance. Because many DVRs have redundant disk drive options the availability of DVRs for recording is very high.

NVRs, or network video recorders, work similarly to DVRs except they do not accept analog video signals as input. The NVR acts as a large database server for digital data streams and allows those streams to be sent anywhere they are commanded or programmed to send the information to when an alarm event occurs. NVRs have all of the advantages of a network including redundancy, system level diagnostics, and system level automatic backups of data. Because NVRs operate on the network it is very important to calculate the expected recording and display data loads on the network to be sure that the network can process these high data rate streams without causing network bandwidth problems or delaying video or alarm data transmission to their destinations.

The decision to use tape or digital recorders (DVR or NVR) depends on the requirements for using the video in the first place. These requirements include immediate assessment, legal proceedings, surveillance, or law enforcement activities. Many of these activities may be regulated by laws within a jurisdiction or by agencies concerning collection, use, and storage of the recorded video information.

Video Monitor

Both analog and digital video monitors convert an electrical signal to a visual scene on the face of the output display. For maximum picture detail, the monitors should have a bandwidth (resolution) at least that of the cameras being used in the assessment system. Monitors are similar to home television receivers in function but generally have wider bandwidths and do not have RF tuning. Low-impedance (75 ohm) or high-impedance (looping) inputs are normally provided. High-impedance looping allows a single video signal to drive multiple inputs (loads).

The use of black-and-white or color monitors is no longer strictly based on cost, because the two types are now comparably priced. Some applications might benefit from the use of color monitors, particularly indoors. For exterior applications, the cost of installation and maintenance of a lighting system that will allow for color images may be prohibitive. For example, low-pressure sodium lights will work very well with black-and-white cameras, but due to their lack of spectral content, will not produce useful color images. Use color monitors if they provide an advantage, not just because they are available. In an exterior perimeter protection system where there is a need to differentiate between a person and a small animal, only the classification level of resolution is required. Color cameras and monitors will not provide any significantly useful information at this point. If an unauthorized human causes an alarm, it can be assumed to be an attack and the response force can be deployed. At this point, additional interior cameras, which can be color, can help track the adversary. Color and black-and-white monitors may also be mixed in a video subsystem.

The corresponding maintenance issues may offset the added capability of color monitors (and cameras) when using color video. For example, questions arise as to color rendition (is the jacket black or dark blue), monitor setup, and white balance levels, due to different perceptions by human observers. Some observers may prefer more red or green, or different brightness and contrast. These individual differences can compromise the effectiveness of the video assessment system.

While aiming and focusing cameras, personnel should verify that each zone is presented approximately the same way on the monitor. Generally, the assessment zone should occupy 75% of the monitor area and be centered on the screen. A representation of this is shown in Figure 8.8. This will make alarm assessment easier by presenting a consistent view to the operator.

System Compatibility

The matching of monitor performance to other system components is an important concern since the video picture monitor

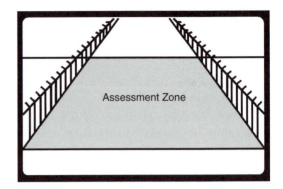

Figure 8.8 Monitor View of an Assessment Zone. Each assessment zone, interior or exterior, should be centered on the monitor and occupy approximately 75% of the monitor area

is the final output in most assessment systems. Monitors use the same dimensions for horizontal resolution as video cameras—television lines. The number of active scan lines limits the vertical resolution of both monitors and cameras. There are commonly 340 television lines for a 525-scan-line system; hence, the horizontal resolution alone may be specified. Monitor resolution is frequently expressed with a certain level of screen brightness or illuminance. Separate degrees of resolution are specified for the center (where resolution is normally highest) and corners of the screen. Monitors having 700–800 television lines of horizontal resolution are often used in 525-scan-line-rate systems operating at up to 10 MHz of horizontal system bandwidth. As more and more high-definition digital monitors are installed at facilities, matching will remain a cost and performance criterion.

An ideal monitor would be capable of displaying white, black, and an infinite number of shades in between, whereas a bistable monitor could display only white or black regardless of video input. Monitors capable of 10 discernible shades of gray or better have produced acceptable results in existing assessment systems. Terry (1992) has published an evaluation of color monitors.

Video Controller

The video controller is the main interface between the alarm sensor system and the alarm assessment system. In a digital network-based system this controller is the database controlled by the alarm sensor software and the network video recorder database that provide the same functionality as described next. The controller will automatically control the inputs and outputs of the switcher, keep track of the recorder, and display the scenes on the monitor.

The video controller consists of a microprocessor, minicomputer, or other logic interface that automatically provides control of the switcher, recorder, or any other device needing information transfer to the assessment system. With this type of system control, all alarm data, switching/recording commands, and status information can be transferred between the video system or NVR and the host system through one communication line or the digital network. This arrangement frees the host to process other data while the video controller is handling the video assessment data. In complex assessment systems, the video controller might be required to interface with time/date generators, character insertion devices, video presence detectors, environmental housing controls, and any other part of the assessment system requiring current information. Several large matrix-switching controllers are available that include some of these capabilities. In a digital network video based system many of these functions are located at each camera. The camera then synchronizes with the information database from the network video server or the alarm sensor software that contains the time and date; character insertion information; network node failures for determining offline cameras; and supports the ability to remotely reprogram the network addressable cameras.

Additional Design Considerations

The video assessment system should be designed as a component of the total intrusion detection system. Many interactions between the video system, intrusion sensors, and display system should be considered during conceptual design. Examples include:

- site/sector layout—layout of sensors so that assessment is possible at a reasonable cost;
- video/sensor interference—design of the assessment system so as not to contribute to the cause of sensor nuisance alarms;
- monitor location—location of video monitors in the display system; and
- construction—common construction and installation requirements, techniques, and locations.

Site/Sector Layout

One requirement of a perimeter assessment system is to display as much as possible of the clear zone including both the inner and outer fences. Camera/lens selection and positioning must ensure detection and classification of any visible cause of fence and sensor alarms in the clear zone at any time. For these reasons, it is important that the following criteria be observed: (1) the inner/outer fence spacing should be relatively uniform; (2) minimum width restrictions for the clear zone should be considered; (3) grading or removal of vegetation of the clear zone should be performed; and (4) adequate area illumination must be provided. Deviations from these criteria will generally reduce system efficiency and increase overall system cost by increasing the camera and equipment specifications to achieve an acceptable level of system effectiveness. As noted previously, each exterior assessment zone should use one fixed camera per zone to provide the assessment capability.

The effect of using more than one camera to assess a single alarm on interior locations should be considered. At smaller or lower-threat facilities, with only a few cameras or with particular video-coverage requirements, multiple cameras per alarm may provide acceptable assessment without an undue duplication of display and recording equipment. Large systems will tend to be simpler if each alarm is assessed by only one camera since decisions regarding which cameras are to be switched will be simpler and the operator will be able to concentrate on a limited selection of live and recorded video for review.

Video and Sensor Interference

Typical exterior systems require installation of camera towers near the area where sensors are installed. Tower height and location must be chosen so that pole vibration caused by wind does not create a source of seismic energy sufficient to cause buried sensor cables to generate an alarm. In addition, camera towers should be placed to prevent their use by an adversary in crossing the perimeter or isolation zone. Power, video, sync, and control lines must be placed where noise cannot be induced between video cables and sensor cables.

Monitor Location

Video monitors should be installed in the system control console in a location that allows effective, rapid assessment without interference from other system controls and outputs. Additional details regarding this aspect of system integration will be addressed in the next chapter.

Construction

Installing signal and power-distribution cables and modifying buildings for equipment installation will be common for many parts of an intrusion detection system. Decreased construction costs and more effective system design will result from combining sensor subsystem and assessment subsystem requirements, such as conduit and junction box installation. Room for system expansion should

be included within these construction elements.

Alarm Assessment by Response Force

Video alarm assessment can be complemented by visual checks from guards. There are situations in which alarm assessment will be performed by the guard force. If the video assessment system is not operable (due to maintenance or weather) or if video assessment is not available for a particular situation (for use within some classified facilities), the guard force must be able to assess the alarm.

Regardless of whether alarms are assessed using video or guards, the alarm must be assessed quickly after it is reported to be most effective. For those facilities that use towers, guards in towers can provide effective assessment if the number, design, and placement of the towers are adequate to provide complete visual coverage of the perimeter. Patrols or roving guards who are sent to investigate an alarm can provide effective assessment only if they are able to respond in a timely manner (i.e., before the intruder or nuisance source disappears) and there is still ample delay in the system. System design to enable effective alarm assessment will be discussed in more detail in the next chapter.

Integration with Safety Systems

Today it is a common practice to add many CCTV cameras to a facility to help in determining the presence of a safety critical event. While these measures may reduce labor costs, there may also be a decrease in security system effectiveness. In large or complex facilities, it may be better to separate these functions so that the security force will not be distracted by safety events that may mask a malevolent attack on the facility. In simple facilities with low-level threats, co-location of these functions may be acceptable, but this may still compromise security system effectiveness during an attack.

Legal Issues

Proper attention to the right to privacy is a major consideration when using CCTV systems. It is generally inappropriate to locate cameras in locker rooms, bathrooms, or other places where employees or visitors have a reasonable expectation of privacy. Use of hidden or covert cameras is legal under many circumstances, but to be certain, consultation with an attorney is recommended to be sure that legal authority exists for this use. It is also a liability to indulge in the use of dummy cameras at a facility. This establishes an expectation of protection, which can create a liability if a person is under attack and believes that the attack has been noted and help is on the way. It is an accepted legal practice to post signs informing people that an area is under video monitoring or surveillance. These signs are often placed at facility entry points to minimize the number of signs and to alert visitors and site personnel of the presence of CCTV. The use of recorded video information must meet certain standards to be admissible as legal evidence. Depending on the jurisdiction, the following may be required: minimum quality of image, time/date stamp, percent of scene occupied by the subject, and the presence of an eyewitness. In addition, in many states the presence of a unique scene identifier is also required. This identifier serves to conclusively establish where the image was recorded. For example, it is necessary to differentiate one office or hallway from another. Electronic images are now using digital watermarks to assure image integrity and eliminate tampering, but they have achieved varying levels of legal acceptance in some states. To be certain that recorded images will meet legal requirements, consultation with an attorney or law enforcement agency in the jurisdiction is recommended.

Camera Selection Procedures

Camera selection should be based primarily on the sensitivity required for a full video output signal in the lighting environment in the area to be assessed. The sensitivity must match the lighting design goals, regardless of the imager. The resolution of the imager is next in importance because it will determine the number of cameras required for a given straight-line perimeter selection. The greater the resolution, the greater the spacing between the cameras can be. The object resolution required should be determined before camera selection, but in practice, the desired object resolution may be slightly modified when camera choices are limited.

Camera format is an important consideration in the camera selection process. The format size determines the sensitivity of the image tube, with smaller formats having reduced sensitivity as well as lower resolution. The tradeoff in this situation is price, but the cost of the camera is only part of the total system cost. Format size also affects the field of view, which dictates the number of lenses available in a variety of focal lengths. The requirements of special design lenses for nonstandard focal lengths should be extensively evaluated before committing to such action.

During the selection process, evaluation of cameras should be undertaken under the real lighting environment expected at the site. In many cases, the experience of other facilities can help to reduce the number of options considered. Manufacturers' literature should not be the sole criteria in camera selection. The specifications, or the conditions under which specifications are developed, may be unrealistic in relation to the design problem at hand.

Other considerations in the selection process include the difficulty of maintenance, packaging of the camera for the environment in which it will be used, maintenance support from the manufacturer, and documentation supporting the equipment. Documentation should include operating, adjustment, and maintenance procedures; theory of operation; block diagrams; schematics; and manufacturer and commercial replacement parts lists. Serious consideration should be given to eliminating any manufacturers' product that does not include this documentation.

Acceptance Testing

A video assessment subsystem requires a conscientious approach to installation and maintenance in order to assure maximum performance. An incoming inspection should be made of any cameras purchased for evaluation or for final system installation. Obviously, different parameters will be evaluated for the two situations. Evaluation cameras will be compared to other cameras purchased for the same purpose. Upon receiving cameras for final installation, camera performance should be evaluated to determine conformity with the manufacturers' specifications, compatibility with the design criteria, and consistent performance from camera to camera. Experience has shown that final inspection at the manufacturers' plant is not consistent, and performance may deviate considerably from the specifications. Frequently equipment has been damaged or had parts shaken loose in transit. We recommend operating the equipment continuously for a few hundred hours before final installation (equipment burn-in), which decreases maintenance problems during the installation phase of perimeter construction. Any problems discovered at this point should be referred to the manufacturer for resolution while still under warranty.

Exterior cameras should be installed according to manufacturer specifications and focused at night under the same type of lighting expected in normal operation. If possible, cameras should be evaluated for their resolution capabilities prior to purchase. One simple method of checking for camera resolution is to use appropriately sized targets in the assessment zones and verify that they can be classified. For example, at Sandia we use a set of targets shaped as a 1 ft diameter circle, a 1 ft square, and a 1 ft high triangle. The targets are painted black on one side and white on the other. By placing the targets at the far field of an exterior perimeter assessment zone and having an operator view the image and recognize (classify) each of the distinct shapes, we can rapidly determine if the system resolution is adequate. The targets can also be moved to bright and dark lighting areas to verify that the images are still identifiable using the appropriately colored side of the target—black for dark spots, white for bright spots. The size of the target can be varied depending on the expected threat at a facility, and resolution charts can be used to determine resolution in interior or exterior assessment zones. One-foot targets simulate the cross-section of a crawling person; larger or smaller targets may be more useful at other facilities, based on the threat. Additional aids in determining resolution include the use of a large resolution chart in the assessment zone or the use of some test targets made by others, such as the Rotakin. The United Kingdom employs a Rotakin test target to evaluate performance of CCTV systems. It was developed in 1989 and is included in the CENELEC (European Standards Committee) CCTV Application Guidelines Standard EN 50132-7. The test target can be used to establish system performance (image quality/resolution), appropriate fields of view, performance of temporal compression-based systems and camera shuttering, and recording rates. The Rotakin is usually employed on a stand giving a total height of 1.8 m, but may also be leaned against a fence or building or laid on the ground to simulate human attack tactics. Due to the lack of accepted resolution standards or requirements for private security system integrators, the system designer or security manager should determine what resolution is needed and specify this when placing contracts or buying equipment.

Camera performance can also be verified in a laboratory using a test bench. This will allow measurements of resolution, focus, and sensitivity and can be a more cost-effective approach to some performance testing. The initial verification of camera performance using a test bench is not sufficient to assure acceptable performance in a protection system. Some CCTV cameras are shipped prefocused; however, the environment that these cameras are focused in may not be the same as the operating environment at a facility. Initial testing and verification should be followed up with appropriate indoor or outdoor testing to confirm that cameras will perform as required. Final adjustments to camera focus, sensitivity, depth of field, and field of view to account for actual lighting or other environmental conditions can be performed at this time.

Exterior lighting surveys should be performed using high-quality light meters and a grid pattern, for example, at 3 ft intervals, 1 ft above the ground. An initial survey should be conducted at lighting installation, and then conducted yearly thereafter. A preventive maintenance schedule for light replacement should also be prepared. Depending on the size of the facility and the available budget, all lamps can be replaced at the same time or lamps can be replaced as they fail. In many cases, lamp replacement in exterior areas will require the use of a bucket truck or similar equipment. If the equipment is permanently available at the site, there will be greater latitude in the maintenance schedule than if the equipment must be rented. This equipment can also be used in the replacement or maintenance of exterior

cameras as well. Over a period of time, enough data can be collected to establish a routine replacement cycle for lamps. In addition, consideration of lighting initiation is important. A variety of approaches exist, such as using one photosensor to activate all lights; one photosensor per light, per side, or per sector; or manual activation.

Interior lighting should also be evaluated on a continuing basis but will not require as substantial an effort as exterior assessment areas. Specifications exist for the amount of light that should be present to enable various tasks, such as reading, inspections, or general office work (Illuminating Engineering Society, 1981). In most indoor applications, the lighting provided to illuminate the work being performed is also adequate for CCTV cameras, but this should still be verified. Particular attention should be paid to the movement of furniture or other objects in internal assessment areas to eliminate shadows or blind spots.

As noted earlier, the speed of the video subsystem should also be tested to be sure that alarm sensing and video capture happen rapidly enough to capture the actual intrusion event. Performance tests on the number of alarms that can be captured and reported within 1 s, camera switching times, and recording times can also help determine if the system is still performing as expected. In addition to performance tests on the video subsystem and its components, use of acceptance tests for any video subsystem provided by a vendor or systems integrator is strongly encouraged. These tests should address adequacy of resolution under actual operating environments, speed of recording, number of alarms that can be acquired and stored for review in 1 s, and related details, such as light-to-dark ratio. The desired specifications and statement of acceptance testing should be included in the terms and conditions of contracts with vendors.

With incoming inspection and equipment burn-in prior to installation, maintenance problems should be minimized for the short term. Camera adjustment will likely consume most of the maintenance time. Optical focus of the camera lens has consistently been a major time-consuming factor during initial installation. The day-to-night illumination levels and energy spectrum changes are responsible for most of these problems. Optical focus is more reliable if accomplished at night under the appropriate scene lighting from the final camera location. Cameras in sealed environmental housings typically pose a serious restriction to this procedure, and many attempts have been made to circumvent or substitute this procedure with others. Awareness of these conditions should reduce problems.

Maintenance problems are best resolved by a competent on-site staff capable of understanding the complexities and interrelationships of all the concepts used in the original system design as well as having a background in electronic systems troubleshooting. Specific, periodic maintenance requirements should come from the equipment manufacturer in the form of printed documentation. Also, it is useful to have a specification for nuisance alarm rates, as this will allow some number of nuisance alarms to occur without penalty. The value of occasional nuisance alarms is that they maintain confidence that the system is working. An example of a nuisance alarm specification might be one nuisance alarm per zone per day. The number should be small enough to allow continuing operation under expected varying conditions, but not so high that a vulnerability is created. This can occur if the allowable number is set too high, or by having so many nuisance alarms that the guard force is tempted to ignore the alarm over time. Any recurring nuisance or false alarms should be investigated for possible system improvement. As with any security equipment maintenance performed by outside personnel, all equipment should be checked after the maintenance activity

to assure that systems are fully operational and unmodified.

Equipment logs should be kept that detail replacement or repair of various system components and appropriate spares should be kept on hand. Depending on the budget and site size, 10–20% of each component (cameras, monitors, lamps, VCRs, etc.) spares are recommended, especially for cameras. If cameras are replaced by newer models or different types, they should be tested for compatibility and performance and appropriate notes made in the maintenance log. There should also be contingency plans explaining what will be done if CCTV capability is lost for varying periods of time or at one or more locations. These may include assigning a guard to the location until the system is repaired or deploying portable systems.

Manufacturers' equipment documentation should be preserved at the site as well as at a central document storage location. Any equipment modifications made on-site should also be documented and stored at these two locations. A maintenance log of all camera repairs and adjustments should be kept to provide a historical record of each piece of equipment. Maintenance trends can be established to identify recurring problems and equipment failures. This practice will substantially reduce repair time and identify any equipment performing in a substandard manner.

Summary

This chapter describes assessment of alarms through the use of a video subsystem. Assessment and surveillance differ, with the major difference being that an assessment system associates immediate image capture with a sensor alarm to determine the response. Surveillance systems are those that collect video information without associated sensors.

In addition, the relationship between detection and assessment is explained in some detail. Because it is a basic security principle that detection is not complete without assessment, assessment of sensor alarms is required to complete the detection function. Assessment may be accomplished by dispatching guards to an alarm location or through the use of CCTV cameras. The preferred approach is to use cameras, particularly in those instances when an immediate response is required. Cameras provide a faster method of assessing alarms and thus allow a faster response to any malevolent attacks.

A video alarm assessment system consists of cameras at assessment areas, display monitors at the local end, and various transmission, switching, and recording systems. The major components include: (1) camera and lens to convert an optical image of the physical scene into an electrical signal; (2) lighting system to illuminate the alarm location evenly with enough intensity for the camera and lens; (3) transmission system to connect the remote cameras to the local video monitors; (4) video switching equipment to connect video signals from multiple cameras to monitors and video recorders; (5) video recording system to produce a record of an event; (6) video monitors to convert an electrical signal to a visual scene; and (7) a video controller to interface between the alarm sensor system and the alarm assessment system.

The determination and use of resolution is described in some detail, and the relationship of resolution to camera placement is also explained. Application of resolution is explained through the use of three levels—detection (presence of an object), classification of the object (person versus rabbit), and identification of the object (Joe, not Frank). Based on tests conducted at Sandia National Laboratories, a resolution of 6 lines per foot is suggested in order to classify a crawling human target. The level of resolution required depends on the expected threat, their tactics, the target asset that is to be protected, and the way the video

information will be used. Alarm assessment system performance must support protection system objectives. Where an immediate on-site response is needed to protect high-consequence targets, the system resolution and timing must be sufficient to enable a timely response, while the delayed response associated with lower-consequence loss assets can tolerate some reduction in system performance. An immediate on-site response may be necessary to protect high-consequence targets, while delayed responses can suffice for lower-consequence targets.

The alarm assessment subsystem must be designed as a component of the intrusion detection system. Interactions between the video system, intrusion sensors, and display system must be considered.

Security Principles

Detection is not complete without assessment.

Humans make poor detectors but are good at assessment.

For an effective on-site response, the time between an alarm and assessment must be short.

Resolution of CCTV cameras falls into one of three classes—recognition, classification, or identification. The appropriate category will establish the resolution required for the assessment system.

Speed of the video assessment subsystem must allow for the capture of images in time to acquire the cause of the alarm in order to make an accurate assessment.

References

Damjanovski, V. *CCTV*, 3rd ed. Boston: Butterworth-Heinemann, 2000, 7–153.

Fennelly, L.J. *Handbook of Loss Prevention and Crime Prevention*, 3rd ed. Boston: Butterworth-Heinemann, 1996, 253–267.

Greenwoll, D.A. An evaluation of intensified solid-state video cameras. SAND90-2566 1991;1–60.

Gill, M. "CCTV: Is it effective?," in Gill, M., ed., *The Handbook of Security*. New York: Palgrave Macmillan, 2006, 438–461.

Illuminating Engineering Society of North America (IES). *IES Lighting Handbook*, Reference Volume. New York: IES of North America, 1981, 8.2–8.55.

Kruegle, H. *CCTV Surveillance: Analog and Digital Video Practices and Technology.* Burlington: Elsevier Butterworth-Heinemann, 2007, 47–69.

Malone, T.P. An evaluation of fiber optic closed circuit television transmission systems for security applications. SAND90-2556 UC-515 1991;1–24.

Mackworth, N.H. "Researches on the measurement of human performance," in Sinaiko, H.W., ed., *Selected Papers on Human Factors in the Design and Use of Control Systems.* New York: Dover, 1961, 174–331.

Terry, P.L. A laboratory evaluation of color video monitors. SAND93-0051 1993a;1–24.

Terry, P.L. Initial laboratory evaluation of color video cameras. SAND91-2579 1992;1–30.

Terry, P.L. Initial laboratory evaluation of color video cameras (phase two). SAND91-2579/2 1993b;1–51.

Tickner, A.H., Simmonds, D.C.V., et al. "Monitoring 16 television screens showing little movement." *Ergonomics* 1972;15(3):279–291.

Tickner, A.H., and Poulton, E.C. "Monitoring up to 16 synthetic television pictures showing a great deal of movement." *Ergonomics* 1973;16(4): 381–401.

Ware, J.R., Baker, R.A., and Sheldon, R.W. "Effect of increasing signal load on detection performance in a vigilance task." *Perceptual and Motor Skills* 1964;18:105–106.

Questions

1. Discuss the following application considerations:

   - 100% of the detection area should be assessed.
   - A single camera should be used for one sector.
   - Coaxial video cable and power cables should be located separately.
   - A pan/tilt/zoom camera system should not be used when immediate on-site assessment is required.
   - The camera view should be free of any blockage, such as fence lines, to assess an exterior perimeter sector.
   - Cameras and lights should be left on, even when there is no alarm.

2. Compare video alarm assessment and video surveillance. What are the strengths and weaknesses of these methods?

3. How could the placement of video equipment (poles, cables, camera housings) disturb intrusion sensors?

4. Why do we say detection is not complete until after the alarm has been assessed?

5. How could an intruder avoid being assessed in a system? How could this be minimized, and how much more would it cost?

6. How could assessment time be reduced?

7. Using the formulas provided in the text, calculate the maximum usable assessment zone for 1/2 in. format camera with 600 lines of horizontal resolution and a 20 ft assessment zone width using the specified lenses:

Lens	6 mm	12 mm	25 mm	50 mm
Near field distance				
Far field distance				
Maximum usable zone				

If you knew that the sensor detection volume was 300 ft long, which lens would be best? Why? Is there a better standard lens size available that could be used? Why or why not?

8. Using Figure 8.6, the computer room, propose a new design using two cameras and two different sensors.

9

Alarm Communication and Display

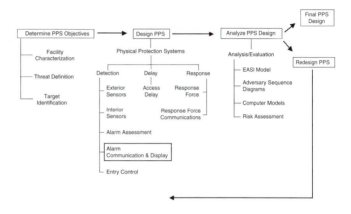

Alarm communication and display (AC&D) is that part of a PPS that transports alarm and assessment information to a central point and presents the information to a human operator. New developments in electronics, computer, and network technology have changed the design of alarm communication and display systems over time. It is now possible to quickly collect and process a wide variety of information; the challenge is to effectively present this information in order to enable decisions about what actions are needed. Equipment and techniques that are available for reporting alarms to an operator are described in this chapter. Because many AC&D systems also integrate the functions of intrusion detection systems and entry control, some information is also provided for use when considering these functions.

As AC&D systems become more network-based, the complexity of designing, procuring, operating, and maintaining them will also increase. As a result, this chapter is only a brief overview of the elements that comprise an effective AC&D system. The speed of technology development far outpaces the revision cycle of books like this one, which is one reason why this chapter only describes the system at a high level. Another reason is that, to be truly thorough, another whole book could be written, and that is not our goal. To help address the complexities of network-based AC&D system characterization, a survey tool that begins to characterize the security aspects of an enterprise network is provided in Appendix B.

The two critical elements of an AC&D system are:

1. the transportation or communication of data
2. the presentation or display of that data to a human operator in a meaningful manner

Evolution of Alarm Reporting Systems

In general, security alarm systems use simple contact closures, such as magnetic switches mounted on doors, to detect an intrusion. Early systems communicated this information using annunciator panels, which had a set of colored lights for each sensor to indicate the alarm status in security zones. Typically, red lights were used to signal sensor detection, yellow to indicate the zone was in access (alarms disabled), and green to show the secure operational state. On an alarm, the operator would manually correlate the alarm to a specific area, then switch the appropriate camera (if present) to a monitor, and determine the proper response. If no CCTV cameras were available, a guard was dispatched to the area to investigate the cause of the alarm. This system, though time consuming, did have some advantages: the simple electrical components were well understood; there was a direct correlation between the lights and a specific sensor; and the system was easy to maintain.

Annunciator panels also have several limitations. Cost can be very high because separate circuitry is used for each zone; a large amount of physical space may be needed for a panel that monitors a large number of zones; and the indicator lights can display only a limited amount of information.

As more sophisticated technology became affordable, alarm communication systems were developed to transmit multiple alarm signals simultaneously, incorporate computer control, and add video capability through CCTV integration. Each of these subsystems offered improvements, but when installed as independent units created a system that was difficult to operate and learn to use. They also put a heavy load on human operators in crisis situations. Modern systems integrate technology components into a coordinated and effective system. When combined with appropriate procedures, and trained people, these systems represent the best method to collect, assess, and respond to security events at a facility.

AC&D Attributes

The most useful AC&D systems have specific characteristics. Systems must be designed to withstand the environments in which they are placed. If a component will experience wide temperature variations, such as in an exterior environment, the equipment must be designed to withstand those variations without failing. Robustness and availability are measures of system performance in all probable environments.

AC&D components and systems should be designed to last a long time. The individual components should be reliable and have a long mean time between failure (MTBF). A reliable system requires less maintenance and is more trusted by operators. Other aspects of reliability include reliable communication and display of alarm data, and no loss of information. No communications system has 100% guaranteed information delivery; however, modern communications equipment can approach that goal by implementing techniques for checking and verifying data and reporting disabled communication links.

Electronic components will eventually fail. Good AC&D systems take this chance of failure into account and provide redundant or backup capability for critical components. By maximizing the robustness, reliability, and redundancy of AC&D systems, the time the system is inoperable or down for repair can be minimized, thereby maximizing its availability.

Alarm information must be available to security personnel in a timely manner. The AC&D system speed should be a small fraction of the overall alarm assessment and response force time. These times will vary from site to site, but AC&D speed should be a negligible factor in calculating response or assessment times.

The AC&D system is a major component in the overall PPS. Because the PPS protects the site's critical assets, it follows that the AC&D system must also be secure from attacks by adversaries. For example, procedures should limit who has access to AC&D displays and the system configuration, and only authorized persons should have access to AC&D information, components, and wiring. As part of this protection, the alarm communication infrastructure should also be secured from access by attackers.

AC&D systems must be easy for an operator to use. While a multitude of sensors can provide considerable data, this data must be displayed in a fashion that presents the essential information to the operator. In addition, the user must not be overwhelmed with data, interaction with the system must be efficient, and users must be able to perform necessary operations quickly and easily. A system that is easy to use also reduces the amount of training and retraining needed.

Each of these general characteristics plays a part in the overall effectiveness of an AC&D system, but the single most important measure of AC&D effectiveness is how well it quickly and clearly communicates alarm data from sensors to the system operator. When an alarm event occurs, the AC&D system must communicate to the operator the following information:

- where an alarm has occurred;
- what or who caused the alarm (assessment data); and
- when the alarm happened.

The operator should also know how to respond. This can be accomplished through training and AC&D system prompts. Moreover, all AC&D activity must occur in a timely fashion, so AC&D system speed is a measure of its effectiveness.

The difficulty with this effectiveness measure is its relationship to the response time of a human operator. Measuring operator response is a very difficult process. Electronic communications systems, on the other hand, are quantifiable. This dual character of AC&D systems makes measuring system effectiveness more complex. Communications systems can be understood, network topologies modeled, and system times measured. When people are involved, however, softer sciences such as ergonomics, human factors engineering, and physiology studies are also needed.

The AC&D system is divided into several subsystems: communications, line supervision and security, information handling, control and display, assessment, and offline subsystems. These are discussed in detail below.

Alarm Communication Subsystem

The communications subsystem transfers data from one physical location to another. Specifically, an AC&D communications subsystem moves data from the collection point (sensors) to a central repository (display). If the central repository consists of multiple computers or displays, then the communication subsystem may also move data throughout the repository.

The basic concepts of AC&D communications incorporate a design model, detailed system functions and how they relate to the other AC&D requirements, size of the system and the topologies used, and the combination (in hierarchies) of simple system configurations. Alarm communication systems have several characteristics that drive the design. These characteristics include the quantity of alarm data, need for high reliability, and speed at which data must be delivered. The following discussion details each of these system characteristics and describes the role of these characteristics in system design.

If a sensor activates, the alarm communications system must assure that accurate data pertaining to this activation is received by the AC&D computers. Assured message delivery means the communication system must be reliable. In addition, alarm data must be transmitted in a timely manner. Both human-factor considerations and interactions between the AC&D and assessment systems drive alarm-reporting speeds.

Human factors require alarms to be reported with no perceptible delay. For a human operator, no perceptible delay is a few tenths of a second. Interactions between the AC&D and the assessment system require reporting times to be a small fraction of the total assessment time. Although total assessment times can vary widely, AC&D and assessment system interaction should only take milliseconds. Such reporting speeds require fast alarm communications since communications times are only a part of the total alarm reporting time.

Other factors are also important when designing an effective alarm communication system. Physical media must have sufficient bandwidth to handle the communications for the system when operating at full capacity. Communication protocols, which are the special set of rules for communication, are important considerations in a system design. System speed dictates the types of protocols used in the system and protocol overhead must be appropriate for the types of data being transmitted. In addition, channel bandwidth and protocol overhead must be balanced to provide the required system speed.

The best possible communications system would provide instant communications with 100% first-time message transmission reliability. In reality, it is not possible to meet this standard. Moreover, high-speed, high-reliability (redundant) systems are expensive. A good communications subsystem design balances the cost of the system with its performance. Depending on the design, a range of protocols can be used to balance speed, reliability, and cost.

To ensure that messages reach the operators in the highest security or most complex systems, redundant hardware is required to handle cases of hardware failure, and the system must be able to automatically route messages through the redundant hardware as required. In addition, the protocols used should detect and correct message errors and duplicate messages. The Open Source Interconnection (OSI) Reference Model describes one way to think about communications systems by dividing system functionality into seven groups known as layers. From lowest to highest, these layers are physical, link, network, transport, session, presentation, and application. For AC&D systems, interest focuses on those OSI layers that provide robustness, redundancy, and speed. The layers of interest are those at the lowest level—the physical, link, and network layers. These layers are described in Table 9.1.

Table 9.1 *OSI Model Layers as Applied to AC&D Systems.*

Physical Layer	The physical layer provides mechanical, electrical, functional, and procedural methods used to transmit information from one place to another. It deals with the media (wire, fiber, etc.) and functional topology (star, bus, point-to-point) characteristics of a communications channel
Link Layer	The data link layer provides protocol delimiters and framing information. This layer also performs basic error-checking
Network Layer	The network layer provides addressing, sequencing, flow-control, receipt/ acknowledgment, and error-handling services. The network layer takes higher-level data and packages it for transmission

Physical Layer

The physical layer describes the electrical and mechanical aspects of a communications channel. It also describes the functional and procedural methods used by a channel. It includes the type of communication media, such as wire or fiber cables, network architectures, such as loops, stars, or buses, and low-level protocols such as EIA-422 (Electronic Industries Association) or direct current line supervision.

Communication media types relate to the physical characteristics of materials used to build a link. Common media types used to move data from one physical spot to another are twisted-pair copper wire, broadband copper wire, fiber-optic cable, and RF communications links.

Twisted-pair copper cable is the most common media type in use today. This cable supports many different electrical protocols and is easy to install and maintain. Its long history of use in telephone circuits makes twisted pair almost ubiquitous. Twisted-pair cables provide two wires (a pair) for a communications link. Twisted pair's weakness is its susceptibility to electromagnetic interference. Lightning, power surges, and common mode signals are all easily coupled into a twisted-pair link. Twisted pair also has distance and bandwidth limitations. High bandwidth signals can be transmitted reliably over only relatively short distances. Therefore, twisted-pair cables are best used for paths of less than 0.6 miles in length.

Broadband cables are similar to twisted pair. Both cable types use copper wire, and the cable provides two conductors to implement the communications link. The difference is in the physical layout of the cables. Broadband cables take advantage of the special electrical characteristics of various wire configurations to improve the cable parameters, thereby increasing distance. Some twisted-pair cable can be broadband if the number of twists in the wire is constant over the entire length of the cable.

The most common broadband cables are coaxial cables. Coaxial cables are typically used to transmit video or high-speed network data. As with twisted pair cable, coaxial cable is susceptible to electromagnetic interference sources such as power surges and lightning and can support many different types of electrical protocols. Coaxial cable, because of its special physical configuration, is more expensive than twisted-pair cable. Broadband cables are best used for paths of fewer than 1.2 miles in length.

Fiber-optic cables use glass or plastic fibers to transmit data using light. Fiber cables are a very high-bandwidth media. Properly installed, fiber is robust and reliable. Other advantages of fiber include its immunity to electromagnetic interference of all types and its long transmission distance characteristics. Multimode fiber can operate over distances of 1.2 miles or more. Special single-mode fibers can extend that distance as much as 12 miles.

Fiber is more expensive and more difficult to connect than copper wire cables. Special tools and training are required to properly connect fiber systems. Because fiber cable does not use electricity, it is not well suited for slow or low bandwidth signals. In addition, fiber is excellent for transmitting fast digital data, but it is not well suited for analog signals.

RF (radio frequency) links use radio transmitters and receivers to send data. The media is actually the electromagnetic signal that passes between a transmitter and receiver. RF links are not typically used in AC&D communications because of their poor security characteristics.

Network Architecture

Network architectures describe how components of a system are interconnected. The most cost-effective method of connection for a given installation often depends on the layout of the sensors. These connections, or wiring configurations, can be point-to-point, star, loop, bus, rings, or a combination of these configurations.

The simplest wiring configuration is point-to-point—devices are connected directly to one another. An example of this connection type is shown in Figure 9.1. Point-to-point connections are used as the basis for other architectures. The simplicity of a point-to-point connection makes it easy to use.

The star architecture, shown in Figure 9.2, uses a collection of point-to-point connections to wire multiple devices back to a single central point. Star networks are commonly used to bring sensor data back to a field panel. Star networks are easy to understand and use, but they are not redundant. This approach can be cost-effective for layouts in which the alarm display system is centrally located among a group of sensors.

The star method of transmission is characterized by the use of a separate wire pair between each sensor and the alarm display system. Each wire pair is independent, and there are many physical routes into the alarm display system. This can be an advantage because then a single-point failure only disables part of the system. The disadvantages are that there may be excessive cabling and that expansion sometimes requires putting multiple sensors on one input line because there is no room left for adding more cables.

Loops use point-to-point connections to chain devices together. Figure 9.3 shows a typical loop configuration. Loops start and end at the same physical location. Loops are more efficient users of media than star networks. Loops can also have redundancy if each point-to-point connection is bi-directional. Special physical layer functions must handle the forwarding of message traffic around the loop.

Devices in a bus network share the same common media. Like loops, bus architectures are efficient users of media. Because devices share the media, the protocol must arbitrate which device is actively communicating at a given time. However, the bus network is not as reliable as other networks. A single device failure can cause all communications to cease. Also, bus networks are not implicitly redundant. A bus network connection is shown in Figure 9.4.

A ring is a special case of the bus network topology, as shown in Figure 9.5. Rings, like buses, share the same physical media. Rings, however, connect devices together in a circle rather than a line. A ring is a

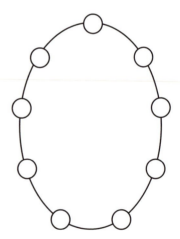

Figure 9.3 Loop Wiring Configuration

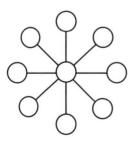

Figure 9.1 Point-to-Point Wiring Connections

Figure 9.2 Star Wiring Architecture

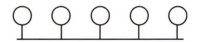

Figure 9.4 Bus Wiring Configuration

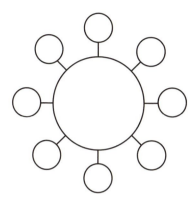

Figure 9.5 Ring Wiring Configuration

special bus with redundant features. Rings also share the reliability features of bus networks. Ring networks are not as reliable as loop or star configurations because, like rings, a single device failure can cause communications to cease.

The basic network building blocks can be combined to form more complex networks. Hierarchical networks combine one or more basic networks in a nested fashion. One common AC&D hierarchy combines star networks with bus or loop networks to connect sensors to the AC&D system computer. Hierarchies can be used to provide redundancy to networks that do not implicitly have redundancy.

Hierarchical networks add complexity to an AC&D communications system. While hierarchical networks can be efficient, they are difficult to use, and in some cases can slow system performance. Performance degradation is most apparent when the communications system uses too many levels of nested networks.

Security Considerations

An alarm reporting system is of little value if the communication link from the sensor to the control center fails to report alarms due to accidental or intentional damage. Physical protection techniques, such as metal conduit, can be employed to prevent or delay physical access to the line. A communications line protected by metal conduit

is most secure if the joints are securely welded. For long distances, burial of the communication line is costly but will delay an attacker. Extra wires or fibers should be included in the cable when burying it to allow for either future expansion or individual line failure. It is recommended that either the cable in conduit be encased in concrete or the cable path be covered with concrete or asphalt and that manhole protection be provided. If the entire area surrounding the cable path is paved, then digging will be discouraged, and the exact location of the cable will be more difficult to detect by an adversary. The recommended placement for communications lines is to run them inside a secured area. This limits access to those persons with authorized access to the area.

Low-Level Protocols

Direct current (DC) protocols use a steady direct current to detect changes in line resistance. DC protocols are low speed and are distance limited. The available bandwidth for a DC signal is low, so only a very limited amount of data can be passed. This protocol is commonly used to transmit sensor switch status.

The many alternating current (AC) protocols use a time-varying signal to transmit information. AC protocols are most commonly used over twisted-pair phone lines. In such an application, data are transmitted using tones or other modulation methods (modulation is provided by a modem). Data can be sent long distances over copper cables using AC protocols.

Digital signals can be considered a type of AC signal because they use time-varying signals to transmit data. Digital signals, however, transmit data in a binary fashion. Digital data are either ON or OFF. Modulation methods may be used to send this binary data. Digital signaling protocols are usually paired with network layer functions to improve the reliability of message transmission.

The Electronic Industries Association (EIA) has developed several standard electrical protocols for sending asynchronous digital data, including EIA-232, EIA-422, and EIA-485. These three standards are commonly used to transmit medium-speed data between computers. Serial protocols using EIA electrical standards must be used in conjunction with good link and network layer functions. The EIA standards detail electrical and mechanical issues but do not specify link and network layer functionality. Without good link and network layers, serial protocols are not reliable.

There are also several high-speed network protocols commonly used in AC&D communications, including Ethernet, token ring, and fiber-distributed data interface (FDDI) protocols. These protocols are considered high-level protocols and provide a rich set of communications services. Network protocols are reliable and can be redundant. Unfortunately, network protocols are not always the best choice because they are expensive. Moreover, providing a rich set of services adds overhead that can affect speed.

Link Layer

The link layer handles packaging data for transmission and may add delimiters and framing information to allow the data to be sent. Outgoing data is formatted for transmission, and incoming data is unpacked or deformatted. The unpacking allows the link layer to perform error-checks.

Error-checking is an important feature of the link layer. Communication systems cannot be perfect transmitters of information because errors sometimes occur. Error detection allows the link layer to notify higher layers when things go wrong. The ability of a link layer to perform error-checking depends on the protocol used. Simple protocols, such as DC analog signals, may provide a simple good/bad status, while network protocols perform error checks on each packet of transmitted information. Network protocols allow for

higher levels to request retransmission of problem packets. Thus, network protocols can be more reliable than simple DC signals.

Network Layer

The network layer provides the overall redundancy and reliability of a communications system. Network layers handle flow control, receipt/acknowledgment, and routing. While the lower layers of the OSI model do not guarantee message delivery (i.e., reliability), the network layer provides this capability.

More reliable network layers make good use of flow control. Flow control determines which device is communicating and when. Also, flow control keeps track of messages and determines if duplicate messages have been sent. The higher-level protocols provide detailed flow-control features. Lack of flow control can cause loss of messages or receipt of duplicate messages at the receiving devices.

These functions provide message acknowledgment services to sending devices. In reliable communications systems, receipt/acknowledgment guarantees a sender that a message has been delivered one time. Combining receipt/acknowledgment and flow control provides the system with the ability to re-send missed messages, thus increasing system reliability.

Redundant systems must provide multiple communications paths, and routing is a function of the network layer that selects a particular path. When failures occur, routing allows a communications system to pick alternate paths. The routing function is most common in higher-level protocols.

Line Supervision and Security

Good communications systems use protocols that allow for error detection. In AC&D systems, errors induced by adversaries or attempts to spoof or disrupt communications are important to discover. Techniques used to detect these induced errors or disruptions are called line supervision, which provides communications system security. Line supervision is the process of monitoring the communication link to assure that it is operating correctly and that data has not been altered during transmission. Communication links can be divided into two categories—passive and active. A signal is sent over a passive link only when an alarm occurs. A break in the link will prevent alarms from being reported, and the break will not be discovered unless a test of the system is performed. In contrast, a continuous signal is transmitted over an active link, allowing immediate detection of breaks in the link.

Vulnerabilities exist for all physical media. Landlines are vulnerable to environmental disturbances and attack; radio links are vulnerable to jamming or attack at the transmitter and receiver. Radio transmissions are also more susceptible to electrical interference and weather-related phenomena than are landlines, which typically have been buried or enclosed in a grounded metal conduit. In addition, radio transmission can be intercepted by anyone at even great distances, but landlines require that a potential attacker gain physical access to the line in order to determine what information is being transmitted. These vulnerabilities necessitate the use of line supervision, in addition to physical protection measures, to provide secure communications.

Types of Supervision Supervisory systems monitor the communication link to ensure that it is operating correctly and that data has not been altered during transmission. Supervisory systems can either be static or dynamic. Static systems always represent the secure condition by the same signal. This signal can be easily discovered and characterized by an adversary, who might then substitute a counterfeit signal and easily defeat the static system. Dynamic systems, on the other hand, generate a continually changing signal to represent the secure condition. Such systems are more difficult to defeat. Most

modern dynamic systems use encryption techniques to provide supervision.

A fiber-optics communication system is more self-protecting than equivalent copper-wire systems. LEDs or lasers transmit the signal over glass fibers. Tampering with glass fibers is difficult to accomplish and easy to detect. In addition, the principles of fiber operation make the substitution of counterfeit data difficult. For these reasons, fiber optics are more secure.

The goal of a static supervisory system is either to detect access to the protected line or to prevent successful substitution of a counterfeit signal. Systems may use DC or AC supervision. Each system can be described by its sensitivity, which is the amount that the current can vary from the nominal value before an alarm is produced. Typical systems have sensitivity ranges of 2–30%.

DC supervision employs resistors at the end of the line to maintain a constant current in the line. A specific current outside the normal range indicates an alarm condition, such as a sensor alarm or a tamper alarm. A highly sensitive system is only slightly more difficult to defeat than a much less sensitive system and is considerably more prone to nuisance alarms. The extra expense for high sensitivity is unwarranted. DC supervision is relatively inexpensive and provides adequate protection against casual threats such as vandalism and accidental cutting of the cable.

AC supervision monitors the amplitude and the phase of the imposed AC signal for alarm conditions. Greater electronic expertise is required to defeat this scheme, but only slightly more effort is necessary. Little can be done to counter an attack by a knowledgeable adversary. As with the DC system, high sensitivity does not significantly improve the security of AC supervision. The greater expense and only slight increase in security that AC supervision provides make DC supervision a more attractive choice for AC&D systems.

Dynamic supervision alters the secure signal over time. An adversary has great difficulty in first determining the nature of the secure signal and then substituting a counterfeit signal. The ideal dynamic supervisory technique uses a random number sequence or key to encode each data message. The major problem associated with such an encoding scheme is storing the key information. Security is reduced when the number of keys is reduced.

Theoretically, dynamic supervision techniques are vulnerable to a sophisticated attack. An attacker may be able to record the output from a transmitter and play it back to the central site at a slightly slower rate. The reduced data rate may not be detected. Eventually, enough secure signal data may be accumulated to cover the time required for an intrusion. To combat this, a dynamic system must employ unique messages and two-way transmissions to detect the attack.

Encryption Systems Modern block encryption systems can be used to reduce the number of random encryption keys required for line supervision. With such systems, protection of the key information must be maintained, and key information must not be transmitted over the communications channel. To do so would allow an adversary to use recorded data and brute force techniques to ultimately defeat the system. The security of encryption systems, therefore, depends on key management.

Encryption systems work best on block, or contiguous, data. However, the simple binary data provided by sensors is not in block form. Additionally, many encryption schemes require that the block data be unique for every transmission. Uniqueness can easily be provided using message-counting techniques, but adding a unique number to each sensor message increases the message size and requires communications links with greater bandwidth.

Encryption keys cannot be automatically distributed. Most encryption systems provide mechanisms to manually key the equipment. This requires an authorized person to key each encryption station in the AC&D system. In addition, some systems require new keys to be inserted in a specific order. Another issue is that while keying is in process, parts of the system are off-line.

Although encryption provides good line supervision and security, the expense of manual key management and the need for greater link bandwidths has prohibited its use for sensor line supervision. Encryption is best used for links between data-gathering equipment and the central computers or between computers in the AC&D system. However, encryption is necessary for communication lines outside the secured area.

If the transmitter and the receiver do not use exactly the same random number key for a transmission, then the decoded data is incorrect, and the system must reset. Often, the same sequence of random keys is used every time a reset occurs. It is possible for an attacker to record no-alarm data after one reset and use this to cover an intrusion.

Data transmission errors can cause the data to be rejected. An error may result in rejection of a block of data, or in some systems, all subsequent data. One solution is to implement error-detection or -correction techniques before verification or decoding. Another solution is to ignore a single block of erroneous data and then require that several contiguous transmissions be erroneous before an alarm is reported. However, requests for retransmission and indications of acceptance or rejection of data are not secure practices. An attacker could substitute data infrequently enough to be ignored by the system, yet get immediate feedback as to whether the false data has been accepted.

These examples show that use of encryption alone is not sufficient to protect AC&D communications. By defeating the protocols used to send data, there are many possible ways to defeat encryption systems. AC&D system users and designers should be cautious when evaluating or using encryption systems to ensure that such protocol attacks are not possible. Physical protection and line supervision are primarily intended to protect the communication link between the link's endpoints. The link may still be vulnerable at the interface with the sensor, at various junction boxes along its route, and at the entry to the central console. At these points, additional security can be achieved by employing enclosures equipped to indicate intrusion or tampering. This tamper indicator should be treated as a sensor and be provided with a separate reporting circuit rather than as a series or parallel part of another sensor circuit. If this is not done, the system cannot differentiate between a tamper alarm and a line open or a line short.

Information Handling

An AC&D communications system moves alarm data from sensors to a central location. This central location is usually a single computer or is sometimes a collection of computers. The central computer processes the alarm data into useful information. These processing functions make up the information-handling subsystem.

The information-handling subsystem provides functions to model the real-time state of the sensor. Alarm-handling functions, such as assessment or access status, are also performed. Alarm data is organized and categorized by geographic location, priority, or other common characteristics. The information-handling subsystem may then use expert systems or alarm analysis techniques to prioritize information for display. This subsystem can then trigger control actions such as video switching messages.

System states store information on the operational status of system components, keep track of which components or consoles are in control, and store information on operator status. In other words, it stores all relevant system information. The sensor state stores information about sensors. Some of this information includes:

- sensor name (a descriptive name for the sensor)
- sensor location (the geographic location of the sensor)
- sensor type (a description of the sensor type)
- sensor history (summaries of the sensor activation history)
- maintenance data (information on the maintenance history of the sensor)
- other data (as needed for alarm analysis)
- alarm status of sensor

The most important data stored in the sensor state of the system software model, however, is the current alarm status of the sensor. This data includes both the activation and access (i.e., disabled) status of the sensor. The sensor model reflects the real-time status of every sensor attached to the AC&D system. It is critical that the information-handling system models all sensors completely and that the model accurately reflects actual conditions around the site.

Sensor Data Issues The raw data that drives the information-handling system is the sensor alarm data. Each sensor provides information on its status (secure, in alarm, in access, in tamper, or failed) so that individual alarm points are modeled in the sensor model. The information-handling system then combines and categorizes this information.

Most sensors are combined into groups. Therefore, individual sensor information is best utilized when it is combined with information from other sensors. In many ways, a group of sensors can be thought of as a super-sensor that is an aggregate of all its component sensors. Sensors are usually grouped geographically. Sensors closely related in space are usually handled as a single entity. For example, it makes sense to group sensors that are in the same room or to group complementary sensors protecting a single perimeter sector. Geographic sensor groupings are also easier to display to operators. Even when sensors are grouped, the system must provide the capability to present a status of individual sensors.

Prioritization is a method used to assign relative importance values to various sensors or groups. Generally, sensors closest to the asset are given a higher priority than those farther away. This is an example of a simple static prioritization scheme.

Besides prioritizing by proximity to the assets, priorities can also be set dynamically. Dynamic priorities are usually set on groups of sensors. For example, if more than one constituent sensor in a group is active, that group may be assigned a higher priority than other sensors or groups. Sensor or group priorities are used to direct the system and operators to those events that are most important. There are many different prioritization schemes that can be employed. The goal is to use a system with a scheme that provides the operator with the best information to assess the situation.

Alarm information is commonly displayed based on priority and time of arrival. Those events with the highest priority and occurring most recently are displayed first. It is also possible to group and prioritize sensor information based on likely activation sequences.

Given the location of sensors and the likely path taken by an adversary, it is possible to construct timing sequences of likely attack paths. If sensors placed in those paths activate at times predicted by the timing sequence, then the probability of intrusion is greater. The information-handling system can perform such analysis on alarm data. Those sensor activations that match the sequence analysis may be displayed with higher priority.

Alarm handling is the sequence of operations that the information-handling system performs to process sensor alarm data. There are several operations involved including acknowledgment, assessment, and access.

Acknowledgment is a user action. The user may acknowledge alarms explicitly through some action, or the acknowledgment may take place in conjunction with some other operator action. An acknowledgment tells the alarm-handling system that the operator has seen the alarm. Unacknowledged alarm points usually flash and cause an audible signal to the user. Acknowledged alarms can cause the information-handling system to bring up real-time video or other assessment actions. The information-handling system then keeps track of the acknowledged state of sensors.

Assessment, which is the process of determining the cause of an alarm, is another operator function. When operators request assessment video, the information-handling system controls video switching equipment and video storage equipment and then cues the appropriate video for the specified sensor or group. The information-handling system may then enter data concerning the assessment into the system log files.

Access is an optional operator function. An accessed sensor is one for which the system will ignore intrusion alarms; however, tamper alarms will be reported and displayed to the operator. Sensors will often be placed in access during daytime operations at a facility or to allow maintenance activities in an area. The alarm status of accessed sensors is not displayed to the operator unless it is a tamper alarm. While the information-handling system may continue to track sensor status, that status is not reported. Requested accesses are controlled by the information-handling system. Some systems require two or more operators to concur with access requests. The information-handling system enforces this two-or-more person concurrence.

Intelligent Alarm Analysis Intelligent alarm analysis is a new area of research focused on applying alarm processing and sensor fusion techniques to provide information that is more useful to the central alarm station operator. The goal is to correlate and integrate a variety of inputs to improve the confidence in an event. Inputs include sensor information and features from several sensors, environmental data, knowledge of sensor performance under certain conditions (e.g., weather and visibility conditions), sensor priority, and recent operator feedback. Intelligent alarm analysis also incorporates trend analysis using historical knowledge of nuisance-alarm data to identify installation, setup, or maintenance problems. Future research includes integrating site data, such as sensor configurations and target locations, to predict intruder movements and intentions and then aid in dispatching a response force. Intelligent alarm analysis is a high-order process that takes a global look at the intrusion detection system to enhance the information passed to the operator.

Alarm Control and Display

The control and display subsystem of the AC&D system presents information to a security operator and enables the operator to enter commands affecting the operation of the AC&D system. The ultimate goal of the subsystem is to promote the rapid evaluation of alarms. The alarm display equipment (operator's console) receives information from the sensors. There are several concerns that must be addressed in the design of the operator's console, including the following:

- what information is presented to the operator;
- how the information is presented;
- how the operator communicates with the system; and
- the arrangement of the equipment at the operator's workstation.

An effective control and display subsystem presents information to an operator rapidly and in a straightforward

manner. The subsystem also responds quickly to operator command. However, the display subsystem should not overwhelm operators with detail—displays should show only necessary information, and control functions should be limited to those that make sense in the context of the current display.

Examples of information that can be presented to aid in zone security include the following:

- the access/secure/alarm/tamper status of the zone
- the geographical location of the zone
- the time of the alarm
- information about any special hazards or material associated with a zone
- instructions for special actions
- telephone numbers of persons to call
- maps of the secure area

Related considerations include ways of alerting the operator to the fact that action is required. A major system design task is to specify the various details of the operator interface. For example, the type of display equipment, the format, and other visual features of the information that is to be displayed, and the design of the input equipment must be determined. The human factor considerations of various hardware components and software techniques are discussed in the following sections.

Ergonomics—Human Factors

The control and display subsystem must be designed with the human operator in mind. Meeting standard personnel occupancy conditions relative to temperature, humidity, noise, and general comfort factors provides an environment that enhances an operator's effectiveness and reduces frustration and fatigue. For example, adjustable lighting allows illumination levels to be chosen as desired for enhancement of the viewing contrast on cathode ray tube (CRT) displays. Additionally, the console design should facilitate the exchange of information between the system and the operator, such as alarm reports, status indications, and commands.

A good human interface improves the mechanics of issuing commands and of deciphering the information presented. Thus, the amount of data displayed should be limited to only the data required by the operator. Also, data should be presented in a manner that makes their interrelations obvious. On the other hand, the techniques for transferring information from human to machine should limit the opportunity to make errors without compromising system efficiency.

As a result of these requirements, the work area design must consider the following factors:

- what the operator must be able to see—people, equipment, displays, and controls;
- what the operator must be able to hear—other operators, communications equipment, and warning indicators; and
- what the operator must be able to reach and manipulate—hand or foot controls and communications equipment.

Points to Consider

The space around the operator consists of zones of varying accessibility and visibility. All displays should be approximately perpendicular to the operator's line-of-sight and should be easily visible from the normal working position. Indications and operator inputs should be prioritized and the most important ones placed in the primary interface area, as illustrated in Figure 9.6. Displays in this primary interface area do not require extreme eye or head movement from the operator's line-of-sight. Placing the principal items to be viewed within a 30° viewing cone will avoid such extreme movement.

Frequently used operational displays should be located in the secondary area. Eye movement, but not head movement, from

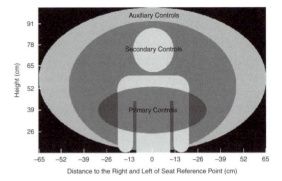

Figure 9.6 Placement of Operator Controls in an AC&D Console. The primary areas include the computer monitor and keyboard. The secondary area includes alarm assessment monitors

the normal line-of-sight may be required. Infrequently used support displays, such as backup systems and power indicators, may be placed beyond the secondary area.

Because the operator's attention is not always directed to the display panel, audible signals are effective for alerting the operator to a significant change of status. Audible alarm characteristics, such as pitch and volume, can be used to separate classes of alarms (e.g., security, safety, or maintenance). Computerized voice output may also allow the operator to keep his or her eyes on the area under observation. Care should be taken when using audible signals to keep the types and number of signals to a very small number. Signals must be unique and be distinguishable in the rich audible environments commonly found in AC&D control rooms.

Displays are generally placed in the center of the console. Controls are located on, below, or around the displays and must be readily identifiable. Clear labeling, color-coding, well-spaced grouping, and coding by shape accomplish this identification. Labels should be large enough to be clearly identifiable. Locating a control near the appropriate display minimizes searching and eye movement. Touch panels locating controls on the display eliminate the need for many other control devices.

System consoles should provide a visual signal in conjunction with any audible signals. A visual signal, such as a flashing light or blinking message, should be used to identify the significant information. Colored lights or indicators display the status of alarms more clearly. For example, traffic light colors of red, yellow, and green are easily recognizable as indicators for alarm/action, caution/abnormal, and proceed/normal, respectively.

Support equipment should be located in relation to its importance and frequency of use. Communications equipment such as microphones, telephones, additional CCTV monitors, and controls must be given the console space necessary for their functions. Equipment that is not necessary for display and control functions should not be located in the operator's immediate workspace. Locating computers and automatic control circuitry (i.e., CCTV switching equipment and communication electronics other than microphones and controls) in a separate room offers several advantages. More space can be available for maintenance personnel and operator activities are not interrupted by maintenance. Distracting noises, such as fans, are reduced. The equipment can be secured from unauthorized tampering, and equipment environment conditions can be different from those of the operators (e.g., equipment may have additional cooling and humidity requirements).

When more than one person at a time operates the console, it is necessary to consider the interrelationships among the operators and equipment. Essential equipment should be duplicated for each operator, but operators should have common access to secondary or infrequently used equipment.

Ergonomics—Graphical Displays

Well-designed graphical user interfaces (GUI) provide a capability for enhanced display of security alarm information in computer-based systems. Conversely, a poorly designed interface can quickly overwhelm an operator. This section describes types of graphical information that can be displayed on a computer monitor screen and offers guidance on how best to display that information. Limits on the complexity of the user interface are proposed, and guidelines are suggested for the display of maps and sensors.

Foremost, a good graphical annunciator has a limited number of features. Current GUIs provide a wealth of features for displaying information. A good display limits the ways information is displayed and places constraints on which operations are allowed.

The window, a rectangular region on the display screen, is the primary method of displaying information in today's GUI. A window can be any size up to and including the entire display screen, and multiple windows can be visible at any one time. A window can contain text, graphics, or controls. Multiple windows of various sizes allow maximum flexibility when displaying information. A good alarm display, however, should limit the size and number of windows. No more than three windows should be visible at any one time. One of these windows should be the full size of the screen and should contain an overview of the system status. A smaller window containing subordinate information can be displayed as needed. Subordinate windows should never be larger than one-half of the screen. A third window may be displayed that contains menus or other operational controls. Limits on the number and size of windows allow operators to quickly find important information. Windows should not have to be resized or moved to view information.

A menu is a list of available commands. When a command is selected, a function is performed. Menus are usually displayed along the top of a window and can be nested. That is, selecting an item causes a subordinate menu to be displayed with additional items. Menus provide a clear and concise method of organizing system commands. A menu structure should not be too large or over-nested. A good menu should have no more than nine items and should not be nested more than three levels. Users tend to get lost in deeply nested menus. Limiting the number of items in a menu reduces the time required to find a particular item, and limiting the number of nested levels makes a menu structure easier to use. Complicated menu structures are intimidating to new users, and experienced operators find them annoying.

Although menus can display system commands in an easy-to-use structure, common commands should not be placed in menus but should be available as buttons. A button simulates the action of a pushbutton switch. An operator can push a button to initiate system action. Depressing a mouse button or key on the keyboard activates the buttons. Only the most important commands should be placed on buttons, and only those commands that are valid in the current context should be available. Buttons can be very flexible. Sensor or map icons can be made to act as buttons. Buttons can be grouped into button bars. A button bar organizes buttons into a single area on the screen for ease of access. Buttons can be context sensitive, although changing a context button should be done in a consistent manner. Generally, if a button is performing the same function on different screens the location of the button should not move, but some systems change the button function based on context. Good examples are the access and secure functions for a sensor. If a sensor is in the secure state we might show an access button. However, if the button is in the access state it makes no sense to show an access button. In this case, it is more appropriate to show a secure button, to allow the operator to change the state of the sensor automatically. Some systems display the access or secure button in the same location on the screen, but only the appropriate button is visible based on context. If they are used correctly, context-sensitive buttons can

help the user interface, but perhaps the best use of context-dependent controls is to direct the user's actions. Good user interfaces only allow the operator to control functions that make sense based on the system state. If there are no sensors in alarm, it makes no sense to allow the user to assess an alarm. This type of context-sensitive user interface is a great aid in making the AC&D system easy to use. Button flexibility must not be overdone. Visible buttons should be limited to a maximum of nine. Buttons should have good descriptive text labels that indicate their function.

The primary advantage of GUIs is the capability to display maps or graphics of the secured area. Maps allow the user to quickly relate a security alarm to its location. Several map sources are possible, and all these sources fall into one of two groups: either scanned copies of paper media or electronically created graphics.

Either group provides a useful graphic for alarm annunciation. Of all the possible graphics sources, the best is a stylized sketch based on a topographic map or other hardcopy map. Standard maps usually have too much detail for effective use in security applications. Effective displays require small-scale maps of about 1:5000. An operator can create a sketch based on a larger-scale map and can eliminate unnecessary detail, while providing the necessary scale. Any maps provided for annunciation should be interactive. In other words, the system should represent sensors on the map and provide mechanisms for the operator to display and control those sensors by performing operations on the graphic.

To support an interactive map, sensors or sensor groups should be displayed on the graphic. All sensor graphics or icons should use the same graphic, be of the same size, and use consistent colors. When feasible, the sensors should be displayed together as a single icon. This type of display can reduce screen clutter. No map should contain more than 50 sensor or group icons, although the total number of sensors displayed can vary based on the complexity of the map graphic. A sensor icon should represent the associated sensor, and sensor states should be displayed using unique colors and shapes.

Grouped sensor icons should indicate the state of the worst-case sensor associated with the group. For example, if any sensor in the group is in alarm, the group icon should indicate an alarm. A sensor in alarm could be the worst-case sensor state, but other sensor states are possible and should be displayed.

Graphically displaying information on a map does not eliminate the need for textual display of information. Dedicated areas of the display should be provided for descriptions of sensors. A good system will also provide some type of online or quick help. Also, text should be limited to vital information only; details can be placed in subordinate windows.

Although color can be an effective aid in highlighting important information, it should be used sparingly. A user should not be dependent on colors to operate a system, since about 10% of the population has some form of color blindness. The number of colors should be kept to seven or fewer. Every additional color visible on the screen adds to the perceived complexity of the display. Menus, buttons, and backgrounds should be in consistent shades of color, with gray being a very common color choice. Maps should be black and white or use low-saturation colors. The primary colors should be reserved to indicate sensor status—red for alarms, yellow for access, and green for secure status.

The overriding design philosophy for any security system must be the operator first. Operators must always be in command of the system. To achieve this goal, follow these design rules:

1. Minimize the number of actions required to perform any command. An operator should only have to click the mouse once or depress a single key for any major operation.

2. Only valid operations, based on context, should be available. For example, the operator should not be able to access a sensor if it is already accessed.

3. The system should use prompts to guide the operator through complex operations. A context-based command selection (see item 2) could be used to direct operators' actions without removing their control.

4. Annunciator systems should never override an operation in progress. If the user is assessing an alarm, then the system must never replace the information currently present for assessment to notify of a new alarm. The assessment should continue, and a nonintrusive notification of the new event should occur. The operator can then decide whether or not to abort the current operation. This principle applies in all situations.

5. Systems should not annoy the user. Avoid using loud, continuous alarms or bright, flashing displays. The user is the most important factor to successful system operation.

6. Options should be available for performing any single command. What is simple for one user may be complex for another. Commands available as menu items, buttons, and keystrokes result in a friendlier system; the user could then select the preferred method.

The purpose of any AC&D system is to enhance site security. If a system fails in its security task, then it is a failure as a system. Fancy graphics cannot salvage an ineffective system. A simple-to-use system is much more likely to succeed than an unnecessarily complex one. Consider a simple user interface and limit the total number of maps, sensors per map, buttons, menus, dialog boxes, and colors.

Figure 9.7 State-of-the-Art AC&D System. Components are placed to make the operator most effective

Assessment

Figure 9.7 shows a typical operator's console for an effective control and display subsystem. The horseshoe shape of the equipment bay allows the operator to view and reach all racks conveniently. The console provides all functions necessary to:

- assess alarms;
- use the CCTV subsystem;
- request system status;
- change sensor state;
- reconfigure console monitors;
- log into the system;
- recalibrate any touch-sensitive panels on the CRTs to initiate sensor self-tests;
- select the primary or standby mode of operations;
- issue duress alarms; and
- silence audible alarms.

Graphics Monitors

In a computer-based AC&D system, one color graphics monitor is situated directly in front of the operator seated at the console. Under normal operating conditions, the monitor displays the site map. The site map indicates the overall security status of the facility and functions as a locator for selection of detail maps.

The site map is a symbolic representation of the entire facility. The map displays messages concerning the security status of the facility and presents buttons by which commands are given to the system. Perimeter sectors and vehicle gates are reproduced in their relative positions. Sensored buildings are drawn to represent their relative sizes, shapes, and positions within the facility and are identified by building number. Selecting a building or perimeter sector causes its detail map to appear on the graphics monitor. Note that the map is a stylized sketch of the site and not an actual scale drawing of the site. The site map should show a large-scale representation of the facility with only those elements necessary for the security functions shown.

The detail maps are representations of buildings, areas within buildings, and perimeter sectors. Buttons across the bottom of each map allow the input of commands to the system. Such maps show the locations of sensors and cameras and are available for all buildings containing sensors and cameras as well as for all perimeter sectors. The symbols for cameras and sensors can be touch-sensitive, allowing their use for entering commands to the system. The buttons at the bottom of the display may also be touch-sensitive and provide an alternate method for entering commands.

CCTV Monitors

Four black-and-white CCTV monitors are included in an automated AC&D system design to allow operators to view scenes generated by the site cameras. Three monitors automatically display scenes for alarm assessment or scenes manually chosen by the operator for status determination. One monitor is available for assignment by the operator and is normally used for surveillance rather than for alarm assessment. Figure 9.8 shows the arrangement of these four monitors.

One primary CCTV monitor displays live video coverage of the highest priority alarm zone, while the monitor next to it replays the images that were automatically recorded

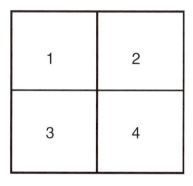

Figure 9.8 Arrangement of CCTV Monitors in a Display Console. Monitor 1 displays the current live image of the zone with the highest priority alarm; Monitor 2 displays the recorded video of the same area; Monitor 3 displays the recorded video of the next highest priority alarm; and Monitor 4 is available for operator use

when the alarm occurred. If additional alarms are awaiting assessment, a third monitor displays alarm scene coverage for the alarm that has been assigned the next highest priority by the system. The fourth monitor is always available for manual use by the operator. The system designer must decide whether the three automatic CCTV monitors will only display an image on an alarm or will always present some video information. The most effective systems will only display scenes of zones that need assessment of an alarm. The system should allow the operator to switch video to any monitor, but this selection should be over-ridden in the event of an alarm.

Input Devices

The operator can communicate with the control and display system through the use of one or more input devices. Such input devices include a typewriter keyboard, a function keyboard, a touchscreen, a mouse, or a track ball. The appropriate input device should be selected for the intended use. The input command structure should be designed to be natural and easy to use, and should also be protected against input errors.

A CRT display often employs a typewriter keyboard for input. Keyboards are best suited for lengthy input requiring alphanumeric input, such as password entry, assessment annotation, or combinations of letters, numbers, and other keys that supply commands and queries. The use of such a keyboard may be unsatisfactory for several reasons.

Operator commands that are not chosen naturally make the system difficult to learn and confusing to operate (e.g., typing the letters ACK for acknowledgment). Requiring several keys to specify a zone or command increases the opportunity for error and degrades operating speed. Small, closely spaced keys also promote errors. Confusion between I and 1, between O and 0, and between upper and lower cases may occur. A system that is intolerant of input errors may produce results ranging from annoyance and time loss to a complete loss of operator control.

A special-purpose keyboard, on which each key is clearly labeled to identify its function, may be a preferable input device. Function keyboards are effective for rapidly entering security responses, such as acknowledge or secure. A limited range of computer inputs improves system security. The design should provide the operator with only enough keys to perform tasks. If a standard keyboard is necessary for computer program modification, then the keys that are not necessary for day-to-day operation should be covered or ignored by the system. Desirable keyboard features are tactile feedback in which the operator can tell that the key has been depressed enough to be activated, audible feedback, and instantaneous response.

A touchscreen overlaying a CRT display is the most versatile and easy-to-use input device. Input simply requires touching the appropriate words or symbols displayed on the screen. Touch panels are used for command entry because it is natural to point to a location on a map. Entering a command by pointing is less error prone than typing the command at a keyboard. Touchscreen technology, however, is fairly expensive. As computer use has become more prevalent, the use of a mouse or trackball is a more cost-effective method.

Personnel at some facilities prefer to use a computer mouse or trackball for entering commands on a CRT display. This tendency has increased in recent years with the advent of the personal computer. The mouse or trackball is used to move a pointer to the appropriate symbol on the screen. Pressing a switch on the mouse enters the desired command. Often a system will have more than one type of device for operator input.

Operator Interface
The operator interface is utilized to communicate with and control the AC&D system. Lighted pushbuttons should only be used with small systems. Commercial interfaces are available to support a keyboard, a mouse,

or a touch panel as an interactive device for computer-driven displays.

Many agencies require not only a record of the information received from the alarm system but also of the actions taken, judgments made, and the parties responsible for legal purposes. Keeping a manual record of such information is feasible for small AC&D systems, but provision should be made for automatic record keeping in computer-driven systems. A full keyboard provides flexibility in such record keeping but consumes significant time in an environment requiring rapid interaction. A preferred approach utilizes mouse or touch-panel selection of predefined messages.

Offline Systems

This section describes several simple subsystems that perform noncritical functions for the AC&D system. These subsystems are noncritical because they are not necessary for the AC&D system to perform its primary function of displaying and controlling alarm points. Offline systems are critical for configuration and maintenance of an AC&D system.

Event Logs
The purpose of the event logging system is to record all events that happen on the AC&D system. An event is any sensor change, operator command, or operator assessment. System failures also generate events. All events are saved on the system for possible later review. Each event is tagged with the current date and time.

A logging system is useful for record archiving and performing system maintenance. As noted above, many facilities have a legal need to archive event information. Maintenance personnel can review historical logs of sensor activations. Analysis of the log data can disclose sensors that are out of alignment or expose sensors that have long-term problems.

The logging system may also be used to assess operator performance. When all operator commands and actions are logged on the system, analysis of the event logs can reveal how well specific operators are handling AC&D operation. Such operator assessments can be used to tailor refresher-training courses.

If enough detail is recorded in the event logs, the logs can be used to generate training scenarios. As actual alarm data is received, it is recorded in the event log.

With a flexible logging system, alarm activation events from the log can be played back to an operator as if they are real alarm events. A playback system also allows the event logging system to be used as a training tool for operators. The event logs can also be used after the fact to reconstruct the events leading up to an adversary intrusion.

Use of Databases
Many systems keep event data in a relational database. The use of a database allows more than one console to view log information. This ability can be most useful because while the system is running maintenance, training, or supervisory functions, personnel can be viewing the event logs.

Event Printer
Many AC&D systems use a printer for each system event. This event printer provides a hardcopy backup of the event log. Also, operators can make use of the hardcopy events to generate shift reports or review previously assessed alarms. With modern computer hardware and redundant storage systems, the event print may be unnecessary. However, many operators are comfortable with the event printer and use it in daily operations. If the AC&D system provides a supervisor's console for viewing event logs, the designer should consider eliminating the event printer.

Supervisory Consoles
A supervisor's console may be employed by an AC&D system for the retrieval of previously stored data. This database console provides a means of retrieving system event logs and generating reports. Supervisory consoles allow authorized users to configure the AC&D system, review and analyze event data, and act as backup display consoles. Adding extra consoles allows supervisors and maintenance personnel to perform their functions without interrupting the primary AC&D operators.

AC&D System Design

AC&D systems are the glue that holds the PPS together. AC&D systems must integrate with a variety of other systems and must do so in a seamless manner. This section describes how an AC&D system must integrate with other components of the PPS. AC&D systems usually connect to the entry control systems, assessment systems, and operators. In addition, the AC&D system should have a redundant design so that it is robust. AC&D systems must also integrate with operational procedures so that users know how to use the system effectively.

Interface with Entry Control Systems

In a high-security system, intrusion detection functions and data handling must always take precedence over any other system or event. This precedence includes entry control, for which functions are less critical because a decision to grant a user normal access to an area can be delayed for a few seconds without a significant operational impact. Intrusion attempts must be communicated immediately for the security forces to have time to intercept the intruder. Intrusion detection events have a higher priority than entry control events, and thus an integrated AC&D system must handle security events before any others.

Integration with Assessment Systems

AC&D systems should employ CCTV cameras to provide visual surveillance of the facility and rapid remote assessment of the causes of intrusion alarms. CCTV systems often use video recorders or digital frame-grabbers to provide an instant replay of an intrusion upon an alarm. Recordings of video coverage can also be saved for later evaluation or documentation. A computer-controlled video routing switch drives the subsystem. The signals from any camera, recorder, or frame-grabber can be displayed on any monitor.

When an intrusion alarm is generated, the CCTV subsystem rapidly records scenes of the assessment zone. When an alarm is displayed for assessment, both live and recorded CCTV scenes from the assessment zone are displayed. The AC&D system selects and automatically displays the four to eight highest priority assessment scenes for video recording when more than four simultaneous alarms occur.

A VCR, DVR, or NVR records critical scenes for post-incident analysis. When high-priority alarms are received, all four images on assessment monitors are recorded or grabbed simultaneously.

System Security

It is generally desirable to protect AC&D system data from interception by outsiders and from compromise by insiders. Outsider protection is primarily established by locating critical equipment inside the PPS boundary and by installing substantial barriers within the boundary. The outsider must cross the boundary and defeat the barriers before gaining access to significant system parts. At least one of each redundant part and all critical single parts of the AC&D system should be protected in this way. Access controls also restrict entrance into critical areas.

Insider protection employs technological and administrative measures to enforce control in all situations where a single insider could significantly compromise the system. Insider protection also uses technology to detect when procedures or technologies indicate possible compromise of sensitive system components and to respond appropriately to such conditions. This response may involve a technological appraisal of the system or dispatch of a guard to an incident location.

Administrative measures can provide insider protection for such common activities as system maintenance and console operation. Access controls limit an insider's access to critical equipment. Some facilities implement the two-person rule for system maintenance, while other facilities require an extensive system check following any activity during which the system could have been compromised. Configuring the AC&D system to incorporate accountability for actions provides a restriction on malevolent activity by the persons making decisions.

Technological measures for insider protection include line supervision on sensor communication and digital encoding on databases. Tamper indicators limit access to processors and displays. Encryption technologies are available and can be used on critical communications lines that pass outside of protected areas or require higher levels of security. Use of encryption technology should be limited to those areas of critical need because of the high maintenance for distributing encryption keys.

Operator Loading

AC&D systems must be easy to use. As previously stated, the single most important measure of AC&D effectiveness is how well the system communicates alarm data from sensors to the system operator. If the operator's mind is occupied, then AC&D effectiveness is compromised. Operators must have time available to handle AC&D alarms. Operators must not be loaded with ancillary tasks that prohibit proper attention to the display. Operators who handle the telephone, the radio, write reports, deal with personnel access, make badges, and operate the AC&D console may be overloaded and can miss important events.

Many sites reduce operator loading by having several operators in the control center. Each operator has an AC&D console, a telephone, and a radio. The work is divided among operators in a prearranged fashion. Dividing the work among several persons reduces individual workloads, but may cost more. Another scheme for reducing workloads relies on a secondary alarm center to handle routine matters (such as nonemergency calls and making badges) while the primary alarm center handles all off-normal activity. This planning keeps the primary center operators focused on high-priority events while allowing all events to be handled.

The AC&D Console as an Overload Source

AC&D consoles must be carefully designed to prevent information overload of the operator. AC&D systems can be very large. It is extremely difficult to present an operator with an entire system status on one display. Use of the proper display technologies, display techniques, priorities, console ergonomics, and system hierarchies all play a part in how well operators handle information.

Event Conditions

An AC&D system must be able to operate in different environments and conditions, and operators must be effective in all three. Table 9.2 summarizes and compares these conditions.

Most systems handle normal and abnormal conditions without problems, and operators are not overwhelmed with

Table 9.2 *Event Situations at a Facility.*

There are three expected operating states at a facility—normal, abnormal, and malevolent.

Normal Conditions	The site is operating normally. Common day-to-day site operations are being performed properly. No special circumstances or conditions are present
Abnormal Conditions	Some abnormal conditions are present. Operators are handling such abnormal conditions as single sensor faults, safety-related events, bad weather, etc.
Malevolent Conditions	Adversary attack or many abnormal conditions are present. The total of abnormal conditions is extreme

data. Good systems handle malevolent situations equally well. The system presents data in a prioritized manner and limits the data displayed to that which the operator needs for job performance. The ultimate test of a high-security AC&D system is how well it handles malevolent situations without overloading the operator. Lower security systems may be able to tolerate higher operational loads, but should still be driven by the need to make the operator most effective.

AC&D systems must be reliable. Every component of an AC&D system is subject to some kind of failure. It is essential to determine which components are likely to fail and the effect such a failure would have on the system. Backup equipment and procedures must be provided to maintain the desired level of security. Backup equipment can operate full-time in parallel with the primary system or it can be activated by automatic or manual switchover. Backup protection and coverage can be provided entirely by increasing the use of manpower. When priorities and procedures for backup operation have been established, security personnel must practice the procedures on a regular basis.

Consoles

AC&D systems are often designed with two-operator consoles. Such equipment redundancy provides hardware reliability because the system can be operated equally well from either console. In some cases, the consoles improve human reliability by implementing the two-person rule, which requires each action to be performed by both operators. In this situation, an equipment failure at either station disables the system. An intermediate approach allows the system to be operated from a primary station with oversight surveillance at a secondary station. The secondary station can assume the primary function in case of equipment or personnel failure at the primary station.

Computers

To be effective, the AC&D system must be computer-driven but not computer-dependent. Failure to provide redundancy for operational functions makes the system computer-dependent. Redundancy is readily available today because computer-processing power is relatively inexpensive.

The use of two host computers, as in a typical automated AC&D system, provides system redundancy. A primary console is connected to the main computer and a secondary console is connected to the backup computer under normal operating conditions. If the main computer fails, then a bus switch automatically connects the primary console to the backup computer. The security operators are notified of the switch, but operations continue normally. Both consoles are unavailable only when both hosts fail.

Uninterruptible Power

Computer-based systems require highly reliable electrical power in order to function properly. Battery-driven, uninterruptible power supply (UPS) systems prevent momentary outages at the computer. Long-term power sources such as diesel generators can handle outages greater than a few minutes or an hour. Besides the AC&D computers, other subsystems may be driven by the UPS to ensure the reliability of the AC&D system. The communication subsystem, individual sensors, and even lighting may be provided with such backup power.

Shared Components

Although many of the AC&D components are redundant, to allow for the possibility of component failure, some components do not have duplicates. For example, duplication of the CCTV subsystem is very expensive, so it is seldom provided. Such components are placed on a shared bus that is normally connected to the main computer. The bus switch automatically connects the shared bus to the backup computer if the main computer fails. As long as one of the host computers is functioning, the shared components are available. An arbitration scheme defines which command center will exercise control over shared resources in a particular situation. If additional security-related computer-based functions (e.g., badging systems) are required, they should operate on separate systems. Data from these systems may be shared with AC&D systems.

Compatibility with Operational Procedures

The hardware system must agree with procedures and regulations. Regulations are written to make sure that minimum requirements are met. Procedures, established by site managers, are statements of rules to be followed and include responsibilities of personnel to produce an efficient and effective protection system. It is necessary to determine what equipment is needed to implement procedures and how the proposed equipment will affect the existing procedures.

Selection of tamper/line-fault detection capabilities is an example of the important interaction between equipment and procedures. If indications of tampering or line faults are routinely ignored, then the equipment purchased to provide these capabilities is essentially wasted. However, if reports are prepared for maintenance personnel because of tamper/ line-fault indications, then true hardware problems will be corrected and some instances of malevolent tampering may be discovered after the fact. The full benefit of tamper/line-fault detection capabilities will only be realized by a response procedure that requires the system to be inspected when an indication is received. Also, the likelihood of apprehending an intruder will be significantly increased.

Summary

The alarm communication and display system is a key element in the successful and timely response to a threat. The system controls the flow of information from sensors to the operator and displays this information quickly and clearly. The alarm communication and display system collects alarm data, presents information to a security operator, and enables the operator to enter commands to control the system. The ultimate goal of the display system is to promote the rapid evaluation of alarms. This chapter discusses communication, information handling, control and display devices, equipment placement, the assessment system interface, operator loading, and offline equipment.

An alarm communication and display system should provide the following:

- Fast reporting time—if something is happening, the operator is informed quickly.

- Line supervision of all cables.
- Easy and quick discovery of single-point failure—once discovered, it should be repaired, or at least isolated, without affecting the entire system.
- Isolation and control of sensors—a path should be provided so that individual sensors can be checked and isolated.
- Expansion flexibility—accommodating new sensors in a computer system should be easy; the communication network should have the same sensor expansion capability.

Finally, an alarm communication and display system is an integrated system of people, procedures, and equipment. The equipment collects alarm data and presents the information so that people can quickly assess the alarms. Design of the system must address what information is presented to the operator, how the information is presented, how the operator communicates with the system, and the arrangement of the equipment at the operator's workstation. Operators then respond to the data according to approved procedures. The system may be a simple alarm panel display or a complex multicomputer control and communication system. In either case, the system must be designed with the specific needs and resources of the site in mind.

Security Principles

AC&D systems are used to reduce the load on human operators to assist their performance during a malevolent event.

The alarm communication subsystem collects and sends information to the operator.

The alarm control and display subsystem processes information and presents it to the operator quickly and clearly.

Questions

1. Discuss the following application considerations:

   a. A means of detecting a system failure (for example, line supervision) must always be provided.
   b. Backup power is essential.
   c. Spare equipment must be stored on site.
   d. Trained maintenance personnel are essential.
   e. The console arrangement must be easy for an operator to learn and use.
   f. Consoles that require lengthy command formats to be keyed into a computer should not be used in an AC&D system.
   g. The use of delicate equipment or software that is easily broken or disabled by careless operator actions should be avoided.

2. In what kind of situations would it be most logical to use a star communication network? A loop communication network?
3. What are the reasons for using a supervised alarm communication link?
4. What techniques can be used for physical protection of alarm communication lines?
5. What information does the console operator need when an alarm occurs?
6. What equipment is needed for display and control?
7. Who should be on the project design team at your facility?
8. What are the advantages and disadvantages of independent subsystems for alarm communication and display?

10
Entry Control

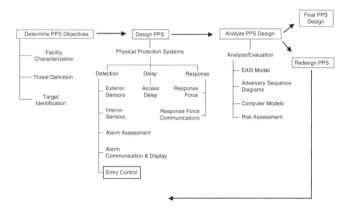

An entry control system allows the movement of authorized personnel and material into and out of facilities, while detecting and possibly delaying movement of unauthorized personnel and contraband. Entry control elements may be found at a facility boundary or perimeter, such as at vehicle gates, building entry points, or doors into rooms or other special areas within a building.

The objectives of an entry control system used for physical protection are:

- to permit only authorized persons to enter and exit;
- to detect and prevent the entry or exit of contraband material (weapons, explosives, unauthorized tools, or critical assets); and
- to provide information to security personnel to facilitate assessment and response.

In this text, entry control is defined as the physical equipment used to control the movement of people or material into an area. The term access control refers to the process of managing databases or other records and determining the parameters of authorized entry, such as who or what will be granted access, when they may enter, and where access will occur. The terms are often used interchangeably in industry; however, there are advantages to differentiating between the two. Many industrial access control systems include software to manage the database of those having authorized access, as well as the physical means of restricting entry or exit. Because the technical issues associated with the installation and use of entry control equipment are different than the administrative controls required to manage authorized access, they require separate consideration in order to achieve an effective and integrated subsystem.

The performance measures of entry control subsystems include throughput and error rates. Throughput is a measure of the time it takes for an authorized person or material to successfully pass an entry or exit point. Technology components that require longer throughput times may not be applicable in all situations, such as entry to an industrial facility at shift changes. Error rates will be discussed in more detail in the section entitled "Personnel Identity Verification (Biometrics)."

Personnel Entry Control

Personnel entry control is the portion of an entry control system used to authorize entry and to verify the authorization of personnel seeking entry to a controlled area. This verification decision is usually based on determining whether the person (1) is carrying a valid credential, (2) knows a valid personal identification number, or (3) possesses the proper unique physical characteristic that matches the person's characteristic recorded at enrollment (biometrics, such as fingerprint, hand geometry, etc.). These three concepts are summarized as what you have, what you know, and what you are. With the exception of biometric devices, entry control devices may be used independently of the authorized person. A physical characteristic match will verify the person's identity; a credential or an ID number will only verify that the person requesting entry has a valid credential or knows a valid number. Combinations of entry control technology can be used effectively to protect access to a facility. These combinations can reduce throughput, but will make the system harder for an adversary to defeat. Methods of personnel entry authorization that will be discussed include personal identification number, credentials, and positive personnel identity verification or biometrics.

Personal Identification Number

Systems are available in which a memorized number, referred to as a personal identification number (PIN), is used. To gain entry the user enters the PIN on a keypad. Some systems use a coded credential to locate the reference file associated with that badge number in the access control database. In this case, an individual

requesting access first inserts the coded credential and then enters a memorized number via a keypad. This number is compared to the one stored in the reference file for that person. If the numbers are the same, the person is granted entry. The memorized number may be selected by the individual enrolling, or it may be assigned. A four- to six-digit number is commonly used. This simple method does have weaknesses: (1) an individual could pass the PIN and credential to an unauthorized individual; (2) the PIN could be observed surreptitiously by an adversary (shoulder surfing); or (3) the PIN could be obtained by coercion. In addition, people often write PINs down, making it easier for an adversary to obtain the PIN.

There are two primary considerations for selecting a secure PIN. First, the PIN should be long enough, and second, the PIN should not be a number that is too meaningful to the individual to whom it is assigned. The PIN must have enough digits to prevent easy guesses. This is especially important where a PIN is the only criteria for granting entry. For a population of a few hundred, a four-digit PIN should be sufficient. Four digits allow for a total of 10,000 combinations, which is much larger than the number of people in the population. The probability of guessing a correct PIN is low under these circumstances.

If a person is allowed to choose his or her own PIN, choosing a PIN that is too meaningful to that person should be strongly discouraged. Birthdays, partial social security numbers, phone numbers, and other numbers may be easy for the individual to remember but may also be easy for an adversary to guess. Other easy numbers to remember like 1-1-1-1, 1-2-3-4, and similar sequences should also be avoided.

Some systems provide a maximum number of PIN entry attempts before disallowing the credential or generating an alarm to the central control system. Using the PIN in combination with credentials and biometrics helps to raise the level of security.

Credentials

There are many types of credentials used in personnel entry control. Those that will be discussed in this chapter are:

- photo identification badge
- exchange badge
- stored-image badge
- coded credential

The first three require a manual check by a guard and require a high degree of vigilance. Coded credentials are checked automatically.

Photo Identification Badge

The photo identification badge is a common credential used for personnel entry control, but it is not always effective. A false photo identification badge can be made, or an individual can make up their face to match that on a stolen badge in an effort to gain unauthorized entry. Also, because this kind of badge is manually checked, guard inattentiveness can reduce its effectiveness, especially at times when large numbers of people are entering a facility.

Exchange Badge

A badge exchange system requires that matching badges be held at each entry control point. When an employee presents a badge and requests entry, a guard compares the individual to the photo on the corresponding exchange badge held at the entry control point. If the two match, the guard exchanges the badges and allows entry. The exchange badge may contain more information than the employee badge and may be a different color. The employee's badge is held at the entry control point until the employee leaves the area, at which time the badges are again exchanged. In this way, the exchanged badge worn within the secure area is never allowed to leave the area. This reduces the possibility of a facility badge being counterfeited, lost, or stolen. The badge exchange system does not prevent someone from making up their face to match the image on a stolen badge in order to gain unauthorized entry.

Stored-Image Badge

The use of a stored-image (video comparator) system requires a guard to verify an individual's identity based on visual characteristics. A securely stored image is used for comparison with a real-time image of the individual requesting entry.

Two of the most important features of such a system are enrollment capability and access time. Enrollment capability is the maximum number of images that can be stored by the system. The access time is the time required from entry of the identification number until the stored image is displayed for viewing. These systems use a coded badge or keyboard to find the stored image for display and visual comparison by the guard.

Stored-image systems are not based on a unique, measurable characteristic, such as a fingerprint, so they are not considered to be personnel identity verification. However, they have an advantage over manual photo identification systems in that it is difficult to tamper with the stored image. In this way, the stored-image system is comparable to badge exchange systems. Nonetheless, they are still susceptible to the use of make-up to disguise an unauthorized person.

Coded Credential

Coded credential systems, also called key-card systems, are commercially available with a wide range of capabilities, including:

- maintenance of entry authorization records for each coded credential;
- provision of unique identification code numbers that can be read by a machine;

- termination of entry authorization for an individual without the necessity of recovering that individual's badge or credential; and
- provision for several levels of entry authorization, such as entry only at selected entry control points or only at certain times of the day.

Entry authorization records can be updated each time entry is requested using a coded credential. Each entry action and its time of occurrence, entry location, and the coded credential identification number can be recorded and listed on request. Many coded credentials are in the form of a badge that is worn or carried while in a facility. A technical introduction to the use and application of coded credentials is available (Wright, 1988).

There are many techniques available for coding a badge. The most common techniques include magnetic stripe, wiegand wire, bar codes, proximity, and smart cards.

Magnetic stripe encoding is widely used in commercial credit card systems. A strip of magnetic material located along one edge of the badge is encoded with data. These data are then read as the magnetic strip is moved through a slotted magnetic reader. The measure of the resistance of a magnetic material to changes in the stored information when exposed to magnetic field is called its coercivity. The coercivity is defined as the magnetic intensity of an applied field required to change the information. The unit of magnetic intensity used to describe the coercivity is the oersted.

Two materials have been used as the magnetic stripe medium. The one most commonly used for credit cards is a 300 oersted (low coercivity) magnetic material. This material is relatively easy to erase. The coercivity of the second magnetic stripe material is in the range of 2500–4000 oersteds (high coercivity). This material is the one most commonly used in security credential applications and is

very unlikely to be accidentally erased. Common household magnets are not strong enough to erase high-coercivity stripes. Less common rare-earth magnets, on the other hand, do produce field strengths strong enough to alter high-coercivity magnetic stripes.

The use of alphanumeric encoding allows both the badge-holder's name and a badge number to be included. Credential forgery is relatively easy since data from the magnetic strip can be decoded or duplicate badges encoded by the use of commercially available equipment. This vulnerability can be mitigated to a great degree through the use of proprietary, nonstandard encoding and reading techniques. The use of proprietary systems, however, may limit the ability to interface with other equipment or subsystems. This may also limit choices when considering upgrades or expansions.

Wiegand wire technology has been in existence for some time, and the wiegand signal output format has become a de facto industry standard. The code is produced by a series of parallel, embedded wires that have special magnetic properties. The wires are typically arranged in two rows (see Figure 10.1). Encoding is determined during card manufacture. Cards are swiped through a slotted card reader, much like the way magnetic stripe cards are read.

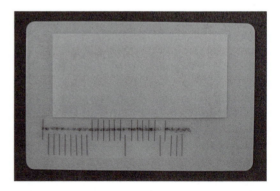

Figure 10.1 Weigand Wire Badge. The metal wires produce a unique code that is determined when the card is manufactured

While this technology is not used too much anymore, the weigand data protocol is still in common use.

The bar code, widely used in retail trade to automatically identify products at the point of sale, is sometimes used on coded credentials. The varying widths of the bars and spaces between them establish the code. To read the card, an optical sensor scans the bar code and transmits the information to a decoding unit. Typically, the bar code is printed on the credential and is used in much the same way as a magnetic stripe. Unless the bar code is covered with an opaque covering, it is relatively easy to duplicate. This opaque covering is becoming more commonplace as the bar code badge moves into the security credential market. Two-dimensional symbologies (2D bar codes) are also used on security credentials and are capable of storing more information than their ID counterparts.

The proximity badge is one whose information can be read without the badge being physically placed into a reader device. Proximity badges can be classified by the method of powering the badge, operating frequency range of the badge, and read-only or read/write capability (Wright, 1987).

The electronic proximity identification badge, a small RF transponder/transmitter, must be powered in some way. A long-life battery packaged with the unit powers active badges. For some types of badges the battery power is applied only when the badge enters the interrogation field. For others, the badge continuously broadcasts and the reader antenna picks up the RF data as the badge enters the reading field. The passive badge draws its power from the reader unit through the RF signal as it enters the interrogation field.

Proximity badges fall into two groups according to frequency. The low-frequency badges are in the 125 kHz range, and the high-frequency badges range from 2.5 MHz to over 1 GHz. A read-only badge contains a specific code usually fixed at the time of manufacture and cannot be changed.

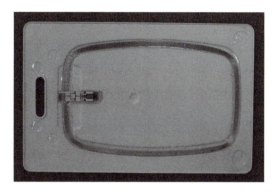

Figure 10.2 A Passive Proximity Badge. The embedded coil and the RF chip are visible through the transparent back

The read/write badge, on the other hand, usually contains a larger data field than read-only badges and can be programmed by the system manager as required. The proximity badge of Figure 10.2 has a transparent back showing the embedded components.

While relatively new in the United States, smart card technology has been in use for more than a decade in France. The smart card is the size of a standard bank credit card with an integrated circuit embedded in the card. Gold contacts on the surface of the card (see Figure 10.3) allow for communication with a reading

Figure 10.3 Smart Card with Embedded Microprocessor. The processor contains specific user data, which gives this device high security protection

device. Contactless smart cards use RF communications to talk to the reader and do not have the gold contacts. Cards with only memory circuits serve much the same function as magnetic stripe cards: badge number, user's name, and other information can be stored and read. A true smart card includes a microprocessor that makes the card smart and sets it apart from memory cards. The size of memory on the smart card ranges from 8 to 64 KB, with projections of 1 MB available in the future.

The main advantages of the smart card are its large memory and its high degree of resistance to forgery or compromise. These advantages must be considered relative to the high cost of smart cards. Many smart cards have the ability to encrypt communications, which adds another level of protection. When facility populations are large and the security level is not extremely high, the cost of smart cards is prohibitive. However, issuing smart cards to a small population for use at a very high security facility or to limit access to certain areas in large facilities may be appropriate. Examples of the latter case might be entry into areas containing precious metals or executive suites. A facility may also have extensive administrative concerns such as training, health care records, or property control; a smart card that combines one or all of these record-keeping functions with security features could be cost-effective.

Homeland Defense Presidential Directive 12 (HSPD12) is a presidential directive signed by George W. Bush in August of 2004 that directs the entire Federal Government and all contract agencies to use a single high-security credential. The credential is based on Federal Information Processing Standard 201 (FIPS 201) and uses both contact and contactless smart card technology. The implementation of this new credential is scheduled to be completed in the 2009–2010 timeframe. This directive primarily impacts federal and federal contractor facilities but may also have some impact on private industry.

For example, personnel driving vehicles into federal or contractor facilities on a routine basis may be required to obtain a federal ID. Oversight for the development and testing of the credentials and related equipment (readers and entry control systems), as well as issuance procedures, is being provided by GSA and NIST. For more information on HSPD-12 see http://www.smart.gov/, http://csrc.nist.gov/piv-program/, or http://www.smart.gov/iab/. Considerable information can be obtained by conducting an Internet search on HSPD-12 or FIPS 201. Caution must be used when reviewing information obtained through a web search because a considerable number of vendor sites will appear in the search results. Some vendors state that their products are HSPD-12 compliant but do not mention certification. Compliance may simply mean that the vendor believes that their product meets all the requirements; to be certified, their product must be submitted to GSA and NIST for testing. Upon successful completion of the testing, the product will be placed on the government official approved products list, which can be found at http://fips201ep.cio.gov/apl.php.

Personnel Identity Verification (Biometrics)

Personnel identity verification systems corroborate claimed identities on the basis of some unique physical biometric characteristic(s) of the individual. Commercial equipment is available that uses hand or finger geometry, handwriting, eye pattern, fingerprints, speech, face, and various other physical characteristics. All personnel identity verification systems consider the uniqueness of the feature used for identification, the variability of the characteristic, and the difficulty of implementing the system that processes the characteristic.

Biometric devices can differentiate between verification and recognition. In verification mode, a person initiates a claim of identity, presents the specific biometric feature for authorization, and the equipment agrees. In recognition mode, the person does not initiate the claim; the biometric device attempts to identify the person, and if the biometric information agrees with the database, entry is allowed.

Many biometric technologies use error rates as a performance indicator of the system. A Type I error, also called a false reject, is the improper rejection of a valid user. A Type II error or a false accept is the improper acceptance of an unauthorized person. Often these error curves are combined and displayed graphically to show the equal error rate. This is the crossover point where Type I errors equal Type II errors. This point is not necessarily the point at which the device should be operated. The equal error rate does not occur at the point where Type I or Type II errors are both lowest. It is a figure of merit that may be useful when comparing various biometric devices. Figure 10.4 shows an example of the graphical display of error curves and the equal error rate.

When selecting or deploying biometric devices, consideration of the security objectives is required to assure that the

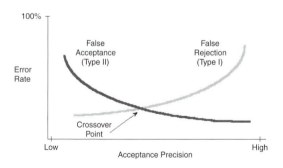

Figure 10.4 Equal Error Rate Graph. The false-accept and false-reject occurrences at a specific sensitivity of a biometric device can be plotted and their crossover point determined. This point is not where the device should be operated but can be used as a figure of merit when comparing devices

device will operate as required. Some systems may be set to operate in an area where the device will minimize false rejects, whereas others may minimize false accepts. The device cannot minimize both error types simultaneously, so a decision must be made as to the balance between false accept and false reject rates. This has a significant implication to system operation. A low false accept rate compromises system security, but allows all authorized users entry. False rejects, on the other hand, can deny access to authorized users in order to maintain high security. The security manager will undoubtedly hear about the cases of false rejects, particularly if senior managers or other influential employees are denied access. Adversaries, on the other hand, are unlikely to report that entry was obtained due to false acceptance!

Hand/Finger Geometry

Personnel identity verification using the hand geometry system is based on characterizing the shape of the hand. The underlying technique measures 3D features of the hand such as the widths and lengths of fingers and the thickness of the hand (see Figure 10.5).

The hand-read sequence is initiated by presenting a coded credential or by entering a PIN. The user then places the hand on a reflective platen; the device has guide pins to help the user properly align fingers. Although the guide pin arrangement is best suited to the scanning of right hands, the left hand can be enrolled and scanned by placing the left hand on the platen palm up. A solid-state camera takes a picture of the hand, which includes a side view for hand thickness. Due to the combination of infrared illumination and the reflective platen, the image of the hand appears as a silhouette to the camera. The system measures the necessary lengths and widths and creates a representation of the hand called a feature vector. Figure 10.6 shows an example of a hand geometry unit.

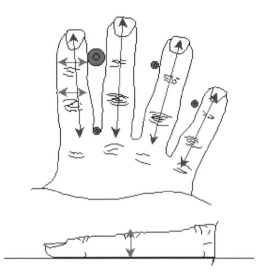

Figure 10.5 Hand Geometry Measures. Certain aspects of the hand, such as widths and lengths of fingers and thickness of the hand, are measured and used to create a user template

During verification, the feature vector is compared with previous measurements (the template) obtained during enrollment. If the feature vector and template match within an allowable tolerance, verification is successful. Testing of a hand geometry system at Sandia National Laboratories indicates that Type I and Type II error rates of less than 1% are achievable (Holmes et al., 1991). A report on the use of a hand geometry unit in an operational environment has also been prepared (Ruehle and Ahrens, 1997).

A similar system uses two fingers to verify identity. This two-finger geometry system measures finger lengths and widths of the index/middle finger pair. Because only one guide pin is used (between the two fingers), the left or right hand fingers work equally well. The functional concept of this device is similar to the hand geometry system.

Handwriting
Signature verification has been used for many years by the banking industry, although signatures are easily forged. Automatic handwriting verification systems have been developed that use handwriting dynamics, such as displacement, velocity, and acceleration. Statistical evaluation of these data indicates that an individual's signature is unique and reasonably consistent from one signature to the next. Transducers that measure these characteristics can be located in either the writing instrument or tablet. These systems provide low security and are best used in applications where authorizing signatures for a transaction are already in use.

Figure 10.6 Hand Geometry Unit. The hand is placed on the platen and a small camera takes a picture. Specific measures are used to create a feature vector, which is compared to the stored user template

Fingerprints
Fingerprints have been used as a personnel identifier for more than 100 years and are still considered one of the most reliable means of distinguishing one individual from another. The art of processing human fingerprints for identification has been

greatly improved in recent years by the development of automated systems. Such systems, which rely on image processing and pattern recognition, have application in personnel entry control. A variety of commercial systems are now available that perform fingerprint verification. Figure 10.7 is an example of a fingerprint verification system.

Most fingerprint verification systems use minutia points, the fingerprint ridge endings and bifurcations, as the identifying features of the fingerprint, although some systems use the whole image for comparison purposes. All fingerprint identification systems require care in finger positioning and accurate print analysis and comparison for reliable identification.

Optical methods using a prism and a solid-state camera are most often used to capture the fingerprint image. Dry or worn fingerprints can be difficult to image using optical methods, so special coatings have been applied to the optical platens to enhance the image quality. The purpose of these coatings is to ensure a good optical coupling between the platen and the fingerprint.

Figure 10.7 Fingerprint Identification Unit. A PIN is entered into the keypad and the index finger is placed on the center reader. The system then compares the fingerprint to one stored in a file to grant access

Ultrasound is another fingerprint imaging method. Because it is able to image below the top skin surface to the lower layers where the fingerprint is not damaged, it is not as susceptible to dry or worn fingerprints. Due to the raster scan required by the ultrasonic transducer, ultrasound imaging is not as fast as optical methods.

Direct imaging sensors that use solid-state devices are also available for acquiring fingerprint images. Capacitive, electric field, and thermal methods have been commercially developed. It is thought that the projected lower cost of these devices, due to the efficient manufacture of silicon chips, will make fingerprint verification devices common on the desktop for secure computer log-on. Overcoming the difficulties of hardening delicate silicon chips for everyday use has delayed their widespread implementation. Electrostatic discharge, finger oil, and sweat are harsh on silicon devices.

Eye Pattern

The retina is the membrane lining the more posterior part of the inside of the eye. It contains light-sensitive cones and rods and nerve cells. A retinal scan identity verifier is shown in Figure 10.8. The pattern of blood vessels in the body is unique, and the pattern on the retina of the eye can be assessed optically through the lens of the eye. A circular path about the center of vision is scanned with a very low-intensity, nonlaser light from infrared light-emitting diodes (LED). The intensity of the reflected light versus beam position during the scan indicates the unique location of the retinal blood vessels. To enroll, the user must look into the verifier and stare at an alignment target while the optical scan is being made. Several such scans are usually taken and algorithmically combined to create the reference profile. If the device is to be used in the verification mode, a PIN number is usually assigned at this time as well.

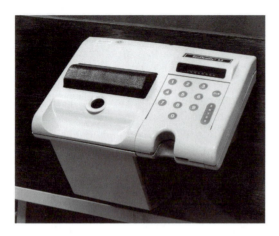

Figure 10.8 Retinal Scan Device. The user enters a PIN, then looks through the verifier, and aligns a target. A scan of the retina is made and compared with the stored image. As good as this device was, users did not accept it and it is no longer available

Verification, which requires only a single scan, is done in a similar manner. The retinal scanner can also operate in recognition mode. In this mode, the entry of a PIN is not required. Because the entire enrollment file must be reviewed, verification processing time increases as the number of enrollees is increased. Data from an operational evaluation in a laboratory environment indicates that Type I and Type II error rates of less than 1.5% are achievable (Holmes et al., 1991). User acceptance of this unit was very low, due to the unfounded fear of damage to the eye by the LED. As a result, this technology is no longer available.

Another technology uses the iris to accomplish identification. The iris is the colored portion of the eye that limits the amount of light allowed into the eye. This system uses a video camera to image the iris structure of the eye (see Figure 10.9). The unique structure of an iris can be used to identify an individual. This system operates in the recognition mode, so entry of a PIN is not required. A distinct advantage for this system is that the camera images the iris at a distance of about 10.12 in., so no physical contact between the face and the scanner is required. In addition, the eye is externally illuminated with visible light, so there is no LED shining in through the lens. Consequently, user acceptance is better than for the retinal scanner.

Data from a laboratory test of a prototype iris scanner indicated some difficulty with glare off glasses. This caused some Type I (false reject) errors. No Type II (false accept) errors were observed in the laboratory test (Bouchier et al., 1996). Later devices incorporated glare detection and compensation features to counteract problems. Transaction times range from 4 or 5 s (by practiced users) up to 15 s (for those new to the system). Approximately 2% of the population cannot be enrolled due to blindness or other iris damage, people whose eyes are extremely dilated (no iris to work with) or very dark irises, so they require another method of granting secure access. Both retinal scan and iris scan devices offer high levels of security protection in an entry control subsystem.

Voice

Voice is a useful attribute for identity verification and is appropriate for automatic data processing. Speech measurements useful for speaker discrimination include waveform envelope, voice pitch period, relative amplitude spectrum, and resonant frequencies of the vocal tract. The system may ask the user to speak a specific predetermined word or to repeat a series of words or numbers selected by the system in order to verify access.

While this technology currently offers low security, it is an attractive alternative due to its ease of deployment and acceptance by the public. Voice recognition systems need only be installed on one end of a telephone system, and perhaps centrally located, reducing the number of units required. In addition, most people have experience with using telephones, so training is minimal, and distrust of the

Figure 10.9 Iris Scan Device. The user aligns the eye with the camera in center, then waits for a scan to be completed and grant access

technology is low. As a result, several units are currently being marketed for security applications, and further development is active.

Voice systems also have some associated procedural issues. A person's voice can change due to sickness or stress, so a procedure or backup method of access must be provided to accommodate these instances.

Face

Facial verification systems use distinguishing characteristics of the face to verify a person's identity. Most systems capture the image of the face using a video camera, although one system captures a thermal image using an infrared imager.

Distinguishing features are extracted from the image and compared with previously stored features. If the two match within a specified tolerance, positive identity verification results.

Although facial systems have been proposed and studied for a number of years, commercial systems have only been available recently. Developers have had to contend with two difficult problems: (1) wide variations in the presentation of the face (head tilt and rotation, presence or absence of glasses, facial hair changes, facial expression changes, etc.) and (2) lighting variations (day versus night, location A versus location B, etc.). Performance of currently available face systems has not yet approached that of more mature biometric technologies, but face technology does have the appeal of noncontact and the potential to provide face-in-the-crowd identifications, for identifying known or wanted criminals. This latter application could be useful in casinos, shopping malls, or other places where large crowds can gather.

Other Techniques

Keystroke technology (typing patterns) has been developed and marketed for secure computer log-on. Other verifier techniques based on such things as ear shape, gait (walking patterns), fingernail bed, and body odor have been studied, but little development has been attempted.

Because each biometric technology has some limits in terms of inability to enroll certain people, procedures dealing with this event must be developed. Examples include cataract interference with retinal scanners; very dry or heavily damaged skin (scars, etc.) can cause problems with fingerprint devices; some signature and some speech systems have problems handling certain people because their results are not repeatable. In addition, authorized users may occasionally suffer injuries such as broken fingers or hands, eye injuries or surgery, or other medical conditions, which may temporarily affect their ability to use a biometric device. Additional technology or guard intervention may be required to address this problem. For additional information, Jain et al. (1999) have written a thorough review of biometric techniques and their application. Others (Rejman-Greene, 1998) have discussed biometric devices and security considerations.

Personnel Entry Control Bypass

When coded credentials or biometric technologies are used to allow personnel access into rooms, the use of keyed locks as a bypass route should be considered. This bypass will be useful in case of a component or power failure. The possible vulnerability introduced by this alternate access path can be countered through the use of a BMS or other door sensor. In the event that the door is opened, an alarm will be recorded and can be investigated. This will happen whether a key is used or if the lock is picked or broken. For areas or rooms where multiple entry doors exist, only one door need be equipped with a keyed lock.

Contraband Detection

Any item that is prohibited from an area is contraband. Contraband screening typically occurs when entering a secure area. Unauthorized weapons, explosives, and tools are contraband because they can be used to steal or to gain access to or damage vital equipment. Drugs, cell phones, radios, computers, and computer media are some additional items that could be considered contraband at a facility. Where these items are a part of the threat definition, all personnel, materials, and vehicles should be examined for contraband before entry is allowed. Methods to screen for weapons, tools, and explosives are discussed in the following sections. The technologies discussed include: manual search used for all threats; metal detectors used for weapons, tools, and bomb components; package searches (X-ray systems) used for weapons, tools, and bomb components; and explosives detectors used for both the bulk explosive charge and for trace explosives residues. Additionally, there is a brief discussion of chemical and biological agent detection and their role in facility protection.

Manual Search

Manual search should not be overlooked as a contraband detection method. Screeners performing manual searches can be very effective if they are properly trained to recognize the threat items and if they remain vigilant. Advantages of manual searches are low hardware investment cost and flexibility. Two disadvantages of manual search, compared to the technologies described below, are slow throughput and higher labor costs.

Metal Detectors

One system employed for the detection of metal is a magnetometer. The magnetometer is a passive device that monitors the earth's magnetic field and detects changes to that field caused by the presence of ferromagnetic materials. This method detects only ferromagnetic materials (those that are attracted by a magnet). Materials such as copper, aluminum, and zinc are not detected. While most firearms are made of steel, some are not and therefore will not be detected by a magnetometer. Although magnetometers have not been used for contraband screening for many years, research and development of a modern magnetometer has been conducted in recent years. Although the term magnetometer is often used to refer to metal detectors in general, this device differs greatly from modern active metal detectors.

Most metal detectors currently in use to detect contraband carried by personnel actively generate a varying magnetic field over a short period of time. These devices either detect the changes made to the field due to the introduction of metal to the field or detect the presence of eddy currents that exist in a metallic object caused by a pulsed field. The magnitude of the metal detector's response to metallic objects is determined by several factors including the conductivity of the metal, the magnetic properties of the metal (relative permeability), object shape and size, and the orientation of the object within the magnetic field.

At present two methods can be used to actively detect metal: continuous wave and pulsed field. Continuous-wave detectors generate a steady-state magnetic field within the frequency band of 100 Hz to 25 kHz. Pulsed-field detectors generate fixed frequency pulses in the 400–500 pulse-per-second range. Due to the complex shape of the waveforms employed, the pulsed fields may have frequency components from zero to several tens of kilohertz. Unfortunately, the only manufacturer of continuous-wave metal detectors is no longer in business, thus they are not commercially available.

A typical coil configuration for continuous wave metal detection is illustrated in Figure 10.10A. A steady-state sinusoidal signal is applied to the transmitter coil located at one side of the detector arch. This coil produces a magnetic field of low strength. The receiver coils are mounted on the opposite side of the arch such that a person being screened passes between the transmitter and the receiver coils. The signal is detected by the receiver coils and is then routed to a balanced differential amplifier, which amplifies only the difference between two signals. When there is no metal present within the arch, there is no difference in the signals at the inputs to the differential amplifier; therefore, there is no output signal from the amplifier. When a metallic object enters the arch, the changes it makes to the magnetic field disturb the balance of the receiver coils. The unbalanced field produces a difference at the differential amplifier resulting in an output signal. This signal is then further amplified and phase-checked. If the signal exceeds a selected threshold, an alarm is generated. The phase detection permits some optimization of detection for either ferromagnetic (high relative permeability) or nonferromagnetic (low relative permeability) metals.

A typical coil configuration for a pulsed-field metal detector is shown in Figure 10.10B. The coil arrangement is similar to that of the continuous-wave metal detector. The greatest difference to the coil configuration is that the balanced

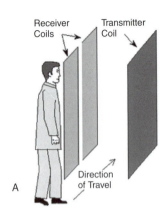

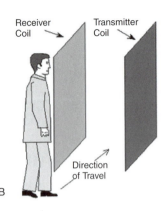

Figure 10.10 Metal Detector Technologies. A represents a continuous wave device and B a pulsed wave device. Continuous wave devices are no longer available.

receiver coils are not required for pulsed-field operation. The multiple transmitter coils produce magnetic field flux patterns that lessen the effects of object orientation on detector response. The low-inductance transmitter coils are driven with a series of pulses that produce short bursts of magnetic field (as short as 50 μs), 200–400 times per second. During the time that the magnetic field is present, the receiver amplifiers are switched off. Following the end of the transmitted pulse, the receiver amplifiers are switched on for a period of time, typically a few tens of milliseconds. When there is no metal present in the arch, the output of the receiver amplifiers is the low background electromagnetic noise. When there is a metallic object present in the arch, the collapse of the magnetic pulse induces an eddy current in the metal. This eddy current decreases rapidly as a function of the resistivity of the metal but persists long enough to be present when the receiver amplifiers are switched on. The signal is then further amplified and phase-detected. If the signal exceeds a selected threshold, an alarm is generated. The phase detection again allows for optimization for detection of ferromagnetic metals or nonferromagnetic metals. Modern digital technology allows for more analysis of the signal, resulting in better discrimination between different types of

metals and real targets and the harmless metallic objects carried by people being screened.

When a portal metal detector is used to detect very small quantities of metal such as gold, detection may be very difficult. In the case of a continuous-wave detector, the use of a higher-than-usual frequency will enhance detection; in all cases very high sensitivity operation will be required. Because high-sensitivity operation will sharply increase the NAR, an area for personnel to change out of steel-toed shoes and to remove other metallic items from their body may be required. Handheld metal detectors can detect even very small quantities of metals and may be better suited to the task of screening very small items. The disadvantage of handheld metal detectors is the requirement for active guard participation in the screening process and the time required for the search. Handheld metal detectors can also be considered intrusive due to the proximity of the metal detector to the person being screened. This can be especially intrusive when the screener and the person being screened are of opposite sex. Many sites, notably airports, provide same-sex operators to address this unease.

Because the magnetic field is not confined to the area between the coils and metal detectors are sensitive to metal moving outside the physical boundaries of the detector, care must be exercised in determining detector placement. Any movable metallic objects either in front or to the side of the detector, such as doors, forklifts, and carts, can cause nuisance alarms. Electromagnetic transients, such as radio transmitters, power-line fluctuations, and flickering fluorescent lighting, can cause false alarms.

Metal detectors are designed to be tolerant of some nonmoving metal in their immediate area. Reinforcing steel in concrete floors and walls and other metallic building materials can be tolerated to some degree; however, installing a metal detector against a steel support beam is not recommended. Large quantities of metal can cause severe distortions in the magnetic field. In some cases, the metal detector will not operate and may generate an error alarm; in other cases the detector may continue to operate but have areas of extremely low or high sensitivity. These distortions may lead to missed targets or unusually high nuisance alarms due to innocuous items. Metallic items, such as safety equipment, metal trash cans, chairs, and other items, may not completely interfere with a metal detector if placed close to the detector but can cause distortions to the detection field. For this reason, some installations institute a no-move rule for these metallic items within the vicinity of the detector following installation testing.

Package Search

Packages may be searched for contraband manually or by active interrogation. Active interrogation methods used to detect contraband objects include a family of X-ray approaches: single energy transmission X-ray, multiple-energy X-ray, computed tomography (CT) scan, and backscatter X-ray. In general, these methods are not safe for use on personnel; however, a backscatter X-ray technology for screening personnel will be discussed

in the next section. Simple single energy transmission X-ray imagers are used to find metallic items (i.e., weapons, tools, and metal components in bombs) and the other techniques are designed to image materials with low atomic numbers. The atomic number (Z) is the number of protons in the nucleus of an atom. Examples of low-Z contraband materials are explosives, drugs, and some foods. Low-Z atoms include hydrogen, oxygen, carbon, and all the elements up to aluminum, which is Z number 26.

A conventional single energy transmission X-ray package search system produces an image for an operator to inspect. This approach is effective when the operator is properly trained and vigilant and when the image is not too cluttered. Metals strongly attenuate X-rays, while less dense and low-Z materials do not. Conventional X-rays will not penetrate the heavy materials sometimes used for shipping containers or in vehicles. Higher-energy X-rays or multiple-energy X-rays can be used to assess the contents of the larger and denser shipping containers and vehicles. Because most of the development of low-Z screening devices is directed toward the detection of explosives, these technologies are discussed in detail below. While discussion of these devices is focused on explosive detection, most of these technologies can be adjusted to search for drugs as well.

Explosives Detection

Explosives detection technologies are divided into bulk and trace methods. This division is based on the target of the technology—macroscopic (bulk), detonable amounts of explosives or the particle and vapor (trace) residues associated with handling explosives. Bulk technologies have the advantage of targeting specific threat amounts of explosives. Trace techniques target residue that can lead a screener to perform secondary screening. Usually, the bulk techniques utilize ionizing radiation that is not suitable for use on people due to safety considerations. Methods of bulk explosives detection and trace explosives detection are presented in the following sections. References on explosives detection include an excellent description of various technologies (Yinon, 1999), a survey of commercially available equipment (Theisen et al., 2004), and a survey of existing and potential standoff technologies (National Academy of Sciences, 2004).

Bulk Explosives Detection Bulk explosives detection technologies measure characteristics of bulk materials, thereby screening for the presence of explosives. Some of the bulk characteristics that may be measured are the X-ray absorption coefficient, the X-ray backscatter coefficient, the dielectric constant, gamma or neutron interaction, and microwave or infrared emissions. Further analysis of these parameters can result in calculated mass, density, nitrogen, carbon, and oxygen content, and effective atomic number (effective Z). While none of these characteristics are unique to explosives, they are sufficiently unique to indicate a high probability of the presence of explosives. Fortunately, many materials that share similar bulk characteristics with explosives are not common among everyday items. Some bulk detection devices are sensitive enough (minimum detectable amount is less than the threat mass) and are specific enough (low NAR) to allow for effective automated detection explosives. Automated detection provides significant advantages, including reduced labor costs and lower reliance on human interpretation of images for detection.

X-ray technologies are continuing to grow more sophisticated and are widely deployed in many configurations from portable package imagers to very large systems capable of imaging a large truck and its cargo. Using backscatter technologies, people can be safely imaged, although X-ray technologies are most commonly used for package searches. These devices usually serve a dual purpose. The package being searched for guns or other contraband is simultaneously analyzed for the presence of explosives.

Simple, single energy transmission X-ray scanners do not provide enough information to make the explosives search, so a method to extract more information is needed. Dual energy technologies measure the mass absorption coefficient and enable approximation of the effective Z number. The image displayed can be highlighted using colors to draw the operator's attention to areas of the image with a low Z number that matches explosives. Backscatter technology can image low Z using the relatively large amount of X-ray energy scattered back in the direction of the source by low-Z materials. These areas appear bright in the backscatter image drawing the operator's attention.

Computed tomography (CT) is an automated technology for explosives detection that provides detection of small threat masses. The X-ray source and detectors are mounted on a gantry that spins around the package, imaging the contents from many different angles. A computer uses that data to construct a 3D representation of the contents. CT scanners are the only X-ray approach that can extract enough information to calculate the material's mass, density, and mass absorption coefficient. This extracted information can be used for automated detection of materials that may constitute a threat. Compared to simple transmission X-ray devices, CT devices have significantly higher purchase and maintenance costs due to the heavy spinning gantry. CT also suffers from relatively high NARs (up to 20%) compared to trace technologies, mainly from foods and some polymers.

For vehicle and cargo-container searches, high-energy X-ray devices are available. Often these devices are large and built into fixed sites, even into their own buildings, for screening commercial cargo shipments. The high-energy illumination is highly penetrating, allowing a reasonable image to be produced through the engine compartment or the filled trailer of a commercial truck. The method for producing the high-energy light is immaterial. Gamma-ray devices that use a radioactive source instead of an X-ray tube are also used for this purpose. Backscatter X-ray technology may be combined with high-energy technology to provide low-Z detection.

Low-dose backscatter X-ray devices can safely examine people for hidden items, providing an image of the body beneath the clothes. A person entering a scanner booth must be scanned two times, front and back, to ensure that no explosives are secreted on the person. The radiation dose to a person being screened is about 10 microrem. This low dose meets the NRC requirement that personnel must not receive a radiation dose above 100 millirem/year (10 CFR Part 20, Section 20.1301 (a) (1), 1991). Radiation exposure should always be kept as low as reasonably achievable (10 CFR Part 20, Section 20.1301 (d) (3), 1991). Figure 10.11 illustrates a typical computer-enhanced image obtained with various materials located on the subject. These devices are currently being tested by the Transportation Security Agency (TSA) for possible use in airports and subway systems.

Nuclear technologies interrogate a vehicle (or package) using gamma rays or neutrons. Gamma-ray devices are similar to high-energy X-ray devices which were discussed. Thermal neutron activation (TNA) devices determine the nitrogen content of a material. A thermal (low energy or slow) neutron is absorbed by the nucleus of nitrogen-14, producing excited nitrogen-15. This excited atom radiates a gamma ray of specific wavelength and detection of this specific gamma ray is evidence of nitrogen content. Because many explosives are nitrogen-rich, these devices can automatically detect their presence. Both the neutrons and the gamma rays are very penetrating, making them suitable for large, dense item searches. Pulsed fast neutron absorption

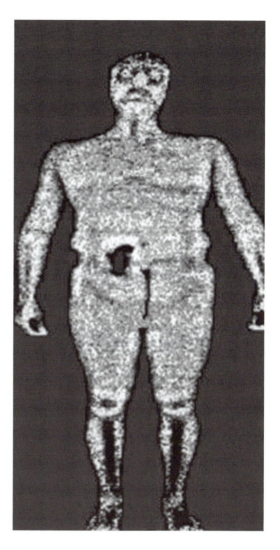

Figure 10.11 Computer-Enhanced Output of an X-Ray Personnel Scanner. The subject appears to have what looks like a weapon in the belt. These systems are being tested by TSA in selected US airports

(PFNA) can determine carbon and oxygen content. Here, "fast" means high energy (several MeV). International law prohibits the irradiation of food with energies above 10 MeV due to concerns of making the food radioactive, so there is a potential risk if a system using more than 10 MeV is used to screen food shipments. When combined with TNA, a PFNA device can also measure nitrogen content.

In theory, measuring carbon, nitrogen, and oxygen content allows more specific identification of explosives and better rejection of nuisance materials (that may be nitrogen-rich). The major drawbacks of these devices are their cost (for vehicles from about $500,000 and up, TNA is less expensive), size, throughput, and use of radioactive materials in the neutron source or neutron generator tube. Some small (<100 lb) TNA package search systems are commercially available.

Quadrupole resonance (QR) technology is a promising commercial technology that uses pulsed low-energy radio waves to determine the presence of nitrogen-rich materials. QR is very sensitive (detects small threat masses) for some explosives. Contraband can be shielded from the radio interrogation with a thin covering of metal, but the device can detect the presence of the shielding and warn the operator. A QR scanner is compact, relatively low cost (about $100,000), and does not subject the package to ionizing radiation. Hand-held QR systems are in development and may provide a useful tool for manually screening people for explosives.

Raman analysis uses laser interrogation followed by analysis of the spectrum of scattered light to identify materials. Portable, lightweight systems have been developed for hazardous materials detection, including explosives. A laser can shine through some containers (such as glass) or directly on the suspect material surface. Small but visible amounts of material are required for detection. As currently configured, this new technology could be useful for screening through bottles or plastic bags, but it is not appropriate for package searches.

Technologies for standoff detection of explosives are in great demand because of the need to detect explosive devices from a safe distance. But at present, standoff detection remains an area of much research and few commercial products, which is especially true for the detection of suicide bombers and large vehicle bombs. Infrared

cameras can be used to image people for concealed objects that could be explosives. Passive and active millimeter-wave (approximately 100 GHz, sometimes called terahertz or THz) imaging systems are available that operate similar to infrared systems, but in a different part of the frequency spectrum. Laser methods that look for characteristic fluorescence or atomic emission are another example of techniques under development. Standoff detection of explosives is a difficult challenge (National Academy of Sciences, 2004). Vendor claims regarding the performance of standoff detection devices should be investigated to verify their performance against the defined threat in the expected environment.

All of the bulk explosives detection technologies have strengths and weaknesses. A successful system based on bulk detection techniques may consist of a combination of two or more of these technologies. If enough information is gathered on a suspect material through this combination, a real determination of the presence of explosives may be made.

Trace Explosives Detection   Use of trace explosives detectors has become common for checkpoint screening in the last decade. Trace vapors and microscopic particles are associated with explosives and their handling. Detection technologies for trace explosives include ion mobility spectrometry, colorimetry, chemiluminescence, mass spectrometry, fluorescence, and canine olfaction. Key performance metrics for trace detectors include limit of detection (the smallest detectable amount) and selectivity (ability to distinguish one material from another). Many trace detectors are amazingly sensitive, detecting less than a nanogram. Still, vendor claims regarding detector performance should be verified prior to purchase. True detection of explosive traces leads a screener to search further for the materials in their threat definition.

Sampling is a key part of effective trace detection because the trace residues must be collected and then delivered to a detector for analysis. Swipe sampling, where a fabric swab is rubbed across the object (i.e., person, package, or vehicle), is the most efficient method of collecting particle residues from hard surfaces and produces the most collected mass for analysis. The collected sample on the swab is vaporized by heating and directed into a detector. Vapor sampling, where the air next to the object is collected (often with some agitation), is most efficient for sampling from inside containers or from soft surfaces. Because it does not require touching the object, vapor sampling is less invasive than swipe sampling.

The challenge involved in detecting trace explosives vapors is evident after consideration of the low-vapor-phase concentrations of several common high explosives. Concentrations in the parts per billion or parts per trillion range are typical, with further reductions in vapor pressures encountered when the explosive constituent is packaged in an oil-based gel or solvent (for example, RDX in C-4 plastic explosive). Explosive molecules also readily adsorb upon most materials at room temperature and decompose upon moderate heating or exposure to large doses of energy; hence, transport and collection of vapor-phase explosive molecules is achieved only at the expense of significant sample loss.

In an ion mobility spectrometer or IMS, the analyte molecules in an air sample are negatively ionized using a radioactive Ni-63 source and chloride dopant, then passed into a drift cell through a shutter, which opens periodically (about every 20 ms). Within the drift region, the ionized species move down an electric field gradient against a counter-flow of an inert gas. The ions separate by mobility, with the lightweight species and their smaller cross-sections progressing more quickly upstream than the larger species. At the end of the drift region, the ions strike a Faraday plate that records the output voltage as a function of ion drift time. A typical IMS drift cell is about 5 cm in length with an electric field gradient of 200 V/cm. Under these conditions, the drift times of the explosives molecules range from 5 to 15 ms. While common high explosives form negative ions, some of the emerging explosive threats like triacetonetriperoxide (or TATP) also form positive ions. IMS instruments with both positive and negative ion analysis capability are now commercially available.

IMS-based detectors provide high sensitivity (nanogram quantities) to dynamite, military-grade TNT, and plastic explosives compounds, at instrument costs of $40,000 for bench top models or $25,000 for handheld units. The combination of selective ionization and time-of-flight separation achieved in the drift region provides enough specificity for screening applications. Interferents and NARs are low in the field, with some exceptions such as compounds used as fragrances in lotions and perfumes. Sensitivity, ease of operation, instrument robustness, and low maintenance are advantages of IMS. Although their purchase cost is lower, the handheld detectors have higher maintenance requirements and need AC power for operation beyond a few hours.

Several vendors offer technologies where a color change is evidence of explosive presence. Generally these kits have some materials like a spray, test paper, or ampoule that gets consumed during the test. Chemical reactions produce the color changes. Frequently, multiple solutions are used in sequence to determine what explosive (if any) is present. The great advantage of this method is low cost and portability. Disadvantages include high NAR and disposal of consumable chemicals. Some have a strong smell.

Chemiluminescence detectors use photochemical detection. The vapor sample is collected and separated into its components using a fast gas chromatograph. The sample is then heated so that any nitrogen compounds that are present will decompose to form nitrogen oxide (NO). Reaction of NO with ozone forms an excited state of nitrogen dioxide (NO_2), which emits a photon that can be detected using a phototube. The coupling of the photoemission and the chromatograph permits identification of nitro-based explosive compounds. Without the gas chromatography step, one would only know that a nitrogen-containing material was present. With the chromatographic separation, identification of several explosives in a single sample is possible in under a minute.

Chemiluminescence detectors have excellent sensitivity (pictogram quantities) to common high explosives, including compounds with very low vapor pressures such as RDX and PETN. However, the chemiluminescence instruments are also the most expensive of the commercial detectors, have the longest analysis time, and require more maintenance than other trace detectors.

It is possible to place another detector after the chromatography step, for example, an electron capture detector (ECD). ECDs take advantage of the high electron affinity of nitro compounds to identify trace explosives in a vapor sample. Electron capture technology itself cannot determine the specific explosive detected, but by coupling the ECD with another technology such as a gas chromatograph (GC), the type of explosive can be identified. GC/ECD is more commonly used for laboratory analysis than for routine checkpoint screening. Advantages of GC/ECD are low cost, good specificity, and low limits of detection. Disadvantages are long analysis times (minutes are typical) and frequent GC column maintenance.

In mass spectrometry, ions are processed in magnetic and electric fields to determine their mass-to-charge ratio. Quadrupole mass spectrometry and quadrupole ion trap time-of-flight are two examples of this method. A wide variety of mass spectrometer configurations are available.

In a quadrupole mass spectrometer, the sample molecules are negatively ionized with an electrical discharge, accelerated in an electric field, and then focused onto an ion detector with the magnetic field of a quadrupole. Selected mass numbers characteristic of explosives can be monitored individually or a range scanned continuously. The mass of the parent ion and characteristic fragment or daughter ions can be determined. Alarms are produced when a threshold current is exceeded for a given mass number or combination of mass numbers.

A quadrupole ion trap time-of-flight mass spectrometer collects ions in the trap, where they orbit. Periodically the trap is emptied and the time for the ions to travel to the detector is measured. The time-of-flight depends on the square root of the mass (kinetic energy) of the ion. IMS is similar to time-of-flight mass spectrometry, except IMS occurs at atmospheric pressure and mass spectrometry occurs under vacuum. Alarms are produced from the mass spectrum in the same way as described above.

Mass spectrometry is the gold standard of the analytical chemistry laboratory. Advantages of mass spectrometry are specificity and low limits of detection. These devices can be easily reprogrammed to detect additional analytes, a desirable feature in a world of evolving threats. However, high costs, high maintenance requirements, and the need for expert operators have slowed the deployment of mass spectrometers for routine screening. Newly developed instruments are better suited to explosives detection in checkpoint settings, and improvements continue.

Amplifying fluorescent polymers can change their fluorescence in the presence of some explosives. Systems have been developed with a fluorescence that quenches in the presence of an explosive molecule like TNT. The TNT molecule quenches the fluorescence of all the monomers (thousands of them per molecule), thus amplifying the effect many times. Highly sensitive detection of low picogram to femtogram quantities are possible. The polymers are coated onto capillary tubes and placed adjacent to a photomultiplier tube. Vapors are drawn through the tube, and changes in the fluorescence above a threshold produce an alarm. Advantages of these systems are small size, low cost, and high sensitivity. Not all explosives will produce a response with the existing polymers and research to develop coatings for more explosives is ongoing.

Canine olfaction is used widely in law enforcement and the military for locating hidden explosives. Where mobility is required, such as building searches or quickly relocating detection capabilities, canines excel. Detection is actually made by the handler who observes the dog behavior. Canines and their handlers require constant retraining to continue to identify synthetic compounds such as explosives. Moreover, the reliability of canine inspection is subject to the vigilance and skill of the handler and the health and disposition of the dog. Canine teams also require frequent breaks, which may create the need for multiple teams. While acquisition costs are low, the labor of the handler is a recurring cost. As a result, the use of canines is less common at fixed checkpoints, where commercial explosive detectors are gaining greater acceptance as the preferred method for screening.

Trace explosives detection portals have been developed over the past decade and are now deployed at many airports. A trace portal collects particle and vapor samples from a person after agitating the person's clothing with short bursts of air. These pulses of air help dislodge explosives residues, while the air surrounding the person is filtered. The filter collects explosives vapors and particles for several seconds, and then the filter is heated to desorb any collected explosives into a trace detector (ion mobility spectrometer or mass spectrometer). Screening time ranges from 10 to 25 s. Advantages include automated detection, high sensitivity (nanograms), and noninvasive screening of the whole person. Disadvantages are size, cost (approximately $150,000), and maintenance. For comparison, swipe sampling of a person is possible, but would likely be considered invasive and would require more than a minute per person.

A summary of many commercial explosives detectors is available (Theisen et al., 2004). Commercial trace explosives detectors must be carefully selected to meet the needs of each facility. Vendor claims should always be verified through testing in the appropriate operating environment. The sensitivity, nuisance alarm resistance, response time, operating and maintenance costs, and list of explosive materials in the threat definition are all factors to consider when selecting a detector.

Chemical and Biological Agent Detection
Chemical and biological agent detection is typically performed with point sensors, searching for evidence of an attack at the site perimeter. In the case of chemical agent attack, an adversary may attack suddenly with large (and therefore quickly lethal) concentrations, and the security system goal is an early warning for successful interruption and neutralization of the adversary. Military and environmental chemical (trace) detectors have been developed over the past century for this purpose. Some modifications may need to be made if continuous operation over extended time periods is required. Careful consideration should be made regarding NARs. Because the response to a chemical attack must be fast and complete, nuisance alarms or drills may not be tolerated well by those required to respond. Chemical detectors normally sample air at various perimeter locations and may not be appropriate for use in checkpoint

screening. Some chemical sensors use optical methods to achieve standoff detection.

Biological agent detection differs from chemical detection in two ways. First, most biological agents are not immediately lethal, so response time may not be as critical as for chemical attacks. Second, detection methods usually involve filtering air for several hours and then analyzing the filter (several more hours). As a result of this delay, it can be difficult to detect the biological agent in time to prevent exposure; however, once the agent is identified any personnel who have been exposed can be treated. As a result of this limitation, biological detection is a very active area of research at present. Other materials that cross the site perimeter, such as water (via rain, streams, piped potable water) and air (pollen, pollutants), can also be monitored, but these are usually considered as part of environmental monitoring, not contraband detection.

Locks

Locks are important elements in the entry control system of a facility since they secure the moveable portions of barriers. However, locks should generally not be relied upon as the only means of physical protection for significant areas at a facility. Because an individual with enough skill and time can compromise them, locks should be used in conjunction with complementary protection measures, such as periodic guard checks and sensors.

In all applications, the goal should be to make the lock delay time and capability closely match the penetration resistance of the rest of the secured barrier (balanced protection). It would be unwise to select a lock that is either significantly stronger or weaker than the rest of the barrier (the door and wall). This section presents information that will be helpful in selecting the appropriate match for an

application. Chapter 11, "Access Delay," describes delay concepts more thoroughly.

A detailed discussion of locks and locking systems is beyond the scope of this chapter, but some high-level information will be presented that will allow the novice to understand the major issues and recognize the essential considerations in selecting and applying locks. There are two specific areas that must be considered— defeat resistance and application considerations.

The most common applications of locking devices are padlock, door lock, switch lock, cabinet lock, and cam lock. The following description applies to padlocks, doorlock, and cabinet locks.

Major Lock Components

The two major components in most locks are the fastening device and the coded mechanism. The fastening device is most often referred to as the latch or bolt assembly. The coded mechanism is the key cylinder in a key lock or a wheel pack in a mechanical combination lock.

Fastening Device

The fastening device is composed of a latch or bolt assembly located within the lock case and a strike for door locks or a shackle for padlocks. The latch or bolt extends into the strike or shackle securing the lock when projected into the locked position.

The difference between a bolt and a latch is that a latch will automatically retract as the door is closed, whereas a bolt stays in the same position unless it is intentionally moved. A mechanical bolt is a uniformly thick, moveable device intended to block motion perpendicular to its direction of travel. A bolt is constrained in its extended position by interference with a solid obstacle. Latches are beveled and spring loaded so that they will automatically retract. Latches are more convenient, but more vulnerable, than bolts. The latch or bolt assembly types are latchbolt, deadlatch, or deadbolt (intermittent or positive). A description of each type follows:

- Latchbolt—A beveled latch that is projected by spring action and retracted by end pressure, knob (lever), or code mechanism.
- Deadlatch—A latch and pin that is projected by spring action and retracted by knob (lever) or code mechanism. A deadlatch has a pin that is depressed as the door is shut, placing an obstacle in the path of the spring latch, which restricts its movement.
- Intermittent Deadbolt—A bolt that is not permanently coupled to a code mechanism and that is projected or retracted by the knob or code mechanism. Intermittently coupled key locks can often be defeated by bolt manipulation without operation of the key mechanism (Figure 10.12).
- Positive Deadbolt—A bolt permanently coupled to a code mechanism and projected and retracted only by the code mechanism. When a positively coupled deadbolt is fully extended, it cannot be unlocked by exerting end pressure. Figure 10.13 illustrates the operation of this device.

Strike

Typically, bolts and latches are mounted on the door. The door is locked when it is closed and the bolt or latch projects into a recess in the strike located in the doorjamb. A strike is used to strengthen the recess into which a bolt or latch projects. Strikes may be active or passive. The only function of a passive strike is to strengthen the recess. Some locking devices are designed to function either mechanically or electrically, for example, a mechanical lock mounted on the door combined with an active strike on the doorjamb or a passive strike mounted on the doorjamb combined with an electric bolt lock mounted on the door.

An active strike allows the door to be opened when pressure is exerted on the door. The operation of electric bolts and latches is controlled by the application of power to either a solenoid or an electric motor. A solenoid becomes an electromagnet when power is applied. The solenoid then exerts a magnetic force on the appropriate mechanism, which removes a barrier allowing the user to retract the bolt or latch. An electric motor can be used to perform the same function as the solenoid. While this is more secure, it is also more expensive. An active strike can be either fail-safe or fail-secure. The difference is that the fail-safe device unlocks when power is removed, and the fail-secure device locks when power is removed.

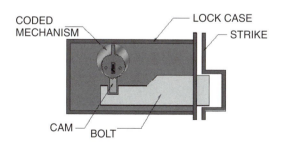

Figure 10.12 Intermittent Deadbolt Assembly. As the key turns in the lock, the cam slides the bolt open or closed. The key rotates one time in the coded mechanism

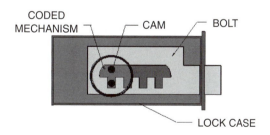

Figure 10.13 Positive Deadbolt Assembly. In this case, the key must be turned multiple times to allow the cam to fully open or close the bolt

Hasps and Shackles

A hasp is a metal fastener with a minimum of two sections. The two sections are attached either to a moveable and a fixed barrier or to two moveable barriers. When the barrier is closed, the two sections of the hasp are positioned together in such a manner that the shackle of a padlock can be inserted through both to fasten the two sections together. Only a few varieties of hasps are commercially available. Most are not comparable in quality (in terms of resistance to forcible attack) to the high-security padlocks that might be used in conjunction with them. Since the lock and hasp work together to provide security, the proper hasp selection and its installation are critical to providing the required protection. Hasp designs usually vary considerably due to different mounting requirements. Hasps can be either mounted with nonremovable bolts or welded directly to the door or frame. A shackle is typically a U-shaped steel bar used to couple a door to the door-jamb by means of a hasp. Often padlock bodies and shackles are hardened, with shackle exposure ranging from exposed to totally concealed.

Coded Mechanism

The coded mechanism is located in the lock body and, when decoded, moves or permits movement of the latch or bolt to the retracted (unlocked) position. There are two major types of coded mechanisms, keyless and key.

Keyless Coded Mechanisms A keyless lock is a device that is operated by the use of a code to gain access. These locks include:

- mechanical combination
- electromechanical combination
- mechanical entry control lock
- electromagnetic keyless control

A mechanical combination lock is a lock with a number or letter dial rotated to certain positions in a particular order during a given number of turns in the prescribed direction, after which the bolt can be withdrawn. Combination locks are incorporated into padlocks and door locks. They range from simple locker-room variety padlocks to highly developed security vault door locks; however, the basic principle of operation is the same for all combination locks.

The dial is usually divided into sections marked with numbers. An index mark is located on the door lock's dial ring or, in the case of a padlock, on the padlock body. In the door lock, the dial and dial ring are usually the only visible portions of the lock. When the dial is rotated, its motion is transmitted to code wheels located within the lock case. Correct positioning of the wheels allows the bolt to be retracted.

Electromechanical combination locks are very similar in operation to mechanical ones; however, they rely on electronics rather than mechanical parts to accept the combination. One such lock has a liquid crystal display (LCD) that shows the numbers selected by turning the dial.

Mechanical entry control locks allow local entry through a door based on entering a sequence of numbers by pushing appropriately numbered buttons. This type of lock system allows controlled entry into rooms or buildings without a central computer-controlled system.

Electromagnetic locks rely on the strength of powerful electromagnets to secure a door. A steel strike plate is typically mounted on the door with the magnet mounted on the doorjamb. Holding strength in this type of lock is from 600 to 1200 lb. Simple electromagnetic locks are inherently fail-safe because the magnet does not work when power is removed. Fail-secure electromagnetic locks employ a solenoid activated bolt that works in conjunction with the magnetic portion of the lock.

An alternative design is the shear-type electromagnet lock. This lock mounts into recesses in the door and door jamb, thus hiding it from view. The part mounted in the door recess will typically have movable steel bolts or strike plates that are attracted to the electromagnet in the doorjamb when the door is closed and the current is applied. The strength of commercial electromagnetic shear locks ranges from approximately 2000 to 2700 lb.

Key Coded Mechanisms Key locks are locks that operate through the use of a mechanical key. If the correct key is used, the key and key mechanism retract the bolt or latching and allow access. Most key locks fall into five general classes: warded locks, wafer locks, pin-tumbler locks, disk locks, and lever locks. In addition, key locks also include some unique options and variations of these general classes of locks.

Warded locks incorporate fixed wards or obstacles (external and/or internal wards) in the lock structure that a key has to clear in order to rotate and operate the bolt or latching mechanism. The key for a warded lock has ward cuts placed at designated locations to allow key rotation. Warded locks were once popular as door locks and may still be found in some older hotels and residences. The warded door lock is easily picked. In addition, warded skeleton keys (passkeys) are easy to fabricate and are readily available through commercial sources. Since the warded lock cannot be keyed with a master key, it has limited usefulness and versatility. If a warded lock is compromised, it should be removed from service since it cannot be re-coded for a different key.

Large lever locks are commonly used in prison security applications. These larger locks are resistant to picking, primarily due to their massiveness and the strength of the springs on the levers. A further refinement incorporated into some lever locks requires that the key be turned several times in order for the bolt to be completely retracted. In this case, a lock would have to be picked once for each required key rotation.

Disks are flat rotating plates that a key must align. Rotating disk locks are highly pick-resistant locks that operate using a specially cut cylindrical key that rotates individual disks in the cylinder to different turn angles. When the key is inserted and rotated, the disk notches align, allowing a locking bar to drop into position. This action frees the otherwise constrained plug containing the disks and allows the plug to rotate.

Pin-tumbler locks, patented by Linus Yale in the 1800s, offer more security than warded or wafer locks. However, in their standard form, pin-tumbler locks are also vulnerable to picking and impressioning. The standard pin-tumbler lock consists of a cylinder case that contains a cylinder plug or core. The lock case houses several small, spring-loaded pins placed in line and extending into the keyway. The top (or driver) pins are forced down by the springs into the plug to prohibit plug rotation. The cone-shaped end of each bottom (or key) pin rests against the inserted key; if the key is properly cut, it raises the break between the top and bottom pins so that each break is even with the outer surface of the cylinder plug (shear line). When the pins are thus aligned, the cylinder plug can be rotated.

Pin-tumbler locks are usually manufactured to high-tolerance specifications and offer a number of different possible key codes. They can easily be master-keyed for tens of thousands of possible combinations. Very complex master-keying systems can be developed using pin-tumbler locks. The pin-tumbler lock is widely used in padlocks and door locks, as well as for special applications, such as keyed electronic switches.

Installation Considerations

Generally, the farther the lock is from the face of the door, the more protected is its position. This protection can also be provided by the use of a guard plate that covers as much of the cylinder as possible while still permitting the key to be turned.

Hardened guard rings should be recessed and have sufficient taper and rotation to withstand forcible defeat.

Special security screws should be used to mount security hardware located outside the secured area and, depending on application, sometimes those mounted inside the secured area. The two basic varieties of security screws are those that cannot be moved once installed and those that may be removed only with a special tool once installed. Adversaries are likely to have access to the special tool.

If screws are used where they are accessible by an adversary, they should be installed with their heads welded to the device they are securing. Screws used for mounting security devices should be hardened. If the hardware is mounted on wood, a higher level of security may be achieved by using screws long enough to embed themselves in the underlying structure.

The possible vulnerability associated with keyed locks can be balanced by the use of a BMS or other door sensor. Then if the door is opened using a key or by picking the lock, an alarm will be recorded and the unauthorized entry detected. This simple measure will work against insider or outsider threats and can be very cost-effective, particularly if sensors already monitor interior doors to critical areas.

In summary, the use of locks should apply the same principles as the other elements already discussed in this text—balance among the subsystem elements and proper selection of the appropriate technology for the specific threat under consideration. In addition, key control for keyed lock systems requires strict adherence to procedures. For nonkeyed locks, use of keyed locks as bypasses should be considered to allow a backup method of entry in case of equipment failure or power loss. Once again, keys should be strictly controlled.

System Integration and Installation Issues

There are a variety of issues that must be considered when installing the entry control components of a protection system. At the highest level it must be determined if the entry control functionality and the AC&D functionality are to be implemented on the same host computer or separately, that is, in fully integrated or parallel systems. Questions that must be considered include: Will the entries and exits from a security area be under CCTV surveillance? Are there any requirements for local masking of sensors? Will there be any electronic connection between the AC&D/entry control subsystems and the contraband detection equipment? These issues and many others must be addressed at the design stage of the protection system.

There are many AC&D systems that incorporate entry control features. Fully integrated AC&D and entry control systems are attractive for a variety of reasons. Often there is a reduced cost for both hardware and software to the user when a fully integrated system is installed rather than two separate systems. For example, the field panels that collect alarms also have card-reader interfaces and door-strike relays on the same board. Installation is simplified due to this integration. It is important that the AC&D system be informed when the entry control system authorizes a person to open a door, because the door sensor alarm signal must be suppressed for some period of time to allow the person to proceed into the area without causing an alarm. Door sensor masking happens automatically in a fully integrated system, but this function must be implemented by some other means, usually with user-provided hardware, when installing independent systems.

On the other hand, fully integrated systems may suffer performance degradation due to the integration. The reporting of alarms must take priority over handling entry control requests. Although this requirement seems obvious, laboratory testing reveals that in some systems alarms take several seconds to be received by the AC&D system because the system was busy processing entry control requests. Care must be taken when selecting a fully integrated system to ensure that system AC&D performance is not degraded by the entry control function. This is why system testing under normal, abnormal, and malevolent conditions should be performed to verify system performance. It is not sufficient to test a system under only normal operations; this level of performance may not represent the most critical operating state of the system. This limitation is partially compensated for through the use of high-speed microprocessors and communication protocols.

Entry and exit through doors, turnstiles, and gates area are not normally recorded by the CCTV system. However, when the security level is sufficiently high and the traffic level is low, CCTV and time-lapse video recording may be used. Recordings of the visual information, along with entry and exit logs, can be useful in determining the sequence of events when security incidents occur. In addition to event-logging cameras, door and gate sensor alarms should be subject to the same video assessment requirements as other sensors in the area being protected.

Often the use of contraband detection equipment at an entrance is in the local alarm mode of operation. Because of the high number of nuisance alarms expected from metal detectors due to pocket clutter, metal detectors are seldom operated unattended. Security personnel are needed at the metal detector to oversee that procedures are followed, pocket clutter is searched, and alarms are resolved. Frequently the resolution of metal detector alarms involves manual search by pat down or by the use of a handheld metal detector. X-ray machines employed in package search require an operator to interpret the image that is generated.

Automated image analysis of X-ray images for contraband is still years away. Despite the fact that security personnel are usually in attendance at contraband screening points, it is sometimes advantageous to monitor this equipment at the central alarm monitoring station. Metal detector alarms may be monitored and the image generated by X-ray machines duplicated at the alarm monitoring station for secondary screening by security operators.

Another serious concern when designing an entry control system is the impact of fire codes. It is often desirable to maintain secure control for exit as well as entrance to an area; this is frequently difficult to implement without violating fire codes. A fire door normally must have a single-hand/single-motion exit device. Exit control hardware such as card readers and electric strikes can be installed but can be easily bypassed by any fire-rated exit hardware. Signs indicating that the fire-exit hardware is not used except for emergencies, but without stating consequences for violators, may encourage some users to bypass the exit controls. When fire doors do have controlled entrance and free exit, an additional means of local masking of the door alarm must be implemented. Masking the alarm for exits is usually accomplished through the use of a request for exit sensor. These infrared sensors detect persons approaching the door from inside the security area and alert the system that the door is about to be opened. This method is useful during normal operating hours at a facility. An additional method of addressing fire code requirements while maintaining secure control includes the use of delayed exit hardware, in which the door can be opened only after a short period of time. This allows for the use of CCTV to monitor activity at the exit or for the extension of the time delay while verifying the emergency condition. These systems have been useful at schools and other locations where false fire alarms have been initiated to disrupt normal activities. The method used is determined after careful examination of federal and local fire codes and security systems implications. In no case should lives be placed in jeopardy; however, in some facilities critical assets must remain protected even in emergency conditions. Some examples are semiconductor fabrication plants, commercial nuclear reactors, and certain drug manufacturing facilities. In these cases, exit from the facility may lead to an additional secure but safe area or include the use of procedures. Interfacing of biometric devices with the site's entry control system is another problem that arises during system design. Most biometric identifiers are implemented as the entire entry control system, rather than a component of a larger entry control system. Consequently, even when the biometric device has a data interface to a larger system, there is no industry standard for that interface. This sometimes forces the designer to trick components into operating in unison when combining card readers and PIN pads with biometric devices. A simple approach is to place the biometric device and the entry control system's unlock relays in series. A more elaborate integration is possible if the biometric devices have a card-read buffer or a shared data storage area. In this case, the biometric device captures the card-reader data stream. After the biometric verification is successfully completed, the device sends the buffered data to the entry control system. In this method, the entry control system is not aware that the biometric device is connected. In a few cases, the entry control system has a device-specific interface that allows biometric templates to be stored on the entry control system's host computer. This is an example of integration at the highest level.

Procedures

As with any protection technology elements, entry control systems require a procedural component as well. These procedures address issues such as presenting badges upon entry, wearing them in plain view while inside the facility, and how to protect the badge or other credentials when off-site. In addition, there should be a rule prohibiting the disclosure of any PIN numbers. The practice of tailgating or allowing others behind to enter without completing the entry control process should also be prohibited. Enforcement of this procedure is recommended. All employees should receive training on the proper use of company entry credentials and understand that this is a serious issue at the site. Encouraging employees to challenge those who try to tailgate or providing telephones near entry points to report this practice should be considered. Although it is courteous to hold doors open for fellow employees or others, this custom can compromise security at a facility, particularly if an employee has been recently terminated or if a visitor has not received authorization to enter. Along with this, employees should not allow access to other employees who have forgotten or lost their badges.

Other considerations when installing entry control equipment include determining how many tries will be allowed before an access request is invalid, what to do if access is denied this way, and establishing a preventive maintenance schedule on equipment. Regular calibration of metal detectors should be performed. When using metal detectors, it is recommended that the procedure for those detected with metal be to remove the metal and re-enter the detector. A variation of this procedure is to use handheld portable wands to scan those who have been detected. Once an object is found, it should be removed and the scan repeated. This process should be repeated until there are no further detections. It is important to repeat the scan after a metal object is found, because the detection of one piece of metal does not indicate that this is the only piece of metal.

Allowing entry after finding a metal object without an additional scan can create a vulnerability in the protection system. If explosives detectors are used at a site, careful thought will be required to determine what to do if a detection occurs. This response can be problematic, because there are a number of elements that may generate a nuisance alarm, or an adversary may have been legitimately detected. If cameras are used to verify identity before access, users should be instructed or trained to remove sunglasses, hats, or other image blocking items, and told where to stand and which direction to face. In addition, random searches of packages, briefcases, and purses can be implemented along with technology components. In this case, the company policy on prohibited items such as guns, other weapons, explosives, drugs, alcohol, recording devices, and cell phones should be included in employee training and as a part of visitor control.

Administrative Procedures

In addition to the procedures that complement use of entry control technology, a system of access controls will also need to be established. This system defines who gets access to the facility, during which hours, how many different levels of access are required, and where people can enter. It will also include procedures for employees who forget or lose credentials, visitor control, and may handle other functions such as parking passes. An explicit part of these procedures should describe access for people with disabilities or temporary medical conditions, like a broken leg or hand. Backup procedures will also be required where biometric devices are used—both for employees who are temporally unable to use the system and for visitors who cannot be enrolled. These exceptions may be handled through the use of oversized bypass gates or by directing people to manned locations for assistance.

Procedures must exist for handling visitors. Clearly, all but the smallest or simplest facilities need a procedure to provide for the authorized access of visitors. The appropriate employee should make the request for access, and this request should include certain pertinent data, such as day and time of visit, the point of contact, and the purpose of the visit. Procedures may also require the signature of a manager to authorize the request. If biometric devices are used to allow entry, either visitors need to be temporarily enrolled in the database or the escorting employee will be required to provide access at the time of entry. The placement of internal telephones at entry points may also be useful when handling visitors. A list of employee phone numbers or a help desk should also be provided.

Many large facilities designate a special office or manager to administer the access control process. An important aspect of these controls will be database management. The access control system database should be continually updated to reflect employee separations, leaves of absence, or suspensions. In addition, it should track visitor credentials and assign a duration time for their use. Access to the database should be limited and may require the consent of two employees to protect against insider tampering.

The office or individual assigned to manage access controls should also be the location that issues employee and visitor credentials. This function will include the previously described tasks, as well as replacement of old or lost employee credentials, removal of old or inactive credentials from the database, addition of new credentials, and collection of visitor credentials at the end of the visit. Because this can be a time-consuming process, it is recommended that the access control computer be separate from the AC&D host computer, particularly if this computer will also generate the credential. Personal computers are fairly inexpensive and the dollars to be saved by performing both of these functions on the same computer do not justify compromising operational security.

Summary

This chapter describes entry control systems and equipment for personnel entry control, contraband detection, and detection. These systems meet the objective of allowing the movement of authorized personnel and material through normal access routes while detecting and delaying unauthorized movement of personnel and material into and out of protected areas.

Methods of personnel entry authorization include credentials, personal identification numbers, and automated personal identity verification. Two types of errors are encountered in these systems: (1) false rejection and (2) false acceptance. Most credentials can be counterfeited. Also, during the process of entry authorization, the credential rather than the person is verified. Although personnel identity verification systems verify a unique personal physical characteristic, such as hand geometry or eye retinal pattern, they require more sophisticated equipment and personnel to operate and maintain the system. These systems will also require backup methods for access for those unable to enroll or to temporarily use the biometric device.

Contraband includes items such as unauthorized weapons, explosives, drugs, and tools. Methods of contraband detection include metal detectors, package searches, and explosives detectors. Metal detectors should be placed at entrances and exits, and explosives detectors should be placed at entrances. Explosives detection includes both bulk and trace techniques. Recently, there has also been considerable activity in the area of WMD, including large explosives, chemical and biological agents. If these are capabilities of the defined threat for a facility, some technologies exist that can aid in detection, although considerable research is still needed to improve their performance.

An effective entry control system permits only authorized persons to enter and exit, detects and prevents the entry of contraband material, detects and prevents the unauthorized removal of critical or high-value materials, and provides information to the protective force to facilitate assessment and response. The entry control system is an important part of the detection function of an integrated PPS. When combined with entry control procedures and a process for access control, entry control provides another method of providing balanced protection-in-depth at a facility.

Security Principles

Entry control refers to the technology used to restrict entry or exit at a facility. Access control includes the databases, procedures, and rules for access that complement technology.

An entry control system is one of the tools that may be used to achieve balance and to establish protection-in-depth at a facility.

Entry control technology falls into one of three classes—something you know, something you possess, or something you are.

Contraband detection requires the presence of human operators to make the final decision as to the presence of the contraband item.

References

Bouchier, F., Ahrens, J.S., and Wells, G. Laboratory evaluation of the IriScan prototype biometric identifier. SAND96-1033 1996;1–12.

Holmes, J.P., Wright, L.J., and Maxwell, R.L. A performance evaluation of biometric identification devices. SAND 910276 1991;1–29.

Jain, A., Bolle, R., and Pankati, S., eds. *Biometrics: Personal Identification in Networked Society.* Boston: Kluwer Academic Publishers, 1999, 1–411.

National Academy of Sciences. *Existing and Potential Standoff Explosives Detection Techniques*, the National Academies Press, 2004. http://www.nap.edu/catalog/10998.html, last accessed November 2006.

Rejman-Greene, M. Security considerations in the use of biometric devices: Elsevier Science. Information Security Technical Report 1998, 3(1):77–80. http://sciserver.lanl.gov/cgi-bin/search.pl.

Ruehle, M., and Ahrens, J.S. Hand geometry field application data analysis. SAND97-0614 1997;1–51.

Theisen, L., Hannum, D.W., Murray, D.W., and Parmeter, J.E. *Survey of Commercially Available Explosives Detection Technologies and Equipment.* Washington, DC National Institute of Justice Office of Science and Technology 2004. http://www.ncjrs.gov/pdffiles1/nij/grants/208861.pdf, November 30, 2006.

US Nuclear Regulatory Commission, 10 CFR Section 20.1301 (a) (1) and (d) (3), 1991. http://www.nrc. gov/reading-rm/doc-collections/cfr/part020/part020-1301. html, last accessed November 2006.

Wright, L.J. Proximity credentials—a survey. SAND87-0080 1987;1–27.

Wright, L.J. Coded credentials—a primer. SAND88-0180 1988;1–20.

Yinon, J. *Forensic and Environmental Detection of Explosives.* Chichester: Wiley, 1999, 1–285.

Questions

1. Discuss the following application considerations:

   a. Controlled, free space should be provided for entering personnel.

   b. Employees should not use real devices and systems to practice with or for fun.

   c. A "back out" route should be provided for unsuccessful users.

   d. Swinging metal doors may interfere with entry control devices (e.g., X-ray package search machine and SNM or metal detectors).

   e. Enrollment information should be kept under security control.

   f. Security personnel should be able to observe entry control equipment (e.g., personnel or via CCTV).

   g. Special requirements (e.g., fire lanes, break out doors, etc.) should be considered when designing entry control system.

   h. Alternate entry control procedures should be provided for the people who do not fit the system (i.e., the handicapped).

   i. Measures should be taken to compensate for system failures (e.g., power failures and equipment breakdowns), usually with parallel components.

2. In what situations would a protective force (guard) be used for entry control? What impact could this have on the physical protection system, the cost, and so on?

3. Why should portal doors, walls, and roof provide the same delay as the perimeter or building walls in which they are installed?

4. Why should portal doors be interlocked so that only one door can be unlocked and opened at one time?

5. Discuss entry control problems created by a vehicle portal.

6. What problems would be created by a totally automated entry control system?

7. What problems do you expect to encounter with an explosives detector system?

8. Why might we need a metal detector at the exit of the facility?

11

Access Delay

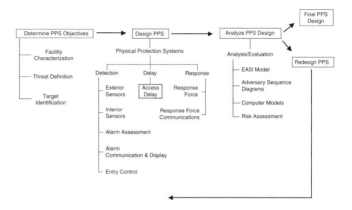

An effective PPS requires that any malevolent act committed by an inside or outside adversary must be detected so that the response force, including on-site guards, local police, and others, can interrupt the adversary's attack before the goal is achieved. Because it is usually not feasible to maintain a large enough guard force to place guards at all asset locations, some type of adversary delay is needed. After an adversary has been detected, delay elements will prevent completion of the malevolent act, provide delay until an adequate response force can arrive, or until additional remotely activated delay and response systems can be activated. Other means of improving the probability of interruption should also be considered. Against an outsider threat, early detection at the site perimeter, as opposed to detection inside a building or vault, increases the available response force time after detection. Minimizing the amount of time required to complete the assessment decision will also improve the total response time.

Figure 11.1 is a simple illustration of the functions of a physical protection system

and the barriers in that system. Although in this example the adversary is considered to be an outsider, the logic is also true for an insider. The time required for the adversary to achieve the final objective is labeled adversary task time. At some point in the scenario, the adversary must be detected. This point is labeled T_0. In Figure 11.1, the adversary task time is represented by a dotted line to point T_0, because this is where detection begins. If the adversary goal is to enter a room or a building, the task time may be very short. If the goal is to accomplish sabotage or theft of critical assets, the adversary task time will most likely be longer. After event T_0, some time will be required to assess the alarm and the level of the threat. If the assessment shows a valid intrusion, the response force is notified. To counter the threat, some amount of time is then required to move the appropriate response force to the desired location.

For an immediate on-site response, the objective of a PPS is to assure that an adequate response force arrives in a timely manner to prevent an adversary from stealing or damaging a critical asset. The

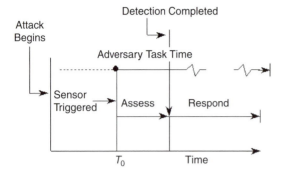

Figure 11.1 Role of Delay in a Physical Protection System. At time T_0, the adversary is first detected. The delay elements serve to slow the adversary down and allow time for the response force to interrupt the adversary

role of barriers is simply to increase the adversary task time following detection by introducing impediments along any path the adversary may choose, thereby providing the needed time for the response force to arrive and react. Some barriers might deter or, if the adversary is unable to complete penetration, even defeat some threats. Since the degree to which the barriers are able to fulfill these two roles is uncertain, they can be considered only as potential obstacles to delay adversaries who are well equipped and determined. The delay provided by physical barriers is highly dependent upon the tools and techniques used by the adversaries. Often the delay time is unknown and testing is required to determine the range of realistic delay times provided, especially for unique barriers using custom construction.

Barrier Types and Principles

Access delay barriers may take the form of passive barriers, guards, or dispensable barriers. Passive barriers include structural elements such as doors, walls, floors, locks, vents, ducts, and fences. The presence of guards can also provide delay to adversaries using stealth or covert tactics to gain entry. Guards may only provide minimal delay to adversaries using force, unless in fixed and protected positions. Dispensable barriers are those that are deployed only when necessary during an attack. Each type of barrier has advantages, and a well-designed PPS will combine all three types to achieve maximum effect.

The presence of guards offers a flexible and continuous delay element. Guards can be easily shifted around a site, and shifts can be arranged to cover the entire work schedule. At the same time, the use of guards is a significant operational expense, and superior adversary numbers can overwhelm guards. In addition, as people, they are subject to compromise. Passive barriers are always in place and will fail secure, that is, even if they fail the delay value will remain. Many passive barriers are also commercially available, reducing their cost and increasing their accessibility. Most passive barriers are weak against explosive attacks, however, and they generally impose operational and aesthetic limits on a facility. Dispensable barriers have the advantages of being compact and rapidly deployable. Examples of dispensable barriers include chemical fogs and smokes, foams, and irritants. When implemented properly they can also maximize delay at the asset location. Due to their dispensable characteristic, they are somewhat threat independent. For example, the time delay provided by a fog or smoke will largely be the same regardless of the tactics or capabilities of the adversary. Dispensable barriers do have some associated safety and operational concerns, such as spurious activation or possible injury to those caught in the material.

Traditional barriers, such as chain-link fences, locked doors, grilled windows, masonry walls, and even many types of vaults, are not likely to delay a small group of properly equipped and dedicated adversaries for a significant length of time. Although the role of delay in a PPS is easy to define, the implementation of barriers is not a simple task. Ensuring that the necessary barriers are in effect at all times during all operational states of the facility requires special attention. Often, the use of compensatory measures, such as additional guards, is required to offset the decreased delay and increased risk encountered during certain operations such as fire drills, temporary movement or storage of critical assets, or maintenance by contract employees. Further, barriers that impede normal operations, such as vehicle traffic between buildings or personnel access to common areas such as cafeterias, will not be acceptable to a facility.

Barriers must be considered in relation to the adversary's objective. If the objective is theft of assets, barriers that are penetrated or destroyed on the way into the facility may not provide delay for departure from the facility. Some barriers, such as emergency exits, provide some delay from the outside but, due to safety requirements, allow rapid exit from the inside. With the exception of a few barriers provided by natural elements such as rugged coastlines, high cliffs, mountain-tops, and vast distances, physical protec-tion must be provided by barriers that are carefully planned and positioned in the path of the adversary. The degree of delay afforded depends on the nature of the physical obstacles employed and the tools used to breach them.

To aid alarm assessment and intercep-tion of the adversary at predictable loca-tions, consideration should be given to installing detection systems and barriers adjacent to each other so that the barrier is encountered immediately after a sensor. This arrangement serves to delay the adversary at the point of detection and increases the probability of accurate assessment.

The principle of balanced design ensures that each aspect of a barrier configuration affords equal delay, or in other words, no weak links exist. For example, an adver-sary is not likely to burn a hole in a door to crawl through if the door locks or hinges are clearly easier to defeat. The principle of delay-in-depth is similar to protection-in-depth for detection systems. Multiple layers of different barrier types along all possible adversary paths will complicate the adversary's progress by requiring a variety of different tools and skills.

System Considerations

Most security barriers at industrial facil-ities are designed to deter or defeat infrequent acts of casual thievery and vandalism. In today's environment of esca-lating threats, these traditional fences, walls, doors, and locks may present very little deterrence or delay. The contribution of delay after detection to system effective-ness is extremely important. Each addi-tional minute required by the adversary provides additional time for assessment and for the response force to interrupt the action. A few minutes of delay may have a significant effect on the outcome of an adversary intrusion.

Using the design basis threat, assump-tions about the adversary's level of tech-nical skill and appropriate equipment are made. If barrier upgrades follow the balanced design concept, the adversary's path may not change, but this may require use of different tools. Upgrading a barrier to force the adversary to use more sophis-ticated tools should complicate the logis-tics, training, and skill required by the adversary even though the penetration time may not, in some cases, change significantly.

Aspects of Penetration

A barrier is penetrated when an indi-vidual can pass through, over, under, or around the protective structure. In this text, the penetration effort is assumed to start at a distance 2 ft in front of the barrier and to end at a point 2 ft beyond the barrier. Penetration time includes the time to traverse the barrier. Consideration must be given to the type of path made through a barrier. For example, cuts through reinforcing rebar in concrete may be very jagged, and cuts made with thermal tools may require cooling. These effects will lengthen the delay time of the barrier. Very thick walls require a larger hole for crawling through than do thin walls, also increasing delay time for the adversary.

A vehicle barrier is penetrated when the ramming vehicle passes through or over the barrier and is still a functioning vehicle, or a second vehicle can be driven through the breached barrier, or the vehicle barrier is removed or bridged and a functional vehicle passes through or over the barrier. The type of vehicle perceived to be a threat will have a considerable effect on the performance of the barrier. A chain-link fence may be capable of stopping a motorcycle or a small all-terrain vehicle (ATV), but would be completely ineffective against a large truck.

As an adversary encounters a series of progressively more difficult barriers, it becomes increasingly difficult to transport and set up sophisticated tools, especially if the adversary must crawl through a series of small openings. The proximity of the target area to vehicular traffic should also be considered. When the adversary is forced to carry heavy equipment for long distances, the delay times may increase significantly. For this reason, some facilities place barriers outside perimeter detection. In this case, the barriers are used to force the adversaries to change tactics and abandon their vehicle. This will slow down adversaries' progress by forcing them to walk or run and to carry their tools on foot, but until they are detected this delay is not included in system effectiveness measures. The use of vehicle barriers outside of the detection and assessment zone is not recommended.

Barrier penetration time is a function of the attack mode, which is governed by the equipment required. Categories of attack tools considered in this chapter are:

- hand tools—sledgehammers, axes, bolt-cutters, wrecking bars, metal cutters
- powered hand tools—hydraulic bolt-cutters, abrasive saws, electric drills, rotohammers, abrasive water jets
- thermal cutting tools—oxyacetylene torches, oxygen lances
- explosives
- vehicles—trucks, automobiles, trains, boats, planes, helicopters, motorcycles, and ATVs

The availability and capability of battery-powered tools has greatly expanded over the past decade. Battery-powered tools are now available which can power small hydraulic systems and cutters of all types. These tools are light, powerful, and disposable. The proliferation of these tools should be kept in mind when evaluating delay elements of a physical protection system.

Figure 11.2 presents a graphic example of a simple scenario for theft using conventional barriers. The scenario starts with the adversary just outside the fenced area and ends when the adversary has exited the fenced area with the stolen asset. In this example, the adversary can accomplish the theft in about 3 min if not interrupted by the response force. Of course, responders may not be available to interrupt the adversary unless there is detection at some point in the scenario, an accurate assessment is made, and they have time to respond.

To illustrate the response times needed for various protection system goals, assume that a perimeter detection system with an immediate alarm assessment capability exists just inside the fence of the example facility. If the goal is to intercept the adversary before penetrating the building, the response force must arrive within about 1 min of the alarm. If the goal is denial of the adversary sabotage task at the asset, the response force must arrive

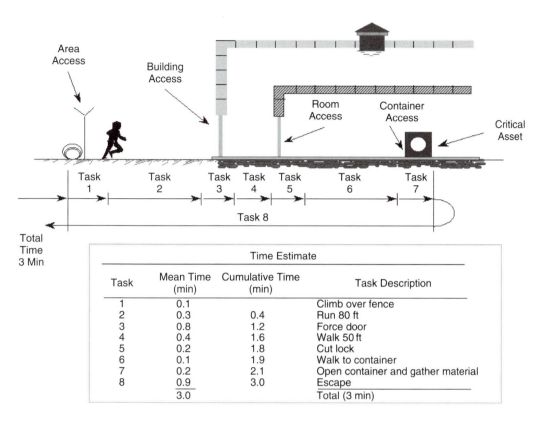

Figure 11.2 Adversary Theft Path. The adversary must complete all eight tasks on the path to successfully steal the asset

at that location within about 2 min of the alarm. If the goal is containment of the adversary within the fenced area after an attempted theft, the response force must intercept the adversary within 3 min of the alarm. Because of the short penetration times of many conventional barriers and the resulting short total adversary scenario times, enhanced or new barriers may be needed to lengthen the delays and gain adequate time for the response force.

Perimeter Barriers

Perimeter barriers form the outermost protective layer of a PPS; their function is to exclude unauthorized personnel from an area. The standard chain-link fences commonly used as perimeter barriers around industrial facilities cannot

be considered a serious deterrent to any dedicated adversary. These fences, however, do serve to establish a visible legal boundary around a facility and can hold signs advising outsiders of trespassing violations or use of deadly force in some cases. Fences can be rammed through with a vehicle, climbed over, crawled under, or cut through in just a few seconds. Improving this type of fence with a few rolls of barbed tape or concertina wire will increase the delay only by a nominal amount. Almost any type of perimeter barrier that is a few yards high and on the order of 30 ft wide can be bridged with portable bridging aids such as ladders or ropes in a minute or less.

However, even though it is difficult to define a perimeter barrier that is cost-effective and will delay intruders for a period of several minutes, the merits of upgraded perimeter barriers are significant. First, coupling vehicle and personnel barriers into a perimeter, inside and adjacent to the perimeter detection system, will delay the intruder at the point of detection for some finite period of time, thus improving the assessment function. Second, if a meaningful delay of the intruder at the perimeter is achieved and the response force responds promptly to the assessed alarm, it can intercept the intruder near the point of the alarm. Without such a delay, it is unlikely that the intruder will still be at the point of alarm when the response force arrives. Third, when it is necessary to protect a site against an adversary whose target is assets stored in a variety of easily penetrated buildings located within the site, a positive protection zone incorporating detection and assessment, delay, and response at the perimeter may be the most reasonable or attractive option. Finally, where necessary, consideration should be given to using a vehicle barrier around a site perimeter inside the perimeter sensors to force an intruder to travel on foot and to carry any needed tools and weapons.

Fences

Security fences topped with rows of barbed wire, general-purpose barbed-tape obstacle, or barbed-tape concertina (BTC) do not prevent intrusion. However, placing rolls of barbed tape on or near standard fences can moderately enhance their capability to delay intruders (Kodlick, 1978). Roll arrangements are limited only by availability of land and funds for upgrading.

Attaching one roll of barbed tape to the outriggers of an existing security fence is probably the most cost-effective addition that can be made because an intruder must now bring additional aids or bulky equipment to climb over the fence. Reversing the outriggers to point toward the inside when installing the barbed tape eliminates the handgrip used by intruders in climbing over the fence, but studies have shown that the direction of the outriggers makes very little difference in fence-climbing times (Kodlick, 1978).

An additional enhancement involves placing barbed-tape rolls either horizontally on the ground or against the fence fabric. Usually the barbed tapes are placed on the inside of an outer perimeter fence and on the outside of an inner (double) fence. This prevents accidental injury to the casual passerby, both outside and inside a site or facility. When rolls of barbed tape are placed horizontally, they are staked to the ground. Care must be taken to prevent excessive plant growth and collection of debris in the rolls. In addition, rolls of barbed tape will obscure CCTV views in the clear zone and increase assessment time.

An example of the triple-fence system in use at some facilities is shown in Figure 11.3. Mounds of BTC are stacked against the middle fence. The mound consists of six rolls of BTC and is approximately 6.5 ft high and 9 ft wide. The penetration time for this system is several minutes, depending on the method used. The advantage of this system is the additional bulky equipment required by the adversary to penetrate the barrier. The disadvantages include the accumulation of debris that would collect between the fences creating a maintenance problem and the degraded CCTV performance due to the number of opaque barriers that would appear on the CCTV monitors. This would have the effect of hiding any adversary progress through the mounds of BTC, making assessment difficult if not impossible. Other drawbacks of the triple-fence system are land area required, safety issues, and cost of implementation. The few minutes of delay the BTC mounds add may not be justified by the high cost, especially for larger sites (Kane and Kodlick, 1983).

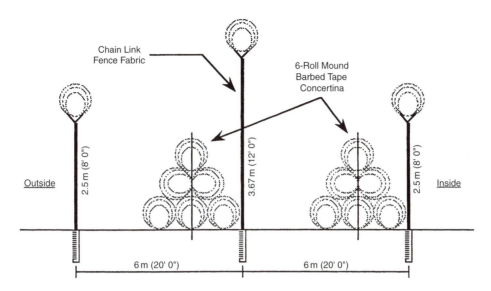

Figure 11.3 Triple Fence System with Barbed Tape Rolls. The mound of barbed tape contains six rolls. Penetration time using simple hand tools is on the order of several minutes, but the tape rolls will block effective CCTV assessment

Gates

Gates establish specific points of entrance and exit to an area defined by fences and walls. They function to limit or prohibit the free flow of pedestrian or vehicular traffic and establish a controlled traffic pattern. Gate barriers and perimeter fences should be equal in delay effectiveness. Gates often require additional hardening features because, as a consequence of their weak hinges, locks, and latches, they are considered easy to defeat. In addition, a vehicular driveway is often aimed directly toward a gate, making the gate susceptible to ramming by a vehicle.

The orientation of vehicle gates and their driveways could reduce the probability of their being breached by vehicles. Driveways constructed with multiple turns on each side of the gateway will reduce the approach and departure speed of vehicles.

The use of multiple hardened gates in a vehicle portal at the perimeter is an option for upgrading vehicle portals. These gates can be interlocked, requiring one gate to be closed and locked before the other can be released and opened. The area between the gates provides a holding area to allow sufficient time to determine if contraband materials or unauthorized persons are attempting entry or exit.

Vehicle Barriers

Entry of private motor vehicles into secured areas should be minimized as they can be surreptitiously used to introduce tools and explosives by an unwitting owner/driver. Ground vehicles can be used by adversaries to penetrate perimeter barriers. Cars and trucks can crash through most fences. In order to minimize the probability of breaching any secured area, vehicle barriers should be installed inside the detection and assessment zone to ensure valid delay. The following design considerations should be examined and coordinated when selecting the type and location of the vehicle barrier system:

- Define the threat that the barrier system is intended to stop (including weight of vehicle, impact velocity, and other physical characteristics).

- Define the asset and determine the area to be protected before selecting the vehicle barrier location.
- Examine site-specific considerations such as terrain, road layout in and around the secured area, buildings and parking lot layout, climate conditions, and the traffic patterns around the area.
- Design a vehicle barrier system, keeping the entire PPS in mind.

Once the layout of a barrier system has been designed, the next step is to select the types of barriers that are best suited to protect against the defined threat vehicle (see Figure 11.4). In order to provide full penetration resistance, barriers must be selected to fit the particular situation and be installed properly. Barriers that are difficult to defeat should be installed in areas that cannot be monitored continuously but may be periodically checked by roving guards. For example, deeply buried, concrete-filled pipes can be constructed so that they will be difficult to defeat, thereby delaying an adversary long enough to be detected by a guard on patrol. Cable barriers can be easily defeated with hand-carried cutting tools. These barriers should be located only within areas that are well patrolled or sensored and under CCTV assessment. Another factor in the selection and placement of a vehicle barrier is the height at which it will impact the vehicle. The optimum height for any barrier depends on its construction and the anticipated threat vehicle. It has been determined by tests that a height of 30 in. works best for most vehicles (Sena, 1984).

All barriers can eventually be breached if the adversary is allowed enough equipment and left unchallenged for a sufficient amount of time. Denying rapid vehicular access forces the adversary to physically carry any tools or breaching aid to other

Figure 11.4 Massive Concrete Vehicle Barrier. These barriers are used to prevent large vehicle attacks into a facility, but require careful integration with response tactics to assure that the barrier does not interfere with response actions. In addition, note the shadows cast by the wall, which can make video assessment in these locations difficult at different times of day. (Photo courtesy of Don Utz/Kontek Industries)

barriers or to consume time in attempting to move the vehicle through the vehicle barrier. If the adversary is prevented from using a vehicle to penetrate a secured area, this will force slower movement on foot inside the area and prevent a rapid means of escape. Examples of well-designed vehicle barriers are shown in Figures 11.5 and 11.6.

A barrier system must be capable of stopping a defined threat vehicle at a specific distance away from a secured area, regardless of where the attack begins. The stopping capabilities of stationary and movable barriers must balance each other so that no weak section will be present in the system. Two-way protection with barriers may be necessary in some situations, such as preventing a threat vehicle from entering and leaving a secured area.

In order for the vehicle to be stopped, the vehicle's kinetic energy, which is proportional to the square of its velocity and to its mass, must be dissipated. Most current vehicle barriers are designed to stop vehicles through one or more of the following methods:

- Vehicle arrestor—Absorbs virtually all of a vehicle's kinetic energy and applies a low to moderately resistive force to gradually stop a vehicle in a relatively long distance. Examples are weights that are dragged by a vehicle and accumulate with distance traveled or piles of loose sand. After crashing through a fence, gate, or other barrier, the weights are attached to the vehicle by the force and momentum of the crash.

- Crash cushion—Absorbs a large portion of a vehicle's kinetic energy and provides a stiff resistive force to stop a vehicle in a reasonable distance. Examples are liquid-filled plastic containers and arrays of empty steel barrels that are backed by strong supports.

Figure 11.5 Example of a Vehicle Barrier. Two Delta Scientific DSC501 portal vehicle barriers installed between massive concrete barriers. Note that the concrete barriers are installed in an "L" arrangement to force incoming vehicles to slow down. The two vehicles in the background are outside the facility. (Photo courtesy of David Dickinson/Delta Scientific Corporation)

Figure 11.6 Proper Installation of High-Security Vehicle Barrier. Note that the hydraulic vehicle barriers are flanked by fixed bollards and steel channels that complete the vehicle barrier system across all potential entry paths. The hydraulic barriers are spaced approximately 25 ft from the inbound guard post to provide some standoff protection from explosive devices, and both the inbound and outbound vehicle lanes are protected. Hydraulic barriers should always be kept in the raised position until a vehicle has been authorized and cleared for entrance. (Photo courtesy of David Dickinson/Delta Scientific Corporation)

- Inertia device—Exchanges momentum and kinetic energy with a vehicle during impact. This device provides a stiff resistive force to stop a vehicle in a reasonable distance. Examples are relatively small concrete shapes and sand-filled barrels that are not anchored.
- Rigid device—Provides very highly resistive force to stop vehicles in very short distances. The vehicle dissipates almost all of its own kinetic energy as it deforms during impact. Examples include massive concrete shapes and steel structures that are well anchored.

The United States Department of State (DOS) has set performance standards for both perimeter and portal vehicle barriers.

Manufacturers desiring to be included in the DOS-approved vehicle barrier list must submit their product to a full-scale crash test witnessed by a DOS representative or delegate. The test ratings include the speed of the vehicle, the mass of the vehicle, and the post-crash penetration distance of the vehicle.

Structural Barriers

Structural barriers include walls, doors, windows, utility ports, roofs, and floors. Most industrial building walls and locked doors can be penetrated quickly. In addition, most buildings include forcible entry points, such as windows and utility ducts that provide intruders with easy routes for entry or exit. In less than 5 min, an adversary with explosives and cutting tools can make a crawl hole through a reinforced, 18 in. thick concrete wall. Tests at Sandia National Laboratories show that the concrete is readily removed by explosive charge (White, 1981). The cutting of the 19 mm diameter reinforcing rebar inside the concrete provides most of the delay. Locked personnel doors can be opened or penetrated within time periods that range from a few seconds to a few tens of seconds. Door or building windows equipped with expanded metal grills offer little delay to determined adversaries.

Hardening a building shell of conventional construction so that it will resist forcible penetration for a significant amount of time would probably require major change and would not, in most cases, be practical or cost effective. Furthermore, doors must be opened or unlocked during working hours for operational needs and for use as rapid emergency exits for personnel safety, which would provide an easy adversary path through walls. Factors such as these tend to limit the delays that can be achieved through building hardening.

Walls

Walls of buildings, vaults, and other structures are usually considered to be more resistant to penetration and less desirable as targets for forcible entry than are doors, windows, vents, and other conventional wall openings. Most existing walls, however, can be breached if adequate tools are used. A wall may be the optimum path for forcible entry by an adversary. Large vehicles can successfully breach cinder block, wood frame, and many other common wall types via ramming. Depending upon the strength of the wall and the type of vehicle used, the vehicle may or may not be operable after the impact. Explosives are especially effective in producing holes large enough to

crawl through. Upgrades to existing walls or new wall designs can significantly extend the penetration delay against hand, power, or thermal tools. Against explosives, upgrading walls or increasing wall thickness usually results in moderate delay increases; however, the amount of explosives needed increases substantially with wall thickness. Upgrading walls can also force an attacker to selectively increase tool requirements and alter penetration methods.

The most common types of walls in facilities are:

- reinforced concrete
- expanded metal/concrete
- concrete block
- clay tile
- precast concrete tee sections
- corrugated asbestos
- sheet metal
- wood frame

Reinforced concrete walls are commonly used in structures used to store and protect sensitive materials. Due to their structural reputation and rugged appearance, concrete walls are almost universally believed to be formidable barriers. Testing has shown, however, that standard reinforced concrete walls can be penetrated rapidly (White, 1981). Concrete walls are designed to support structural loads and, except for vault walls, are not normally designed specifically to thwart or delay penetration. In conventional construction, strength and thickness of concrete and size and spacing of reinforcing materials are determined based on structural requirements.

Two or more reinforced concrete walls in series provide longer penetration delay times than one wall with a thickness equal to their combined thicknesses. Penetration of multiple walls requires multiple individual efforts and the transport of tools through preceding walls. If explosives are used, contained internal pressure from the explosive charge could possibly cause collapse of the roof and surrounding structures, creating further barriers in the form of rubble.

Reinforcement of concrete can be employed to extend the penetration delay time in most designs. Even though the explosion penetrates the concrete, the reinforcing rebar usually remains intact to the extent that it must be removed before entry can be accomplished. Removing the rebar often requires more time than is needed to remove the concrete; therefore, using additional rebar, increasing rebar size, or decreasing center-to-center rebar spacing can be advantageous. Further suggestions for upgrading the barrier potential of existing walls or for consideration in design and construction of a new structure include the use of earth cover or other overburden to delay access to the wall itself or the use of thick or multiple concrete walls to extend delay time and force explosives amounts to impractical limits. The employment of overburden is inexpensive yet effective against all methods of attack.

Doors

In all structures the weakest portion ultimately determines the value of a barrier. The principle of balanced design is especially pertinent to doors. Doors are classified as:

- standard industrial doors
- personnel doors
- attack- and bullet-resistant doors
- vehicle access doors
- vault doors
- blast-resistant doors
- turnstile gates

Penetration delay times through walls can be increased through the use of thicker or composite materials. Doors, however, are often one of the weakest links in a structure due to the design restrictions imposed by the door's functional requirements and associated hardware.

For example, many buildings with heavy concrete walls provide pedestrian access through hollow steel doors. The barrier value of the wall is relatively high, but it is weakened by the use of ordinary doors, frames, and hinges that can be quickly penetrated.

Consequently, the principle of balanced design requires that doors and their associated frames, hinges, bolts, and locks be strengthened to afford the same delay as that provided by the floors, walls, and ceilings of the parent structure. Conversely, if the door assembly cannot be enhanced, it may not be cost-effective to upgrade the building structure. In recent years a number of major door manufacturers have made attack- and bullet-resistant doors (Insulguard, Overly, and Norshield). When properly installed, these doors may offer a substantial increase in penetration resistance over standard industrial doors. The following examples discuss standard personnel doors.

Personnel doors vary in type, style, and class, but most common exterior doors are $1^3/_4$ in. thick with 16- or 18-gauge (1.5 or 1.2 mm) steel surface sheets. Construction is usually hollow core or composite with or without glass or louvers. A composite door core consists of a noncombustible, sound-deadening material, usually polyurethane foam or slab. Light-gauge vertical reinforcement channels are sometimes used inside hollow core doors to add strength and rigidity to the door assembly.

Steel pedestrian doors are found in single or double configurations and use a wide variety of locking devices. Exterior doors usually swing outward, regardless of their functional design, and have their closing devices attached internally. Hinges are mortised with either removable or nonremovable pins. Additional doors are provided for emergency exits, as required by fire and life safety codes. The requirements for panic bar devices on all emergency exits make the door to which they are attached only a one-way barrier.

This safety requirement provides a variety of exit modes to outside attackers after a building has been breached, as well as giving an insider an easy way to defeat the delay. Certain exceptions to life safety codes and crash bars are permissible. As discussed in Chapter 10, "Entry Control," a commonly used system employs a 30 to 45 s delay incorporated into the emergency exit door. Under normal circumstances, the delay mechanism will prevent opening of the door for the prescribed time. However, if a fire alarm is pulled or the automatic fire suppression system is activated, the delay mechanism is overridden and the door will open immediately. Penetration times for lightweight sheet steel doors vary depending on the attack tools used. The following sections describe the attack modes against which standard doors are weak.

Standard Doors

An attack that uses explosives is a very noisy mode of entry and produces obvious evidence of penetration, which can help in detection of an attack. The explosives used can range from a small homemade bomb to very potent charges. The use of a thermal cutting tool offers an alternate entry method. Power tools can also produce a hole big enough to crawl through in approximately 3 min.

Standard key-locking mechanisms, if accessible, can probably be picked. Picking time varies with the type and physical condition of the lock but averages about 1 min for a skilled locksmith. A pipe or strap wrench used on key-in-knob locks reduces penetration time to tenths of a minute. These methods do have some limitations, however. Picking tools are effective only if a keyway is available; a pipe wrench is effective only if locking hardware is exposed. Many doors need no entrance modes at all (only exit modes) and, therefore, can be fully flush-mounted with no external hardware. If keyways are required, there are several high-security locks on the market that require quite long pick times. In addition, use of door sensors will mitigate lock vulnerabilities.

On external doors, hinge pins are usually exposed and are natural attack targets. Even nonremovable hinge pins can be readily defeated with hand tools. Thermal tools or explosives can also be used for rapid removal of hinges. About 1 min is required to defeat the hinges (typically three) on an external door. Hand tools are an effective means of penetrating louvers, windows, or mesh on doors. A large crawl-through hole can be made through plate, tempered, or wired glass in 15 s. Louvers can be forced apart or mesh and glass can be cut in approximately 30 s.

Improved designs are necessary to upgrade the penetration resistance of industrial doors to match the delay provided by the remaining structure. Penetration times for industrial doors vary greatly; the minimum penetration time is about 10 s. Removal of internal panic bars is desirable, but fire and building codes may disallow this. External doors are also susceptible to breaching by vehicle ramming and commercially available search and rescue tools. Examples include special shotgun rounds used by police to quickly breach doors, and hydraulic spreaders used by fire departments.

The following discussion applies to facilities with older standard doors to be upgraded when complete door replacement is not an option. At new facilities or where complete door replacement is necessary, new high-security, attack-resistant doors should be used.

Steel pedestrian doors mounted in stamped steel frames are frequently found in existing structures. These doors offer little resistance to forcible attack; however, they can be upgraded in various ways to increase their penetration delay time. The upgrades and design concepts described in the following paragraphs are intended to balance the overall door structure, including the door face, frame, hinges, exit devices, louvers, glazing, and locks, and to protect it against forcible penetration attempts with hand, power, or thermal tools.

Eliminating all unnecessary doors is the first step in upgrading existing facilities. Eliminating all windows, louvers, and external knobs and keyways is the next level of upgrade. One structural enhancement is the addition of steel plates to door surfaces; this increases the penetration resistance of a door to hand and light power tools. Heavy-duty hinges should be used to support any added weight, and frames should be grouted with concrete to strengthen the supporting structure. Wood cores, particularly redwood, placed between door plates increase the delay times for thermal cutting tools by a factor of three to four times that of an air void.

Hand tools can be used to attack the lock/frame area of a door in order to force the frame strike away from the lock bolt. A forced separation of $1/2-3/4$ in. is usually sufficient to pry open a door. A method has been devised to prevent easy access to the lock/frame area. A sheet steel strip can be either welded or bolted to the door. This strip should be the same height as the door and at least 2 in. wide with a 1 in. overlap onto the adjacent doorframe. In addition, the frame should be grouted with concrete mix at least 18 in. above the frame strike location. Holes can be cut in the doorframe to allow grouting of both sides of the frame. The holes can then be covered with a cover plate, which is welded or screwed into place. A high-security lock could also be installed on exterior pedestrian doors, because lock defeat is one of the quickest and quietest means of gaining entry to a protected area. Replacement of a single conventional lock with a high-security, multiple deadbolt system would virtually eliminate prying attacks.

Hinges can be compromised in approximately 1 min either by removing the pins or by cutting the hinge knuckles. Welding the pin top to the hinge will extend penetration times if only hand tools are used; however, if the hinge knuckles are cut with power or thermal tools, the penetration time is still about 1 min. Upgraded hinges with a stud-in-hole feature are commercially available. This type of hinge extends penetration time. Another method devised to prevent hinge-side door removal employs a Z-strip made from steel, which is bolted or welded to the rear face of the door. This strip is formed so that if the door hinges are removed and an attempt is made to pry the door from its frame, one leg of the Z-strip will come in contact with either the inner frame surface or the rear doorstop surface. Once the Z-strip contacts the doorframe, adversaries must use excessive force and large tools to remove the door. A variety of full length hinge designs are also available that may extend penetration times significantly.

Most exterior doors are equipped with panic hardware that allows rapid exit in case of emergency. However, this safety equipment also makes a door more vulnerable to defeat. Panic (or crash) bars can be defeated in about 1 min by using small hand tools. This method of defeat produces less noise than thermal cutting. Where noise is not a factor, hand or power tools can be used. One possible method of upgrading a panic bar-equipped door employs a bent metal plate with a drill-resistant steel section fastened to it. The plate prevents chiseling and wire hooking of the panic bar. The drill-resistant section extends penetration time considerably if the area between the panic bar and the horizontal leg of the plate is attacked. If any other location on the door is selected for penetration, manipulation becomes considerably harder. Electronic control devices are also available for use with emergency exit hardware. These devices require the push bar to be depressed for a predetermined amount of time before an electronic deadbolt is released. This allows a security officer time to assess the situation via CCTV or to respond to the door alarm, if necessary. Figure 11.7 shows an upgraded exterior

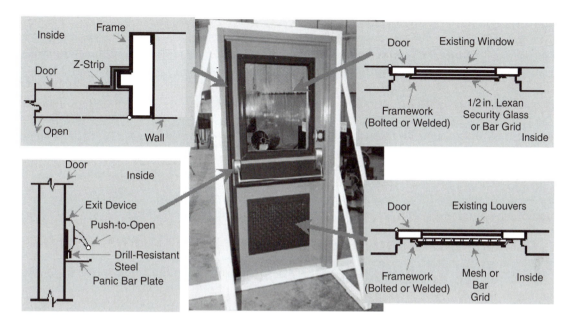

Figure 11.7 Upgraded Door. The door has a Z-strip added to prevent prying, a plate to prevent defeat of the panic bar, and hardened glass, frame, and louvers

door incorporating many of the features described above. One additional recommendation is the removal of exterior doorknobs or other hardware from emergency exit doors. This will reduce the possibility of any prying attack from the outside, but does not compromise rapid emergency egress.

The use of either louvers or glazing material should be minimized for exterior doors since these assemblies can be easily penetrated with hand tools. Either removal of all door louvers and glazing or a reduction in size (less than crawl-through size) is recommended. Possible upgrades include the addition of a screen or a bar grid to the interior of the louver or glazing.

Windows and Utility Ports

Windows provide only minimal penetration delay to adversaries and require enhancement to provide significant penetration resistance. The location of the window affects the required upgrading. Windows should follow the balanced design principle so that they will not be the weak link in a barrier system. This section describes frames, glazing materials, and protective coverings, as well as other suggestions for improving window penetration delay times.

In addition to doors and windows, industrial facilities have many unattended structural openings, such as ventilating ducts, utility tunnels, and service openings, which can be used as intrusion paths by adversaries. Few existing structural openings would delay a determined adversary for very long, especially if the openings are designed to provide easy access for maintenance. These openings can function as a concealed pathway and, therefore, should be barricaded and sensored. The term utility port is used in this discussion to include all types of unattended framed openings other than doors and windows. Often these openings contain grills installed for safety and ornamental reasons, which also function as insect, rodent, and bird barriers. These openings provide very little security. Standard windows and utility ports constitute potential weak links in a barrier system and may require enhancement to provide significant delay. Windows without enhancement have little penetration delay time, because most windows can be penetrated with hand tools in less than 30 s. Utility ports may have lift-off covers that are not equipped with locking devices or interior barriers.

The strength and weight of the frame material of a window vary widely with the class of window and manufacturer. Some manufacturers fabricate a security sash; however, this term can be misleading since the frame material is not hardened. Where windows are installed in doors, the metal strips separating the glass have proven to be weak. For example, a hand tool can be used to accomplish penetration in a few seconds. However, several special window frames contain concealed materials that resist cutting tools. If a window can be opened and closed, the window-locking mechanism may constitute a weak link, and, if forced, this window can be opened. The position and operation of the locking mechanism of a window vary with type and manufacturer. The mechanism should be located so that it is not readily accessible from the exterior. The installation of more substantial locking devices or fixed windows could be considered as possible upgrade options.

Window frame attachment to the structure may be improved by the use of additional or heavier fasteners or by welding the frame fin, but these techniques may not affect the delay time through the window unless additional upgrades are made to the glazing materials and protective coverings. Glass glazing materials include standard, tempered, wire, and laminated glass. These types of glass provide a barrier to the elements but will not provide significant delay times.

Standard glass materials are highly frangible. Penetration by hand tools generally requires only a few seconds. Where a higher level of penetration resistance is required, thick security glass can be used. In addition, standard glazing materials are often upgraded with a protective grill of expanded steel mesh or other forms of metal grills. Tempered glass is formed by the reheating and sudden cooling of a base glass. Although tempering greatly increases its mechanical strength and thermal stress characteristics, the glass can still be easily broken with moderate force. It can be shattered into gravel-size pieces by hand tools (impact) in a few seconds.

The primary use of wire glass is in fire doors and fire windows. The 1/4 in. thick material is fabricated with diamond, square, or hexagonal wire patterns. Penetration of wire glass can be achieved using hand tools in approximately 20 s. Laminated glass is manufactured as a safety and security glass; however, not all types of laminated glass are recommended by manufacturers for use in security areas. Laminated glass is composed of two or more panes of annealed float, sheet, or plate glass bonded to a layer or layers of plastic that range in thickness from 0.050 to 0.090 in. Safety glass that is 1/4 in. thick can be penetrated in 30 s, while 9/16 in. thick security glass requires 1.5 min of work with hand tools to produce a crawl-through hole. Security glass is not transparent armor. It is simply more resistant than standard glass to forcible penetration.

Transparent plastics can be used as substitutes for most glass; however, some are combustible and their use is restricted by fire codes. Acrylic plastics such as Lucite™ and Plexiglas™ up to 1 in. thick can be easily broken with hand tools in less than 10 s. The impact resistance of polycarbonates, on the other hand, approaches the same performance level as that of bullet-resistant glass. Tests show that 1/2 in. thick Lexan® resists hand-tool penetration for up to 2 min (Nuclear Security Systems Directorate, 1989). Thermal tool attacks require about 1 min, but they also result in combustion and release of toxic gases.

Both acrylic and polycarbonate plastic panels up to 1 in. thick can be easily cut with power tools.

Glass/polycarbonate composite glazing contains a tough core layer of polycarbonate laminated between two outer layers of glass. The glazing was originally developed for use in prisons to replace vulnerable security glass. In tests using common hand tools and miscellaneous pipe, bars, and steel sections, glass/polycarbonate composites were penetrated when hand tools and fireaxes were used, but the thickest panels resisted forcible entry attempts for 10 min when miscellaneous steel tools were used (Nuclear Security Systems Directorate, 1989).

The penetration resistance of a window or utility port may be increased by the installation of protective coverings, such as grills, bars, expanded-metal mesh, or screens. Similarly, grids and grates constructed of steel mesh, expanded metal, bar stock, tubing, or bars can be used to reduce the size of the opening in utility ports to prevent crawling through the port. Use of these coverings should occur at or after appropriate detection to be effective in protection. The degree of improvement in windows should be dictated by the balanced design concept. With the proper selection of enhancements (protective coverings, grills, mesh), different glazing material, or methods of frame attachment, the delay time of windows may approach the delay time of doors or even walls for some threats.

In addition to doors and windows, most tunnels used to link buildings are not protected very well. Access may be controlled only by lift-off covers or manholes that are not equipped with locking devices or interior barriers. Pipe channels used inside buildings are often quite congested, but still allow space for maintenance work. Ducts associated with heating, ventilating, and air-conditioning systems could provide an adversary path. Tunnels, manholes, roof, wall openings for equipment, and ductwork can be enhanced by installing interior barriers or a series of barriers.

An option that may be considered in future designs for new buildings is the use of smaller-than-man-size windows and multiple, small openings for utility ducts. The use of very narrow (4 in. or less) windows will increase penetration time, since even with the glazing removed. the opening will need to be enlarged to create a person-size hole. Windows could be removed from existing structures to allow the original window opening to be upgraded to the same penetration delay as the adjoining wall.

Roofs and Floors

Roofs and floors function as climatic barriers, provide working surfaces, and, to some degree, function as protective barriers; however, their use as physical protection against penetration by determined adversaries is generally not considered. The penetration threats include hand, power, and thermal tools, and explosives used alone or in combination.

Construction methods and materials used for roofs and floors are similar. The basic materials may vary slightly in total thickness; type and quantity of steel reinforcement; and the concrete strength required to carry the loads. In general, floors offer more resistance to penetration than roofs do, because they are protected by the main structure and are designed to accommodate heavier loads than roofs.

Contemporary roof types used on many structures include:

- prestressed concrete tee beam
- metal subdeck and reinforced concrete
- metal roof deck with lightweight concrete
- metal roof deck with insulation
- metal roof
- reinforced concrete beam and slab
- wood sheathing with membrane

The following suggested enhancements do not apply directly to any one roof type, but rather to the roof elements. The most cost-effective enhancements appear to be those placed below the roof line; they could be applied to either new or existing facilities. Available roof enhancements include:

- membranes enhanced with embedded screen;
- several inches of rigid insulation added;
- concrete reinforced with deformed steel bars and expanded steel mesh;
- larger rebar formed into multiple rows or layers for reinforced concrete;
- on corrugated roofs, the number of fasteners should be increased, and additional structural members installed;
- joints on metal systems should be secured with mechanical fasteners or with a continuous weld and heavier gauge material; and
- reinforcement of the flange area of precast concrete tee beams with larger rebar.

Penetration tests have indicated that barriers placed below the roof are sometimes more effective against penetration than those in the roof itself. Such barriers may be used in some existing structures without major modification. Placing these enhancements below the roof line provides the structure with some protection against direct attack and could make a second penetration necessary. This second penetration could be constrained to take place in a confined area and could force the use of tools from other tool classes in order to complete penetration. The exact position of a barrier below the roof line is a factor in its effectiveness. The optimum distance below the roof appears to be 10–12 in. This distance may create a hole effect or the restriction of the operating space needed for the tool and the available crawl space. The enhancement materials used within

barriers could range from quarry screen to expanded steel bank vault mesh or floor gratings.

For new facilities, the use of significant earth covering can provide considerable delay through both the roof and the walls. Both buried and cut-and-cover structures effectively use earth covering to provide access delay and blast mitigation.

Dispensable Barriers

Dispensable barriers are those that are deployed only when necessary, that is, during an adversary attack. Two categories of dispensable barriers have been developed: active and passive. Active dispensable barriers can, on command, stop or delay an adversary from accomplishing the objective. Several types are under development. This section identifies the major components of an active dispensable barrier system and describes some of the attributes of dispensable materials.

A typical active dispensable barrier system includes:

- a process for decision-making to determine when the dispensable barrier is to be activated;
- command and control hardware to implement this decision;
- the material that is deployed to physically delay access or incapacitate the adversary;
- the dispensing mechanism; and
- a guard force located on site.

The activation decision mechanism may involve either a member of the guard force, some form of intrusion sensing, or the combined action of both the guard force and sensors. The major compromise is between assurance that activation can and will occur in an adversary attack (reliability) and assurance that the probability of inadvertent activation is low (premature activation). Hardware design and effective operational procedures can reduce the probability of inadvertent activation to as low a value as required.

The command and control hardware accepts the activation decision and must operate the dispensing hardware. Command and control hardware stands between the decision mechanism and the dispensing hardware. Because the activation decision mechanism and the dispensing hardware may be separated by large distances, electromagnetic radiation, lightning, earthquakes, power surges, and other possible severe environments must be considered in the design. The command and control hardware improves personnel safety and assures that, if inadvertent activation occurs, authorized personnel in the area have time to avoid personnel hazards.

The dispensable material is normally stored in a compact form and, through a chemical or physical reaction, is expanded to an effective delay state. The same properties that permit compact storage and rapid expansion make activated delay systems attractive in physical protection applications where operational considerations are dominant. Dispensing hardware consists of storage tanks, activation valves, pressure regulators, safety valves, filters, power sources, and plumbing hardware. The specific hardware design is unique for each material and application, but many of the components are similar. This uniqueness of design and limited application are factors that increase the cost of the dispensing hardware. Further, the dispensing hardware itself must be protected from use or disablement by an adversary.

Dispensable barriers will only delay an adversary for a finite time. They are best used in conjunction with passive barriers such as turnbuckles, tie-downs, or cables. At some point in time, the adversary will defeat any delay mechanism. Therefore, the response force must respond and achieve control in a shorter time than the dispensable barrier delay time.

Dispensable barriers require the adversary to be prepared to do more than just evade the response force. They must also be able to successfully defeat the dispensable barrier. Dispensable barriers usually have the effect of isolating the adversary visually, acoustically, at a particular location, or sometimes in combination. This increased requirement on the adversary can significantly increase the probability that the overall PPS will perform as desired.

Passive dispensable barriers present many of the same benefits as active dispensable barriers but they differ in one important aspect. Passive dispensable barriers do not require any command and control system. The dispensing mechanism is activated by the penetration attempts of the adversary. Elimination of command and control hardware significantly reduces the cost of passive dispensable barriers compared to active dispensable barriers.

While structural barriers are attractive due to their simplicity, dispensable barriers offer an alternative that, in some applications, is more operationally acceptable and may be cost-effective. Specific dispensable materials and associated dispensing hardware that are being developed and tested include:

- rigid polyurethane foam
- stabilized aqueous foam (see Figure 11.8)
- smoke or fog
- sticky thermoplastic foam (see Figure 11.9)
- various entanglement devices

Rigid foam encasing has been used for long-term storage of assets or for protection when transporting materials between sites. Stabilized aqueous foam has been used in government installations overseas. This material has the added benefit of being a fire retardant, so it can add safety benefits if needed. Pepper mace or other irritants can also be added to aqueous foam to further delay an adversary. Smokes and fogs are easy to dispense

Figure 11.8 Dispensing of Aqueous Foam. The foam rapidly expands and fills the area near the asset location. This isolates the adversary visually and acoustically from the environment

and are commercially available in the form of dry ice or other fogging machines, such as those used in theatrical applications. Sticky foam has been used as a passive barrier in some specialized applications and has been considered for use in less-than-lethal applications, such as prison cell extractions or crowd control. Entanglement devices include coils of wire or nets suspended from ceilings and the dropping of shredded paper or other similar items from above onto an adversary. These items are most effective when combined with smoke or fog barriers, as they will not be immediately obvious to an adversary entering an area where the smoke has just been deployed. Obviously, safety issues will be a large part of the decision as to the use of some dispensable barriers.

Figure 11.9 Sticky Foam Test. The adversary has picked up the asset but is unable to move due to the sticking action of the foam. The asset was also secured with heavy wires and turnbuckles anchored into the board the asset was placed on as a passive barrier

Due to their higher cost, dispensable barriers are generally deployed very close to the assets being protected. This is also the most effective location for delay elements in general. Although it is feasible to fill an entire building with smoke or fog, it would be very cost-prohibitive. A more desirable approach is to deploy the obscurant only in the room where the assets are stored. By deploying the dispensable materials close to the target, the issues of cleanup and collateral contamination are also reduced.

During evaluation at Sandia National Laboratories, different materials performed relatively better in single system attributes, but none of the materials is superior in all, or even most, of the qualities that have been discussed. The selection of an optimum dispensable barrier material for a given application is often a compromise among the following major attributes associated with dispensable barriers:

- exert a minimum impact on operations;
- protect volumes;
- provide adequate safety to personnel;

- may operate independently of barriers;
- may offer multiple activation options;
- have a long storage life;
- provide protection-in-depth; and
- can be cost-effective.

Cutting-edge technologies that combine both delay and response are currently being developed and deployed for protection of high-value assets. Two examples are the remotely operated weapons system (ROWS, Figure 11.10) and the millimeter wave system (Figure 11.11). ROWS can be equipped for lethal denial by using conventional lead bullets, or it can be less-than-lethal if loaded with rubber bullets or fragmenting rounds. The system is operated by a security officer located in a remote, well-secured location. As such, the officer is removed from danger and can better assess the situation and respond appropriately. Millimeter wave systems use high-frequency electromagnetic waves to stimulate the nerve endings in an adversary's skin. The adversary perceives a severe burning sensation even though no physical harm is being

Figure 11.11 Nonlethal Denial System. The millimeter wave system shown above creates a burning sensation in the adversary's skin without actually causing any physical harm or damage. These systems are still in the prototype stages

Figure 11.10 ROWS with the Ballistic Cover Raised. This system has two sighting cameras (one infrared) as well as one targeting camera attached to the scope. The system can be designed to fire up to 0.50-caliber rounds. The operator is safely removed from any potential firefight

done. The pain and burning sensation is sufficient to drive away virtually any intruder.

Procedures

Due to the form of most passive barriers, they do not generally require any additional maintenance other than normal cleaning, periodic inspection, or upkeep. Fences, doors, windows, and other delay elements should be repaired or replaced if loose or broken. Maintenance procedures for dispensable delay systems vary widely depending upon the system design. Generally, passive dispensable systems do not require any sort of maintenance other than checking for obvious damage and appropriate pressure in pressurized designs. Active dispensable systems require routine exercising of the command and control system with artificial loads. The design life for dispensable delay systems ranges from 10 to 25 years.

Certain access points such as utility ports, ducts, or drainage pipes can be sensored to provide an alarm when disturbed. If the sensor is placed early in the delay time of the access point, an effective combination of detection and delay can be achieved. Even in the absence of immediate CCTV assessment, a procedure for responding to any alarm from one of these sensors can be implemented. Selection of an appropriate sensor with a high P_D and a low NAR for the area will assure that guards will only be dispatched occasionally. This will provide a balance between effective protection and cost.

Summary

A close examination of the large variety of paths or scenarios an adversary can select to penetrate a given facility will probably indicate that existing barriers do not ensure that adversary delay time will always be sufficient for an adequate response force to react. Further, if the adversary has not been detected prior to encountering a particular barrier or during penetration, the effectiveness of that barrier may be negligible. Most conventional barriers such as fences, locks, doors, and barriers for windows provide short penetration delay against forcible (and perhaps stealthy) attack methods that do not use explosives. Against thick, reinforced concrete walls and other equally impressive-looking barriers, explosives become a more likely method of penetration by the adversary. Ensuring that meaningful barriers are in effect at

all times of the day and night may be difficult to accomplish without adversely affecting normal facility operation. Often, the use of compensatory measures, such as additional guards, is required to offset the decreased delay and increased risk encountered during certain operations such as fire drills or maintenance by contract employees.

On the positive side, a barrier system can be configured or enhanced to provide effective delay times. For instance, the presence of multiple barriers of different types along all possible adversary paths should complicate the adversary's progress by requiring that they be equipped with a number of different barrier attack tools and skills. Locating barriers next to detection alarms should aid in accurate assessment of and response to adversaries.

If the facility to be protected has not yet been constructed, barriers can be incorporated into its design. For example, placing the facility either underground or aboveground with massive overburden is an option that should be seriously considered. Using balanced design principles, appropriate detection systems, and response forces, a facility can be made highly resistant to outsider and insider threats and to the method of transportation used by adversaries (foot, land vehicle, or aircraft).

Consolidating assets into a single room or vault is often one of the most effective ways to reduce response time and the cost of delay upgrades. Having assets scattered throughout a site requires the guard force to accurately assess the threat location and contend with the possibility of diversionary tactics by the adversaries.

Finally, the use of dispensable barriers, such as entanglement devices, or dispensable chemicals such as obscurants, irritants, and foams offer significant potential for increasing adversary delay. These dispensable deterrents should be coupled with passive structural-type barriers to synergistically increase delay times. Also, conventional breaching techniques and equipment used by an adversary may be so ineffective that they would choose not to continue attacking that barrier. Any activated dispensable barrier will, of course, require protection of the complete activation system to avoid or to adequately delay disablement by an adversary.

Security Principles

Access delay follows detection in an effective physical protection system.

The performance measure for access delay elements is time. Delay time for the adversary will depend on the barrier to be breached and the tools that are used.

Delay elements include passive barriers, guards, and dispensable barriers.

As a part of protection-in-depth, delay-in-depth should be implemented.

Delay barriers should provide balance along adversary paths.

Dispensable barriers must be used in combination with passive barriers to provide the most effective delays.

References

Kane, J.W., and Kodlick, M.R. Access denial systems: Interaction of delay elements. SAND83-0362 1983;7.

Kodlick, M.R. Barrier technology: Perimeter barrier penetration tests. SAND78-0241 1978;1–33.

Nuclear Security Systems Directorate. Access delay technology transfer manual. SAND87-1926/1 1989; 4-3–4-6.

Sena, P.A. Security vehicle barriers. SAND84-2593 1985;12–54.

White, I.B. Explosive penetration of concrete walls. SAND80-1942 1981; 1–84.

Questions

1. Would an adversary always choose the fastest penetration method? What situations would lead an adversary toward making a slower penetration effort?
2. Why are a variety of hand tools considered to be used for some barriers but only very limited penetration equipment for the more substantial barriers?
3. What are some of the ways that a perimeter fence line can be upgraded to increase the delay time for vehicle penetration?
4. Where is the best placement for a vehicle barrier in a double-fence system?
5. What are some of the ways that a perimeter fence line can be upgraded to increase the delay time for adversaries on foot?
6. Why is it important to ensure that the floor, ceiling, and walls of a room are balanced—that is, provide the same delay? What would help determine the need for this degree of protection?
7. Why is it important to use multiple barriers and different barriers?
8. What are some of the advantages and disadvantages of using explosives as a means to gain access to critical assets?
9. Why do you think we say that dispensable barriers near the target can be a very cost-effective delay mechanism?

12

Response

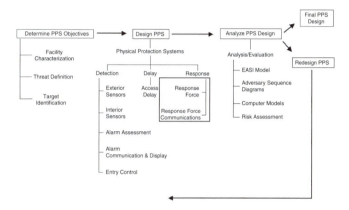

As discussed in previous chapters, an effective PPS must perform the functions of detection, delay, and response. The last of these functions, response, will be presented in this chapter. The response function includes responding personnel and the communications system that is used. The composition of the response force varies from facility to facility. A part of or all of the response force may be located on-site or off-site. The response force may include proprietary or contract guards, local and state police, and, for some incidents, Federal agencies such as the FBI, DEA, or Customs. In this text, guards will refer to the on-site personnel who are available to respond to an incident; response force is a more general term meant to include any response personnel who may be involved in the response at a particular facility, both on-site and off-site. These responders may include security guards, medical, fire, or other safety personnel, or others.

Response may be broken into two major categories—immediate on-site response (timely response) and after-the-fact recovery. Depending on the needs and objectives of a facility, it is prudent to decide in advance which type of response will be used at the site under various conditions. Protection of different targets may require different response plans. For example, stopping an intruder about to sabotage a critical valve in a refinery may require an immediate on-site response, while recovery may be a better technique for theft of low-value company property. For a recovery-based response, the use of videotape for after-the-fact review can be very effective and legally acceptable. It should be apparent that timely response will require better detection and delay than a response strategy that focuses on recovery of the asset. A recovery strategy may not be acceptable for all assets. For example, recovery of stolen documents or information may not be meaningful, because the thief may already have copied or distributed the information. In a like manner, once an incident of workplace violence has occurred, the capture of the perpetrator is commendable, but there is still the aftermath of the event to consider. This aftermath may include legal action by the victim or the victim's family against the facility, bad publicity for the facility, poor employee morale, and regulatory action against the facility.

Because of the wide variety of response force personnel that can exist, it is difficult to provide information concerning the specific procedures or tasks that the response force may be expected to perform. Depending on the threat, consequence of loss of the asset, and the particular facility, the response force must either prevent adversaries from accomplishing their objective or work to recover the asset. Recovery efforts may include investigation of the incident to find the culprit, filing insurance claims, or pursuit of the adversary immediately after the incident. Specific task assignments to accomplish these functions will be reflected in variations of qualification standards, training requirements, and performance standards as measured by realistic tests, governed by policies and procedures at the facility. In this chapter, the PPS function of response has been divided into five parts— general considerations, contingency planning, communication, interruption, and neutralization.

General Considerations

Staffing of the response force is fundamental to the performance of the response function. Proprietary guard forces are those in which the members are direct employees of the facility. Contract services also exist for facilities that prefer to contract this service out to others. There is considerable debate as to which of these two options is best at a facility (Fischer and Green, 2006). It is likely that the answer will depend on the goals and objectives of each corporation and facility. Facility size, assets, location, cost, and other factors may favor use of one system over the other. Many facilities use a combination of the two, which can provide flexibility. Hertig (1999a) has written a paper discussing the considerations of contract

versus proprietary forces. In addition to the use of contract and proprietary guards, some facilities also hire members of local law enforcement to help at night or at periods of heavy demand, such as morning or evening rush hours. Use of local law enforcement officers is appealing because these officers have the legal authority to arrest or detain suspects and to use appropriate force. It is important to reiterate at this time that people make bad detectors, so the investment in guards may not be effective if the PPS is heavily dependent on guards for this function. A more cost-effective solution would be to reduce the number of guards and add technology to supplement guard duties. This will provide better PPS performance at a lower cost than the addition of more people.

Regardless of which type of guard force is used at a facility, the key to effective guard use is training. Hiring contract forces may reduce costs, but does not absolve the hiring facility from responsibility for their actions. For this reason, it is important to provide training at the facility or to incorporate training expectations into the terms of the contract with the vendor.

The details of the legal issues that are associated with guards and the response force are too numerous and complex to be dealt with at any length in this text. These issues, however, generally fall into categories of civil and criminal law and liability. Under civil law, intentional torts such as assault, battery, false arrest and imprisonment, defamation, invasion of privacy, malicious prosecution, and negligence are common. Criminal law is pertinent when dealing with trespassers, illegal drug use, sexual assault, receiving stolen property, and fraud. In these cases, the guard force may need to collect evidence to present to law enforcement officers for further legal action. Another area of law that has application is labor law. Labor law addresses issues such as wrongful termination, activities by labor unions, and strike surveillance. Consideration of these legal issues and others is required to protect the corporation and its employees from legal action. Because each state has different laws concerning these various elements, it is recommended that local law enforcement or attorneys be consulted for guidance in establishing procedures. Hertig (1999b) has written an excellent overview of legal issues and the security function. In addition, some actions, such as kidnapping, require notification of federal agencies, which will then have legal jurisdiction. This principle also applies to bombings at private facilities or attacks on government property.

Response Force Performance Measures

The two measures of an immediate response are the time for arrival and neutralization effectiveness. The time it takes to arrive is used to establish interruption; neutralization is a measure of response success, given arrival. Interruption is a measure of the detection, delay, communication and response functions of the PPS and is represented by the probability of interruption (P_I). Neutralization measures response force numbers, training, tactics, and use of any weapons or equipment and is represented by the probability of neutralization (P_N). The use of these two terms to measure overall PPS effectiveness (by taking their product) was described in Chapter 1; additional information about how these measures are used is provided in the next chapter, "Analysis and Evaluation."

Interruption refers to arrival of response personnel at a location that will prevent the adversary from progressing in their attack. Interruption may be accomplished with one person or multiple personnel, depending on the threat. For example, arrival of one person at a location may be sufficient to scare away teenage vandals, but more motivated threats may require more capable response personnel. For low to medium threats, interruption alone may be an effective response, but for more capable medium to high threats, neutralization of the adversary may become necessary. Interruption depends on reliable, accurate, and fast alarm reporting and assessment, as well as dependable communication and effective deployment to the proper location. These are all elements of the PPS.

Neutralization refers to any confrontation between the adversary and responders and is defined as defeat of the adversary. Some threats may require more than just response presence in order to be defeated, and neutralization is used to measure this aspect of response effectiveness. Effectiveness elements include response tactics, procedures such as use of force and after detainment actions, training, number of personnel who respond to the alarm, and the equipment they carry. Neutralization, then, is more a measure of training and capability. Neutralization may use the entire force continuum including presence (interruption), verbal commands, physical restraint, intermediate force weapons such as batons and pepper spray, or deadly force (at some high-security locations). The techniques used will depend on the defined threat, but the response force must be at least equal to the adversary in terms of equipment, weapons and number to successfully neutralize the adversary.

Contingency Planning

Contingency planning is an important part of a facility's ability to successfully resolve an incident. Prior planning will help a facility manager identify potential targets, respond to different threats, interact with outside agencies, and determine what level of force guards can use in various situations. Well-documented procedures should be developed in advance as a major part of contingency planning.

A critical part of the design and analysis process of a PPS is the identification of assets. This was covered completely in the previous chapter on target identification. Once assets are identified at a facility, the security manager can evaluate the likely routes an adversary may use to approach the facility boundary and the specific asset. This information will assist managers in developing detailed tactical plans to address various threats to the facility. In addition, it will be useful in determining guard patrol routes and schedules. Based on the adversary goal and the consequence of loss of the asset, different response force strategies will be used. These strategies include containment, denial, and, occasionally, assault.

Containment is the strategy used against an adversary with theft as their goal. This refers to the ability of the guards and the response force to prevent the adversary from leaving the site with the stolen asset. A denial strategy is used when the adversary goal is sabotage or violent attack. In this case, the guards or response force must prevent the adversary from completing the task of sabotaging equipment or carrying out a violent attack on another person. It should be apparent that in order for a denial strategy to be successful, the response force must be present at the location and time of the sabotage or attack. A containment strategy for a sabotage goal does no good, because the response will come after the sabotage event has been completed. On occasion, the response force may need to use force to overcome an adversary. This is most common in hostage incidents or when dealing with mentally unstable individuals.

Tactical planning should also be part of contingency planning in general. Procedures and plans for guard actions in the event of an adversary attack should be well established. The chain of command and the succession of command in case of emergency should be well known. Related to this is the need for a defined location for a central command center that is always ready for use (i.e., in hot or cold standby). Plans must be made to ensure that members of the response force possess or have rapid access to the proper equipment consistent with the defined threat. Tactical plans must contain specific details for the response force to deploy successfully. Response strategies of containment, denial, and assault must be well planned and practiced.

The role of the guard force should also be factored into the facility contingency plan. A guard force whose key role is the containment of adversaries until additional help arrives will deploy differently than a guard force capable of recovery operations. It is possible that there will be two sets of guards at a facility: one group checking credentials, patrolling, and serving the deterrence/delay role, and another, more highly skilled group with primary responsibility for response to a malevolent event.

Security personnel, due to their access and familiarity with a facility, are a natural choice for assistance under abnormal conditions at a site, such as hurricanes, flooding, fires, or blizzards. The facility may ask security personnel to help in the event of a natural disaster, bad weather, or accident. These services are reasonable but should not compromise the protection of assets at the facility. Procedures should be developed in advance with input from facility safety personnel, management, legal counsel, local law enforcement, and other public safety agencies, particularly the local fire department, if they will be depended on to provide aid. These procedures should be documented and included in guard training. Part-time peace officers working at the facility should also be knowledgeable of these procedures and of any hazards that exist at the facility. These procedures do not need to be specific to each abnormal condition, but can be used as applicable. For example, in case of heavy rain or snow, the procedure may require early arrival of facility maintenance personnel to place rugs at doorways to prevent slipping or other site-preparation measures, such as snow removal. The procedure may also include notification to employees of a delayed work schedule announced via local radio, employee voicemail, or through a hotline. The guard force should be aware of these procedures and understand their role at these times. In the event of a power failure or a fire, security personnel may be used to assist in evacuation of buildings and crowd control until the all-clear signal is issued or another determination made. These procedural elements can then be applied as needed for a particular emergency. The security manager alone cannot create these procedures; rather, they must represent a cross-section of input from various components of the facility.

Natural or man-made disasters that cause business at the facility to cease may also require the help of the security organization or from external agencies. During a natural disaster, local law enforcement priorities may be to protect the public before protecting facilities. Industrial needs may be last on the list; therefore, resources beyond local law enforcement may be required. Hurricane Katrina is a good example of this—resources were focused on saving people by moving them to safer and higher ground, not protection of commercial industry. If the stoppage is due to an adversary attack, there must be processes and procedures in place to resume operation as soon as possible, while still collecting and preserving evidence. In the event of an abnormal incident, use of daily operational procedures, such as daily backup of computer files or storage of backup records at an off-site location, may reduce the effect of a catastrophic event. Abnormal conditions may reveal weaknesses in the security protection at a facility and provide an opportunity to improve asset protection. The security organization can play a role in assisting the facility to resume normal operation after an abnormal event, and certainly will be involved in the investigation of any malevolent attacks and their aftermath.

Security managers should consider using support from outside agencies as they do their contingency planning. A facility may create support agreements with local or state law enforcement agencies or mutual aid agreements with other local sites. To facilitate this, a written support agreement with outside agencies or sites should be developed. This written agreement should detail the interaction between site guards and these agencies. The agreement should be developed with input from all participants affected by the agreement and approved by each organization. Issues such as the outside agency's role in an incident, off-site pursuit by guards, and communication should be considered. The roles of outside agencies should be well defined and communicated among all participants. Security managers may also consider use of other agencies for recovery support. These decisions will need to be based on the agency's response time, training, equipment, and availability to support the facility. In addition, security managers may decide to provide their guards with off-site credentials and authority to facilitate the response force's ability to operate outside of the facility's boundaries. This may be an important consideration during deployment or pursuit.

Communication will be a key factor in the interaction between facility personnel and other agencies. Since different agencies may not operate on the same radio frequency, the security manager will need to evaluate alternate means of communication during abnormal or malevolent conditions. A dedicated landline may be used for initial notification to outside agencies, and preplanned routes and containment positions may help resolve on-scene communications concerns.

Joint Training Exercises

A critical factor that will influence the ability for a neighboring agency to successfully support a facility is joint training. The facility security manager should plan and conduct periodic training exercises with outside agencies that provide response support. The scope of this training will be dictated by the agency's support role. If the outside agency will act primarily in a containment capacity, then primary containment positions and areas of responsibility should be practiced. However, if the support agency will be conducting recapture or rescue operations, more detailed training and facility knowledge will be required.

One method of addressing aid from and coordination with outside agencies is through the use of a Memorandum of Understanding (MOU). An MOU should be established to prioritize facility support from outside agencies and should answer questions such as: Where does the specific facility response fall? Are there other facilities with critical needs in the area? This is a very important step when organizing external support for a facility. There may be multiple facilities with critical needs within a particular area or jurisdiction, and these priorities should be known in advance so appropriate plans for facility protection can be created, practiced, and continually updated.

Use of Force

Different threats may require guards or other responders to employ a wide variety of force to address any given situation. Response force personnel should have the ability to apply multiple levels of force to stop an adversary's actions. This will include the guard's presence as a deterrent or delay, the use of less-than-lethal force, and when justified, the use of deadly force. The range of force tactics available is referred to as the force continuum. The force continuum begins with presence of a guard, and progresses through verbal commands, use of less-than lethal-force, and finally, deadly force. The facility

should have a written policy to provide clear guidelines to guards in the use of force. The decision about which weapons, if any, to be issued to the guard force should be in alignment with the threats to the facility.

A use of force policy should be based on using the minimum amount of force necessary to stop an adversary's actions under varying but expected conditions. Typically, the amount of force used will be dictated by the adversary's actions. For example, an unarmed adversary who is refusing to follow the instructions of a guard but does not present any other threat should be handled with less force than an adversary who is armed and posing a threat to the facility or guards. This type of policy will typically require guards to have the ability to employ less-than-lethal force weapons such as impact (baton) or chemical (mace) weapons.

The use of armed guards at a facility must carefully balance the value of the asset with the additional legal liability and training costs that will arise. Armed guards are used at banks, armored car companies, private facilities located in high-crime areas, large shopping malls, and large industrial complexes with multiple high-value assets. The use of armed guards at a location will be determined by the design basis threat to the facility. Armed response is usually left to local law enforcement, but if an armed threat is expected, guards may be required to carry guns. Facility guards must still receive training in interaction with local law enforcement, when to call for assistance, and in proper use of whatever force is authorized at the facility.

Training

After developing a use-of-force policy, supervisors should provide response force personnel with training to ensure that all personnel are well versed in the policy and use of their weapons. Managers should consider semi-annual or quarterly training and qualifications to ensure that their personnel are capable of successful application of the facility's policy and weapons. Documentation of all training records will be useful in the event of any legal challenges or post-incident reviews.

When designing a training program, it is important to consult the facility security manager and the PPS designer. The facility security manager is most familiar with the functional performance and task requirements of guards. The manager is also responsible for a separate training agenda that deals with policies, procedures, and basic training not specific to system operation, such as arrest powers, use of force, and communications. The designer is most familiar with the operations and limitations of the PPS equipment and the other PPS functions of detection and delay. From the designer's point of view, the objectives of training are to maximize the ability of the response force to use the PPS in carrying out its basic mission, which is protection of the assets of the facility. The training program at a facility should explain corporate policies and procedures and their relationship to legal and operational aspects of the protection system. At a minimum, a review of legal do's and dont's, as well as training in interpersonal contact, use of the force continuum, and incident reporting should be included. Because each state requires varying degrees of training for security guards, careful consideration of state requirements and facility objectives will be required to construct a suitable training program at a particular facility. Thibodeau (1999) and Baker (1999) have written excellent articles on guard training programs.

Communication

Communication is a vital part of the response function. The proper performance of all other system functions depends on communication. Information

must be transferred through this network with both speed and reliability. Communication to the response force must contain information about adversary actions and instructions for deployment. The effectiveness measures for response communication are the probability of accurate communication and the time required to communicate to the response force. The communication network includes voice and other systems that allow guards and response forces to communicate with each other. The successful operation of a PPS requires a reliable response force communication network that is resistant to being used to the advantage of knowledgeable and determined adversaries, as established by the design basis threat. An excellent description of communications problems after the 9/11 attacks is provided in a recent book (Dwyer and Flynn, 2005).

Normal Use

The most common system used to maintain effective control and coordination of the guard force at a facility consists of low-power, battery-operated, handheld radios. These radios are small, lightweight devices that allow rapid reporting of conditions found during routine patrols and enable rapid deployment of the response force during security events. A typical radio operates on any one of two to six frequencies or channels. The maximum range for reliable communication between two radios is 1–3 miles. More powerful transmitters and better receivers can be used at security headquarters and in security vehicles. These units can allow reliable communication up to ranges in excess of 12 miles.

In most cases, the radio systems used for response force communications are conventional, narrow-band, frequency modulation (FM), clear-voice radio systems. In this context, clear voice means that no attempt has been made to encode or scramble voice transmissions.

As a result, effective eavesdropping is possible on- or off-site by an adversary possessing a receiver that can be tuned to the same frequency. Depending on the site configuration, its area, and on-site building construction, these systems can suffer from deficiencies common to RF communication systems.

The biggest deficiency of this system is the inadequate range of handheld radios. Higher output power from the handheld units, use of RF repeaters across a site, or a multiple-receiver system can minimize this deficiency. An RF repeater receives voice transmissions from the handheld units and transmits them again on a separate frequency to all other units within the system. By placing the repeater at a high location, the range of the radios increases. A multiple receiver system consists of several remotely located receivers connected to the central monitoring station by a landline. A microcomputer monitors the signals received by all multiple receivers and transfers the information to the central station from the remote receiver receiving the strongest signal.

Conventional radio systems have several advantages including simplicity, ease of operation, efficiency, and low cost. If proper transmission procedures are followed and strict communication network discipline observed, routine communications using these systems is very clear, and routine daily business can be conducted efficiently.

Eavesdropping and Deception

Although conventional radio systems are generally adequate for routine communications at most facilities, transmissions within the security network should resist threats from intelligent and resourceful adversaries. Conventional clear-voice radio systems have some serious disadvantages. Adversaries possessing only a conventional receiver, which can be tuned to the proper frequency, can easily monitor conventional transmissions at locations remote from the site. Even if the frequency is unknown, scanners can automatically search and determine the frequency in use. When using a conventional radio system, it should be assumed that adversaries are eavesdropping on transmissions. Security personnel should determine what information is released during routine operations and how an adversary might use that information. Even information released during training exercises might be extremely valuable to an adversary. Conventional radio communications should be limited to only those transmissions that are absolutely necessary and that cannot be communicated by more secure methods, such as telephones and intercoms. Use of cellular telephones should be avoided, due to the ease of adversary interception of the signal. Depending on the threat to a facility, conventional radios may be sufficient for guard communication.

Similarly, an adversary needs only a transmitter tuned to the operating frequency to transmit deceptive messages. An adversary might use deceptive messages during a facility assault in an attempt to confuse members of the response force. Voice-private radios that make a network resistant to eavesdropping will also make it resistant to the transmission of deceptive messages. If an adversary cannot understand a message because it has been scrambled or digitally encrypted, they will probably not possess the means to transmit a deceptive message in the appropriate format.

Several procedural options can also improve network resistance to eavesdropping and deception. One of the most effective procedures relies on the use of more secure transmission media, such as telephones and intercoms. To help protect against deceptive messages, it is better to use some type of authentication code. An authentication code is known only to members of the response force and can

	A	B	C	D
1	BR	YT	XR	GM
2	PL	MW	BR	UB
3	ED	IM	RE	DF
4	MN	KU	ZI	JC

Figure 12.1 Authentication Code Table. The intersection of a column and row provides an authentication code for use prior to radio transmission. For example, position B2 would yield MW as the authentication code. The column and row identifiers may be changed each day or shift to increase uncertainty for an adversary

verify that a critical or questionable transmission was indeed made by a member of the force. This is a simple and low-cost method to increase secure communications at a facility. An example of an authentication code table is shown in Figure 12.1.

Many technologies and systems provide varying degrees of voice privacy. Greater security generally means sacrificing other desirable operational characteristics. The level of security is related to complexity, cost, message intelligibility, and communications range for several voice-private techniques, as shown in Figure 12.2. As a system becomes more secure, it will also become more complex, cost more, and have more noise in the communication channel that reduces effective range.

A final point to consider when using voice-private radios is the effect that such hardware will have on the communication network's resistance to jamming. Voice-private radios do not improve a network's resistance to jamming—they may even make it more susceptible to a jamming assault. As more secure voice-privacy technologies are used, message intelligibility and zone coverage will generally become poorer, and message survivability during jamming will also become poorer, as shown in Figure 12.2.

Jamming

Jamming refers to insertion of unwanted signals into the frequency channel of a communications system for the purpose of masking desired signals. RF systems are most vulnerable to jamming because the potential attacker can jam the channel

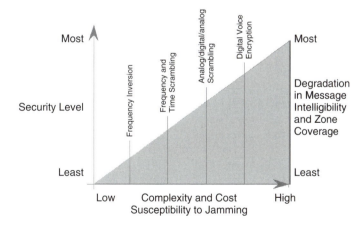

Figure 12.2 Security Level Comparisons. As the scrambling or encryption technique becomes more secure, the radio also becomes more complex, more expensive, and more vulnerable to distortion in the communications channel. In addition, message survivability under jamming conditions is generally poorer in the more secure systems

from a remote location. The adversary can obtain the system's operating frequencies either by monitoring transmissions or by obtaining readily available frequency documentation. It then becomes a simple matter to begin jamming by tuning a transmitter to the proper frequency. If the jamming signal is of sufficient power, it masks the true signal to such an extent that effective communication becomes severely degraded or destroyed. Jamming a single-frequency system that uses handheld radios with 5 W output power can be accomplished by using a similar handheld radio with the same or greater output power.

Developing a communications network that is highly resistant to jamming can be achieved by maximizing the survivability of the radio network, providing alternate communication means to supplement the radio network, use of spread-spectrum radios, and conducting regular jamming exercises.

Survivability of the Radio Network

Personnel training and equipment maintenance can have a significant impact on the survivability of a radio channel during a jamming assault. Methods of maximizing the integrity of the radio network combine training, procedures, and equipment into secure and reliable systems. Procedures requiring periodic maintenance of equipment, particularly batteries and antennas, will contribute to system effectiveness. Another procedure, the use of codes, can also be implemented to aid radio communications. The codes replace commonly used sentences or phrases, such as the 10-codes used in law enforcement. (It is important to note, however, that some jurisdictions in the United States have recently stopped using 10-codes, due to differences in codes across jurisdictions.) Codes make intelligence-gathering by eavesdropping adversaries more difficult, and coded messages, especially digits,

are easier to understand in the event of jamming. If codes are used, they should be used at all times, so they are a natural form of communication among guards. Trying to use unfamiliar codes under the pressures of an adversary intrusion will not help the guard force. In addition, the use of better equipment and additional training on the proper use of the equipment, under normal and jamming conditions, will accustom guards to these operational conditions.

Any communication network will be resistant to radio jamming if alternative methods of transferring the desired information are available and can be used in an efficient and timely manner. If backups to the primary radio links are available, their use must be practiced in jamming exercises in order to be effective during an actual jamming assault. If redundant links are available and each has been effectively used during exercises, a communications network will become increasingly resistant to jamming.

A thorough understanding of jamming geometry can be very helpful in maintaining radio communications during a jamming attempt. Network survivability improves with high-power units and units moved closer together. If the effects of jamming geometry are understood, guards could relay information that might otherwise be jammed.

Alternate Means of Communication

In the event of successful jamming, simply switching to an alternate radio channel may be the easiest method of reestablishing communication. All radios should have a minimum of two channels available for use at any time. The method of selecting between channels must be simple and straightforward. A minimum of four to six channels is desirable, but not always practical. Procedurally, all members of the guard force should know when to change channels and which channel to select. A code that commands a move to a particular alternate security channel is most effective.

In the event of complete and absolute jamming of the primary radio channel, it may not be possible to transmit the command to switch to the backup channel on the radio. To overcome this situation, other means such as plant public address systems, intercoms, or sirens can be used to communicate the command. However, even if the channel switch is successful, the adversary could easily identify the alternate channel and resume jamming on the new channel.

If jamming is a threat to facility communications, lost radio communications should be supplemented through the use of alternate communication means that can effectively relay messages. Some alternate communication means to consider include landline or cellular telephones, intercoms, hand signals, lights, whistles, or pagers. Many of these communication media may already be used for other purposes. Using these means during normal operations creates a network increasingly resistant to eavesdropping and deception, as well as jamming. If alternate communication links are to be effective during a jamming assault, they must be practiced during regular jamming exercises.

Thoroughly exercising proposed anti-jamming techniques under simulated jamming conditions ensures that the techniques will be beneficial during an actual jamming assault. During the confusion and stress associated with an assault, unfamiliar procedures and equipment can only aid the adversary during the attempt to interrupt the information flow within the communication network. Procedures as simple as switching to a backup security channel are not effective until they have been practiced several times by all members of the response force.

Duress Alarms

Duress is an operational situation that the response force communication system should be capable of handling. Adversary action may result in confrontation with one or more members of the response force. It is desirable to know as early as possible that this situation exists. Once the response force is aware of the situation, a prearranged switch to another communication channel might deny the adversary further information on response force actions. A number of duress systems are commercially available and can be installed throughout the facility to relay duress alarms. These systems are also used to allow nonsecurity employees a method of signaling for help in certain applications, such as airports or prisons.

Many manufacturers offer handheld radios equipped with a button that, when pressed, sends an emergency duress signal, including unit identification, to the central monitoring station. In addition to the overtly activated button on the radio or a separate duress transmitter, other duress signaling options have been investigated to some extent. These options include covert, deadman, and holster switches.

A covert device allows the user to send a duress signal while under direct observation by an adversary. Several techniques have been examined. One technique uses a small, balanced magnetic reed switch in the user's shoe, activated by a curling motion of the user's big toe. Placement in this location causes a significant number of nuisance alarms, so may not be desirable. The deadman option consists of a liquid mercury switch firmly attached to a separate duress transmitter worn on the user's belt. If the user falls to the floor or reclines past a certain point, the switch closes and sends a duress signal. There is some resistance to use of this method by guards who may have a tendency to fall asleep while on duty. The holster option includes a balanced magnetic reed switch that is installed in the bottom of the gun holster and activated when the gun is removed. This alarm could be activated by the user himself or herself or by an adversary removing the user's gun. Of course, this system will only be effective when using armed guards.

Spread-Spectrum Systems

In recent years, communication systems that can provide a very high resistance to radio jamming in certain applications have become available. These systems are known as spread-spectrum systems. The term spread-spectrum describes various techniques that result in transmission on different bands. Spread-spectrum radios are used in law enforcement and at some government facilities. Due to their high cost, they may be issued only to a limited subset of security personnel, guards, or other response force members. The spread-spectrum system most applicable to response force communications is the spread-spectrum, frequency-hopping system. Frequency-hopping technology will be discussed throughout this section.

With narrow-band FM systems, information is transmitted on a discrete frequency.

The transmitter and the receiver must be tuned to and remain on that frequency while information is transmitted, or the information will be lost. The bandwidth of these systems is typically about 25 kHz. The frequency output from the transmitter of a frequency-hopping system spreads it over a frequency band 10 MHz wide. If a 10 MHz band is used, the system could create 400 or more discrete frequency channels. According to the input received by the transmitter from a digital code generator, the system could then transmit alternately on these frequencies for short periods of time. The digital code generator, synchronized with the digital code generator in all receivers, determines the order. The dwell time on each of these frequency channels is quite short, and information transmitted during this short period would probably not be detectable by conventional receivers.

This combination of properties forces an adversary to jam a large portion of the RF spectrum, while synchronized radios within the frequency-hopping network continue to look for information within only that bandwidth required for information transmission. Figure 12.3 shows the output spectra of a conventional,

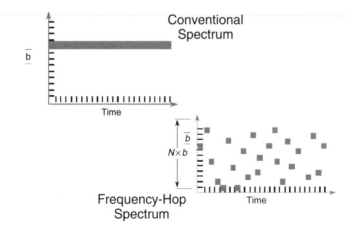

Figure 12.3 Jamming of a Conventional Radio Spectrum and a Spread-Spectrum Frequency-Hopping Radio System. In a conventional radio, only one bandwidth must be jammed, but in a spread-spectrum system, a series of frequencies must be jammed at the proper time

narrow-band FM system and a spread-spectrum, frequency-hopping system. The bandwidth required to transmit the information is labeled with the letter b in both figures. The successful jammer must effectively jam the bandwidth b in the conventional radio or the bandwidth $N \times b$ in the spread-spectrum system (where N is the total number of hop frequencies, or channels, in use). In most commercial frequency-hopping systems, N is approximately 250; but it is as large as 2000 in some systems. The information bandwidth, b, is typically 25 kHz in both figures.

Interruption

In addition to tactical planning and training, it is important for the response force to practice deployment at the specific facility in exercises, so they will know what to do in the event of an adversary intrusion and when a timely response is required. Results of good practice give realistic estimates of response force times. Field exercises should be used to verify that tactical training has resulted in the desired capability and that the overall tactical plan is realistic. In order for the response force to plan and practice, the threat must be characterized in advance. This threat quantification should also address whether the adversary's objective is theft, sabotage, or something else.

One test of guards' proficiency at timely response is to determine if they can arrive in enough time after notification to interrupt the adversary. The responders require certain skills in addition to speed. Skills requiring testing include physical fitness, use of force under stress, use of intermediate force, tactical movement, accurate response communications, asset and facility familiarity, and use of PPS features to their advantage. In those cases where the guard force is armed, periodic proficiency testing in marksmanship will also be required.

Some of these skills can be evaluated in simulation courses in the classroom. Others, especially the testing of the application of the skills, can only take place in the facility or something quite similar to it. The measure of proficiency being tested under engagement simulation exercises in these circumstances is the response force's ability to interrupt an attack. For an immediate on-site response, the most acceptable level of proficiency is the prevention of damage to or loss of assets.

Interruption is defined as the successful arrival of the response force at an appropriate location to confront the adversary. Although the goal is to capture or detain the adversary, interruption refers only to arrival. Because most industrial facilities will not have the option of a force-on-force battle, it is assumed that arrival of members of the response force will effectively end the adversary intrusion at these locations. If the adversary is considered to be violent, response force actions and equipment should align with the threat. This requires accurate communication with and the effective deployment of the response force.

Neutralization

At facilities where an armed conflict between the response force and adversaries is expected, force-on-force training exercises must also be conducted. This set of actions is termed neutralization and is measured by who wins the battle. Although this is the traditional definition of neutralization, in truth, neutralization against some adversaries can be achieved without an armed conflict. For example, vandals could be "neutralized" by a security guard arriving and confronting them. If the vandals run away, or better yet surrender, they can be considered to be neutralized—they have been defeated. By broadening out the traditional definition of response, we can add another measure of response effectiveness, even at sites where guards are unarmed. This measure can then be used in an analysis to support the overall effectiveness measure of a PPS. In addition, this measure can be used in contracts with companies that provide guard forces and used as a method of selecting the best service provider.

Deployment describes the actions of the response force from the time communication is received until the force is in position to neutralize the adversary attack. The effectiveness measures of this function are the probability of successful deployment to the adversary location and the time required to deploy the response force.

Members of the response force must be trained in the details and procedures established in contingency planning. In addition, they must be trained in tactics that increase their chances of successful deployment and arriving at the adversary location. These tactics include:

- knowledge of facility security priorities and vulnerabilities;
- precautions to avoid diversion;
- proper movement in and around buildings;
- proper nighttime response;
- proper deployment from a vehicle; and
- how to work as a response team member.

Additional details concerning neutralization, including how it can be measured, are provided in the Vulnerability Assessment book (Garcia, 2005).

Procedures

In addition to the training and response procedures already described, procedures regarding normal operations should also exist for on-site guards and off-site response personnel. Aside from logistical issues such as shift scheduling and coverage, key control, guard patrol routes,

post orders, and incident reporting procedures are all parts of an effective response system. Depending on the operating hours at a facility and the threat and assets to be protected, on-site guards may be required around the clock or less often. If the assets to be protected are low-consequence loss items, on-site guards may only be required during normal business hours. At larger more complex facilities with 24 h operations, on-site guards, perhaps in reduced numbers for off-shifts, may be necessary. The number of guards required to protect a facility will depend on the number of shifts, the number of guards required per shift, the tasks that guards are expected to perform as part of normal operations, the number of guards needed to respond to a malevolent threat, and the response strategy at the facility. Guards may be located in fixed positions, on continuous patrol on foot or by vehicle or in a combination of the two. Variations in personnel availability due to sickness, vacations, or company-required training must be incorporated into shift scheduling.

At many facilities the issue of key control presents a major problem to the security force. As a general guideline, the number of keys issued should be limited, and procedures concerning key-copying, return of keys at the end of a shift or upon termination of employment, and periodic re-keying of locks should be considered. Related details to key control were discussed in Chapter 10, "Entry Control." An additional procedure that should be incorporated into key control is the use of on-site guards to unlock doors for employees during normal or off-hours, rather than issuing keys to all employees. Procedures detailing the telephone number for employees to call for assistance and the proper method of validating employee access, particularly during off-hours, should exist. This will help limit the number of keys issued and provide on-site guards with another opportunity to collect information about keys and operational status across the facility.

For example, if a door is supposed to be unlocked each morning at 7:00 A.M. and it is not one morning, a report should be generated to look into the reason for the oversight. After-hours access may be limited to only certain manned doors or gates and may require supervisor or manager advance authorization. In this case, security guards must be notified of this authorization. In those cases where automated personnel entry control is used, these issues are addressed through the use of access control rules within the system software.

During each guard shift, post orders, which are the procedures that guards are required to comply with while on duty, should be available at each guard station. These orders generally cover activities such as guard tour frequency and reporting, notification lists and phone numbers in case of a malevolent attack or abnormal event, and any other special instructions. Post orders will also normally detail the format and information required for a guard to provide when reporting an incident, notifying other security personnel of a need for maintenance on a protection system element, or other noteworthy events. Blank forms for this purpose are often provided to facilitate this process.

Summary

This chapter discusses the PPS function of response in terms of general issues, contingency planning, communication, interruption, and neutralization. Contingency planning includes tactical planning, interaction with outside agencies, the facility's use of force policy, and additional duties of the guard force. The importance of relating the strategy of the response force to assets and potential adversary actions is discussed. Several issues associated with interacting with outside agencies and the need for joint training exercises are emphasized. These include establishing radio

frequencies for communication, off-site pursuit tactics and permissions, roles and responsibilities for each cooperating group, and the chain of command during a response action. A written use of force policy and training in the application of this policy is also essential. Additional procedures describing guard force daily operations, such as guard force assistance during safety events or bad weather at a facility, after-hours access, and post orders, are also presented.

Depending on the threat, the successful operation of a PPS may require a reliable response force communication network resistant to eavesdropping, deception, and jamming. Voice-private radios can improve a network's resistance to eavesdropping and deception and are desirable during both normal and emergency operations. Digitally encrypted radio transmissions tend to be more secure than analog transmissions, but are also more expensive. The use of various scrambling techniques can create additional operational problems. Most voice-private radios tend to make a network more susceptible to jamming unless other precautions are taken. Development of procedures requiring proper maintenance of equipment, training in equipment use and communications, and use of alternate communication media are valuable jam-resistant techniques. Spread-spectrum radios that provide resistance to jamming may be considered by facility security managers, if warranted by the design basis threat.

The elements of interruption and neutralization are also discussed. The importance of a well-trained response force arriving at the appropriate location in a timely manner when an immediate on-site response is required cannot be overemphasized. Careful planning, training, and testing of response force capabilities is necessary. Practicing functional response skills on the job is analogous to maintenance and operational practice concerning equipment. As with equipment design, evaluation of human performance in carrying out PPS tasks is a necessary step in assuring that the total PPS—equipment together with people and procedures— is able to achieve its performance goal.

An important consideration in all response elements is the need for training. Facility security managers should not underestimate the value of training in all areas of the response system. This includes joint exercises with support agencies, facility contingency plans, response force deployment, recapture operations, use-of-force policies, and weapons and equipment proficiency training. The effectiveness of the response force should be periodically evaluated by limited scope performance drills and written examination.

This chapter concludes Part Two of the process of PPS design and evaluation. At this point, PPS objectives and design tools and considerations have been reviewed. The final piece of the process—analysis and evaluation—will be addressed in Part Three.

Security Principles

Contingency planning forms the basis of an effective response force. This includes corporate policies and procedures, training, determination of response force tactics, use of force, and normal operating procedures.

Response to a malevolent event can be immediate, requiring a response force capable of timely response, or after-the-fact recovery, which is accomplished through a greater range of activities.

Response force strategies include containment, denial, and assault.

A vital element of response force effectiveness is communication.

The measures of response force effectiveness include response force time for interruption and probability of communication. The probability of neutralization can be used at sites where an immediate response is present and guards are expected to engage with the adversary.

Interruption describes arrival of the response force at the appropriate location. It is assumed that for most industrial facilities, arrival will cause the adversary to surrender or abandon the intrusion. For high-security sites, neutralization, or defeat of the adversary after interruption, is another aspect of response force effectiveness.

References

Baker, D.R. "Curriculum Design," in Davies, S.J., and Minion, R.R., eds, *Security Supervision: Theory and Practice of Asset Protection*. Boston: Butterworth-Heinemann, 1999, 127–133.

Dwyer, J., and Flynn, K. *102 Minutes: The Untold Story of the Fight to Survive Inside the Twin Towers*. New York: Henry Holt and Company, 2005, 352 pp.

Fischer, R.J., and Green, G. *Introduction to Security*, 7th ed. Boston: Butterworth-Heinemann, 2006, 40–43.

Garcia, M.L. *Vulnerability Assessment of Physical Protection Systems*. Boston: Butterworth-Heinemann, 2005, 250–253.

Hertig, C.A. "Considering Contract Security," in Davies, S.J., and Minion, R.R., eds, *Security Supervision: Theory and Practice of Asset Protection*. Boston: Butterworth-Heinemann, 1999a, 227–229.

Hertig, C.A. "Legal Aspects of Security," in Davies, S.J., and Minion, R.R., eds, *Security Supervision: Theory and Practice of Asset Protection*. Boston: Butterworth-Heinemann, 1999b, 330–359.

Thibodeau, C.T. "Staff Training and Development," in Davies, S.J., and Minion, R.R., eds, *Security Supervision: Theory and Practice of Asset Protection*. Boston: Butterworth-Heinemann, 1999, 118–125.

Questions

1. Discuss the following application considerations:

   a. A secure radio frequency should be dedicated to security operations.

   b. Purchased weapons should be appropriate for the facility.

   c. Guard and response force personnel should be well trained for deployment and use of weapons.

   d. Open communication and understanding between facility management, security management, and the response force regarding vulnerabilities and realistic response capabilities should not be inhibited.

   e. Response strategy should include a sufficient number of guards in the response force and should not assume unrealistic or nonexistent containment capabilities.

2. In addition to training in corporate policies and procedures in use of force and radio communications, what additional training might be beneficial for members of the response force?

3. What are some of the individual factors that affect response force performance?

4. What is the most important aspect of the response function?

5. What is the difference between tactical training and tactical practice?

6. What might be some general rules for determining the size of a guard force?

7. What outside agencies might be part of a response force at a particular facility?

PART THREE

Analysis and Evaluation

13

Analysis and Evaluation

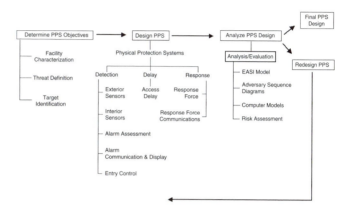

After the PPS objectives have been established and a new or upgraded design has been developed, it is necessary to analyze the effectiveness of the design in meeting the objectives. This analysis can take one of two forms—quantitative or qualitative. A rigorous quantitative analysis is required for protection of assets with unacceptably high consequence of loss, even if the probability of an adversary attack is low. This is a characteristic of high-security systems found at commercial nuclear power plants, prisons, and some government or military installations. This approach can also be applied carefully to museums, refineries, utilities, airports, telecommunications hubs, and large industrial complexes. In each of these cases, the loss of or damage to at least some of the assets can have high consequences—loss of many lives, loss of an irreplaceable piece of culture or history, damage to the environment, or compromise of our national security. The response strategy applied to these assets is usually an immediate on-site response. For a quantitative analysis to be justified the asset must require this level of protection, and

performance measures for system components must be available.

A qualitative analysis is more suitable when evaluating lower security applications. These facilities will have lower consequence loss assets and so will be better able to withstand loss or damage of an asset. Some examples might include retail stores, apartment buildings, small businesses, and restaurants. Some facilities will have a mix of assets, so the PPS designer must balance resources appropriately to provide the most protection to critical assets and lower protection to other assets. In addition, each facility may have other constraints that can strongly influence the protection system design. For example, although school shootings are tragic and emotionally devastating, there is little movement to turn schools into armed camps with many layers of security around them. Designing and implementing an effective system is more dependent on the goals and constraints of a facility, which is why determining objectives is such a vital step in the process.

Analysis of the PPS will establish the assumptions under which a design was formed, relate system performance to threats and assets, and allow a cost–benefit decision to be made. Whether a qualitative or quantitative analysis is used, proper application of the system concepts and principles described in the previous chapters will assure the effective protection of assets at a facility. This chapter will provide an introduction to the analysis process. Chapter 14, "EASI Computer Model for Analysis," will describe the use of a particular model to predict system performance through the use of an analysis tool.

A PPS is a complex configuration of detection, delay, and response elements that can be analyzed to determine system effectiveness. The analysis will identify system deficiencies, help evaluate improvements, and enable cost-versus-effectiveness comparisons. These techniques can be used for evaluating either an existing protection system or a proposed system design. There are several reasons for reevaluating an existing protection system. It is essential that the system design be reviewed and updated from time to time to incorporate advances made in the state of the art in physical protection hardware and systems or to accommodate the introduction of new processes, functions, or assets within a facility. Further, the design of a PPS for a specific facility is expected to vary over time when prevailing circumstances indicate a need for a different level of physical protection. A good example of this is the escalation of threat to a facility. Only by conducting periodic reanalysis can the effect of these changing conditions be seen and quantified.

Adversary Paths

The analysis and evaluation principles and models used in this text are based on the existence of adversary paths to an asset. An adversary path is an ordered series of actions against a facility, which,

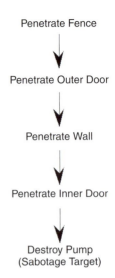

Penetrate Fence

Penetrate Outer Door

Penetrate Wall

Penetrate Inner Door

Destroy Pump
(Sabotage Target)

Figure 13.1 One Sabotage Path to a Critical Pump in a High-Security Facility. Multiple layers of protection must be breached in order for the adversary to be successful

if completed, results in successful theft, sabotage, or other malevolent outcome. Figure 13.1 illustrates a single sabotage path of an adversary who wishes to destroy a pump in an industrial facility. Protection elements along the path detect and delay the adversary. Detection includes not only sensor activation but also alarm communication and assessment. Figure 13.2 describes the security elements along this path.

As described in previous chapters, the protection system design starts with threat definition and target asset identification, and detection, delay, and response elements are specific to the protection objectives and characteristics of the facility. The performance measures previously described for these protection elements are used in path analysis to determine system effectiveness. These performance measures include the probability of detection, delay times, response force time, and probability of communication. At most facilities, many adversary paths to each asset are possible;

Adversary Action	Delay Element	Detection Element
Penetrate Fence	Fence Fabric	Fence Sensor
Penetrate Outer Door	Door Hardness	Sensors on Door
Penetrate Wall	Wall Hardness	Personnel Hear Noise
Penetrate Inner Door	Door Hardness	Sensors on Door
Destroy Pump	Time Required to Sabotage Target	Loss of Pump

Figure 13.2 The Security Elements Along the Sabotage Path. Each element can have detection and delay components

therefore, the identification and evaluation of adversary paths are usually complex processes that can be facilitated through the use of computer models, as described in Chapter 14, "EASI Computer Model for Analysis."

Effectiveness Measures

The goal of an adversary is to complete a path to an asset with the least likelihood of being stopped by the PPS or, conversely, the highest likelihood of successful attack. To achieve this goal, the adversary may attempt to minimize the time required to complete the path. This strategy involves penetrating barriers as quickly as possible with little regard to the probability of being detected. An example of this adversary tactic is a force attack. The adversary is successful if the path is completed before guards can respond. Alternatively, the adversary may attempt to minimize detection with little regard to the time required. This adversary tactic is based on a stealth attack. In this case, the adversary is successful upon completion of the path without being detected.

Recognizing these two extremes of adversary action, effectiveness measures are available to assess system performance. One measure of PPS effectiveness is the comparison of the minimum cumulative time delay along the path (T_{MIN}) compared to guard response time (T_{G}). An adequate PPS provides enough delay for guards to respond. Figure 13.3 illustrates minimum time as a measure of system effectiveness. For an effective system, T_{G} must be less than T_{MIN}. System improvements are achieved by decreasing T_{G} or by adding protection elements with more

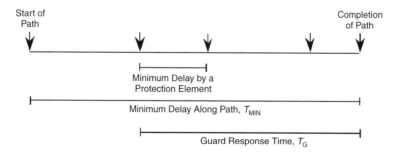

Figure 13.3 Minimum Time as a Measure of PPS Effectiveness. For the system to be effective, guard response time, T_{G}, must be less than the minimum time delay along the path, T_{MIN}. Arrows relate to the tasks of Figure 13.1

delay to increase T_{MIN}. The disadvantage of this measure is that no consideration of detection is involved. Delay without prior detection is not meaningful because the response force must be alerted in order to respond and interrupt the adversary. Therefore, minimum time is often not the best measure of system effectiveness.

Another measure of effectiveness is the cumulative probability of detecting the adversary before the goal is achieved. An adequate protection system provides high probability of detection. Figure 13.4 illustrates the effectiveness measure of cumulative probability of detection. For an effective system, the cumulative detection probability along a path, P_{MIN}, must be an acceptable value. The disadvantage of this measure is that no consideration of delay is involved. Detection without sufficient subsequent delay is not effective because the response force may not have sufficient time to interrupt the adversary.

Due to the deficiencies of each of these measures, neither delay time nor cumulative probability of detection alone is the best measure of system effectiveness. A better measure of effectiveness is timely detection, which combines P_{MIN}, T_{MIN}, and T_G. The principle of timely detection states that system effectiveness is measured by the cumulative probability of detection at the point where there is still enough time remaining for the response force to interrupt the adversary. Figure 13.5 illustrates

the principle of timely detection. Note that the delay elements along the path determine the point by which the adversary must be detected. That point is where the minimum delay along the remaining portion of the path (T_R) just exceeds the guard response time (T_G) and is referred to as the critical detection point (CDP). The probability of interruption (P_I) is the cumulative probability of detection from the start of the path up to the CDP, which is the point determined by T_R. We use P_I to represent this value to differentiate it from the total cumulative probability of detection because it only considers detection up to the CDP. Because P_I represents timely detection, it serves as one measure of system effectiveness. Consistent with the discussion in the previous chapter on response, timely detection considers only detection, delay, and guard response time. It does not consider any force-on-force engagement between the response force and adversaries. It is unlikely that any industrial facility will engage in use of lethal force against an adversary, so these aspects will not be considered in this text. In the event that a force-on-force engagement is expected, additional modeling and simulation tools are available to predict the outcome of the conflict, measured by the probability of neutralization. These tools are beyond the scope of this text; however, they are used in some high-security applications.

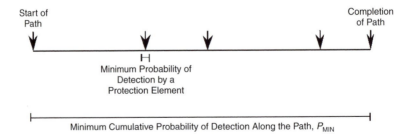

Figure 13.4 Cumulative Probability of Detection as an Effectiveness Measure. P_{MIN} must be an acceptable value, but there is no consideration of delay along the path. Arrows relate to the tasks of Figure 13.1

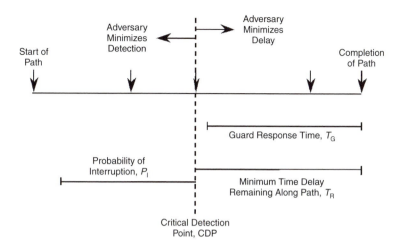

Figure 13.5 Timely Detection as the Measure of System Effectiveness. This is the cumulative probability of detecting the adversary at the point where there is still enough time remaining for the response force to interrupt the adversary. That point is the critical detection point (CDP). We call the cumulative probability of detection P_I, which is the measure of system effectiveness. Arrows relate to the tasks of Figure 13.1

Quantitative Analysis

To calculate P_I, we make an assumption: that the adversary will try to minimize detection before the CDP and minimize delay after the CDP. For the adversary to minimize detection, careful movement is required up to the CDP. This careful movement may include stealth or deceit. After the CDP, detection is less effective because there is not enough delay remaining for the response force to respond. After that point, the adversary is assumed to change tactics and try to minimize delay. This is accomplished by moving as fast as possible, with no concern for detection. It is important to note that the adversary may not choose this attack approach; this is a method used to make a conservative estimate as to system effectiveness. The effectiveness of the system, then, is somewhat dependent on adversary tactics. Adversaries may use combinations of force, stealth, and deceit in order to accomplish their goals. This is why a well-defined design basis threat is so important to system effectiveness. The most successful adversary is assumed to be knowledgeable enough to defeat or bypass

detection along the path up to the CDP and also knows the response force time.

It is a conservative assumption that the adversary will move as quickly as possible after the CDP. Adversary tactics that do not follow this assumed attack mode will increase system effectiveness. For example, if the adversary starts to move quickly earlier in the path, they will be detected sooner, so more time is left to respond. If the adversary tried to minimize detection for a longer time (past the CDP), this added delay can work with remaining detection elements to provide a high probability of detection and allow for an effective response. Of course, an adversary who effectively avoids detection up to the CDP and then minimizes delay can be expected to be successful! This is one reason why protection-in-depth is so important. If the adversary is uncertain as to where he or she has been detected and changes tactics, this change can increase the probability of interruption. Alternatively, by having multiple layers of protection around a facility, the chances of facility success in protection of assets are increased.

In terms of PPS elements, delay time is calculated as a sum and probability of detection as a product, so we have

$$T_R = \sum_{i=k}^{m} T_i > T_G \qquad P_I = 1 - \prod_{i=k}^{k-1} P_{NDi}$$

where m is the total number of protection system elements along the path; k is the point at which T_R just exceeds T_G; T_i is the minimum time delay provided by element i; and P_{NDi} is the nondetection probability provided by element i (i.e., the probability that element i will not detect the defined adversary), which is the complement of P_D. For example, a nondetection probability of 0.2 means that there is a 20% probability the adversary will not be detected, hence, an 80% probability that the adversary will be detected. It is important to note that analysis models use the probability of nondetection, while P_D is the performance measure for detection elements. Obviously, the probability of nondetection cannot be quantified directly. In addition, we assume that detection at each element is an independent variable. P_I is the probability of interruption or the cumulative probability of detection for all elements, as described above.

The following example illustrates the concept of timely detection. Consider the path in Figures 13.1 and 13.2 again. Assume that existing protection system elements provide the time delays and nondetection probabilities given in Figure 13.6 and that detection occurs before delay. If the guard response time is 90 s, the analyst must find the point on the adversary path where the adversary is more than 90 s away from the pump. In this example, that point is at the wall. The time remaining on the path is 114 s after penetration of the wall—30 s to destroy the pump plus 84 s to penetrate the inner door. This means that if the adversary is not detected at the wall, there will not be sufficient time remaining for the guards to interrupt this adversary. Because three detection elements have been passed, the probability of interruption is calculated only using those elements. The outer fence has no detection element, so its probability of nondetection is 1.0. Both the outer door and the wall have detection elements present that occur before or at the CDP. This gives the result:

$$P_I = 1 - (1.0 \times 0.9 \times 0.7) = 0.37$$
(cumulative probability of detection at CDP)
$$T_R = 30 + 84 = 114 \, s \text{ (delay time remaining)}$$

The analyst must repeat this process for many adversary paths, find the most vulnerable path, and decide whether this is a satisfactory result. The most vulnerable path is the one with the lowest P_I. If these results are not acceptable, the system must be improved.

In this example, system performance can be improved. As shown in Figure 13.7, delay at the pump has been increased to 50 s, and detection on the outer door has been improved. In addition, guard

Action	Minimum Time (s)	$P_{ND}(P_D)$	
Penetrate Fence	6	1.0 (0.0)	$P_I =$
Penetrate Outer Door	84	0.9 (0.1)	$1 - (1 \times 0.9 \times 0.7) =$
Penetrate Wall	120	0.7 (0.3)	$1 - 0.63 = 0.37$
Penetrate Inner Door	84	0.1 (0.9)	$T_R = 114 \, s$
Destroy Pump	30	1.0 (0.0)	$T_G = 90 \, s$

Figure 13.6 Timely Detection Baseline Example. Adversary actions along a sabotage path, with associated detection and delay elements

Action	Minimum Time (s)	$P_{ND}(P_D)$	
Penetrate Fence	6	1.0 (0.0)	
Penetrate Outer Door	84	0.2 (0.8)	$P_I =$ $1-(1 \times 0.2 \times 0.7 \times 0.9) =$
Penetrate Wall	120	0.7 (0.3)	$1 - 0.13 = 0.87$
Penetrate Inner Door	84	0.9 (0.1)	
Destroy Pump	50	0.0 (1.0)	$T_R = 50\,\text{s}$ $T_G = 40\,\text{s}$

Figure 13.7 Timely Detection Upgraded Example. Detection has been improved at the outer door and wall, delay has been added at the pump, and guard response time has been reduced to 40 s. The CDP is now located at the pump, thus adding an additional layer of detection and delay to the system

response time has been reduced to 40 s. As a result of these upgrades, the P_I has increased to 0.87. Close inspection of these upgrades will also reveal that the CDP has now shifted to the inner door. Because the guard response time has been reduced to 40 s and the delay at the pump increased to 50 s, the point at which T_R just exceeds T_G (CDP) is now at the pump. Aside from the obvious benefits of increased performance of individual components, these upgrades now allow credit for detection at the inner door, which was not the case in the baseline example. These upgrades were achieved through relatively simple means. Using sensors with higher P_Ds will increase detection; delay at the pump might have been increased by placing the pump inside a metal enclosure with a lock. Guard response time could be decreased by moving guards closer to the target, perhaps part of a reallocation of available personnel closer to high-value assets. Regardless of how the increased performance is obtained, analysis of proposed or necessary upgrades will help the designer or analyst to optimize system performance. In this example, the upgrades added another layer of protection to the system.

Critical Path

Clearly, there are many adversary paths into a facility. The critical path is that path with the lowest P_I. The critical path characterizes the effectiveness of the overall protection system in detecting, delaying, and interrupting the adversary. After a preliminary quantitative analysis of a facility, consideration of upgrades to the facility will be made, starting with the most vulnerable paths. The use of the principle of balanced protection allocates upgrades so that all paths to critical assets have approximately the same P_I. Balancing protection may allow the removal or replacement of some protection elements on paths that are overprotected compared with some other paths. In a similar way, paths that are very weak may be strengthened by relocation of protection elements from paths that have very high P_Is. This is part of the art of systems analysis. A good analyst will be able to propose upgrades that meet system protection objectives while maximizing the use of available funding, equipment, and personnel.

Note that paths differ depending on the adversary objective. Theft implies the adversary must get into and out of the facility to succeed, while sabotage only requires that the adversary get to the asset and have time to complete the act of sabotage to be successful. This difference is extremely important when performing a quantitative analysis, because it will determine how much time the response force has to interrupt the adversary.

Qualitative Analysis

Quantitative analysis is used for assuring protection of critical, high-value assets where testing data is available, either from performance tests run on the PPS or from tests run in the laboratory. When one of these two aspects is not present—either the asset has a lower consequence of loss or the data is not available—a qualitative analysis can be used. As an example, if an asset can be temporarily lost or easily replaced, there may be limited value in looking in detail at the protection system. There may be other assets of high value, perhaps a corporate executive, where a full quantitative analysis is not performed, because it would be too disruptive to rigorously test and validate all aspects of security around an executive or time is not available to do so.

During a qualitative analysis, probabilities are assigned a descriptor, such as low, medium, or high rather than a numerical value. The analyst can create a conversion table, like the one shown in Table 13.1, that can be used to assign these descriptors. The assignments are typically based on subject-matter expertise rather than tests. The table also comes in handy for converting any testing data that is used during the analysis.

To calculate the qualitative equivalent of P_I, the analyst can proceed in two ways.

Table 13.1 *Conversion Table Between Verbal Descriptors of Probability and Numerical Values.*

This table can be used in a qualitative analysis when there are no performance data to support a quantitative analysis or the asset is a lower-consequence target.

Verbal Descriptor of Probability	Equates, Roughly, to the Following Probability
Very Low (VL)	0.1
Low (L)	0.25
Medium (M)	0.5
High (H)	0.75
Very High (VH)	0.9

The simpler method is to compare subjective predictions of delay time in the system after detection to the response force time. If the delay time easily exceeds the response force time, assign a very high probability of interruption; if they are close assign a medium; and so on. The detailed method is to develop a timeline, like the one described earlier in this chapter, and to mentally assign the CDP based on where the analyst predicts the time remaining just exceeds the response force time. The analyst then looks at each point of detection up to the CDP and assigns a verbal descriptor to each location. Probability of interruption is then assigned to be the maximum descriptor over all detection locations up to the CDP.

Applying this approach to the baseline example found in Figure 13.6, the analyst would have to predict where the CDP was. If the CDP is assumed (correctly) to be the wall, then the analyst might assign a VL to the first two locations and an L to the third location. The probability of interruption would be assigned an L, by taking the largest of the three scores. If the analyst had incorrectly assigned the CDP as the inner door the probability of interruption would be assigned as a VH, resulting in an incorrect conclusion that the pump was well protected. This example shows that the result of a qualitative analysis depends very heavily on the skill of the analyst.

A qualitative analysis still requires that the analyst follow the process of defining threats and targets and evaluating system performance, but these should be tailored to meet the budget and time constraints for the analysis. Where security components cannot be tested, a basic understanding of equipment will facilitate good design. For example, an understanding of the sources of nuisance alarms for interior sensors can help the designer predict that a PIR will not work well in an application where there are too many heat sources. This understanding can also be used to predict that several microwave sensors will work well because nuisance alarm sources for these sensors are not present and their energy will flood the area. In this way, reasonably effective systems can be constructed, without demanding the same rigor that would be applied in a quantitative analysis.

Beyond these aspects, the basic features of design using a qualitative analysis are the same as the design based on quantitative analysis. Security principles, such as detection before delay, protection-in-depth, balanced protection, orientation of sensors, consideration of operating environment and NARs, complementary sensors, camera resolution, light-to-dark ratio, proper equipment installation and maintenance, and response force training will still play a role in system effectiveness, whatever the type of analysis done. The purpose of the protection system in either case is still to protect the asset.

Summary

This chapter describes the concept of an adversary path for modeling a PPS system. Three possible measures of system effectiveness include delay time, cumulative probability of detection, and timely detection. Of these measures, timely detection is the most important. Timely detection is the principle that system effectiveness is measured by the minimum cumulative probability of detection of the adversary at the point where there is still enough time remaining for the response force to interrupt the adversary. This chapter also establishes the bases for use of quantitative and qualitative analyses. A quantitative analysis is appropriate when the asset has an unacceptably high consequence of loss and performance data is available. A qualitative analysis can be used for lower consequence loss assets or when the rigor of a quantitative analysis cannot be supported. For a quantitative analysis, an immediate on-site response is generally necessary, because the response force time is part of the overall system effectiveness.

Performance measures that are used in a quantitative analysis include the probability of detection, delay times, and response force times. Along each path, the existence of a critical detection point is noted and the relationship between delay time remaining on the path and response time is compared.

Security Principles

Analysis of a protection system uses the concept of adversary paths.

An analysis can be quantitative or qualitative. A quantitative analysis is preferred for high-value critical assets with a high consequence of loss and where an immediate response is required. A qualitative analysis can be used for lower threats and for lower consequence loss assets.

Timely detection states that system effectiveness is measured by the minimum cumulative probability of detection of the adversary at the point where there is still enough time remaining for the response force to interrupt the adversary.

One measure of system effectiveness in a quantitative analysis is P_I, which is the measure of timely detection. In high-security systems, P_N, the measure of neutralization can also be used. The product of P_I and P_N will then represent system effectiveness.

Questions

1. Discuss the differences between quantitative and qualitative analysis. What elements of a protection system would help to determine which type to use?
2. What is timely detection?
3. What performance measures are used in quantitative analysis?
4. Describe what we mean by adversary path, and why this concept is useful in protection system analysis?

14

EASI Computer Model for Analysis

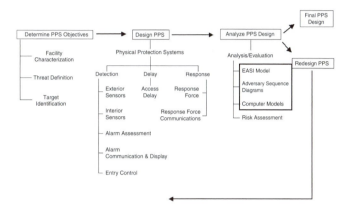

There are many quantitative analytical computer models that can help the analyst evaluate the effectiveness of a PPS. Most of the models follow the same basic format. They provide a mechanism for entering the input data, performing the required computations, and displaying the output. Some are particularly good at analyzing the insider threat, while others are better suited for outsiders. In addition, there are several commercially available products that can be used in qualitative analysis of a PPS. These tools are useful for an initial evaluation of protection system needs and can help in designing protection for lower consequence loss assets. Caution should be used if applying qualitative tools in evaluation of protection systems for high-consequence loss assets, because this analysis may not adequately predict system performance.

Quantitative Analysis Tools

Some selected models that have been used at Sandia National Laboratories are described below. This is not a complete list; some of these models have been replaced with newer models aided by advances in technology, and models are continually being developed, but the list gives an idea of the types of models that have been developed. All of these models are based on rigorous and validated research and development.

- ASSESS (Analytic System and Software for Evaluating Safeguards and Security)—A state-of-the-art proprietary model, in use by the DOE, that incorporates the insider threat into an advanced methodology. The output is a ranking of the threat paths of a facility. This model also analyzes the force-on-force encounters between adversaries and security forces and provides a probability of defeat. This model incorporates the EASI algorithm to predict system performance.

- EASI (Estimate of Adversary Sequence Interruption)—A simple, easy-to-use method of evaluating PPS performance along a specific path and under specific conditions of threat and system operation. This model computes a probability of interruption from an analysis of the interactions of detection, delay, response, and communication and will be discussed in more detail in this chapter.
- FESEM (Forcible Entry Safeguards Effectiveness Model)—A computer model useful for the analysis of a fixed site's effectiveness against a forcible entry and attack by an adversary. The model uses a simulation to analyze a forced entry along an assumed path by an adversary with an assumed set of attributes. This model is no longer in use and has been replaced by EASI.
- ISEM (Insider Safeguards Effectiveness Model)—Another model using assumed paths and adversary attributes that simulates a group of insiders attempting to steal material or sabotage a facility. The input data relating to the effectiveness of the personnel control system, the sensors, portal detectors, and guard force tactics are very subjective. This model is no longer in use and has been replaced by EASI.
- SAFE (Safeguards Automated Facility Evaluation)—SAFE takes the input data relating to the facility, the physical protection features, the adversary paths, and the response force and selects the most vulnerable paths through a facility. The model then applies EASI along the most vulnerable paths and uses BATLE (Brief Adversary Threat Loss Estimator—a

force-on-force engagement model) to determine the probability of neutralization.
- SAVI (System Analysis of Vulnerability to Intrusion)—This model provides a comprehensive analysis of all adversary paths into a facility. Once data on the threat, target, facility, site-specific PPS elements, and response force time is entered, the SAVI code computes and ranks the 10 most vulnerable paths for up to 10 response force times. This model uses the EASI algorithm to predict system performance.
- SNAP (Safeguards Network Analysis Procedure)—SNAP employs the network modeling approach to problem-solving. It requires the analyst to model the facility, the guard force, and the adversary force. SNAP is highly scenario-dependent and uses an assumed attribute method to give a measure of the PPS effectiveness within a certain scenario. For applications in which force-on-force battles are not expected, EASI is the preferred analysis tool.

Each of these techniques utilizes the effectiveness measure of timely detection. EASI was selected as the model to demonstrate in this text because other more complex path analysis tools are based on the EASI model. EASI is simple to use, easy to change, and it quantitatively illustrates the effect of changing physical protection parameters. EASI was developed in the 1970s for use on a hand calculator (Bennett, 1977). Modified versions for use on personal computers now exist (Chapman and Harlan, 1985). The most commonly used form of EASI is as a Microsoft Excel® application. A listing of the Excel code that will run on a personal computer can be found in Appendix C, "EASI Model." In addition, the model is available for download at http://www.bhusa.com/companions/0750673672/default.asp. This chapter will explain the model, the input and the output, and then describe the best way to use the model.

EASI Model

EASI is a simple calculation tool that quantitatively illustrates the effect of changing physical protection parameters along a specific path. It uses detection, delay, response, and communication values to compute the P_I. But, since EASI is a path-level model, it can only analyze one adversary path or scenario at a time. Path level means that the model analyzes the protection system performance along only one possible adversary path or one adversary scenario. Even so, it is able to perform sensitivity analyses and analyze PPS interactions and time trade-offs along that path.

For theft or sabotage attempts to be defeated, the response force must be notified of the attempt while sufficient time remains to respond and interrupt the adversary. Communication of the alarm to an operator and to the response force, therefore, is a factor in the analysis. An adversary interruption occurs in the EASI model if the PPS works properly, resulting in confronting the adversary with a response force large enough to prevent them from proceeding further along their path. The input for the model requires (1) detection and communication inputs as probabilities that the total function will be successful and (2) delay and response inputs as mean times and standard deviations for each element. The output will be the P_I or the probability of intercepting the adversary before any theft or sabotage occurs. After obtaining the output, any part of the input data can be changed to determine the effect on the output. However, because EASI is a path-level model, as systems get larger and more complex, better computer models are needed to perform the analysis of multiple paths. This point will be discussed later in the chapter, in the section titled "Adversary

Sequence Diagrams (ASD)." ASDs provide a graphical method to represent the protection elements in a system, which can serve as the interface between a human analyst and computer software.

The Input

In the EASI model, input parameters representing the physical protection functions of detection, delay, and response are required. Communication likelihood of the alarm signal is also required for the model. Detection and communication inputs are in the form of probabilities that each of these total functions will be performed successfully. Delay and response inputs are in the form of mean times and standard deviations for each element. All inputs refer to a specific adversary path.

The EASI input for the detection function is the P_D for each sensor encountered by an adversary. As discussed in previous chapters, this probability is highly dependent on the capabilities of the adversary. The P_D is the product of the probability that the detector will sense abnormal or unauthorized activities by the adversary (P_S), the probability that an alarm indication will be transmitted to an evaluation or assessment point (P_T), and the probability of accurate assessment of the alarm (P_A). P_S was discussed in Chapter 5, "Physical Protection System Design," and assessment was covered in Chapter 8, "Alarm Assessment." Transmission of the alarm to a predetermined point is part of AC&D evaluation. The relationship among these performance measures for P_D can be summarized as

$$P_D = P_S \times P_T \times P_A$$

The communication of an alarm condition to the response force is input into EASI as the probability of guard communication, P_C. In most PPSs, the likelihood of successful communication to the response force increases with time. The value entered into EASI for P_C is the probability of guard communication associated with the guard communication time included in the response force time (RFT). Evaluation of many systems designed and implemented by Sandia National Laboratories indicates that most systems operate with a P_C of at least 0.95. This number can be used as a working value during the analysis of a facility, unless there is reason to believe that this assumption is not valid. If actual testing at a facility yields a different P_C, this number should be used; if guard communication appears to be less dependable, a lower value can be substituted in the model. Factors that may influence P_C include lack of training in use of communication equipment, poor maintenance, dead spots in radio communication, or the stress experienced during an actual attack. This flexibility allows the analyst to vary P_C as needed to correctly represent this function.

The delay time required by an adversary to travel a given path to a target can be thought of as the sum of the times required to perform certain tasks or travel distinct path segments. For the sake of simplicity, both task times and travel times are referred to as adversary task times. In general, it is not possible to predict the exact time interval necessary for the adversary to perform these tasks or proceed across these path segments. This is due to the fact that the adversary (or the response force) will not always perform a task within exactly the same time. For example, the adversary may take more or less time to get through a door, or the response force might have trouble starting a vehicle. Over a number of attempts, some variation in delay values will be observed. To allow for this expected variation in EASI, these time intervals are modeled as random variables possessing an average or mean value and a standard deviation. The length of each of these successive adversary task times is input into EASI as a mean time and a standard deviation. Standard deviation is discussed in more detail below.

Response time is modeled in EASI as the time between the generation of an alarm signal by a sensing device and the confrontation of the adversary by a response force adequate to halt the progress of the adversary along the path. This time consists of the successive time increments listed below and are shown in Figure 14.1:

- alarm communication time;
- time required for alarm assessment;
- guard communication time;
- time required for the guards to prepare, to gather arms, to start vehicles, and so on;
- guard travel time; and
- time required for the guard force to muster and deploy.

Response time input to EASI is in the form of a single mean time and standard deviation representing the sum of all the elements shown in Figure 14.1. Note that inclusion of these six time segments into the guard response time is different than the response time discussed in Chapter 12, "Response." Alarm communication and assessment times were incorporated into RFT within the EASI model to simplify data entry and handling. The use of RFT should not be confused with P_C. RFT is a measure of the time it takes to receive, assess, and respond to an alarm; P_C is a measure of the likelihood that there will be

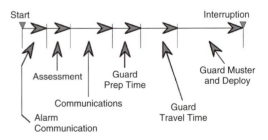

Figure 14.1 Elements of Guard Response Time in the EASI model. This is the required chain of events for successful guard response

successful communication to the response force to carry out the response.

There is one final note on data input to the EASI model. The time data entered into EASI may be in units of seconds or minutes, but not both. Given this constraint, delay and RFT should be in the same unit. If delay times are entered in seconds and RFT in minutes, the discrepancy will affect the accuracy of the output.

Standard Deviation

To use the EASI model as effectively as possible, some knowledge of standard deviation is required. Standard deviation is a measure of dispersion of a set of related data. Suppose the response time of the guard force at a facility is measured five times and gives the results shown in Table 14.1.

Using this data, the average response time is $(9 + 7 + 10 + 11 + 8)/5 = 9\,\text{min}$. The standard deviation is a measure of the amount that a given data point is likely to deviate from the mean of all the data. Quantitatively this is calculated as

$$S_n = \sqrt{\frac{\sum\limits_{i=1}^{n} \left(x_i - x_{avg}\right)^2}{n-1}}$$

$$= \sqrt{\frac{0 + (-2)^2 + (1)^2 + (2)^2 + (-1)^2}{(5-1)}} = 1.58$$

This is the sample standard deviation, based on $n = 5$ observations. If we were to

collect many observations on the response time, the sample standard deviation, s_n, would tend towards S, the standard deviation for the true distribution of response times. The sample standard deviation, s_n, should not be used in the EASI model. This is because five data points are not sufficient to justify this estimate of the population standard deviation. A better approach would be to collect response time data over several months and divide the data into groups of five. Then find s_n for each group using the equation above, and average these values to estimate S, the population standard deviation. This will take a minimum of 30 data points, and 6 values of s_n. This average s_n can then be used in EASI as the standard deviation. As an alternative, tests at Sandia have shown that the standard deviation of a time event can be conservatively estimated at 30% of the mean and, therefore, if there have not been enough tests to establish a statistically significant standard deviation, one can simply use 30% of the estimated mean. These assumptions are equally applicable to delay times, i.e., there is a standard deviation associated with each mean time and the standard deviation can be approximated by using the mean ±30%. Use of the standard deviation for RFT and delay times allows consideration of the fact that guards will not always respond in exactly the same time, and that adversaries may take more or less time to penetrate barriers.

If we were to make many measurements of the RFT, we would expect to find a

Table 14.1 *Guard Response Time Trials.*

Multiple tests were conducted to measure response force time at a facility. X_{avg} is the average of the five trials and X_i is the individual trial result.

Trial Number	Response Force Time (minutes)	$(X_i - X_{avg})$
1	9	0
2	7	−2
3	10	1
4	11	2
5	8	−1

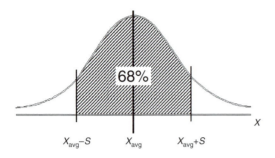

Figure 14.2 Distribution of Response Time Data Points. In a Gaussian distribution, 68% of the values are found within the interval $X_{avg} - S$ and $X_{avg} + S$

Gaussian distribution of data points as shown in the curve in Figure 14.2. In a Gaussian (or normal) distribution, 68% of the values are found within the interval $(X_{avg} - S)$ and $(X_{avg} + S)$. In the above case, this means that we would expect the RFT to be between 7.42 and 10.58 min, 68% of the time.

The Output

The output of the EASI model is an estimate of the probability that a sufficient number of response force personnel will interrupt the adversary at some point before the adversary completes acts of theft or sabotage. The output is the probability of interruption, P_I. If there is one sensor on the path, this probability is calculated as

$$P_I = P_C \times P_D$$

Using the Model

To use EASI, the initial step is the selection of an adversary action sequence. The selection should be based on thorough knowledge of the facility and reasonable assumptions about the adversary. Next, select a physical path to the asset corresponding to the chosen sequence. Visualize the adversary tasks along that path,

and determine the location of sensors. Then, obtain the required data: (1) the probabilities of detection and communication and (2) the mean and standard deviation of task times and response times. Finally, enter the data into the computer and obtain the results. The real value of the EASI model does not end there, however, because the analyst now has the opportunity to change the input data and see what effect this has on the output. A few examples will demonstrate these effects.

EASI Examples

Consider the example where the adversary intends to sabotage a target in a vital area as shown in Figure 14.3. The adversary intends to penetrate the fence, travel to the building, force open a door, travel to the vital area, force open another door, and set and detonate an explosive device on the critical asset. Detection and delay values are shown in Figure 14.4 and the RFT is 300 s.

After entering this data in EASI, the result shows the probability of interruption is 0.48, as shown in Figure 14.4. The analyst may decide that this P_I is too low and that something should be done to improve this result. If a fence sensor

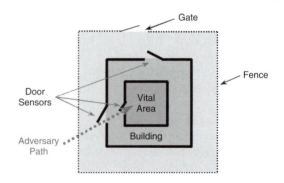

Figure 14.3 Adversary Path to Asset in a Vital Area. The adversary must cross the fence, approach the building, enter the outer door, travel to the asset location, enter an inner door, and then set up the explosive charge at the asset

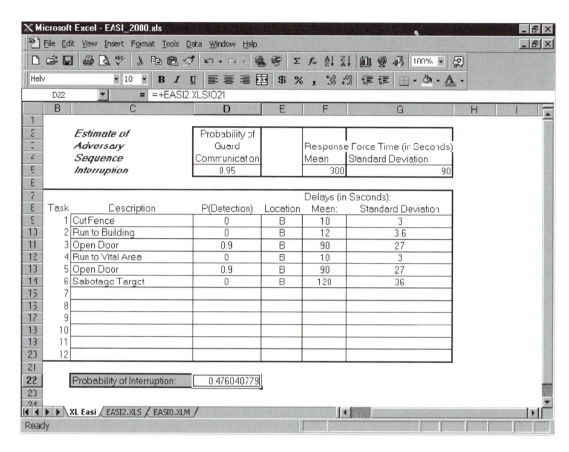

Figure 14.4 Results of EASI Analysis for Adversary Path. P_I is 0.48 for this path

with a probability of detection of 0.9 were added to the outer fence, the input would be as shown in Figure 14.5. The P_I in this upgraded case is 0.58, which may be satisfactory and may justify the installation of the fence sensor system.

If this value is still not acceptable, an additional upgrade could be modeled. For example, if the RFT is also reduced to 200 s, the new P_I is 0.90 (see Figure 14.6). This is a significant improvement and only required relocating guards closer to the target, i.e., low or no additional cost. Or, if preferred, guards could be left at their current location (RFT still 300 s) and delay can be doubled at the asset, perhaps by enclosing it in a hardened case. This would result in a P_I of 0.84 (see Figure 14.7). This is not quite as high as the previous upgrade, but might be

easier or cheaper to implement or operationally be more acceptable. When the P_Is along all paths are approximately equal, the PPS is said to be balanced, i.e., all paths are equally difficult for the adversary to achieve their goal. Note that balance is achieved by mixing detection, delay, and response components and that there are a number of possible combinations that will result in acceptable system performance. This provides the opportunity to select combinations that meet cost and operational requirements without compromising system effectiveness.

These results demonstrate the utility of the EASI model, i.e., the ability to adjust protection elements and their performance in order to predict overall system effectiveness prior to implementation. Further manipulation of detection

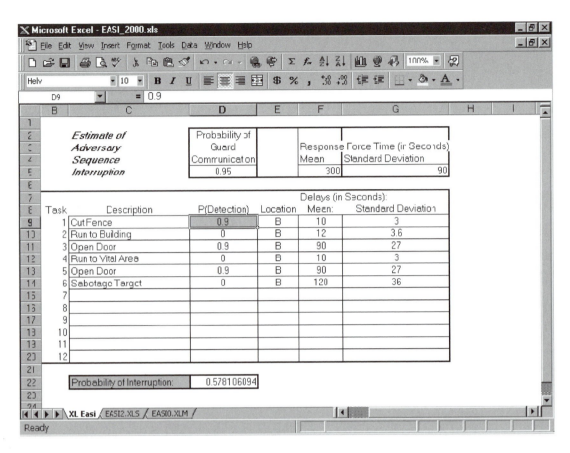

Figure 14.5 Results of EASI Analysis after Upgrade. A fence sensor with P_D of 0.9 was added to the outer fence resulting in an improved P_I of 0.58

and delay components at different points on the path will emphasize the value of the security principles discussed throughout the text. These include detection early on the path and prior to delay, effectiveness of delay at the asset, the relationship among detection, delay and response functions, timely detection, and the principles of protection-in-depth and balanced protection.

Critical Detection Point

As described in Chapter 13, "Analysis and Evaluation," the critical detection point or CDP is the point on the path where the delay time remaining first exceeds the RFT. EASI cannot locate a CDP because the

delay and RFTs are random variables in a distribution, so there is a chance that any point on the path will be the CDP during the actual attack. The concept of a CDP is too important to dismiss, however, because it gives valuable guidance on where to put additional protection, that is, add detection before or at the CDP and delay after.

Many of the more complex analysis tools, like SAVI or ASSESS, that find most-vulnerable paths use only the mean delay and RFTs, because their algorithms fail when variation is introduced. Experience with these tools over the years has shown that effective systems can be designed by assigning the CDP based on the mean times, and then adding detection before this CDP and delay after it. This CDP, based on the mean values, will be what we

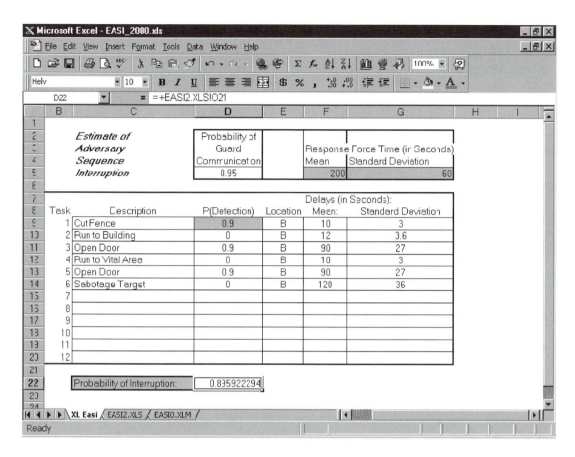

Figure 14.6 EASI Analysis after Reduction in Response Force Time. Reduction of RFT and detection at the fence has increased P_I to 0.90

refer to as the CDP in this chapter, rather than the more precise definition found in Chapter 13. For example, in Figure 14.4, the CDP is at the first door. To illustrate why this CDP is important for effective design, we will incorporate detection ($P_D = 0.9$) at the target itself and show the results in Figure 14.8. The P_I is 0.48, which is the same as the baseline system. In Figure 14.9, 20 s of delay has been added at the fence, again resulting in a P_I of 0.48. Both of these upgrades were on the wrong side of the CDP and both had negligible effect on performance.

While it is practical to set the CDP based on mean delay and RFTs, this must be done carefully, with the understanding that there will be variation in times. In Figure 14.4, the mean time remaining at

the CDP exceeds the mean RFT by only 10 s—not a lot of leeway. Considering that the standard deviation for the RFT is 90 s, while that for the time remaining is 27 s, we see that 10 s leeway is probably insufficient to assure that any detection at this door will be effective. Typically, 30 s or more is desirable. This does not mean that a very large difference between RFT and time remaining on the path is by itself a design criterion, but it could become one if most of the detection is located on the path near the CDP.

Use of Location Variable in EASI

At this point, all but one of the required input elements to the EASI model have

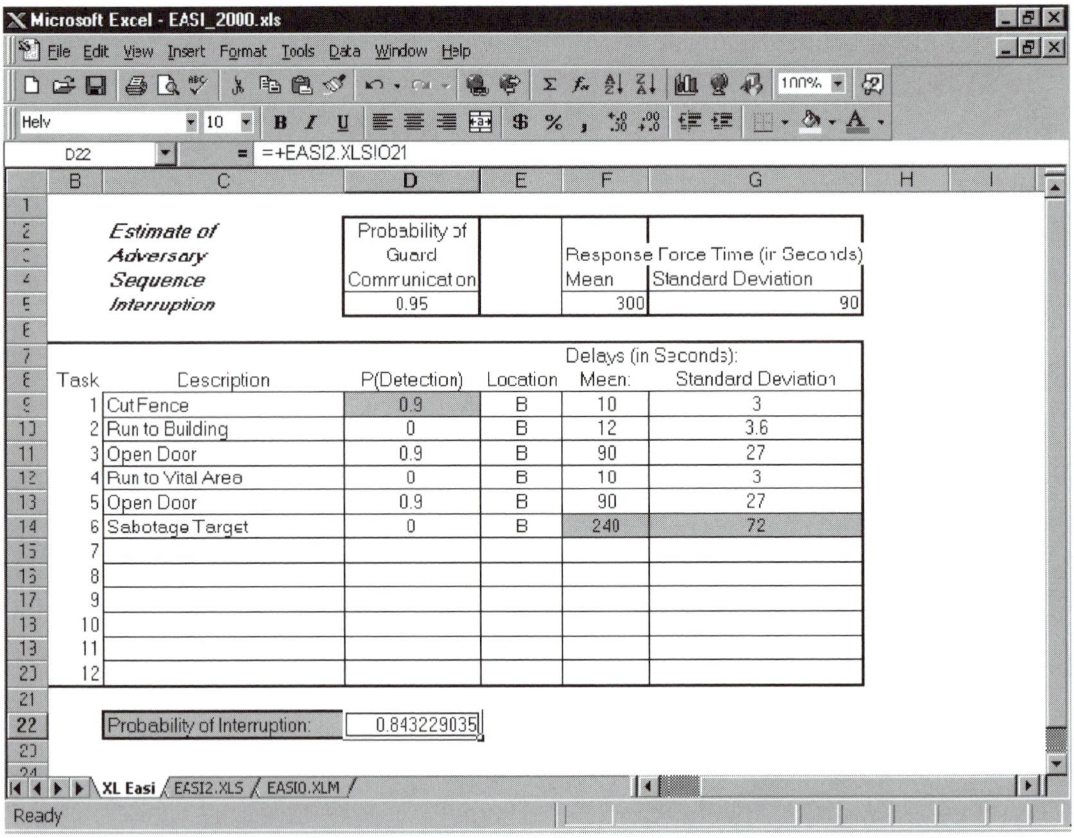

Task	Description	P(Detection)	Location	Mean	Standard Deviation
1	Cut Fence	0.9	B	10	3
2	Run to Building	0	B	12	3.6
3	Open Door	0.9	B	90	27
4	Run to Vital Area	0	B	10	3
5	Open Door	0.9	B	90	27
6	Sabotage Target	0	B	240	72
7					
8					
9					
10					
11					
12					

Figure 14.7 EASI Analysis after Addition of Delay at Asset. With detection at the fence and delay at the target, P_I is now 0.84

been discussed. This last input falls in the column labeled Location in the previous figures. Note that each of these results have a B in this column. The Location column is used to describe where in the model detection falls relative to delay for the specific protection element. Consider that if detection and delay both exist at an element, the detection may start before delay, at the end of delay, or somewhere in-between. Due to these possibilities, EASI allows assignment of detection relative to delay to more accurately model system effectiveness. To do this, entries are B for detection before delay, M for detection during delay (middle), and E for detection after, or at the end of, delay. Where there is no detection associated with the delay the location parameter will not matter. When the location is B, the delay time is calculated using the mean delay time for that element plus/minus the standard deviation; when an E is entered, EASI uses 0 as the time delay for this task. Use of an M indicates that the delay happens somewhere in between the before and end values, so is approximated as one-half the mean plus/minus the standard deviation. The mathematical calculations for these assumptions are shown in Appendix C. Use of this location parameter allows the model to better allocate credit to the standard deviation of the delay time. This in turn allows the analyst to achieve a more realistic view of the probability of interruption by calculating the P_I based on the relationship of detection and delay time at each protection element. This is a complex

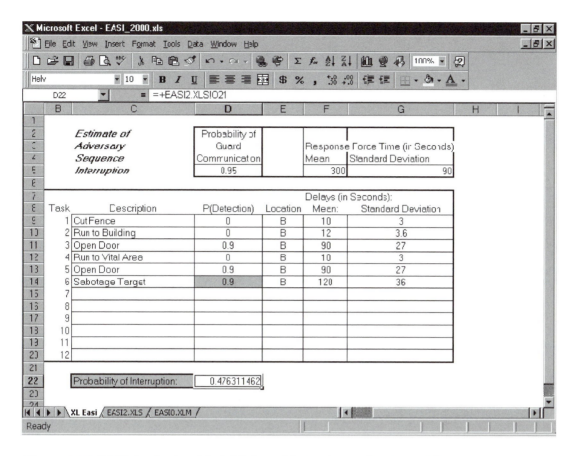

Figure 14.8 EASI Analysis with Addition of Detection at the Asset. The P_I remains at 0.48

point that may be best explained through the use of examples.

For example, a locked door with a balanced magnetic switch sensor might be assigned a location of E. This is because the sensor will not register an alarm until the door is opened a small distance. An attack on the door might be to pick the lock, then enter through the door. In this case, most of the delay came from the time to pick the lock, not to pass through the door, so the detection came at the end of the delay, which limits the effectiveness of the delay. An example of use of the M location parameter might be for the case where an adversary will use an explosive to penetrate a wall. In this case, the adversary must take time to set up the explosive charge, then retreat to a safe distance during the detonation. At this point, the explosion would presumably be detected, but the adversary still has to return to the wall and get through the hole to continue the attack, so some delay still remains after detection. Use of the B parameter in the location column is exemplified by a volumetric sensor in a room monitoring a door. In this case, as soon as the adversary starts to penetrate the door, the sensor will detect the intrusion, and the adversary still must finish penetrating the door to get to the asset. The volumetric sensor detects before the door delay, so use of a B is appropriate.

Adversary Sequence Diagrams

In a typical facility there are multiple options to defeat the different layers of protection. For example, to penetrate a

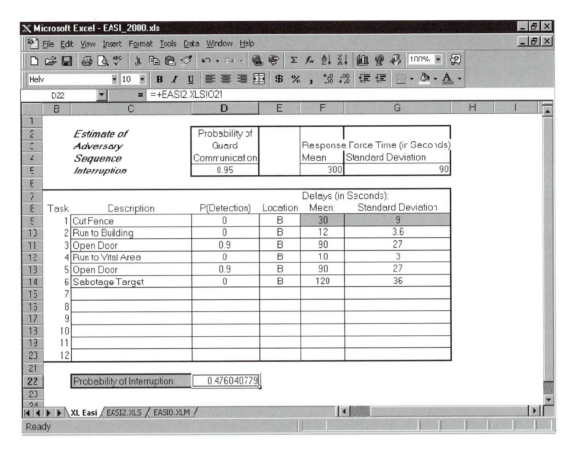

Figure 14.9 EASI Analysis with Addition of Delay at the Fence. The P_I remains at 0.48

locked building, an adversary can defeat doors, windows, walls, or the roof. Because the adversary can attack any option on each layer, the number of paths into the facility easily number into the hundreds or thousands. To apply EASI to such facilities, the analyst needs some systematic method of recording these paths. The method used is termed an adversary sequence diagram (ASD).

The ASD is a graphic representation of protection system elements that is used to help evaluate the effectiveness of the PPS at a facility. It shows the paths that adversaries can follow to accomplish sabotage or theft goals. For a specific PPS and a specific threat, the most vulnerable path (or the path with the lowest P_I) can be determined using EASI. This path establishes the effectiveness of the total PPS.

There are three basic steps in creating an ASD for a specific site. These include:

1. modeling the facility by separating it into adjacent physical areas;
2. defining protection layers and path elements between the adjacent areas; and
3. recording detection and delay values for each element.

The ASD models a facility by separating it into adjacent physical areas. Figure 14.10 shows a representation of an example facility. The ASD represents areas by rectangles, with areas named to model a specific site. The ASD models a PPS by identifying protection layers between adjacent areas (Figure 14.11). Each protection layer consists of a number of protection

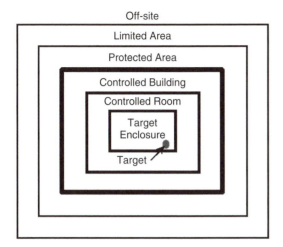

Figure 14.10 Sample Facility Representing Adjacent Physical Areas. Each area is represented by a rectangle

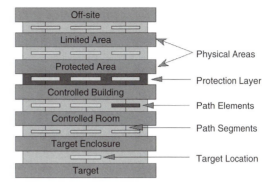

Figure 14.12 Basic ASD for a Facility. Each physical area is separated by a protection layer, which contains the protection elements. A path element can be traversed on entry and exit

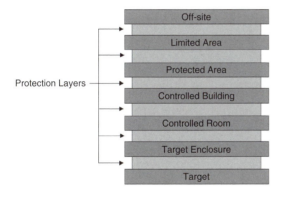

Figure 14.11 Physical Areas and Protection Layers. Each adjacent area is separated from the next by a protection layer, which is part of the PPS

elements (PE), which are the basic building blocks of a PPS. Some types of PEs and target locations used in the ASD are shown in Table 14.2. Acronyms are used to keep the element boxes in the ASD small.

Once the ASD is created, the analyst records P_D, mean delay, standard deviation of delay, and location for each element. Both entry and exit path segments can be modeled. The entry path segment is

from off site to the asset (target), and the exit path segment is from the asset back to off site. A given PE may be traversed once (either on entry or exit), or it may be traversed twice, on entry and in the opposite direction on exit. The ASD as it has been developed so far is shown in Figure 14.12. The adversary attempts to sequentially defeat an element in each protection layer while traversing a path through the facility to the target. The ASD represents all of the realistic paths that an adversary might take to reach a target.

For sabotage analysis, only the entry paths would be evaluated, and we assume the protection elements will be traversed in only one direction. An act of sabotage only requires proximity to the asset long enough to cause damage to the asset; it does not require exit from the facility to be successful. For theft analysis, the protection elements are traversed twice—on entry to the asset and on exit from the asset. A more conservative protection goal, to interrupt the adversary before removing the target from its location, requires only that entry be considered. When the entry and exit case is evaluated, the number of possible paths shown on the ASD is the square of the number of entry paths.

Table 14.2 *Most Common Protection Elements Used in ASDs.*

Each path element has associated detection and delay components. SUR is used to model walls, floors, and ceilings; DOR is used to describe personnel doors. One DOR is required for each different type of door in a layer. A generic target location (GNL) can be used to describe asset locations that are not represented in the existing list.

Protection Elements		Target Locations
EMP Emergency Portal	DUC Duct	BPL Bulk Process Line
GAT Gateway	EMX Emergency Exit	CGE Cage
ISO Isolation Zone	FEN Fenceline	FLV Floor Vault
MAT Material Portal	HEL Helicopter Flight Path	GNL Generic Location
DOR Personnel Doorway	OVP Overpass	IPL Item Process Line
SHD Shipping/Receiving Door	PER Personnel Portal	OPN Open Location
SUR Surface	SHP Shipping/Receiving Portal	TNK Storage Tank
VHD Vehicle Doorway	TUN Tunnel	
WND Window	VEH Vehicle Portal	

Site-Specific ASD

A site-specific ASD is constructed for each asset or set of assets having a common location at a facility. The objective is to correctly model the PPS that exists at a site. This site-specific ASD is created by identifying the protection elements that are present at the facility. Figure 14.13 shows a simplified example facility and PPS layout. Figure 14.14 shows the resulting

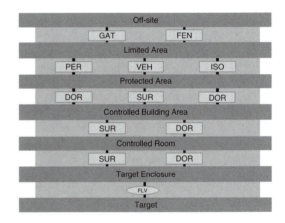

Figure 14.14 ASD of Sample Facility. Functional protection elements are found in each physical layer of the facility

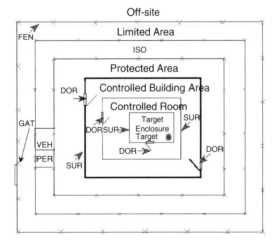

Figure 14.13 Sample Facility and Protection System. Each area contains certain protection features as movement progresses from off-site to the asset (target)

site-specific ASD that is constructed by using the example facility information. Sometimes it will be necessary to deviate from the orderly sequence of physical areas and protection layers of the generic ASD in order to create an accurate site-specific ASD. There are two features in the ASD modeling technique for this purpose—jump and bypass.

A jump is used to model a site element that does not directly connect to the adjacent area shown on the generic ASD. As shown in Figure 14.15, there is a wall

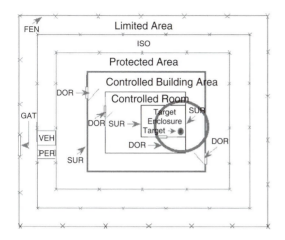

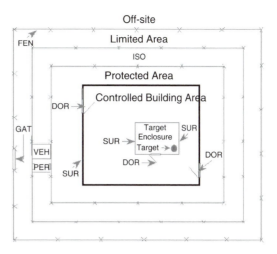

Figure 14.15 Sample Facility with a Common Surface. This connection allows a direct path from one layer to a nonadjacent area

Figure 14.17 Sample Facility that Is Missing a Layer. In this example, there is no controlled room inside the building, so one layer is bypassed

common to the controlled building area and to the target enclosure. This situation is correctly modeled by including a SUR jump element from the controlled building area to model this portion of the common surface. The site-specific ASD (Figure 14.16) then shows a direct path that jumps from the controlled building area to the target enclosure (without passing

through the controlled room) in addition to all other selected indirect paths.

A bypass is used to model the absence of a protection layer. It is possible to bypass features of the example ASD by eliminating all of the elements in a layer. If, as shown in Figure 14.17, a facility has an access area that is itself a building with

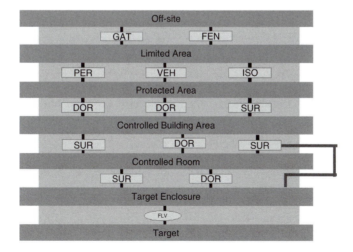

Figure 14.16 Example of a Jump in an ASD. In this case, there is a shared wall between the building and the target enclosure, so there is a direct path between these two layers at this point

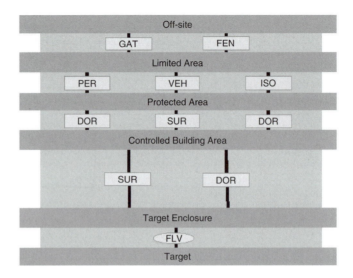

Figure 14.18 ASD Showing a Bypass. The controlled room is not present, so once the surfaces are penetrated, the adversary is at the target enclosure

no other controlled rooms present, the resulting ASD would have a direct connection between the controlled building area and the target enclosure. The bypass is accomplished by eliminating all of the path elements in the layer between the controlled room and the target enclosure. Figure 14.18 shows the ASD with this bypass.

The ASD, then, serves as a useful tool to represent all the detection and delay elements in a PPS. By graphically representing all of the protection elements by layer, the analyst will have a simple picture of adversary paths into a facility and to critical assets. Paths that appear weakest can be entered into the EASI model, and the resulting P_Is can be calculated and compared. When all paths have achieved approximately the same P_I, the analysis is complete and the system can be implemented. The process of calculating P_I over many paths is facilitated by more complex models that make use of computing power and the graphical ASD entered in a separate module; however, these models are not yet commercially available. As a result, the EASI analysis

requires that the analyst successfully select the most vulnerable paths. In industrial applications this is actually easier than it sounds, because once an ASD is drawn, and detection and delay measures collected, system deficiencies are relatively easy to spot.

The ASD can serve as a useful tool to represent all of the detection and delay elements in a PPS. By graphically representing all of the protection elements by layer, the analyst will have a picture of adversary paths into a facility and to critical assets. Then, various paths can be modeled in EASI and resulting P_Is calculated and compared.

Summary

EASI is a very simple method of quantitatively evaluating the effectiveness of a PPS against a defined adversary utilizing a specific path and attack scenario and for an immediate response. The analyst must enter data describing the detection, delay, and response components along the adversary path. The EASI model then performs the calculation and displays a probability of interruption, P_I. If P_I is not satisfactory, additional PPS measures can be incorporated and subsequent analyses run to determine the most cost-effective solutions. The model reinforces the security principles presented throughout the text, including detection before delay, balanced protection, protection-in-depth, response force capability, and timely detection.

EASI only analyzes one specific path, selected by the analyst. EASI uses the probability of detection, probability of guard communication, RFT, and delay times to determine P_I. EASI is a Microsoft Excel® application and a copy of the Excel worksheet is attached in Appendix C, "EASI Model."

In larger more complex facilities, path analysis is aided by the use of ASDs. ASDs are a graphic representation of the physical layers around a facility, the protection elements between layers, and paths to the asset. Once this graphic is constructed and detection and delay values collected, the analyst can review possible paths, identify those that appear to be weakest, and determine the overall effectiveness of the PPS.

Security Principle

The EASI model allows for a quantitative analysis of a protection system, where the asset requires this level of protection and performance data exists to support the analysis.

References

Bennett, H.A. The EASI approach to physical security evaluation. SAND Report 760500 1977;1–35.

Chapman, L.D., and Harlan, C.P. EASI estimate of adversary sequence interruption on an IBM PC. SAND Report 851105 1985;1–63.

Questions

1. What are the limitations of EASI? What are the strengths?
2. What do we mean by path analysis?
3. Using Figure 14.4, add the steps and performance measures shown in Table 14.3 that represent an adversary theft scenario, instead of sabotage. Assume RFT = 300 s and $P_C = 0.95$. What is the P_I? Where is the CDP, based on mean delays and RFT? What detection and delay improvements could be made?
4. Using the initial theft scenario from question 3 above, assume the RFT is 600 s. What is the P_I? What if the RFT is changed to 150 s?
5. Using the sabotage scenario described in Figure 14.4, change the EASI location variable to those shown below one at a time and calculate the change in P_I. Explain your results. Be sure to change data back to the original value before making the next change.

Table 14.3 Data for Question 3.

Description	P_D	Location	Delay Mean	Standard Deviation
1. Remove asset	0.0	B	60	18
2. Exit Vital Area door	0.9	B	10	3
3. Run to second outer door*	0.0	B	20	6
4. Exit outer door	0.9	B	0	0
5. Run to gate	0.0	B	15	4.5
6. Exit facility	0.2	B	12	3.6

* This not the same door that they entered through; it is the other door leading out of the building.

Table 14.4 Data for Question 7.

Threat	Outsiders traveling on foot carrying explosives and metal tools
Travel Times	Running, approximately 10 ft/s
Tilt/vibration fence sensor	0.8 probability of detection
Climb fence/gate	10 s delay (climbing)
Doors in personnel portal (2)	12 s delay per door
Combined badge reader (hand geometry unit/magnetic stripe) in personnel portal	0.85 probability of detection
Badge reader (hand geometry delay time)	8 s delay
Officer at vehicle portal	0.5 probability of detection
	30 s delay
Microwave exterior detection system	0.9 probability of detection
Isolation zone width	50 ft
Detectors on all doors	0.99 probability of detection
Exterior door 1, 6 in. metal	60 s delay
30 cm, reinforced concrete walls and floors	3 min delay
Exterior door 2, 3 in. metal	30 s delay
1.6 mm interior doors	1 min delay
Time to steal material	2 min
Time to sabotage facility	51 s
Standard deviation on all times	30% of mean

a. Task 1, cut fence, change to M.
b. Task 6, sabotage target, change to E.
c. Task 3, open door, change to E.
d. Task 3, open door, change to M.

6. Using the example from Figure 14.4, change the probability of communication to 0.8, 0.7, and 0.5. Record the new P_I for each of these values. Explain your results. What are some possible reasons for lowering the probability of communication in a PPS?

7. Using the ASD in Figure 14.14 and the information in Table 14.4, fill in the details of the ASD for all the protection elements.

8. Create an ASD of a sample facility. Show the physical areas, protection layers, protection elements, path segments, and targets. Remember, if there are multiple distributed targets, you may need to do more than one diagram. Using this ASD, pick a few paths to model using the EASI tool. You may need to use hypothetical values for performance measures.

15

Risk Assessment

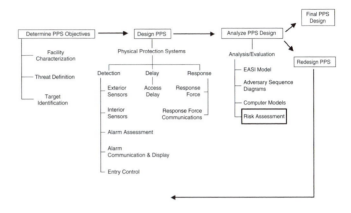

The basic premise of the approach presented in this text is that the design and analysis of physical protection must be addressed as an integrated system. In this way, all components of detection, delay, and response can be properly weighted according to their contribution to the PPS as a whole. At a higher level, the security manager, the facility manager, and senior management must balance the effectiveness of the PPS against available resources and then evaluate the proposed design. Without a methodical, defined, analytical assessment, the PPS might waste valuable resources on unnecessary protection or, worse yet, fail to provide adequate protection at critical points of the facility. For example, it would probably be unwise to protect a facility's employee cafeteria with the same level of protection as the critical production area. However, maximum security at a facility's main entrance would be wasted if entry were also possible through an unguarded cafeteria loading dock.

This chapter will discuss some significant considerations of the PPS designer and facility management as they are charged with answering the question: How do we know if the security system is good enough? In earlier chapters, the concept of probability of interruption of a defined adversary along the most vulnerable path in the facility was developed and identified as the best measure of PPS effectiveness. The next question is: Given a certain P_I, is that good enough?

This question may also be stated as: How much risk is the facility willing to accept versus the cost of reducing that risk? The best answer to this question should consider all risks to the enterprise from all endeavors. This holistic risk across the enterprise is made up of risk elements including financial risk management, liability risk financing, property/net income financing, employee benefits, environmental health and safety, and property engineering in addition to security risk. Thus, security is only one component of risk to the enterprise and must allocate resources within the larger risk picture. The facility or corporate Chief Risk Officer must still combine all of the various risks and help the corporation manage total risk. While the security department may be able to aid in mitigation of risk in other areas, the security organization is only one of many functions that must be depended on to assure that the corporate enterprise manages and limits their risk exposure. Given limited resources to be applied to address all risks, each application of a portion of those resources must be carefully and analytically evaluated to ensure a balanced risk.

This chapter will address how to apply limited security resources within the context of risk to the enterprise and show how the security system reduces overall risk to the facility. In this text, risk is defined as the likelihood of damage or loss multiplied by the potential magnitude of the loss.

Risk Management Approaches

Risk management may take one of several different forms. Good risk programs should include a combination of risk financing (insurance) and risk control tools to treat the risk. The risk approaches used include avoidance, reduction, spreading, transfer, and acceptance (Grose, 1987). Any one or a combination of the five may be appropriate at different times, for different assets, and at different facilities. Risk avoidance is accomplished by eliminating the source of the risk. For example, a company may choose to buy a critical component from another company, rather than manufacture it. This removes the production line for that item as a sabotage target. Risk reduction is achieved by taking some actions to lower risk to the enterprise to reduce the severity of the loss. This is the goal of many security programs—to lower risk by implementing at least some security measures. Risk can also be spread among multiple locations. This may be accomplished by having similar production capability at more than one corporate site. Then, loss of the capability at one site can be managed by increasing production at the other locations. Another example of risk spreading might be the distribution of assets across

a large industrial site. By separating the assets, fewer assets are at risk during any given adversary attack. Risk transfer is the use of insurance to cover the replacement or other costs incurred as a result of the loss. This is an important tool in many security systems. Risk acceptance is the recognition that there will always be some residual risk. The key is in knowingly determining a level that is acceptable to the enterprise, not unwitting acceptance. It is this last approach that will be elaborated in the rest of this chapter.

Risk Equation

One of the basic assumptions of this text has been the need for a method to quantify the way a protection system performs. By understanding how well a PPS protects assets from threats, we can also address the amount of risk that remains after implementation of the design. In order to do this, the following risk equation is used:

$$R = P_A \times [1 - (P_E)] \times C$$

where the terms are as follows:

$R =$ Risk to the facility (or stakeholders) of an adversary gaining access to, or stealing, critical assets. Range is 0–1.0, with 0 being no risk and 1.0 being maximum risk. Risk is measured for a period of time, such as 1 or 5 years.

$P_A =$ Probability of an adversary attack during a period of time. This can be difficult to determine, but generally there are records available to assist in this effort. The value of this probability is from 0 (no chance at all of an attack) to 1.0 (certainty of attack). Sometimes in the calculation of risk, we assume $P_A = 1.0$, which means that it is a conditional risk. That is, the calculated risk assuming that an attack on a facility will occur.

P_E = Probability of system effectiveness. This is the product of the probability of interruption and the probability of neutralization. The principle of timely detection is used in calculating this probability from 0 (the adversary will definitely be successful) to 1.0 (the adversary will definitely be interrupted in their path).

C = Consequence value. This is a value from 0 to 1 that relates to the severity of the occurrence of the event. This is a normalizing factor, which allows the conditional risk value to be compared to all other risks across the site. A consequence table of all events could be created that would cover the spectrum of loss, from highest to lowest. Therefore, by using this consequence table, the risk can be normalized over all possible events. Then the limited PPS resources can be appropriately allocated to ensure the risk is acceptable across the spectrum.

This risk formula incorporates the effectiveness measure, P_I, by subtracting it from 1.0. If $P_I = 1.0$, the risk drops to 0. If $P_I = 0$, then the conditional risk is equal to the consequence value, which determines the upper limit of risk. For those cases where force-on-force incidents can be expected, the system effectiveness measure will change. In these cases, system effectiveness is measured by multiplying the probability of interruption and the probability of neutralization. This product is then subtracted from 1.0, in place of P_I. This system effectiveness considers not only the arrival of the response force, but also the outcome of any force-on-force battle. This is not an expected event in most industrial applications, but this calculation is included for completeness.

The risk equation provides the opportunity to model the effect of some assumptions that we make. For example, if we assume that there will be an attack (i.e., we calculate a conditional risk) P_A drops out of the equation. If we then assume

that C is equal to 1.0, that is, the consequence is the highest we can imagine, this term also drops out. This leaves a conditional risk, R, that is determined solely by the effectiveness of the PPS, which can be useful in establishing the worst case risk—that is, a certain attack by the most capable adversary on the most valuable target. It is then possible to go back and use different consequence values to determine the risk to the enterprise for lower consequence losses. This will allow a prioritization of targets and appropriate protection. Finally, the probability of attack may also be varied, based on available data where possible, and a realistic assessment of risk can be obtained. This three-step process can help in simplifying the complexity of the risk assessment by varying only one term at a time, allowing an appreciation of the influence of each factor on the outcome. In some cases, P_A and PPS effectiveness are not independent. For example, a very effective PPS may deter the adversary from attacking, but for the purposes of this text, we assume independence. The derivation of the terms of the risk equation has been discussed in previous chapters. We are now in a position to see how the overall process works and how these measures can be merged to predict the risk the facility or enterprise faces within the security function. The process of vulnerability assessment (VA) serves as the method of determining the P_I component of risk and then providing upgrades to the existing system to strengthen any system vulnerabilities.

Vulnerability Assessment Process

A team with broad experience is necessary to ensure that a complete and accurate VA is produced. The team must have a team leader who is a security specialist and who can ensure that the VA is correct. The members of the team should be:

- team leader
- security systems engineer

- response expert
- data analyst
- operations representatives
- subject matter experts, such as lock-smiths, explosives personnel, or information systems experts

Some members of the team may only be required occasionally, and others may be needed on a permanent basis. The team leader should be experienced in some aspect of security systems design and project management. The security systems engineer will have an understanding of detection, delay, and response technologies, and the integration of security systems. Response experts will have knowledge of weapons, response force tactics and training, contingency and emergency planning, and investigation techniques. The data analyst will understand how to use a computer model to predict system performance. This person may also be a security systems engineer, a response or delay expert, or a subject matter expert. Depending on the facility and threats, experts in locks, explosives, and other specialized skills may be necessary to assess threats and establish performance goals for the designed system. In addition, operations representatives including safety, production, legal personnel, and other facility experts will be required to provide input on allowable activities or any operational effects of proposed changes.

Once the team is assembled, the first phase of the design and evaluation process can begin—determine system objectives. The output of this stage should be a complete facility characterization, including a description of existing security elements, a design basis threat or threat spectrum, and an understanding of all assets at the facility and their associated consequence of loss. Asset identification and consequence analysis may be aided by the use of a fault tree. At this point, the baseline system can be modeled using EASI and ASDs and an initial P_I

can be determined. These results can be compared to the system objectives and a risk value quantified using the equation above. If the risk value is acceptable, the existing system is satisfactory; if not, system redesign must be done to lower the risk to the facility.

Risk Assessment

It is important to note that in order to truly make cost–benefit decisions, the system effectiveness and associated risk of the current, or baseline system, must be known. It will be impossible to make good cost–benefit decisions without this information, because it is essential to know the decrease in risk and the cost to get there in order to make an informed decision. It is also important to recognize that there will only be a limited amount of funding available to accomplish the security goals. So, if the threat to a facility is high, but there is only enough money to protect the facility against a lower threat, there will be additional risk. Different system performance or effectiveness will be required against different threats. Because system effectiveness is dependent on the threat, there will be different P_Is, and therefore different risk values, for different threats. As threats get more capable or sophisticated, the security system must also perform better. This relationship is shown in Figure 15.1. This analysis can serve as the justification for additional funds to further reduce risk or can serve as the basis for a longer-term plan to increase security over a number of years. The goal of the risk assessment is not to spend as much money as possible, but rather to help decision-makers spend the available money most effectively to reduce security risk to the facility or enterprise. If the results indicate an unacceptably high risk exposure, additional funds can be made available to increase security system effectiveness more quickly. As an alternative, completion of the risk assessment

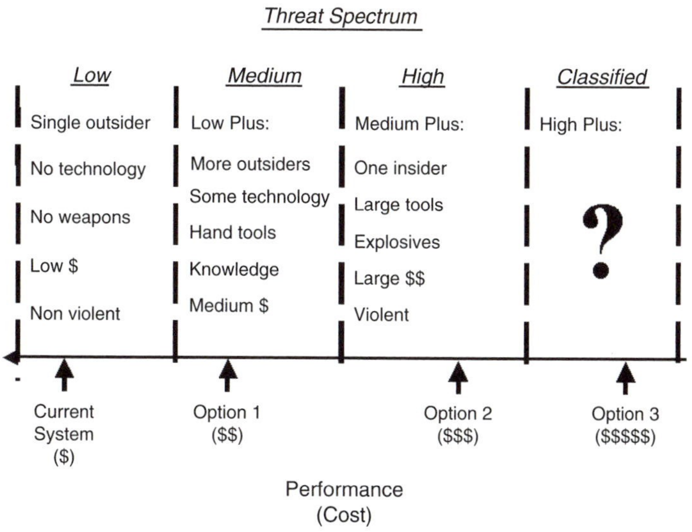

Threat Spectrum

Figure 15.1 Threat Spectrum and System Performance. After the decision to invest in a protection system is made, it will be necessary to determine how much the system helped to decrease risk. If the expected threat is high, but there is only enough budget or other resources to protect against a lower threat, there can still be significant risk

will show which threats have been mitigated by the protection system and which threats still pose an unacceptably high risk to the facility. When these risk assessments are completed, they should be treated as proprietary data and shared only on a limited basis throughout the company.

An additional tool that can be useful in the risk assessment of a facility is the consequence matrix that was introduced in Chapter 4. "Target Identification." Now that a complete discussion of the security system objectives and functions has been presented, it is helpful to look at this again. A sample consequence matrix is shown in Table 15.1.

All of the elements of the consequence matrix have been thoroughly discussed in previous chapters. The probability of adversary attack and threats placed inside the matrix are determined in threat definition. Consequence of loss is determined when identifying targets of adversary attack. Special attention should be paid to any threats that appear in the top left box of the matrix—high consequence

of loss and low probability of occurrence. It is common to hear executives and security managers accept this risk by saying the probability of the event happening is low, so no action is required. This approach can work if the facility is truly prepared to accept the risk; however, low probability is not a zero probability. Full consideration of these events should be part of the analysis that the security organization provides to the corporation and is the best example of the use of conditional risk. For example, the *Challenger* space shuttle explosion, the chemical release and loss of over 10,000 lives in Bhopal, and the Chernobyl reactor accident are good examples of high-consequence, low-probability events. While none of these is a security incident, they could have been. Examples of security incidents include the Oklahoma City bombing, the Columbine school shooting, prison riots where guards or inmates are killed, and the terrorist attacks of 9/11, and on the Bali nightclub and London subway bombings.

Table 15.1 *Consequence Matrix.*

Shaded boxes in the top right corner indicate the threats that must be prevented. The threats in the lower left box may be acceptable as is or with limited procedural changes. The threats in the unshaded boxes indicate the areas in which decisions must be made when allocating resources. Depending on the facility, high-consequence, low-probability events can take precedence over other events.

High Consequence			
Medium Consequence			
Low Consequence			
	Low probability	Medium probability	High probability

The consequence matrix relates the probability of adversary attack, consequence of loss of the asset, and the threat spectrum. This can be a useful tool when presenting reviews of the security function or requests for additional budget to senior management. It puts all of the pertinent information together in a simple and graphic form. These issues can then be related to risk and various options to increase protection system effectiveness. An example of this is shown in Figure 15.2.

Through the use of the risk equation, various security improvement options can be evaluated by relating system performance and, therefore, risk reduction to cost options. In this way, the security organization can present their proposals in a manner in which senior executives can use familiar principles to understand how the security organization helps the overall enterprise and what measurable improvements can be expected in return for a budget investment. These risk values are based on the existence of a measure of system effectiveness or P_E. If a qualitative analysis is used, the P_E measure is more uncertain, possibly leading to incorrect conclusions. This is only acceptable if the assets have a lower consequence of loss or fall into the acceptable risk category.

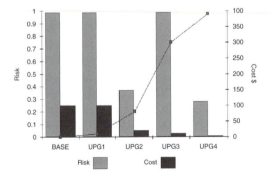

Figure 15.2 Relationship of Risk and Security System Upgrades. Each upgrade option has a level of risk and cost associated with it. This is a quick way to show the cost–benefit of possible options to senior management when trying to decide which option to fund

Performance Testing

In addition to the use of EASI code to calculate P_I, system performance tests, component performance tests, and initial data verifications should be conducted prior to acceptance of the risk associated with the final design for a PPS. Documentation of the actual performance tests is required to support the overall risk calculation. Even after a PPS design is accepted and approved, testing must continue. Some of the classes of tests are:

• Operability tests—conducted daily by facility security personnel to ensure that the PPS equipment is operating properly.

- Performance tests—conducted periodically to ensure that the sensitivity of the PPS equipment is high enough to support the assumed values of P_D used in the analysis models.
- Post-maintenance tests—conducted after maintenance on the PPS equipment to ensure it is working correctly and is at the desired level of sensitivity.
- Whole system and limited scope tests—conducted by the facility to ensure large parts of the system are all working together as assumed in the analysis. Some of the coordinated parts of the PPS that should be tested together might be detection with response and detection with delay.
- Evaluation tests—periodic independent tests on the PPS to ensure that the VA is still valid and that the expected level of PPS effectiveness is being maintained.

The operability and post-maintenance tests are needed whether the basis of analysis is qualitative or quantitative. In fact, all five types of testing can support qualitative risk analysis; the only distinction is that the data enters the risk analysis qualitatively, not quantitatively.

Summary

A recommended process for the design and analysis of a PPS was presented in the preceding chapters. This process culminates in values for C, P_A, and P_E. Once these measures are determined, the risk to a facility by a particular threat can be calculated. Through the use of the risk equation, various proposed upgrades in physical protection at a facility can be compared. The options that give the best cost–benefit to the facility can be implemented. This process allows limited security resources to be allocated to protect assets that are most important. In addition, there is a quantifiable result that can be used to show senior executives what they get for their investment, and it is expressed in terms that are familiar to them. The risk is normalized to the consequence of loss of the asset, and thus the allocation of scarce physical protection resources is appropriately applied to keep all risks at an acceptable level.

Security Principle

Through the use of the risk equation, $R = P_A \times [1 - (P_E)] \times C$, system effectiveness can be used to quantify the risk a facility faces from a specific threat. Use of the risk equation and P_E will enable good cost–benefit decisions to be made and help select the option that reduces risk to an acceptable quantity.

Reference

Grose, V.L. *Managing Risk: Systematic Loss Prevention for Executives.* Arlington, VA: Omega Systems Group, 1987, 47–48.

Questions

1. Why is risk assessment important to the evaluation of a protection system?
2. Pick a facility as an example and plan out the vulnerability assessment that would need to be completed. Include a description of who should be on the team, what tasks the team would need to accomplish, and how the team would report its findings.
3. Using the risk equation and the following information, calculate the risk to a facility.

a. Assume a conditional risk, that is, the adversary will attack.

b. How does conditional risk change when the consequence value changes from High ($C=1$), to Medium ($C=0.5$), to Low ($C=0.2$)?

c. Assume that the P_I for the system is 0.7 for a design basis threat (the maximum credible threat) of three armed criminals with insider assistance. How does conditional risk to a high-consequence asset change if the threat is now reduced to two outsiders and P_I is 0.85? What if I increases to 0.95 against the lowest threat, a single vandal?

4. Using the risk equation and the knowledge that an asset has a consequence value of 0.5, calculate the risk for the following P_As:

a. $P_A = 0.2$
b. $P_A = 0.5$
c. $P_A = 1.0$

What conclusions could you draw from this?

16

Process Applications

This chapter provides a discussion of how the principles described for designing and evaluating a PPS can also be applied to other security applications. Although the basic principles and process can be shown to work within any security application, such as retail, hotels, museums, subways, ports, and critical infrastructure protection, this chapter will discuss only three—executive protection, ground transportation, and cyber systems. None of these areas are discussed in great detail; that is not really the goal. Rather, it is our hope that by showing how the same process and principles are applied, we can establish some common views of security system design, integration, and implementation.

Executive Protection

Executive protection is a specialized area of security that is commonly found in the government and large corporations. While the protection of senior executives is an important part of the overall protection approach for these groups, the process that is used parallels that used in PPS. As with other areas of security, executive protection usually starts with a risk assessment. This assessment may be as a result of a new

policy, a recent security incident, corporate merger, or a periodic review. Whatever the reason, the risk assessment will consider the threat, consequences of an attack on an executive, and the vulnerabilities of the executive's protection system, as well as the impact of a successful attack on shareholders, and any effect on corporate governance.

To keep this discussion simple, we will assume that the protection is provided by a single person and will use the term principal to designate the person receiving protection. While it is true that in some circumstances a multi-person team will provide protection, the basic concepts still apply.

For corporate security managers it is critical to understand the differences between public sector executive protection and corporate executive protection. Two critical differences are that public sector security is generally legally mandated, which requires the public sector executive to accept protection. In the corporate sector, executive protection is not legally required and executives have a tendency to become more involved in reviewing risks and threats, as well as suggested mitigation plans. Further, executive protection costs have implications in private companies that do not apply in the public sector; therefore, careful analysis of costs should be undertaken. For example, issues such as Board-mandated use of corporate aircraft for security purposes need careful independent reviews to comply with Internal Revenue Service regulations and prevent imputed income questions if aircraft (or vehicles) are used for personal purposes.

Determine Protection Objectives—Facility Characterization, Threat Definition, and Asset Identification

When planning executive protection, facility characterization takes the form of checking all the locations that the principal frequents or will visit. It is useful to think of these locations in terms of home, office, travel, and information security. Often, home and office locations have some form of physical protection already in place. For locations that will be visited by the principal, whether on official business or pleasure, it is customary to conduct an "advance" of the location to familiarize those providing protection with the terrain, environment, personnel, layout, and operations at the site. In addition to checking the actual venue, vehicle entry and exit points are identified, and protected paths into the building, to the meeting location, and exit from the building can be prepared, along with backup paths if needed. It is common practice to identify nearby restrooms and designate a private area where an unexpected telephone call can be answered or meetings can be held. This is also an opportunity to identify the closest hospitals or other medical aid, in the event that medical assistance is needed.

The executive's daily routine should be identified, generally by considering questions such as: Does the executive stop for breakfast or coffee each morning? Is it usually the same place day after day?

What about lunchtime? Does the executive belong to a health club? When do they work out? Does the executive take children to and from school, dance lessons, or sporting events? This process can be facilitated by following the principal around for a few days (if possible) and documenting the daily routine. This should be done over several days or a week to detect patterns of behavior and the different environments the principal operates in—predictability and fixed routines increase risks. Checklists that can be used to aid in this process are provided by Holder and Hawley (1998).

After these routines are evaluated, certain information can be developed. Generally, this falls into two basic categories—predictable areas and chokepoints. Predictable areas typically include the executive's residence and workplace and, to a certain extent, the neighborhoods immediately surrounding these locations. A residence and workplace must be defined broadly. A residence, for example, may be a home, hotel, resort, or weekend cabin. The workplace may be an office or conference center. It is in these predictable areas that an attack is most likely to occur because the adversary knows that eventually the principal must enter them. An assailant need only know the approximate time the principal will arrive; insider threats will have greater opportunity and knowledge to pick the time and location for an attack.

Choke points include elevators, narrow or one-way streets, bridges or underpasses, and construction zones. The detail may try to avoid or limit these locations whenever possible; however, if this is not possible, these areas must be added to the locations that must undergo closer routine scrutiny.

Just as with a fixed-site PPS, a threat can be defined for executives. General threat data can be obtained from commercial services that compile information for incidents against executives around the world, by networking with other executives or protection experts, by monitoring local and national news, and by reviewing crime studies for the surrounding home and office areas. Some open sources for intelligence include the FBI Infra-Gard program, the US State Department Overseas Advisory Council (OSAC), the Search for International Terrorist Entities (SITE) Institute, and the Maritime Security Council. Specific threats against an executive that take the form of letters, emails, phone calls, and workplace violence incidents can also be used to determine the threat. Certain sectors, such as financial services, pharmaceutical and energy, or those with executives based overseas, may also be targets of activist groups who may engage in physical attacks on executives, their families, their homes, and vehicles. In some areas, kidnapping and carjacking must be considered. The responsible security official should create processes for the collection of external and internal data and sources to maintain current relevant threat information. A history of prior attempts or recent interest by an activist group against the principal would suggest the need for a more active and effective protection plan.

The executive protection scheme used will vary with the nature of the threat and their goal. Clearly, different techniques will be used to keep protestors away from a principal than if there is a violent threat. Key to the protection of executives is a policy that describes which executives will be protected, at which locations and times of day, and some description of how far these measures can go. For example, the US Secret Service will obviously go to greater lengths to protect the President of the United States than a major company may to protect a senior executive. Typically, mid- and field-level employees operating in foreign markets may be at higher personal risk, and the company at greater financial risk, than in the US. The impact of this threat can be partially mitigated by transferring the risk from the principal's company to insurance companies in the form of Kidnap and Ransom (K&R) coverage. This coverage usually includes the services of a specialized security agency that negotiates on behalf of the customer and the insurance company to recover the employee safely and coordinates with the family. It is always best to establish these policies in advance of an event.

It should be clear that the asset to be protected in this case is the executive; this protection may also be extended to members of the executive's immediate family. Due to their organizational rank, executives often have a high profile and spend significant amounts of time traveling, sometimes to dangerous areas. Given this higher-than-normal risk and frequent absences, reasonable protection of the principle residence to safeguard the executive, their family, and access to corporate intellectual property (hard copies or electronic data on computers in the residence) is warranted. This is another detail that should be addressed in corporate policy.

Protection Functions—Detection, Delay, Response

The primary detection, delay, and response functions for executives generally are provided by the person (protective agent or just agent) providing protection. The agent may be aided by technology, such as portable metal detectors, radios, and weapons. At locations where an effective PPS is installed, protection will be supplemented by these additional layers of security.

Detection by the protective agent is generally a result of direct visual observation and is facilitated by maintaining close proximity to the principal and constant scanning of the surrounding area. Good advance preparation and intelligence gathering enhance the potential for detection. Hands waving, extended articles, or sudden movement are all potential indications of an attack. In addition to direct observation, the agent may be required to interview people at various locations to determine what is normal in that environment. For example, if the executive attends the theater every Friday, the agent would determine the type of activity that is typical on a Friday night.

Additional detection measures include room, building, vehicle, and package searches. Packages may include mail, gifts, luggage, and other items, especially those offered by strangers. A procedural element that can be used to reduce attacks on the principal is screening of all those who work closely with the principal. This is generally accomplished through background checks on employees, vendors, and contractors who are in routine contact with the principal or their family. Awareness training for staff supporting the principal (secretaries, personal aides, domestic staff, etc.) enhances any protection program and can provide early warning signs of a potential attack.

Delay is provided by having the detail place themselves between the principal and potential threats, engaging in physical intervention in the short term, if appropriate, and by evacuation as soon as possible. "Cover and evacuate" are key words in the scope of emergency response and good security planning requires that the advance agent have a plan for relocation. Delay technologies that are used in executive protection include bulletproof vests, armored vehicles, and bullet-resistant glass. Expanding the perimeter can also delay an adversary by adding distance; this may also facilitate earlier detection by the agent of an attack.

Response is always practiced in advance and can range from simply removing the principal as fast as possible to defending the principal from armed attackers. The proper response will vary with the threat, their weapons, the surrounding environment, and legal constraints. Legal issues can be quite problematic, especially overseas, so this should be well-understood before a particular response is used. A variety of defensive tactics can be used (Holder and Hawley, 1998), including:

- Redirection—prevent the attacker from getting closer to the principal by changing their direction of travel.
- Evade—avoid any face-to-face conflict by gracefully getting the principal away from a potential incident.
- Confront—either verbally or physically, if required. Use caution during a physical intervention, be sure this is legal in the jurisdiction and under the specific circumstances, and be certain that the detail has the proper training in defensive skills.
- Survival—situations where life is in imminent danger. These responses can include physical force or an armed engagement (although this is rare in the United States).

In some cases, response may also include the recovery of a kidnapped executive. K&R experts will manage this process if coverage has been purchased; if not, there is an implicit assumption that this is an acceptable risk for the company.

Analysis

In executive protection, analysis is based on knowing the routine and locations the principal will visit, conducting a thorough advance, and incorporating a mix of technology and personnel to prevent successful attacks. In this case, path analysis comes down to understanding the entry and exit paths available to the adversary and the principal; scenarios can be developed in advance that the agent and others can practice to assure effective protection. It is likely that multiple scenarios can be addressed through the same responses, which keeps the system simple. For example, removing the principal from a room or situation prevents many adversary attacks from being successful.

Protection analysis and preplanning for trips are greatly enhanced by technology which allows the use of search engines for monitoring current activity of activists or other threat groups, updates on local country conditions for overseas travel, and access to daily Homeland Security and State Department intelligence information. In addition, sites like Google Earth™ allow preliminary review of areas to be visited, evacuation considerations, alternate safe sites, hospitals, and other details. Much of this information can be consolidated into electronic presentations via laptop or PDA, thus facilitating thoughtful preparation and briefings to other members of a multi-person detail and the principal. Much of the analysis stage of executive protection involves understanding the surrounding environment the principal will be in, coordinating details for visits, and having backup plans in place.

Ground Transportation

For this discussion, we will limit transportation to ground vehicles only (trucks), not rail or water transport. Just as a well-designed PPS contains elements of detection, delay, and response, secure ground transportation protection also contains the same elements. The same physical protection elements (detection, delay, and response) are provided in a somewhat different manner in a transportation security system, but their relationship to the adversary task timeline remains the same. A transportation system can be described as a movable access controlled area with built-in delay systems. Access to the transport vehicle when it is moving is very difficult. Detection is provided by observation of its exterior by personnel accompanying the shipment, either the driver alone or the driver and their security escort, if present. Detection and subsequent assessment are then accomplished primarily by direct human observation rather than relying upon technology and will frequently occur almost simultaneously when personnel recognize that they are under attack.

One major difference in response for vehicles versus fixed sites is that the response force will come to the adversary in transportation attacks. The effect is that the adversary may preposition themselves and prepare the surrounding area for the attack. The adversary can then use the position to their advantage, particularly on remote or overly congested routes. Conversely, the response may include leaving the attack location or positioning the vehicle to frustrate adversary tasks.

Instead of being at fixed stations, guards may be present and move with the vehicle (as in armored car transport). The communication systems, both within the response force itself and to a central monitoring location, become much more complex due to the movements of the vehicle and the large distances that usually exist between the vehicle and the central monitoring location or any response. This response is generally provided by local or federal law enforcement, supplemented by security personnel of the vehicle operator or product owner.

The synergistic balance of technology and the response force is important. If security personnel travel with the vehicle, they provide immediate detection, assessment, delay, and response. If, on the other hand, there is no immediate response, the need for delay may be higher to allow enough time for security personnel to arrive and interrupt the attack. Of course, one option is to accept the risk of a vehicle hijacking or other theft and address this through the use of insurance or other consequence mitigation. An example of consequence mitigation is the use of Banker's dye packs when carrying bond-certificates. Activating the dye packs can make the bonds valueless to the adversary, but recoverable (through reissue) for the owners so that the only real loss is inconvenience.

The synergism that occurs between security personnel and technology is one of the keys to an effective, balanced security system. In many respects, ground transportation security is more challenging than security at a fixed site. Operation in the public domain is frequently required and the same degree of access limitation is not possible as at a protected fixed site. In addition, and perhaps even more importantly, an attack can occur anywhere along a route of up to several thousand miles, giving the adversary a wide choice of potential attack locations. And, in most cases, this choice could be in locations where it will be virtually impossible for any response force to arrive within a useful period of time. As a result of these differences, security personnel in transit play a more dominant role in the security of a mobile system than they do for a fixed site. In all cases, however, the system time delay that is required to provide the response force the time to react must be provided primarily by transportation vehicle technology elements. Well-trained and disciplined personnel can increase their effectiveness by being less routine in their movements and more aware of their surroundings because their mobile PPS positions them to use keen observation and quick reflexes to hamper adversary tasks. The Transportation Research Board (TRB) provides considerable information about all forms of transportation security in their web page, http://www.trb.org/Activities/Security/ TransportationSecurity3.asp.

Determine Protection Objectives—Facility Characterization, Threat Definition, and Asset Identification

In the case of a ground vehicle, the facility is the vehicle itself. Characterizing the vehicle involves the same methodology as a fixed site, but the components vary. First, the structure of the transport vehicle is characterized in terms of walls, ceiling, and floor. This is most often accomplished using engineering drawings and visual observation. Next, any additional physical protection system elements, such as

communication and alarm devices, can be characterized.

Transportation routes should be reviewed in detail, with special attention to potential danger zones or choke points; locations for scheduled stops; possible adversary infiltration and egress routes; and speed and distance, which affect the timing of events. For example, vehicles traveling slower up a steep grade offer adversaries a better target than one moving faster on a level road. Congested areas make it more difficult to detect adversary infiltration and restrict response escape and evasion options. Ground transportation encompasses various operating states, which include

- stopped at a scheduled (predetermined) location, day or night;
- stopped at an unscheduled location, day or night;
- rolling to or from a stop, day or night; and
- moving at various speeds, day or night.

Each state may be affected by different types of terrain and environments.

Prior to designing the system, it is necessary to characterize the facility, identify threats and critical assets, and determine the risk management approach. While transportation threats may have some slight differences in capability (such as more vehicles or tactics that include an ambush or diversion on a road), threat definition is essentially the same. Critical assets can include any high-value cargo that may be of interest to an adversary, including commercial products (CDs, cigarettes, stereo equipment, jewelry, etc.), special parts or assemblies (unique military or industrial components, weapons, explosives, etc.), or shipments of money, drugs, or other marketable items.

Protection Functions—Detection, Delay, Response

Depending on the value of the cargo and applicable regulatory guidelines, security personnel may or may not be present. If present, they may be in the vehicle, in front of, or behind the vehicle. These security personnel continuously observe the vehicle and serve as the detection and assessment elements of the security system. Response force capabilities depend on the value of the asset and the policy of the transporting organization. In addition, some effective means of entry control and interior intrusion detection would provide an intrusion alarm if unauthorized personnel attempt to enter the vehicle. Technology used in vehicle protection could include exterior locks on cargo holds and the incorporation of RF tracking devices on pallets or individual components to aid in recovery of assets.

An attack may occur in remote areas of the route where additional security assistance is not immediately available. The required delay is that time needed by security personnel who accompany the shipment to respond as required. Responses may include escape/evasion, immediate engagement with the adversary, notification to a central monitoring location via overt or covert means of an attack, reduction of the asset's value or consequence of loss, or cooperation with the adversary. If an immediate response is required, the minimum delay time is the time it takes for responders to arrive before the cargo has been removed from the scene or sabotaged. This depends on the time needed to penetrate or remove the vehicle cargo-hold, the number of security personnel with the vehicle, the number of vehicles under attack, and security personnel tactics.

It is difficult to design delay systems that will ensure sufficient delays for all possible sets of adversary capabilities and tactics, but systems using items such as visual obscurants, vault-like structures, gases, hardened containers, razor tape, chains, and so on, can be designed that will successfully delay most of these attacks. Without the delay and immediate response provided by accompanying security personnel, it is very difficult

to design an effective protection system. It is also nearly impossible to develop technology-only security systems that can withstand a well-planned attack for significant amounts of time that will allow for secondary responders to arrive from a more distant location.

It is rare to find security guards in addition to the driver(s) assigned to escort all but the most valuable shipments (armored car couriers are a good example of an exception). If they are used, their number will depend on cost considerations, because they must be on duty from departure until delivery, well-trained and highly capable, and at least match the estimated size, capability, and objectives of the adversary. In most cases, there is either no immediate response or the response is initiation of an investigation with the goal of recovering the assets or apprehending the criminals. It is important to note that responding personnel may be more vulnerable to a surprise attack while they are operating in public areas.

Effective communications are necessary to facilitate the essential detection and assessment function among the responding security personnel should they have to deploy, for organizing and carrying out a coordinated defense, between the vehicle and any central control station for periodic status checks, reporting to notify authorities that an incident has occurred, and for summoning law enforcement or other responders in the event of an attack. The relative degree of importance of each of these operations depends on the policy associated with the asset, corporate procedures, where the vehicle operates, and the risk tolerance of the asset owner.

If an investigative response is planned, then tagging and/or tracking technologies may be all that is appropriate. If there is an immediate response, the design of the transport vehicle must provide sufficient delay so security personnel can respond to an attack and defeat the adversary before the adversary task is accomplished. A well-protected vehicle can provide increased access delay and ballistic protection together with enhanced safety, while potentially reducing the required number of accompanying security personnel. In addition, vehicle entry control and response force communication capabilities are essential to protect cargo in transit.

Primary security requirements for the vehicle may include ballistic protection, entry controls, access delay for the vehicle, and response aids. Methods include:

- a very strong vault wall panel design;
- robust access doors for the cargo compartment;
- tamper indicating seals;
- two-person rules for entry control;
- vehicle immobilization hardware;
- consequence mitigation that eliminate or reduce the effects of asset loss; and
- adversary/asset tagging and tracking technologies to aid in recovery.

Specialized vehicles can be designed that provide delay by incorporating panels of multi-layer corrugated steel, inner and outer stainless steel skins, and other barrier materials on a tubular steel frame. The corrugated steel together with the overall thickness of the wall panels provide access delay and ballistic protection for the cargo. The vault cargo volume should be designed to accommodate as broad a range of container sizes and weights as possible. The vehicle capacity is dependent upon the truck chassis selected for the vehicle and whether cab armor is used. Aircraft-type cargo tie down tracks are typically preferred and are often incorporated in the vault floor and perhaps on the vault sidewalls and roof. This arrangement allows flexible cargo tie down schemes for containers, palletized loads, or sidewall racks. Multiple layers of cargo locks may also be included to secure the cargo to the vehicle and provide further delay.

An entry control system is needed to control authorized access to the cargo area. One example is a three to eight digit individual code entry from a plug-in, limited-view, scramble pad pendant. Electronic locks that accommodate up to 1000 valid user codes with limited-try features and easy code entry and recode are recommended. Output from the entry control system should control an electromechanical door lock incorporated into the door. This type of mechanism incorporates aircraft-quality actuators for operating a locking block upon receipt of a valid entry code. The locking block drives multiple, distributed locking pins that physically secure the door to the vault frame. A passive locking wedge should provide hinge-side locking. The door lock should also be hardened to provide additional forced entry protection.

Immobilization capabilities can prevent an adversary from simply driving the vehicle away if it is captured. The vehicle can include a number of chassis immobilization features that can be activated from the vehicle cab or remotely from one of the escort vehicles. Chassis immobilization methods could include an engine fuel shutoff device, a turbo air shutoff valve, an accelerator linkage disablement device, and controlled braking of the vehicle to bring it to a stop in several seconds after initiation. The immobilization system may be reversible either by a variable timer or by manual resets.

Procedural techniques used for protection of ground transportation vehicles include scheduled status checks with a central monitoring location, parking multiple vehicles back-to-back so cargo doors cannot be easily opened, and varying transport routes and times.

Analysis

For a fixed facility, it is recommended that a combination of a path analysis and a scenario analysis be used to evaluate the PPS. However, for a ground vehicle, there are limited layers of protection that an adversary team must penetrate to gain access to the target. This situation makes a path analysis less suitable for analyzing the effectiveness of the PPS of a material transportation system. A more effective tool for systems with limited layers of protection is the scenario analysis.

In general terms, the analyst must determine the defeat methods the adversary may use to:

- stop the vehicle (if not already stopped);
- penetrate the cargo area;
- acquire or sabotage material; and
- defeat the driver or security personnel, if present.

In scenario development, the analysis should consider likely locations and times of the attack, the use of diversions, vehicle bombs, attacks on personnel during meal breaks, and if the trailer can be separated from the tractor or from personnel and therefore reduce the probability of interruption of the adversary. The level of detail in the scenario must be sufficient to ensure all adversary tasks are fully understood and credible. Questions to consider include:

- How many adversaries will be used to breach the vehicle?
- How many adversaries will be required to acquire and move target material?
- Will the adversary use assault teams to engage the response force?

Once the scenarios are fully understood and defined, an engagement analysis should be conducted to determine if the response force is able to deploy effectively and then interrupt and neutralize the adversary team. This is typically conducted using either computer models, subject matter expertise, or practice exercises, or combinations of these tools. The relationships between the adversary task timeline and the "detect, delay, and respond" timeline remain the same as with a fixed location.

Cyber Systems (Computers and Networks)

Applying the PPS methodology described in this text to computer security is a natural step when providing overall system security (see Figure 16.1). Applying physical security concepts to cyber security, which is the protection of computers and networks from malicious acts, is not, however, a one-to-one proposition. Delay, temporal differences, physical proximity, and jargon all provide hurdles for the security designer to overcome. This section discusses the extent to which the PPS process is applicable to cyber security, explains the similarities and differences between the two, and discusses strengths and shortcomings when applying PPS concepts to cyber security.

Cyber Security Fundamentals

Cyber security, at the highest level, includes securing wide area and local networks, wireless technologies, and controlling network access to protect electronic systems and the data stored on them from malevolent acts. The three tenets of cyber security are availability, confidentiality, and integrity (Froehlich/Kent, 1997). Availability is assurance that a computer or network service is ready for use. Examples of availability include email servers transporting user messages, as well as a desktop workstation being available for processing. Confidentiality is assurance that data is only accessed by those with proper authorization. Personal credit data, medical records and proprietary data are all forms of information where confidentiality is paramount. Integrity is assurance that data is as it was conceived or received as it was transmitted.

Regarding user interaction with data, computer security is concerned with authentication, authorization, and nonrepudiation. Authentication is assuring that

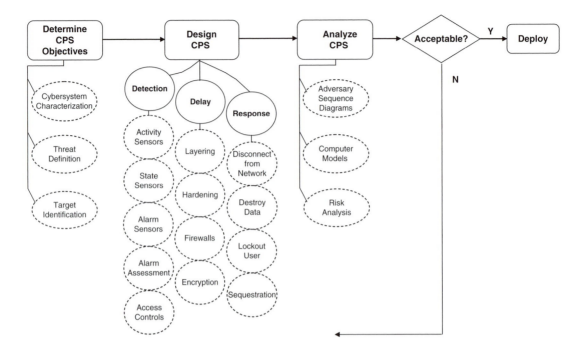

Figure 16.1 Cyber Protection System Design and Evaluation Process. While the tools and procedures used may be different than the tools that are used in a PPS, at a high level the same process steps must be considered in order to result in a cost and performance-effective system.

a user is whom they claim to be. An example of authentication is the act of proving one's identity when logging in to a secure website with something the user knows, has, or is unique about the user, as described in Chapter 10, "Entry Control." Authorization is the determination of a user's rights; examples include the ability to read, write, and/or execute files on a UNIX-like operating system. Nonrepudiation, following authentication, is the condition that user actions can absolutely be attributed to that user. A prime example is the attribution that results when data is digitally signed with a cryptographic key.

Determine Protection Objectives—Facility Characterization, Threat Definition, and Asset Identification

As in a PPS, the first step in cyber protection system (CPS) design and evaluation is to determine the objectives of the cyber security system. These objectives include cyber system characterization, threat definition, and assets that are to be protected.

System characterization in the cyber sense includes the physical and logical inventory of the cyber system. In addition, detailing enterprise policies, policy enforcement, and management within the system in design is essential. The physical components of computer or networked systems include both the obvious hardware (personal computers [PCs], servers, switches and routers, cabling) and the not-so-obvious hardware—personal digital assistants (PDAs) that connect to computers, transient laptops, mobile computing devices, and rogue wireless access points, hard drives, and USB drives. Details of the system design, such as processor architecture, may be helpful, though not necessarily pertinent. Network topology, interconnections, and connections to the Internet, and existing protection and access to these connections are important physical aspects to system characterization.

Logical network topology, network ports and traffic, software applications and versions in use are all parts of logical characterization. Defining the logical topology in parallel with physical topologies aids characterization as they often differ and up-to-date familiarization is favorable. The protocols and processes that reside on the system are also inventoried, and the client-side interfaces—PCs, terminals, and programs with access—that are part of the system and interface with other systems are also described.

Collecting characterization data can be an arduous task—networks are large and complicated, interconnections abound, users add and delete nodes, and technology keeps evolving, which creates the desire for more user features. Software tools that aid in data collection do exist and include the free and ubiquitous Nmap and SolarWinds Engineer's Toolset. Hardware devices, such as Fluke's OptiView Workgroup Analyzer, provide more permanent assistance. Automated network discovery tools and scanners help, though hard investigative work may be needed to form a complete picture of the system. In this sense, cyber systems are much like AC&D systems—not surprising given that most modern AC&D systems use multiple computers operating on networks. As a result, Appendix B may also be useful when characterizing the CPS.

The following aspects of CPS characterization address the policies, procedures, and management of operations. What policies are in place or will be implemented? Are the policies followed or enforced? How? What data is collected to support compliance or enforcement? Answering these questions gives a realistic picture of operations; what is documented can be quite different from what actually occurs. After a thorough CPS characterization, secondary targets of attack are often identified or added to the list of assets that require protection. Other aspects of CPS characterization include reviewing user profiles, access policies, and manual interfaces, such as those used for sharing terminals or passwords.

Just as with a PPS, a good CPS is based on a robust threat definition. The steps taken to efficiently define threats in cyber security are similar to physical security: list information needed to define the threat, collect information on the potential threat or threats, and organize that information to make it useful. Important threat characteristics concerning numbers, resources, capabilities, tools, motivations are compiled. Cyber-specific descriptions of threat characteristics are discussed here.

Cyber adversary capabilities begin with funding, education, and training. Low-level criminals self-finance, while nation-states sponsor hacker teams. Education and training includes computer science education from universities or government agencies, corporate training, industry certification, or just plain teach-yourself hacking skills. Coding capabilities range from kernel level, or operating system core, exploits to high-level visual languages. Assessment capability is an amalgamation of each previous capability that makes up the adversary. A curious teenager has little to no assessment capability, while a nation-state sponsored adversary can assess worldwide networks without ever raising suspicion.

The tools of the cyber adversary include the hardware, software, and computer and network access available for an attack. Hardware can include custom electronics, high-speed personal computers and servers, networking hardware for testing purposes, and telecommunications equipment used for access. Software and exploits range from pre-canned, dated exploits freely available on the Internet, to zero-day exploits, which are exploited software vulnerabilities for which no known patch is available (Naraine, 2006). Social engineering, another tool of the cyber adversary, is essentially lying to attain an end goal. For example, an adversary can impose authority on or feign ignorance to a system administrator over the phone to obtain a password and subsequent unauthorized access. Manual methods of obtaining useful information, such as dumpster diving for passwords and other access information, should also be considered.

Motivation ranges from novice curiosity to government-induced ideology. A sample threat spectrum for cyber security is shown below, from lowest to highest severity threat.

Sample Threat Spectrum

- Threat Level Very Low—Script Kiddie
  Capabilities: No funding, high school-equivalent education; uses canned, detailed scenarios only, intermediate Windows use, no assessment capability
  Tools: Home user, school or public-level access, canned, dated, predetermined exploits
  Motivation: Status among peers, curiosity, random malicious act
- Threat Level Low—Criminal, Disgruntled Employee (Associated Press, 2006)
  Capabilities: Little or borrowed funding, some education and possibly corporate training, advanced use of pre-developed tools, power user of Windows and possibly Linux, noisy, yet accurate assessment
  Tools: Corporate-level access, developed attack tools, dated exploits, minor social engineering
  Motivation: Revenge, monetary gain
- Threat Level Medium—Organized Crime (Day et al., 2006)
  Capabilities: Well-funded, university educated; zero-day exploit development, expert in most operating systems, focusing on Windows; broad

assessment capabilities blend often seen as network noise
  Tools: High-speed network and computer access, zero-day exploit code, customized rootkits, advanced social engineering HTTP and email code
  Motivation: Power, monetary gain
- Threat Level High—Nation-State, Defense-level Adversary (Thornburgh, 2005; Nie, 2006)
  Capabilities: Focused, government-funded training and education; kernel-level coding, disassembly and undiscovered exploit development; expert in all operating systems and hardware; stealth assessment. These threats may also have the ability to introduce weaknesses into a piece of software before it is used. For example, a programmer working for a US-based software company overseas introduces a backdoor to be used later.
  Tools: High-speed, restricted network and computer access, undiscovered exploits, custom rootkits, possibly including virtualization.
  Motivation: Military indoctrination, ideological motivation, desire for higher standard of living

The final step when determining CPS objectives is to identify targets of attack (assets, hardware, and software) within the system. Identifying targets reveals to the cyber protection system designer which assets to best protect using available resources. Target identification consists of specifying undesirable consequences and listing potential targets. Theft is unauthorized acquisition of data. Sabotage in the cyber sense includes data destruction or deletion, and denial of service attacks (DoS). A consequence matrix, such as the one shown in Table 16.1, is an effective tool to summarize objectives. Details of creating a consequence matrix were discussed in Chapter 4, "Target Identification."

Table 16.1 *Consequence Matrix.*

Similar to the matrix shown in Table 15.1, this matrix captures cyber system threat and consequence information.

High Consequence	Industrial Spy (theft/sabotage of source code)		
Medium Consequence		Cracker for hire (data theft, sabotage)	
Low Consequence			Hacker (vandalize web site)
	Low Probability	**Medium Probability**	**High Probability**

The table is populated with adversary type, goals, and likelihood of attack, as well as consequence level. The example of an industrial spy versus a web site vandal demonstrates the cyber analog of the PPS target identification process. Protecting a web server against well-known exploits decreases the success of an adversary with only minor computer education. Implementing the level of protection needed to fend off an expertly trained industrial spy might hamper operations and usability of a public web site.

CPS Functions—Detection, Delay, Response

Specific technologies for each design function are provided only as examples because our purpose is to demonstrate that the same process works for PPS and CPS design and evaluation. In application, there are many technologies that must be integrated to provide effective CPS.

Detection is the first component of an effective CPS. For example, consider an employee stealing proprietary data off the corporate network. Without detection, the employee could download files without fear of being caught. In an integrated CPS, detection is placed as far as possible from the target to allow sufficient delay to deny the adversary. Detection components in a CPS include host and network intrusion detection systems (HIDS and NIDS, respectively), logging and alarms, anti-virus software, network monitoring and diagnostics. Correlation engines are emerging detection technologies that use a combination of the aforementioned technologies to detect malicious events from smaller, disparate indicators.

Delay follows detection and is best placed closer to the target(s). Delay without detection will not be effective because without notice of an attack, we cannot respond, and the purpose of delay is to allow time for an appropriate response. Delay mechanisms in computer security include authorization and access controls, firewalls, honeypots, and encryption.

Access controls, such as incorrect password timeouts and lock-outs, are simple methods of delay. Firewalls, previously and incorrectly thought of as the panacea of computer security, are essentially delay. Firewalls provide a barrier to the outsider as well as the insider, through the use of egress filtering. Honeypots are traps placed on the cyber system that are meant to look like attractive targets to adversaries. Honeypots distract adversaries, theoretically luring them away from the real target(s), thus delaying action against the target for a finite amount of time.

Encryption is currently the most effective, and at the same time the most misused, form of delay. Proven encryption—that is, encryption whose algorithms have undergone public review—properly implemented is infeasible to be broken. Such algorithms include AES, RSA, and Blowfish. A prime example of improper implementation is wired equivalent privacy (WEP). WEP used weak initialization vectors (IV), which modern tools and techniques can break within minutes (Ossman, 2004). Aside from the vulnerabilities introduced due to bad implementation, encryption can be broken by paying or coercing an insider to provide the key.

In computer security, the time between detection and compromise of the target can be short to the point of being negligible. This does not mean that the system cannot be designed following PPS principles, but rather, the time for response is proportionately small—response time must scale down to the speed of the attack and delays. Response mechanisms include automatically deleting files (requires secure backups), eliminating network connectivity, moving files or sequestering the adversary or target system, and human interaction with the system as a result of an alerted system administrator or security officer.

Analysis

After objectives are defined and documented and the CPS is designed, the system is analyzed. Analysis techniques using adversary path analysis and the effectiveness measures for cyber systems are discussed in this section, as well as shortcomings and ongoing work. Systems that protect high consequence networks and data may require quantitative analysis. Qualitative analysis can be used for systems protecting lower-end assets.

Adversary paths in the cyber realm are many and varied. Few system administrators, let alone security engineers, have mapped all possible paths to their respective targets. The use of mapping and scanning tools, such as Nmap, a free open-source utility for network exploration or security auditing (see http://insecure.org/nmap/) and Nagios, an open source host, service, and network monitoring program (see http://nagios.org/), can aid in this arduous task. Hardware network scanners can also be used to determine paths and nodes in a system. Given the defined adversary tools and capability, all appropriate paths to the target must be mapped. This emphasizes the importance of thorough cyber system characterization and objectives definition in general.

Consider this simple example of an adversary sequence. An adversary collects open-source, or publicly available, information about an organization. The adversary discovers an Internet-accessible login that ultimately leads to the desired target by using a low-privilege, default account whose deactivation was neglected. Still using unauthorized access, the adversary then elevates their account privileges using a known exploit, perhaps a buffer overflow. The adversary then has the power to enter the system unhindered and heads straight for the asset.

This example shows the path taken by the adversary, the sensors encountered, and finally the critical detection point. The first sensor is the login of the default account and the notification, if any, of an administrator. This is much like entering a PPS portal using a valid credential (deceit). The next sensor is triggered by the privilege escalation via buffer overflow. Host-based detection may alert administrators and initiate a response. This might be similar to bypass of a BMS on a door. Analysis might show that this point is also the CDP for this path. Now acting as a super-user (due to the increased privileges), the adversary switches to the quickest, brute-force techniques to attain the respective goal, while the system administrators or automated responses only have the time from buffer overflow on to interrupt the adversary.

The performance of each network protection element in an adversary sequence must be determined to support quantitative analysis of high-consequence systems. Calculating the probability of detection (P_D) is still an issue in cyber systems. Neither intrusion detection systems nor alert administrators use standard testing procedures or quantitative data that provide their P_D. Testing host and network sensors at a given point in time may not give absolute certainty of effectiveness under all operating environments, although it does give the analyst a better understanding of the system and a better idea to the designer of where to apply upgrades to improve protection, at least for this single path. Clearly, the large number of paths into a cyber system makes the analysis problem more complex; the number of paths quickly increases given Internet access and the use of remote computing nodes.

Delay times are also difficult to determine for cyber systems. Actions, both adversary and responses, can happen very quickly and protection actions must be proportionate to attacks.

The probability of interruption (P_I) also applies in cyber systems. Knowing the CDP is as crucial in cyber systems as it is in PPSs. Again, times are compressed and response actions, such as denial of availability to the adversary, introducing an air gap, moving targets, or simply trapping the adversary, should be measured for their timeliness and contribution to system effectiveness. Regarding probability of neutralization (P_N), there is a similar correlation to PPS use. If the adversary breaks off the attack due to uncertainty about whether they have been detected or because there is an automated response, we have neutralized them, albeit only temporarily (they can attack again tomorrow). This may be enough against less motivated threats.

Note that neutralizing the adversary by deleting important files eliminates important forensic data, which may be acceptable for some high-consequence assets; in practice, neutralization via this action should be carefully considered.

Qualitative analysis is used for most CPSs today and is appropriate for lower consequence systems, and subject matter experts can achieve success in determining, at a high level, the effectiveness of their systems. This is commonly accomplished through the use of risk assessments, where system effectiveness metrics are measured only by the dollar value of consequence. System effectiveness resulting from quantitative analysis, that is, determining the probability of detection of intrusion detection sensors, delay time of cyber barriers, and response times of networks or personnel, is not the standard for high-end systems. Quantitative analysis methodologies are rarely mentioned (Federal Financial Institutions Examination Council, 2006) and subjective effectiveness metrics (Swanson, 2001) are the norm. Qualitative analysis with graded effectiveness should be migrated to quantitative analysis for high-consequence targets.

Summary

This chapter provided a brief overview of three areas of security application that demonstrate that the process of design and evaluation is the same regardless of the application. Executive protection, ground transportation, and cyber systems were used to demonstrate this. The principles and concepts of determining protection system objectives, how detection, delay, and response functions are combined to provide effective protection, and the use of system analysis techniques are just as applicable to executive protection, ground transportation system protection, and cyber system protection as they are for PPSs. While the specific mix of people, technology, and procedures will change within each application, the combinations of the tools to provide detection, delays, and response to give an effective protection scheme follow the same process, and the same basic principles apply.

References

Associated Press, Feds: Linkin Park Fan Hacks Phone Data. November 24, 2006. http://www.forbes.com/home/feeds/ap/2006/11/24/ap3202377.html, last accessed December 2006.

Day, G., et al. McAfee Company, Criminals 'target tech students'. http://news.bbc.co.uk/2/hi/technology/6220416.stm, December 2006, last accessed December 2006.

Federal Financial Institutions Examination Council (FFIEC), Information Security booklet, July 2006. Information Security, Section: Information Security Risk Assessment. http://www.ffiec.gov/ffiecinfobase/booklets/information_security/02_info_sec_%20risk_asst.htm, last accessed January 2007.

Froehlich/Kent Encyclopedia of Telecommunications, vol. 15. New York: Marcel Dekker, 1997, 231–255.

Holder, P.T., and Hawley, D.L. *The Executive Protection Professional's Manual.* Boston: Butterworth-Heinemann, 1998, 64–67.

Naraine, R. Microsoft Issues Word Zero-Day Attack Alert, December 7, 2006. http://www.eweek.com/article2/0,1895,2068786,00.asp, last accessed December 2006.

Nie, P. Chinese army holds "Vanguard-206B" drill in E. China November 19, 2006. http://news.xinhuanet.com/english/2006-11/19/content_5349105.htm, last accessed December 2006.

Ossmann, M. WEP: Dead again, Part 1., December 14, 2004. http://www.securityfocus.com/infocus/ 1814, last accessed December 2006.

Swanson, M. Security Self-Assessment Guide for Information Technology Systems. NIST Special Publication 800-26, November 2001. Washington: U.S. Government Printing Office. http://csrc.nist.gov/publications/nistpubs/800-26/sp800-26.pdf, last accessed January 2007.

Thornburgh, N. The invasion of the Chinese cyberspies (and the man who tried to stop them), August 29, 2005. http://www.time.com/time/magazine/article/0,9171,1098961-1,00.html, last accessed December 2006.

Appendix A
Threat Tables

Outsider Table.

	Type of Adversary				
Potential Action Likelihood (H, M, L)					
Theft					
Sabotage					
Other					
Motivation (H, M, L)					
Ideological					
Economic					
Personal					
Capabilities					
Number					
Weapons					
Equipment and tools					
Transportation					
Technical experience					
Insider assistance					

Insider Table.

Insider	Access to Asset (often, seldom, never)	Access to PPS (often, seldom, never)	Theft Opportunity (H, M, L)	Sabotage Opportunity (H, M, L)	Collusion Opportunity (H, M, L)

Appendix B
Network Site Survey

Guidance

1. Critical information assets that are electronically available only on individual machines are *not* the subject of this survey. Critical information assets include proprietary data, databases, trade secrets, human resources data, cost data, and other similar information.
2. All critical information assets accessible via networks (not media stored in repositories) *are* the subject of this survey.
3. The purpose of this survey is to collect preliminary information on the cyber protections at each site. These are categorized as:

   a. Detection or Entry Control, such as

   i. Passwords
   ii. Sniffers
   iii. Audits
   iv. Real-time monitoring
   v. Intrusion Detection System software

   b. Delay, such as

   i. Encryption
   ii. Honeypots

   iii. Access layering
   iv. Sequestration

   c. Response, such as

   i. Account disablement
   ii. Real-time responses
   iii. Server/device disconnects
   iv. Network shutdown
   v. File erasure
   vi. Personnel notification

Survey Questions

1. Identify each independent network containing critical information.

   1.1 Who is the network Point of Contact (POC)? Name, location, phone, email
   1.2 How are individual (local and remote) access privileges granted and by whom? How are authorization lists maintained?

      1.2.1 How many local users are there?
      1.2.2 How many remote users are there? At which sites?
      1.2.3 Are there any time-of-day restrictions for access? Describe.

317

1.3 How are device (server or desktop; local and remote) connection privileges granted and by whom? How are authorization lists maintained?

   1.3.1 How many local desktops are there?

   1.3.2 How many remote desktops are there? At which sites?

   1.3.3 Are there any time-of-day restrictions for access? Describe.

1.4 Within that network, uniquely identify each device (server) containing critical information. IP address and server name.

   1.4.1 Identify the major databases or files located on that device (specify the sensitivity of data and approximate number of records or megabytes)

      1.4.1.1 Local users?

      1.4.1.2 Remote users?

   1.4.2 Identify the building and room where the device is physically located.

   1.4.3 What cyber protections exist at these devices or databases:

      1.4.3.1 Detection/Entry Control

      1.4.3.2 Delay

      1.4.3.3 Response

   1.4.4 Identify the subnetwork.

1.5 What kinds of network connections exist from your site to others? (leased lines, fast lanes, private, etc.)

   1.5.1 In what physical locations do these connections enter your site?

   1.5.2 What cyber protections exist at these connections:

      1.5.2.1 Detection/Entry Control

      1.5.2.2 Delay

      1.5.2.3 Response

1.6 Identify each subnetwork.

   1.6.1 Who is the network POC? Name, location, phone, email

   1.6.2 What are the physical connections between this and other subnetworks?

   1.6.3 What cyber protections exist at these connections:

      1.6.3.1 Detection/Entry Control

      1.6.3.2 Delay

      1.6.3.3 Response

1.7 Provide any diagrams of this network, its subnetworks, physical and logical connections, and services provided

2. Identify any interconnections between these networks, whether permanent or temporary.

2.1 What cyber protections exist at these connections:

   2.1.1 Detection/Entry Control

   2.1.2 Delay

   2.1.3 Response

Appendix C
EASI Model

The EASI method calculates the probability of interruption of an adversary action sequence aimed at theft or sabotage. This is the probability that the response force will be notified when there is sufficient time remaining in the sequence for the force to respond. The notification of the response force is called an alarm and the probability of alarm is

$$P(A) = P(D) \, P(C)$$

where $P(D)$ = probability of detection and $P(C)$ = probability of communication to the response force.

In the case of a single detection sensor (or other possible means of detection), the probability of an adversary action sequence interruption is given by

$$P(I) = P(R \mid A) \, P(A)$$

where $P(R \mid A)$ = probability of response force arrival prior to the end of the adversary's action sequence, given an alarm.

An adversary action sequence takes place along a path consisting of a starting point, a sequence of detection sensors, transit and barrier delays, and a terminal point. The transits and barriers can be thought of as tasks the adversary must perform. Current versions of EASI allow specification of where the detection sensors are located with respect to the task delays—before, after, or during the task delay.

If TR is the time remaining for the adversary to reach the terminal point when a sensor activates, and RFT is the response time of the security force, then for adversary interruption it is necessary that

$$TR - RFT > 0$$

The random variables TR and RFT are assumed to be independent and normally distributed[*] and thus the random variable

$$X = TR - RFT$$

is normally distributed with mean

$$\mu_x = E(TR - RFT) = E(TR) - E(RFT)$$

variance

$$\sigma_x^2 = \text{Var}(TR - RFT) = \text{Var}(TR) + \text{Var}(RFT)$$

---

[*] The normal distribution requirement may be approximated by letting TR and RFT be sums of random variables which satisfy the conditions of the Central Limit Theorem

and

$$P(R|A) = P(X > 0)$$

$$= \int_0^\infty \frac{1}{\sqrt{2\pi\sigma_X^2}} \exp\left[-\frac{(x - \mu_X)^2}{2\sigma_X^2}\right] dx$$

In EASI, $P(R|A)$ is approximated using the NormSDist function found in Excel®. Because the method is concerned with the time remaining in the sequence, evaluation of $E(TR)$ and $E(RFT)$ at point p along a path of interest must be with respect to the terminal point. The penetration time through each barrier and the transit time between barriers are considered to be random variables with values corresponding to the level of adversary resources. Then, the expected time from any point p to the terminal point n is

$$E(TR) \text{ at point } p = E(\text{Time After}$$
$$\text{Detection at point } p) + \sum_{i=p+1}^{n} E(T_i)$$

where

$$E(T_i) = \text{the expected time to perform}$$
$$\text{Task } i$$

and

$E(\text{Time After Detection at point } p) =$
   $E(T_i)$ if detection is at the beginning (B)
   $E(T_i)/2$ if detection is in the middle (M)
   0 if detection is at the end (E).

Assuming each task to be independent, the variance of the path time remaining between point p and the terminal point n is

$$Var(TR) \text{ at point } p = Var(\text{Time After}$$
$$\text{Detection at point } p) + \sum_{i=p+1}^{n} Var(T_i)$$
$$(7)$$

where

$Var(\text{Time After Detection at point } p) =$
   $Var(T_i)$ if detection is at the beginning (B)
   $Var(T_i)/4$ if detection is in the middle (M)
   0 if detection is at the end (E).

For two or more sensors, the conditional probability of response force arrival, $P(R|A)$, for each sensor must be calculated as previously described. Then the formula for $P(I)$, the cumulative probability of sequence interruption calculated along the adversary's path from the starting point, must consider detection at the first location, at the second, and so on. For example, for a path with two detection locations:

$$P(I) = P(D_1)^* P(C_1)^* P(R|A_1)$$
$$+ (1 - P(D_1))^* P(D_2)^* P(C_2)^* P(R|A_2)$$

Notice that $P(C_1)$ is included in the first term but not the second; this is because if we do detect at the first location, but do not communicate to the response force based on that detection (due to jamming, etc.), we will probably not get a second chance to communicate at the second location just by the virtue of being detected there. (The probability of this event is $P(D_1)^*(1 - P(C_1))$, which represents the difference between $P(D_1)^* P(C_1)$ in the first probability term and $P(D_1)$ used in the first part of the second probability term in (8)).

The general formula for $P(I)$ based on similar reasoning is

$$P(I) = P(D_1)^* P(C_1)^* P(R|A_1)$$
$$+ \sum_{i=2}^{n} P(R|A_i) P(C_i) P(D_i) \prod_{i=1}^{i-1} (1 - P(D_i))$$
$$(9)$$

Additional Notes on EASI Excel Model

The next pages are printouts of the Excel model. EASI_formula_vu.xls shows the contents of each cell calculation. This can be used to check input after keying in the information if the user has no Internet access to download the model. EASI_200.xls shows the values for each calculated cell. This can be used to locate incorrect manual inputs. Both files refer to the EASI results of Figure 14.4.

The first tab in the Excel file (XL Easi) is a table formatted to look like Figures 14.4 through 14.9. This can be formatted using whichever font or line widths desired, but the data must reside in the appropriate column/row. The data inside the table (columns D through G, rows 9–20) is entered for a specific path.

	A	B	C	D	E	F	G
1							
2			*Estimate of*	Probability of			
3			*Adversary*	Guard		Response Force Time (in Seconds)	
4			*Sequence*	Communication		Mean	Standard Deviation
5			*Interruption*	0.95		300	90
6							
7						Delays (in Seconds):	
8		Task	Description	P(Detection)	Location	Mean:	Standard Deviation
9		1	Cut Fence	0	B	10	3
10		2	Run to Building	0	B	12	3.6
11		3	Open Door	0.9	B	90	27
12		4	Run to Vital Area	0	B	10	3
13		5	Open Door	0.9	B	90	27
14		6	Sabotage Target	0	B	120	36
15		7					
16		8					
17		9					
18		10					
19		11					
20		12					
21							
22			Probability of Interruption:	0.476040779			
23							

Second tab (EASI2.XLS):

All of the information must appear exactly as shown, in the appropriate cell.

	A	B	C	D	E	F	G
1							
2							
3							
4							
5		1		='XL Easi'!F5	='XL Easi'!G5		
6	PC	='XL Easi'!D5					
7							
8				mean	sdev	pad	1-pd
9		='XL Easi'!D9	='XL Easi'!E9	='XL Easi'!F9	='XL Easi'!G9	=$B$5*B9	=1-F9
10		='XL Easi'!D10	='XL Easi'!E10	='XL Easi'!F10	='XL Easi'!G10	=$B$5*B10	=(1-F10)*G9
11		='XL Easi'!D11	='XL Easi'!E11	='XL Easi'!F11	='XL Easi'!G11	=$B$5*B11	=(1-F11)*G10
12		='XL Easi'!D12	='XL Easi'!E12	='XL Easi'!F12	='XL Easi'!G12	=$B$5*B12	=(1-F12)*G11
13		='XL Easi'!D13	='XL Easi'!E13	='XL Easi'!F13	='XL Easi'!G13	=$B$5*B13	=(1-F13)*G12
14		='XL Easi'!D14	='XL Easi'!E14	='XL Easi'!F14	='XL Easi'!G14	=$B$5*B14	=(1-F14)*G13
15		='XL Easi'!D15	='XL Easi'!E15	='XL Easi'!F15	='XL Easi'!G15	=$B$5*B15	=(1-F15)*G14
16		='XL Easi'!D16	='XL Easi'!E16	='XL Easi'!F16	='XL Easi'!G16	=$B$5*B16	=(1-F16)*G15
17		='XL Easi'!D17	='XL Easi'!E17	='XL Easi'!F17	='XL Easi'!G17	=$B$5*B17	=(1-F17)*G16
18		='XL Easi'!D18	='XL Easi'!E18	='XL Easi'!F18	='XL Easi'!G18	=$B$5*B18	=(1-F18)*G17
19		='XL Easi'!D19	='XL Easi'!E19	='XL Easi'!F19	='XL Easi'!G19	=$B$5*B19	=(1-F19)*G18
20		='XL Easi'!D20	='XL Easi'!E20	='XL Easi'!F20	='XL Easi'!G20	=$B$5*B20	=(1-F20)*G19

	H	I	J	K
1				
2				
3	dddd			
4				
5				
6				
7				
8	P(first detn)	cum delays	Cum Var	True Mean
9	=F9	=D9+I10	=(E9*E9)+J10	=IF(C9="B",D9,IF(C9="M",0.5*D9,0))+I10
10	=F10*G9	=D10+I11	=(E10*E10)+J11	=IF(C10="B",D10,IF(C10="M",0.5*D10,0))+I11
11	=F11*G10	=D11+I12	=(E11*E11)+J12	=IF(C11="B",D11,IF(C11="M",0.5*D11,0))+I12
12	=F12*G11	=D12+I13	=(E12*E12)+J13	=IF(C12="B",D12,IF(C12="M",0.5*D12,0))+I13
13	=F13*G12	=D13+I14	=(E13*E13)+J14	=IF(C13="B",D13,IF(C13="M",0.5*D13,0))+I14
14	=F14*G13	=D14+I15	=(E14*E14)+J15	=IF(C14="B",D14,IF(C14="M",0.5*D14,0))+I15
15	=F15*G14	=D15+I16	=(E15*E15)+J16	=IF(C15="B",D15,IF(C15="M",0.5*D15,0))+I16
16	=F16*G15	=D16+I17	=(E16*E16)+J17	=IF(C16="B",D16,IF(C16="M",0.5*D16,0))+I17
17	=F17*G16	=D17+I18	=(E17*E17)+J18	=IF(C17="B",D17,IF(C17="M",0.5*D17,0))+I18
18	=F18*G17	=D18+I19	=(E18*E18)+J19	=IF(C18="B",D18,IF(C18="M",0.5*D18,0))+I19
19	=F19*G18	=D19+I20	=(E19*E19)+J20	=IF(C19="B",D19,IF(C19="M",0.5*D19,0))+I20
20	=F20*G19	=D20	=E20*E20	=IF(C20="B",D20,IF(C20="M",0.5*D20,0))

	L	M
1		
2		
3		
4		
5		
6		
7		
8	True Var	z-values
9	=IF(C9="B",E9*E9,IF(C9="M",0.25*E9*E9,0))+J10	=(K9-$D$5)/SQRT(L9+$E$5*$E$5)
10	=IF(C10="B",E10*E10,IF(C10="M",0.25*E10*E10,0))+J11	=(K10-$D$5)/SQRT(L10+$E$5*$E$5)
11	=IF(C11="B",E11*E11,IF(C11="M",0.25*E11*E11,0))+J12	=(K11-$D$5)/SQRT(L11+$E$5*$E$5)
12	=IF(C12="B",E12*E12,IF(C12="M",0.25*E12*E12,0))+J13	=(K12-$D$5)/SQRT(L12+$E$5*$E$5)
13	=IF(C13="B",E13*E13,IF(C13="M",0.25*E13*E13,0))+J14	=(K13-$D$5)/SQRT(L13+$E$5*$E$5)
14	=IF(C14="B",E14*E14,IF(C14="M",0.25*E14*E14,0))+J15	=(K14-$D$5)/SQRT(L14+$E$5*$E$5)
15	=IF(C15="B",E15*E15,IF(C15="M",0.25*E15*E15,0))+J16	=(K15-$D$5)/SQRT(L15+$E$5*$E$5)
16	=IF(C16="B",E16*E16,IF(C16="M",0.25*E16*E16,0))+J17	=(K16-$D$5)/SQRT(L16+$E$5*$E$5)
17	=IF(C17="B",E17*E17,IF(C17="M",0.25*E17*E17,0))+J18	=(K17-$D$5)/SQRT(L17+$E$5*$E$5)
18	=IF(C18="B",E18*E18,IF(C18="M",0.25*E18*E18,0))+J19	=(K18-$D$5)/SQRT(L18+$E$5*$E$5)
19	=IF(C19="B",E19*E19,IF(C19="M",0.25*E19*E19,0))+J20	=(K19-$D$5)/SQRT(L19+$E$5*$E$5)
20	=IF(C20="B",E20*E20,IF(C20="M",0.25*E20*E20,0))	=(K20-$D$5)/SQRT(L20+$E$5*$E$5)

	N	O
1		
2		
3		
4		
5		
6		
7		
8	Normal values	prod h?*n?
9	=EASI2.XLS!fornorm__a(M9)	=H9*N9
10	=EASI2.XLS!fornorm__a(M10)	=H10*N10
11	=EASI2.XLS!fornorm__a(M11)	=H11*N11
12	=EASI2.XLS!fornorm__a(M12)	=H12*N12
13	=EASI2.XLS!fornorm__a(M13)	=H13*N13
14	=EASI2.XLS!fornorm__a(M14)	=H14*N14
15	=EASI2.XLS!fornorm__a(M15)	=H15*N15
16	=EASI2.XLS!fornorm__a(M16)	=H16*N16
17	=EASI2.XLS!fornorm__a(M17)	=H17*N17
18	=EASI2.XLS!fornorm__a(M18)	=H18*N18
19	=EASI2.XLS!fornorm__a(M19)	=H19*N19
20	=EASI2.XLS!fornorm__a(M20)	=H20*N20
21		=SUM(O9:O20)*B6

Third tab in file (EASI0.xlm):

	A
1	fornorm (a)
2	=RESULT(1)
3	=ARGUMENT("z_value",1)
4	=z_value
5	=NORMSDIST(z_value)
6	=RETURN(A5)

Glossary

The terms in this glossary were derived from physical protection training material prepared at Sandia National Laboratories. In addition to the security terms included in this glossary, many other terms common to other specialized fields have been added.

A

acceptance testing: performance of all necessary testing to demonstrate that installed equipment will operate satisfactorily and safely in accordance with the design plans and specifications.

access control: process of managing databases or other records, and determining the parameters of authorized entry, such as who or what will be granted access, when they may enter, and where access will occur.

access control measures: hardware and software features, physical controls, operating procedures, administrative procedures, and various combinations of these designed to detect or prevent unauthorized access to classified information, facilities, or materials, and to enforce utilization of these measures to protect security and property interests.

access delay: *See* delay.

AC&D: Alarm Communication and Display. Refers to an integrated system of people, procedures, and equipment that collects alarm data and presents the information in a manner that promotes rapid assessment.

acknowledge: to indicate the reception of an alarm signal.

activated delay: any technique that delays an adversary and depends on a sensor to initiate the delay mechanism.

activated denial: any technique that denies access to a target and depends on a sensor to initiate the denial mechanism.

active: refers to a communication link that carries a continuous signal allowing immediate detection of a break in the link.

active infrared sensor: an active intrusion detection sensor that emits infrared light and detects blockage of light.

active lines: scanning lines in the raster that contain video information. (*See* raster.)

active sensor: an intrusion detection sensor that emits a signal from a transmitter and detects changes in, or reflections of, that signal by means of a receiver. (*See* passive sensor).

actual force: force consisting of a physical act, especially a violent act directed against a robbery victim.

actual threat: a credible situation or validated information indicating that facility interests are currently or will be at risk.

adversary: a person performing malevolent acts in pursuit of interests harmful to the facility; an adversary may be an insider or an outsider.

adversary action: a specific act performed by an adversary.

adversary action sequence (action sequence): a required/ordered series of acts performed by an adversary to achieve their objectives.

adversary capabilities: attributes of the adversary, such as knowledge, motivation, and access to equipment that comprise a measure of his or her abilities.

adversary class: adversaries are generally classed as insiders or outsiders, depending on whether they are working inside a facility or must start an action sequence from the outside.

adversary neutralization (neutralization): the termination by the facility guard force of an attack such that the adversary is captured, killed, or forced to flee.

adversary path: an ordered collection of actions against a target that, if completed, results in successful theft or sabotage.

adversary sequence modeling (sequence modeling): using an analytical model to estimate the probability of success of an adversary along a specific path or set of paths.

adversary task: a specific act the adversary must perform in order to advance along a path; for example, penetrate a barrier, travel a certain distance, etc.

AFC: Automatic Frequency Control (usually video/CCTV). An AFC circuit is used to maintain an oscillator at a specified frequency.

AGC: Automatic Gain Control (usually video/CCTV). An AGC circuit is used to maintain an output signal at a constant level over a limited range of input signal levels.

alarm: a warning from a sensor or sensor system that a sensor has been triggered or activated, usually signaled by light or sound; it may indicate a nuisance or false alarm, or a valid alarm.

alarm assessment: process of determining an alarm condition status; appraisal of the credibility, reliability, pertinence, accuracy, or usefulness of an indicated alarm.

alarm priority scheme: a technique or presentation for dealing with alarms from a combination of sensors in a logical order. Alarm presentation sequence based on importance or seriousness of alarm.

alert: communication that informs all security personnel of a facility emergency and of the location of the emergency.

analog signal: a signal that attains an infinite number of different amplitude levels, as opposed to one that can attain only a finite number of levels as a function of time. (*See also* digital signal.)

angular field of view: the measure of the field of view of a lens or surveillance camera/lens combination expressed in degrees. (*See* field of view.)

annunciator: an electrically controlled signal board or indicator primarily used for alarm presentation to guard forces.

aperture: the lens opening that determines the amount of light that will pass through the lens and onto the image plane.

ASD: Adversary Sequence Diagrams. A means of graphically displaying paths that an adversary might take to accomplish his or her objective.

assess: to determine the validity and response to an alarm signal.

assessment: the determination of the cause of an alarm and information regarding the threat.

assessment zone: the volume of space in which assessments are possible.

attack: an attempt by an adversary to defeat the physical protection system and achieve his or her objectives. Attack tactics include force, deceit, and stealth, used singly or in combination.

authentication code: a code known only to members of the response force. It can be used to verify that a critical or questionable transmission was made by a member of the force.

auto-iris lens: a lens whose aperture is controlled by monitoring the video signal amplitude and automatically adjusting the iris to maintain a constant video amplitude output.

automated access control system: electronic or electromechanical system used to authorize movement of personnel, vehicles, or material through entrances and exits of a secured areas. Authorization is obtained by the user entering personal identification information (i.e., through magnetic or proximity cards, personal identification number, or biometric scan), a computer comparison of identification data against an authorized user list, and computer activation of the portal unlock mechanism if the requester is authorized access.

B

background noise: the total system noise, independent from the presence or absence of a signal. The signal is not included as part of the noise.

balanced line: a video transmission line whose impedance to ground from either side is equal, usually 124 ohms in video transmission systems.

bandsplitting (frequency scrambling): a common analog voice-scrambling technique that involves partitioning of an audio channel into several separate frequency bands that are then transposed or interchanged before transmission.

biometric device: automatic device that can verify an individual's identity from a biological measurement of a feature.

bistatic: refers to an active intrusion detection sensor in that the transmitter and the receiver are not collocated in the same unit. (*See* monostatic.)

blackmail: extortion by threats, especially of public exposure or criminal prosecution.

blinding: the reduction of scene information as the result of relatively high light levels entering the lens. The camera lens opening will be determined by the higher light levels, and will close down. Information in darker areas of the scene will be lost.

blooming: the loss of detail in regions of the video picture due to enlargement of an intense and excessively bright spot being displayed on the fluorescent screen of the cathode-ray picture tube; also, charge migration on video camera imagers from high illumination sources.

BMS: Balanced Magnetic Switch. An intrusion sensor usually used to indicate a door opening. The switch is activated by the movement of a magnet mounted on the door.

bridging (or looping) input: a high impedance intermediate termination of a signal line at the input of an amplifier, monitor, or video switcher where the signal line must continue on to other equipment. In video equipment, all outputs have a characteristic impedance of 75 ohms. The bridging (or looping) high impedance input allows several pieces of equipment to use a common video signal without significant loss of signal amplitude. The last input in a single video line must be terminated in 75 ohms.

brightness (luminance): the attribute of visual perception in which an area appears to reflect or emit light, measured in foot-lamberts.

broadband: wide bandwidth transmission system with a single carrier and multiple information channels; it can be fiber-optic or RF (radiated or on cable).

broadband jamming: simultaneous jamming of many adjacent frequencies by one high-power jamming signal.

buffer: a data area shared by hardware devices or program processes that operate at different speeds or with different sets of priorities. The buffer allows each device or process to operate without being held up by the other. In order for a buffer to be effective, the size of the buffer and the algorithms for moving data into and out of the buffer need to be considered by the buffer designer. Like a cache, a buffer is a "midpoint holding place" but exists not so much to accelerate the speed of an activity as to support the coordination of separate activities.

buried-line sensor: a passive intrusion detection sensor that employs a buried transducer to detect seismic and/or magnetic disturbances.

burned-in image: an image that persists in a fixed position in the output signal of a camera tube after the camera has been turned to a different scene.

bypass: a sensor defeat mode in which an intruder defeats a sensor by avoiding its detection zone or detection method.

C

CCD: Charge-Coupled Device. A semiconductor device that is used especially as an optical sensor and that stores charge and transfers it sequentially to an amplifier and detector.

CCTV: Closed Circuit Television. A television system in which the signal distribution is limited or restricted, usually by cable.

Classification: the positive assessment that a detected object is human, animal, or some other object. (*See* detection and identification.)

clear-voice: normal radio transmissions that have not been scrambled or encoded. (*See also* voice privacy.)

clear zone: an area within the storage site perimeter and around the boundary of the storage site free of all obstacles, topographical features, and vegetation exceeding a specified height. The zone is designed to facilitate detection and observation of an intruder, to deny protection and concealment to an intruder, to maximize effectiveness of the security force, and to reduce the possibility of a surprise attack. (*See* isolation zone.)

coaxial cable (coax): a cable consisting of a single conductor surrounded by, and insulated from, a metallic shield, used for the transmission of video baseband and high-frequency signals.

coercivity: the measure of the resistance of a magnetic material to changes in the stored information when exposed to a magnetic field. The coercivity is defined as the magnetic intensity of an applied field required to change the information. The unit of magnetic intensity used to describe the coercivity is the oersted.

collusion: secret agreement between two or more persons for a fraudulent, deceitful, illegal, or malevolent purpose.

common mode: pertaining to signals or signal components that are identical in amplitude, duration, and time; in an operational amplifier, characteristics denoting amplifier performance when a common signal is applied to inverting and noninverting inputs.

communication: the function of transmitting or interchanging information, including both transmission of alarm signals to a central processing station and transmission of response information to security personnel.

communications system: the equipment and procedures used by the security force for sending and receiving messages.

complementary sensors: sensors selected for combination because of their capabilities of mutually providing what the other lacks in terms of probability of detection, nuisance alarm rate, and/or vulnerability to defeat. Multiple sensors will use different detection technologies.

containment: physical barriers, such as walls, transport flasks, containers, vessels, and so on, that in some way physically restrict or control the movement of or access to nuclear material, to information related to the quantities or locations of nuclear material, and to IAEA (International Atomic Energy Agency) surveillance devices.

continuous detection: for a protected perimeter, no detection gaps occur in the detection zones of any of the sensor lines included in the perimeter subsystem.

contraband: materials such as firearms, explosives, or special nuclear material that are not permitted to enter or to leave a particular area; unauthorized material or material that could be used for sabotage, such as SNM (special nuclear material), shielded SNM, weapons, explosives, narcotics, gold, and/or currency.

contrast: the ratio of light and dark portions of a video picture.

control track: for videotape recorders, the area on the tape containing a recording used by a servomechanism primarily to control the longitudinal motion of the tape during playback.

covert sensor: an intrusion detection sensor that is hidden from view, such as a sensor buried in the ground, and that does not radiate any signal detectable from outside of the perimeter. (*See* visible sensor.)

CPU: central processing unit; the microprocessor in computers that provides the computing power.

crawling: the physical act of entering and leaving a detection zone by lying prone to the ground and moving at an approximate velocity of 0.1 m/s through the zone while maintaining a low profile.

crawl test: crawling through an intrusion sensor's expected detection zone to help determine whether or not it is functioning properly is called a crawl test. (*See* detection zone.)

crossover: the point at which the centerlines of two overlapping microwave sensor beams intersect.

Cross-talk: undesired transfer of signals between systems or parts of a system.

CRT: Cathode Ray Tube. A display tube used in television sets and CCTV monitors.

D

deadly force: force that a reasonable person would consider likely to cause death or serious physical injury, which could lead to death.

dead spot: gap in communication system coverage, especially radio coverage.

dead time: the length of time between two successive uses of the line by a particular sensor in a time-division, multiplexed sensor system.

deceit: attempt to defeat a security system using false identification or authorization.

deception: the transmission of misleading messages by an adversary attempting to confuse or deceive.

decoder: in communications, decoding is the use of an inverse algorithm of the one used for encoding a communications message to obtain the original message.

defeat: to prevent someone from accomplishing their goal. Also the act of bypassing a sensor or system of access, personnel, or material control within the facility.

delay: the element of a physical protection system designed to impede adversary penetration into or exit from the protected area.

denial: the effect achieved by safeguards and security systems or devices that impedes or hinders a potential intruder or adversary from gaining access to or use of a particular space, structure, or facility.

deployment: the actions of the protective force from the time communication is received until the force is in position to neutralize the enemy.

depth of field: the maximum distance from a CCTV camera lens that two objects may be separated in a given lens field of view and still maintain acceptable image focus for both objects.

detection: determining that an unauthorized action has occurred or is occurring; detection includes sensing the action, communicating the alarm to a control center, and assessing the alarm. Detection is not complete without assessment.

detection and assessment: the element of a physical protection system designed to discover and to verify unauthorized intrusion attempts.

detection zone: a volume of space or surface area under the surveillance of one or more intrusion detection devices from which an alarm is produced when the volume or surface area is subject to a condition for an alarm.

deterrence: discouraging an adversary from attempting an assault by making a successful assault appear very difficult or impossible.

digital encryption: the conversion of the analog voice signal to a digital signal in the system transmitter, and the encoding of each bit of the digital data stream according to an algorithm dependent upon a pseudorandom code sequence generated within the transmitter.

digital signal: a radio signal made up of a series of digital pulses produced by pulses of one current or voltage value. (*See also* analog signal.)

disgruntled employee: an employee who is very dissatisfied and thus a potential insider adversary.

distribution amplifier: a wideband amplifier having a single input and several impedance-matched outputs for driving multiple signal lines. Distribution amplifiers can be used for video or sync signals.

diversion (divert): an attack, or feint, that draws the attention and force of an enemy from the point of the principal operation.

Doppler effect: the apparent change in the frequency of sound or electromagnetic energy, due to the motion of the object emitting or reflecting sound or electromagnetic energy.

due diligence: (1) The diligence reasonably expected from, and ordinarily exercised by, a person who seeks to satisfy a legal requirement or to discharge an obligation. Also termed reasonable diligence. (2) Corporations and Securities: a prospective buyer's or broker's investigation and analysis of a target company, a piece of property, or newly issued security. A failure to exercise due diligence may sometimes result in liability, as when a broker recommends a security without first investigating it adequately.

duress: a condition characterized by a forcible restraint of liberty, imprisonment, constraint, or compulsion.

duress alarm: an alarm initiated by a security operator to signal a physical attack or other serious problem.

duress code: a prearranged word, group of words, phrase, or other signal (normally aural) that covertly indicates to a knowledgeable person (e.g., guard or alarm console operator) that the individual is under some form of coercion and is acting unwillingly.

duress system: a system that can covertly communicate a response requirement to a security control center or to other personnel who can then notify a security control center.

dynamic: refers to an active communication link that generates a continually changing signal to represent the secure condition.

E

EASI: Estimate of Adversary Sequence Interruption. A dynamic analytical computer model.

eavesdropping: an adversary's unauthorized monitoring of information carried over a radio network.

ECD: Electron Capture Detector. A passive explosives vapor detector.

effectiveness evaluation: an analysis of the capability of a physical protection system to defeat an attack.

electric-field sensor: an active intrusion detection sensor that generates an electric field and senses changes in capacitance caused by an intruder.

element: a distinct part of a physical protection system.

embezzlement: stealing of money or property by an employee to whom it has been entrusted.

EMI: Electromagnetic Interference. Disturbances of equipment operation caused by electromagnetic fields from outside sources.

encryption: in digital communications, encoding an intelligible binary data stream to prevent unauthorized eavesdropping of radio transmissions.

end event: the uppermost gate or event of a logic diagram; a gate that does not input to another gate; the ultimate objective of an adversary in a sabotage or theft fault tree.

enhancement: change or modification to a system that improves its operation performance (i.e., by reducing either risk or cost).

entry control: the physical equipment and procedures used to verify access authorization and to detect contraband; part of the physical protection function of detection.

entry control point: entrance to a site or secured area at that access is controlled and egress is allowed.

equalization: the process of correcting for transmission line losses of the frequency characteristics of an electronic signal.

equalizer: an electronic device used to compensate for low-and high-frequency losses through a transmission system.

equalizing pulses: pulses used to maintain horizontal sync in interlaced scanning that occur at twice the horizontal scan rate.

escort: an authorized individual assigned the responsibility to accompany persons who lack need to know or access authorization within a security area in order to ensure adherence to security measures.

event: an act against a physical protection system that an adversary must perform to achieve his or her objective.

excessive force: unreasonable or unnecessary force under the circumstances.

explosives detector: a device capable of detecting the presence of certain types of explosives. Two types of explosives detectors are: (1) ion mobility spectrometer, which is capable of detecting all types of nitrated explosives, and (2) gas chromatograph-electron capture detector, which is capable of detecting all of the nitrated commercial explosives, including TNT.

extortion: stealing money or property by force or threat, such as blackmail.

F

facility: a plant built or established to serve a particular purpose.

facility characterization (characterization): describing, listing, or drawing the major parts of a facility.

fail-safe: systems that fail or lose power in such a way as to protect an asset. (*See* fail-soft.)

fail-soft: the capability of a physical protection system to operate, perhaps in a reduced capacity, during a failure of some element in the system. (*See* fail-safe.)

false alarm: alarm caused by internal equipment malfunction; because false alarms have no readily discernible cause, they actually are unknown alarms. A subset of nuisance alarms.

false arrest: an arrest made without proper legal authority.

false imprisonment: a restraint of a person in a bounded area without justification or consent. False imprisonment is a common-law misdemeanor and a tort. It applies to private as well as governmental detention.

FAR: False Alarm Rate. (*See* false alarm.)

far-field: refers to the far edge of an assessment or detection zone. In alarm assessment, the far field is the resolution-limited field of view.

feature criteria approach: definition of a physical protection system in terms of the features or elements (such as sensor systems) it must contain. (*See* performance criteria approach.)

field: the video produced in one vertical scan of the camera imager or monitor that consists of 262.5 horizontal scan lines in US television systems. Two fields are required to form a single video frame.

field frequency: the rate at which video fields are created, nominally 60 times each second in US television systems.

field of view: the area visible through the lens of an optical instrument. (*See* linear field of view and angular field of view.)

FL: Focal Length. The distance from the optical center of a simple lens to the plane of focus and which is indicative of the image size produced.

flare: light reflections from polished or shiny surfaces. Such reflections appear as bright areas in a video image.

float-charging (trickle-charging): continuous slow-charging of a storage battery in that the charging rate is just sufficient to compensate for internal losses or normal discharge.

f-number: the ratio of the focal length to the clear aperture in a lens, expressed in the form f/1.8.

foot-candle (fc): the unit of illuminance when the foot is taken as the unit of length. It is the illuminance on a surface one square foot in area on which there is a uniformly distributed flux of one lumen, or the illuminance produced on a surface all points of which are at a distance of one foot from a directionally uniform point source of one candela.

force: an overt attempt to overcome a security system by violence, compulsion, or constraint.

force continuum: description of the range of actions responders may use to counter an adversary. Begins with verbal commands and escalates to deadly force as appropriate.

format: the size of the usable image in a TV camera or lens, or the system used to record video.

frame: a single television picture, made up of two interlaced fields, occurring in 1/30 of a second, and consisting of 525 horizontal scanning lines (US standard).

frame frequency: the rate at which a complete frame is scanned, nominally 30 frames per second.

freeze frame: to display a single frame of video continuously.

f-stop: the lens designation indicating relative diaphragm opening or aperture diameter.

fullband jamming: a jamming signal with a bandwidth greater than or equal to the bandwidth of the signal being jammed.

full duplex mode: refers to a transceiver function that allows receiving and transmitting simultaneously on two discrete frequencies.

G

ghost: a spurious image displaced from the primary image caused by different arrival times of the signals.

guards: the on-site facility security personnel who comprise the response function in a physical protection system.

H

halo: most commonly, a dark area surrounding an unusually bright object, caused by overloading of the camera imager. Reflection of lights from a bright object might cause this effect.

hardened container: container, used for transportation, of such strength and durability as to provide protection to prevent items from breaking out of the container and to facilitate the detection of any tampering with the container.

hardening: enhancing a wall or door to make it more difficult to penetrate.

hoax: a false claim.

I

identification: the positive assessment of a recognized object as a specific person, animal, or thing.

illuminance: the density of the luminous flux incident on a surface.

impostor: an adversary who deceives by using an assumed name or identity.

impostor pass rate: the rate at which persons with false credentials are allowed to pass through an entry-control portal. Also called false accept rate.

IMS: Ion Mobility Spectrometer. A time-of-flight mass spectrometer that measures the mobility of ions at atmospheric pressure; a passive explosives vapor detector.

infrared: light or energy in that portion of the electromagnetic spectrum having a longer wavelength than visible light. Many CCTV cameras have considerable sensitivity to energy in the shorter wavelengths of this region.

insider: a person who, by reason of official duties, has knowledge of operations and/or security system characteristics, and/or position that would significantly enhance the likelihood of successful bypass or defeat of positive measures should that person attempt such an action.

intercom: intercommunication system; a two-way communication system with a microphone and loudspeaker at each station for localized use.

interlaced scanning (interlace): a process of interweaving two separate fields of video information to form a single video frame.

interruption: stopping the progress of the adversary by the response force.

invasion of privacy: an unjustified exploitation of one's personality or intrusion into one's personal activity, actionable under tort law and sometimes under constitutional law. The four types of invasion of privacy in tort are (1) an appropriation, for one's benefit, of another's name or likeness; (2) an offensive, intentional interfer-ence with a person's seclusion or private affairs; (3) the public disclosure, of an objectionable nature, of private information about another; and (4) the use of publicity to place another in a false light in the public eye.

IR: *See* Infrared.

iris (camera): the adjustable opening that controls the amount of light exiting a lens. Its diameter controls both the amount of light used to excite the imager and the depth of field.

iris (eye): the colored portion of the eye that opens and closes to regulate the amount of light allowed into the eye.

isolation zone: restricted access area surrounding a facility that has been cleared of any objects that could conceal vehicles or individuals and affords unobstructed observation or the use of other means for detection of entry into the area. (*See* clear zone.)

J

jamming: an adversary's attempts to prevent radio communications through physical destruction of communications equipment or through transmission of a disruptive radio signal.

jamming geometry: the geometrical relationship between the jammer and the radio units in the system being jammed.

K

K-band: the 11–36 GHz band of frequencies.

L

lag: a result of imager persistence, usually expressed as a percentage of signal remaining three fields (50 milliseconds) after the signal has been removed. Lag produces image smearing and resolution loss when relative motion exists between camera and scene.

land line: a hard-wired communications line, such as a telephone line.

light level: the intensity of incident light measured in foot-candles or lux.

linear field of view: the measure of the field of view of a lens or camera/lens combination expressing the width or height of the scene at a specified distance, stated in meters (or feet). (*See* field of view.)

line-of-sight sensor: an intrusion detection sensor that requires a clear line of sight (LOS) in the detection space; an active LOS sensor requires a clear LOS between the transmitter and the receiver. (*See* terrain-following sensor and LOS.)

line-lock: refers to a condition occurring when the vertical drive (vertical sync in video signal) is the same frequency as the power line.

line sensor: an intrusion detection sensor that exhibits detection along a line. (*See* volumetric sensor)

line supervision: a means to monitor the integrity of communication lines.

local communications: communications that transfer details and tactical information among security personnel once they have arrived at the location of an emergency.

local threat assessment: threat assessment for a specific facility, operation, or geographical area.

logic tree: a logic diagram that graphically represents how a combination of events can end in a specific result. It is a technique used to describe the significant ways an adversary can reach his or her objective by defeating the elements of a physical protection system.

loop: (1) a signal path; (2) an alarm communication and display term that refers to a series of multiplexers connected via dual communication paths to two microprocessors.

LOS: Line of Sight. The distance over which a radio signal may be directly transmitted along the surface of the earth; radio LOS is usually greater than optical LOS.

lossy: refers to a cable having high attenuation per unit length; in the case of a ported coax sensor, attenuation is caused by cable leakage.

lumen (lm): the photometric unit of radiant power. One lumen is the amount of luminous flux emitted into a solid angle of 1 steradian by a point source whose luminous intensity is 1 candela. A steradian is a three-dimensional unit of measure for solid angles. It is a wedge of space that is a radian in angular measurement in the horizontal and vertical dimensions.

Luminaire: a complete lighting unit consisting of a lamp or lamps together with the parts designed to distribute the light, to position and protect the lamps and to connect the lamps to the power supply.

lux (lx): the metric unit of illuminance equal to 1 lumen incident upon $1\,m^2$. One lux is equal to 0.0929 foot-candle.

M

magnetic buried-line sensor: a buried-line sensor that generates an electrical signal when ferromagnetic material passes near the transducer.

magnetometer: a passive device that monitors the earth's magnetic field and detects changes to that field caused by the presence of ferromagnetic materials. This method detects only ferromagnetic materials (those that are attracted by a magnet). Materials such as copper, aluminum, and zinc are not detected.

malevolent act: an illegal action, or an action that is committed with the intent of causing wrongful harm or damage. It includes trespass or theft; industrial sabotage; espionage; loss, compromise, or theft of classified matter or government property; vandalism; and adverse impacts on the national security, program continuity, or health and safety of employees, the public, or the environment.

malevolent action: a deliberate action with intent to harm or destroy installations or people.

matching transformer: a passive device used to convert the impedance of a circuit to the impedance of a transmission line or vice versa.

metal detector: active device that generates a varying magnetic field over a short period of time to detect the presence of metals. These devices either detect the changes made to the field due to the introduction of metal to the field, or detect the presence of eddy currents that exist in a metallic object caused by a pulsed field. The magnitude of the metal detector's response to metallic objects is determined by several factors including the conductivity of the metal, the magnetic properties of the metal (relative permeability), object shape and size, and the orientation of the object within the magnetic field.

microwave reflector: a planar metallic surface or grid designed for passive reflection of a microwave beam and used for the purpose of directing the beam.

microwave sensor: an active intrusion detection sensor that transmits microwave signals and detects changes in the signal caused by a moving object.

mitigating: reducing the severity or harshness of a situation.

monochrome signal: a television signal without color information.

monostatic: refers to an active intrusion detection sensor in which the transmitter and the receiver are together, either the same or nearly coincident. (*See* bistatic.)

multiplexer: a device that allows two or more signals to be transmitted simultaneously on a single carrier wave, communications channel, or data channel.

multiplexing: a signaling method using wire or radio characterized by the noninterfering transmission of more than one signal over a communication channel.

N

NAR: Nuisance Alarm Rate. The expected rate of alarms from an intrusion detection sensor that can be attributed to known causes unrelated to intrusion attempts.

negligence: the failure to exercise the standard of care that a reasonably prudent person would have exercised in a similar situation; any conduct that falls below the legal standard to protect others against unreasonable risk of harm, except for conduct that is intentionally, wantonly, or willfully disregardful of others' rights. The term denotes culpable carelessness. Also termed actionable negligence; ordinary negligence; simple negligence. Expressed in terms of the following

elements: duty, breach of duty, causation, and damages.

neutralize: render ineffective or stop the actions of an adversary.

nuisance alarm: an alarm that is not caused by an adversary intrusion. For example, wind, snow, birds, or system malfunction may cause nuisance alarms.

O

offset: the distance on the ground surface, measured from either the transmitter or the receiver in the direction of the line of sight, in which an intruder can crawl under the beam of a microwave sensor undetected.

off-site: the area outside the plant's or facility's land boundaries, not just exterior to the buildings.

on-site: the area within the plant's or facility's land boundaries, not just interior to the buildings.

outriggers: the angled metal extensions at the top of a fence.

outsider: a person who does not have official business with the facility or has not been granted routine access to a program, operation, facility, or site; a person who is not authorized to enter a protected or vital area.

overburden: a cover of dirt or rocks above a sensitive area to protect it from attack; access delay.

overt: an action that is open and not concealed. An attack using explosives would be an overt attack.

P

P_{As}: probability of assessment; a measure of the speed and accuracy of determining the cause of an alarm.

P_{AD}: probability of assessed detection; the product of the probability of detection and the probability of assessment.

P_D: probability of detection; the likelihood of detecting an adversary within the zone covered by an intrusion detection sensor.

P_E: probability of system effectiveness; the product of the probability of interruption and the probability of neutralization.

P_I: probability of interruption; the cumulative probability of detection from the start of an adversary path to the point determined by the time available for response (T_R).

P_N: probability of neutralization; the measure of response force effectiveness, given interruption. Neutralization uses the force continuum from verbal commands through deadly force to prevent adversary success.

P_S: probability that an intrusion detection sensor will sense an unauthorized action, sometimes also called probability of detection

pan/tilt mount: an electromechanical device used for remote CCTV camera field-of-view positioning.

passive: refers to a communication link that carries a signal only when an alarm occurs.

passive infrared sensor: a passive intrusion detection sensor that detects different infrared energy (heat) over background levels.

passive sensor: an intrusion detection sensor that produces no signal from a transmitter but simply detects energy emitted in the proximity of the sensor. (*See* active sensor.)

path: any physical route taken by the adversary.

performance criteria approach: specification of a physical protection system in terms of the performance expected from it. (*See* feature criteria approach.)

performance test: test to confirm the ability of an implemented and operating system element or total system to meet an established requirement.

performance testing: process to be used to determine that the security features of a system are implemented as designed and that they are adequate for the proposed environment. Note: This process may include functional testing, penetration testing, or software verification.

perimeter: an isolation zone around a protected area or the boundary between off-site and on-site.

PETN: Penta-erythritol tetra-nitrate. A nitrate ester that contains an unstable bond and is the explosive chemical in common plastic explosives such as detasheet and detcord.

physical protection: measures implemented for the protection of assets or facilities against theft, sabotage, or other malevolent attacks.

physical security: (1) the use of people, procedures, and equipment (alone or in combination) to control access to assets or facilities; (2) the measures required for the protection of assets or facilities from espionage, theft, fraud, or sabotage by a malevolent human adversary.

physical security plan: a facility-specific document (or group of documents) that gives a comprehensive description of the measures employed for the physical protection of property, information, equipment, materials, and other assets of interest.

piezoelectric effect: a property of an asymmetric crystal, such as quartz, rochelle salt, tourmaline, or various synthetics, that delivers a voltage when mechanical force is applied to its faces.

PIN: Personal Identification Number.

point detector: an intrusion sensor that has a relatively small detection region usually located close to the sensor.

portal monitor: any electronic instrument designed to perform scans of items, personnel, and vehicles entering or leaving a designated area for the purpose of detecting weapons, explosives, and nuclear material. (*See* explosives detector and metal detector.)

ported: refers to a cable having closely spaced, small holes or gaps in the shield that allow RF energy to radiate.

positive feature: an element of a physical protection system that has a predictable, effective level of performance.

positive personnel identity verification: examination of a unique physical characteristic, such as voice, eye pattern, or fingerprint, of a person to compare with stored data. If the data match, the person's identity is verified.

PPS: Physical Protection System.

primary event: an event considered to be the cause of other events but which itself has no developed cause; the first step in a logic tree. A primary event may be a basic, an undeveloped, or a developed event.

priority: a measure of the importance of a particular alarm relative to site security.

protected area: a specifically defined area, enclosed by one or more physical barriers, to which access is controlled.

protective force: the guard force at a facility whose responsibility it is to respond first to an adversary attack.

protocol: the special set of rules for communicating that the end points in a telecommunication connection use when they send signals back and forth. Protocols exist at several levels in a telecommunication connection. There are protocols between the end points in communicating programs within the same computer or at different locations. Both end points must recognize and observe the protocol. Protocols are often described in an industry or international standard.

psychotic: an insane person who acts in an irrational manner.

PTZ: refers to a pan-tilt-zoom equipped camera.

Q

quiescent: refers to the state of an active intrusion sensor when there is no movement in the detection zone.

R

raster: the blank gray or white picture produced by a monitor when its electron guns are just turned on but not varied in intensity by an applied video signal.

RDX: hexahydrotrinitrotriazine (cyclonite). A nitrogen containing compound that is the primary explosive chemical in C-4 plastic explosive.

real-time: an observation made at the time an event is taking place, or a phrase describing the operation of a computer or a data processing system, in which events are represented or acted upon as they occur.

reasonable force: force that is not excessive and that is appropriate for protecting oneself or one's property. The use of reasonable force will not render a person criminally or tortiously liable. Also termed legal force.

rebar: steel reinforcement bar used to reinforce heavy concrete walls, floors, or other structures.

repeater: a radio device that retransmits received signals for the purpose of extending transmission distance or overcoming obstacles.

resolution (horizontal): the number of independently resolvable elements in three-fourths of the picture width. It is most easily and frequently measured with the aid of a resolution chart, with the resolution units specified in TV lines. Horizontal resolution depends upon the high-frequency phase and amplitude response of the camera, transmission system bandwidth, and the monitor, as well as the size of the scanning beams in the camera image tube and monitor.

resolution (vertical): the number of independently resolvable elements in the picture height. Vertical resolution is primarily fixed by the number of television scanning lines per frame, generally considered to be about 340 TV lines in a 525-scan-line system.

response: the element of a physical protection system designed to counteract adversary activity and interrupt the threat.

response force: the guards and external agencies that respond immediately to counter the threat of an adversary.

response time: the time between the verification of an alarm and the interruption of an attack.

retina: a membrane lining the most posterior part of the inside of the eye. It comprises photoreceptors (rods and cones) that are sensitive to light and nerve cells that transmit to the optic nerve the responses of the receptor elements.

RF: Radio Frequency.

RFI: Radio-Frequency Interference. Undesired radio frequency signals that compete with desired signals in amplifiers, receivers, and instruments.

RF shield: an object, such as a metal building, that will attenuate an RF signal.

risk: measure of the potential damage to or loss of an asset based on the probability of an undesirable occurrence.

risk assessment: process of analyzing threats to and vulnerability of a facility, determining the potential for losses, and identifying cost-effective corrective measures and residual risk.

roll: the vertical movement of an image on a monitor as the result of a temporary loss of vertical sync, frequently present in nonsynchronous switching systems.

roll test: rolling through an intrusion sensor's expected detection zone to determine whether or not it is functioning properly.

run test: running through an intrusion sensor's expected detection zone to determine whether or not it is functioning properly.

S

sabotage: (1) industrial: any deliberate act, not involving toxicological releases, that could have unacceptable impact to programs. (2) toxicological: a deliberate act directed against hazardous materials stored, produced, or used at facilities that could cause a release of a toxic substance that may adversely impact the health and safety of the public, employees, or the environment.

SAVI: System Analysis of Vulnerability to Intrusion. A dynamic analytical computer model using multiple adversary paths.

scenario: an outline of a sequence of events by which an adversary may achieve the objective.

scrambling: processing a radio signal to make it unintelligible to a receiver that does not have the proper decoder.

sector: a defined portion of the physical protection system that may have multiple sensors and dedicated CCTV coverage.

secure: refers to the normal operational state of a sensor during which both intrusion and tamper alarms are displayed at the operators' consoles.

security: an integrated system of activities, systems, programs, equipment, personnel, and policies for the protection of classified information or matter, sensitive information, critical assets and personnel.

security area: in general, an area that requires monitoring of area boundaries and controlling of personnel entry.

security communications network: the procedures and hardware used to carry communications among members of the security force during both normal and emergency operations.

seismic buried-line sensor: a buried-line sensor that detects mechanical pressure, deformation, and vibration transmitted through the ground burial medium to the sensor transducer.

seismic disturbances: mechanical pressure, deformation, or vibration transmitted through the ground.

seismic-magnetic buried-line sensor: a buried-line sensor that is sensitive to both seismic and magnetic disturbances.

self-test: a feature often available on sensors that allows them to be tested readily to determine whether they are functioning properly.

sensitivity analysis: an examination of how a system responds when one or more of its elements are changed.

sensor: a device that responds to a stimulus associated with an unauthorized action, such as an intrusion into a protected area or an attempt to smuggle contraband through an entry.

spoof: to defeat a sensor by means of any technique that allows a target to pass through the detection volume without generating an alarm.

spread-spectrum system: a jam-resistant communication system in which the transmitted signal is much wider than the minimum bandwidth necessary to transmit the information signal.

stand-off attack: an attack on a facility without actually entering it, such as firing a missile from off-site.

stealth: an attempt to defeat a physical protection system by avoiding or inactivating its components in order to prevent detection.

stop-action: in recording systems, the process of electronically holding the picture at one field or frame.

strategy: the overall method planned by the adversary to achieve objectives.

subsystem: a component or group of components comprising one unit or fulfilling one function of the physical protection system.

surreptitious: secret or stealthy, especially leaving behind no evidence of penetration or compromise.

surveillance: the collection of information through CCTV or direct observation in order to detect security events. This process depends on a human to detect the event or activity without the aid of sensors.

sync: synchronizing.

sync generator: a composite of three basic functional units for use in video subsystems: a pulse generator, a timing reference, and a comparator/control unit to lock the pulse generator to the time reference.

synchronization (sync): in a video monitor or image tube, the process of maintaining two or more scanning processes in phase.

sync pulse: a pulse transmitted as part of the composite video signal to control scanning.

T

T_G: guard response time.

T_R: time available for response; the minimum delay along the portion of the adversary path remaining after the point at which the adversary must be detected to allow guard response (T_G); R just exceeds T_G.

tamper alarm: an alarm that is generated when access doors to sensor electronics or wire connections are opened or when the sensor detects a spoofing attempt.

tamper-indicating circuitry: line supervisory circuitry on data transmission lines and switches used to sense the loss of alarm capability.

tamper-indicating device: a device that may be used on items such as containers and doors, which, because of its uniqueness in design or structure, reveals violations of containment integrity. These devices on doors (as well as fences) are more generally called security seals.

tampering: interference in an intentional, unauthorized, or undeclared manner to physically defeat a security device.

tamper protection: (*See* tamper-indicating circuitry)

tamper-safing: the act of applying a tamper-indicating device.

target: the objective of an attack. Also called an asset.

target identification: the process of evaluating a facility to determine locations where an adversary might accomplish objectives.

TDM: Time-Division Multiplexing. An alarm communication system; signals from more than one sensor are transmitted over a common wire at different predetermined times in a time-interval scanning cycle.

terrain-following sensor: an intrusion detection sensor that detects equally well on flat and irregular terrain. (*See* line-of-sight sensor)

test pattern: a chart used to evaluate many of the operating parameters of a video camera or system. It has various line patterns for measuring resolution, circles to evaluate geometric distortion, and a 10-step gray scale for evaluating gray scale response, among other features.

theft: the unauthorized removal of valuable material or information from a facility.

threat: an individual or a group with the motivation and capability for theft or sabotage of assets, or other malevolent acts that would result in loss of assets at a facility.

threat analysis: a process in which information about a threat or potential threat is subjected to systematic and thorough examination in order to identify significant facts and derive conclusions therefrom.

threat assessment: a judgment, based on available intelligence, law enforcement, and open source information, of the actual or potential threat to one or more facilities or programs.

throughput: the rate at which people pass through an entry-control portal, a contraband detector, or an SNM (special nuclear material) detector.

time-division multiplexing (timescrambling): a common analog voice-scrambling technique; dividing a voice signal into small time segments whose transmission is delayed for a brief interval during which a subgroup of the segments is rearranged.

timely detection: the cumulative probability of detecting an adversary while there is still time for the response force to interrupt the adversary.

transducer: a device that receives waves (electrical, acoustical, or mechanical) from one medium or transmission system and supplies waves (not necessarily of the same type as input) to another medium or transmission system.

transient: a sudden, high-voltage spike in an electrical system, caused by arcing or lightning; any short pulse attributable to external causes.

triaxial cable: a double-shielded coaxial cable; a center conductor is surrounded by two concentric, independently shielded conductors.

turnkey: built, supplied, and/or installed complete and ready to operate.

TV: television.

twinaxial cable: a coaxial cable having two center conductors.

twisted pair: a two-conductor transmission line seldom used in video systems due to limited distance and bandwidth capabilities.

two-man rule: a procedure requiring that at least two knowledgeable persons be present to verify that actions taken are authorized.

Type I error: in a positive personnel identity verification system, rejection of a claimed identity when the identity claimed is true. Also called false reject.

Type II error: in a positive personnel identity verification system, acceptance of a claimed identity when the claimed identity is false. Also called false accept.

U

unauthorized person: person not authorized to have access to specific information, material, or areas.

unknown alarms: alarms for which the cause is unidentified.

upgrade: modification of an existing physical protection system to improve the system's effectiveness.

UPS: Uninterruptible Power Supply. A battery-powered, alternating current source that will maintain power to vital equipment even if all site power is lost.

V

vault: a structure or room whose door, walls, floor, and roof are designed to make penetration difficult.

vault-type room: a facility-approved room having a combination-locked door(s) and protection provided by a facility-approved intrusion alarm system activated by any penetration of walls, floor, ceiling, or openings, or by motion within the room.

video distribution amplifier: a wideband video amplifier used for the transmission of a single video signal to multiple video components from individual impedance-matched outputs.

visible sensor: an intrusion detection sensor that is in plain view of an intruder, such as a sensor attached to a fence or mounted on its own support. (*See* covert sensor.)

vital area: an area of a plant or facility containing equipment or material whose failure, destruction, or release could directly or indirectly endanger facility operations or personnel.

voice privacy: refers to the encoding of transmissions for the prevention of eavesdropping on sensitive radio traffic or of receiving deceptive messages. (*See also* clear voice.)

volume protection: monitoring an entire area, such as a room, to detect entry from any entrance portal, walls, floor or ceiling.

volumetric sensor: an intrusion detection sensor that exhibits detection in a volume of space. (*See* line sensor.)

vulnerability: an exploitable capability or an exploitable security weakness or deficiency at a facility of security interest. Exploitable capabilities or weaknesses are those inherent in the design (or layout) of the facility and its protection, or those existing because of the failure to meet (or maintain) prescribed security standards when evaluated against requirements for defined threats. If the vulnerability were detected and exploited by an adversary, then it would reasonably be expected to result in a successful attack causing damage to the facility.

vulnerability analysis: a method of identifying the weak points of a facility.

vulnerability assessment: a systematic evaluation process in which qualitative and/or quantitative techniques are applied to detect vulnerabilities and to arrive at an effectiveness level for a security system to protect specific targets from specific adversaries and their acts.

W

walk test: walking through an intrusion detection sensor's expected detection zone to determine whether or not it is functioning properly.

waveform monitor: an oscilloscope used specifically for measurement and analysis of video signals.

X

X-band: the frequency band extending from 5200 to 11,000 MHz.

Z

zone: a specific volume of space. (*See* assessment zone, clear zone, detection zone, isolation zone, perimeter.)

zone: a space that surrounds (but may not be occupied by) one or more targets and in which the functions of the physical protection system are to be accomplished. For example, if a facility is surrounded by a double fence, the fences and the space between them form a zone.

zoom lens: lens with a variable focal length.

Index

Note: Page numbers followed by "f" indicate figures

Analysis and evaluation of systems (*cont.*)
  introduction to
    objectives and goals of, 5
    performance measures, 8, 248
    process of, 5–6
    qualitative analysis, 273
    quantitative analysis tools, 276
    research about, 8–9
    risk, relationship to, 9
    Safeguards Automated Facility Evaluation
      (SAFE), 274
    Safeguards Network Analysis Procedure
      (SNAP), 274–275
    safety *vs.* security issues of, 2–3
    security, principles of, 271
    study questions, 271
    System Analysis of Vulnerability to Intrusion
      (SAVI), 274, 280, 338
Analytic System and Software for Evaluation
    Safeguards and Security (ASSESS),
    273, 280
Anti-Terrorism Act (1966), 34
Aqueous foam, 237
ASDs. *See* Adversary sequence diagrams (ASDs)
ASSESS. *See* Analytic System and Software for
    Evaluation Safeguards and Security
    (ASSESS)
Assessment
  alarms. *See* Alarms
  evaluation and analysis of systems. *See* Analysis
    and evaluation of systems
  risk. *See* Risk assessment
  vs. surveillance, 128
Authentication codes, tables of, 250–251f

B
Badges. *See* Credentials
Barriers
  aqueous foam and, 237
  dispensable, 237–239
  introduction to, 221
  penetration, aspects of, 221–223
  perimeter
    fences, 78, 224
    gates, 225
    introduction to, 223
    vehicle, 225
  structural
    doors, 230–233
    introduction to, 229
    roofs and floors, 235–267
    walls, 231
    windows and utility ports, 235
  system design considerations, 6
Biometrics
  eye patterns, 195–196
  face, 197–198
  fingerprints, 194–195
  hand and finger geometry, 193–194
  handwriting, 194

  keystroke technology, 198
  voice, 196–197
Bruce, D., xix
Buckle, T., xviii

C
Camera and lens alarm systems. *See* Video alarm
  systems
Camera selection procedures, 153–154
CCIR. *See* International Radio Consultative
  Committee (CCIR)
CCTV
  alarm assessment and, 127–157. *See also* Alarms
  automated alarm communication and display
    systems (AC&Ds) and, 179
  CCTV Application Guidelines Standard EN
    50132-7, 154–155
  fences and, 78, 224
CENELEC. *See* European Standards Committee
  (CENELEC)
Characterization, facility. *See* Facility
  characterization
Choke points, 300
CIAO. *See* United States, Critical Infrastructure
  Assurance Office (CIAO)
Classification, intrusion sensors
  exterior, 69–98
  interior, 101–123
Columbine high school (Colorado), shootings, 295
Combating Terrorism directive (PDD-34, 62)
Communication and response alarm communication
  and display systems (AC&Ds). *See* Alarms
  alternate means of, 252–253
  eavesdropping and deception, 250–251
  introduction to, 173
  jamming, 251–252
  normal use, 249–250
  survivability, radio networks, 252
Computer Security Institute (CSI), 28, 33
Consequence matrix, risk assessment, 291–299
Contingency planning, 245–247
Contraband detection
  entry control and. *See* Entry control
  explosive detectors, 207
  introduction to, 198
  metal detectors, 199–201
  package searches, 198, 201, 204, 216, 302
Contraband detection, 198
  manual search, 198–199
Control, entry. *See* Entry control
Corporate security managers, 299–300
Corporation Commission, 18
CPS. *See* Cyber protection system (CPS)
Credentials
  coded, 189–182
  exchange badges, 189
  introduction to, 189
  photo identification badges, 189
  stored-image badges, 189
Critical adversary path, 264–265